NATIONAL PARK

First Review

PEAK
NATIONAL
PARK

CONSERVATION

RECREATION

RURAL DEVELOPMENT

WAYS AND MEANS

continued ...

Maps

All maps are diagrammatic and are not statutory land use plans. If you wish to clarify or confirm the relevance of a map to your property, read the relevant policy or contact an officer of the Board or of the relevant authority named after that policy. The scale of Maps 2.1 to Map 24.2 is 1cm to 3.2km.

Foreword

This review of our National Park Plan was adopted by the Board on 14th October 1988, following extensive consultation and public participation.

The original National Park Plan was approved by the Board and published in 1978. It set out management policies to conserve the character and qualities of the National Park for this and future generations, and to provide for public enjoyment of the area, while paying regard to the needs of the local community. In the 10 years that followed, much was done by the Board, and by many other authorities and organisations, to implement those policies.

In 1987-88, we reviewed the Plan because we were required by Government to do so, but also because some circumstances and ideas had changed and new legislation had been introduced. Some policies we have changed very little: others have had to be updated or extended to take account of new thinking.

This new Plan is the formal basis for the management of the Park until well into the 1990s. Its sister, the Structure Plan, deals with the Board's land use policies.

Management of the Park is not a matter for the Board alone. It involves a wide range of organisations, whose commitment to the policies is vital to the success of the Plan. We now have wide support for its contents, and all the agencies identified as helping to implement the policies have agreed that they should be named.

The Plan foreshadows an ambitious programme of work over the next 5 to 10 years. The pace of that work will depend, in large measure, upon the resources available to the Board, and to our partners. We look to them, and to Government, for the tools to do the job.

John Beadle
Chairman
Peak Park Joint Planning Board

The Peak National Park

The Parks are an inheritance, not an invention . . .
If we look after them, the future will look after itself.

Abbreviations

AFSDO — Agriculture and Forestry Special Development Order
AIS — Agriculture Improvement Scheme
BMC — British Mountaineering Council
BTCV — Britsh Trust for Conservation Volunteers
BWGS — Broadleaved Woodland Grant Scheme
CARE — Community Action in the Rural Environment
CEGB — Central Electricity Generating Board
CLA — Country Landowners' Association
Co. Co. — Countryside Commission
DoE — Department of the Environment
EEC — European Economic Community
ESA — Environmentally Sensitive Area
FC — Forestry Commission
FGNs — Farm Grant Notifications
FWAGs — Farming and Wildlife Advisory Groups
ha — hectares
HBMC — Historic Buildings and Monuments Commission
IRD — Integrated Rural Development
LARA — Land Access and Rights Association
LNRs — Local Nature Reserves
MAFF — Ministry of Agriculture, Fisheries and Food

MoD — Ministry of Defence
MSC — Manpower Services Commission
NCC — Nature Conservancy Council
NESTWOP — North East Staffordshire Working Party
NFU — National Farmers Union
NNRs — National Nature Reserves
NPP — National Park Plan
Peak Board — Peak Park Joint Planning Board
PPCV — Peak Park Conservation Volunteers
PPJPB — Peak Park Joint Planning Board
PTE — Passenger Transport Executive
RDA — Rural Development Area
RDC — Rural Development Commission
RLMEG — Rural Land Management Executive Group
RUPPS — roads used as public paths
SMR — Sites and Monuments Record
SSSIs — Sites of Special Scientific Interest
TAP — Tourist Action Programme
The Board — Peak Park Joint Planning Board
The 1949 Act — The National Parks and Access to the Countryside Act (1949)
The 1978 Plan — National Park Plan (1978)
This Plan — National Park Plan (1989)
TPOs — Tree Preservation Orders

1 INTRODUCTION

The purpose of National Parks

"Not ours, but ours to look after." [1]

1.1 It is easy to lose sight of the purpose of our National Parks, or to assume that all readers of this Plan for the Peak National Park are familiar with them.

1.2 There are 10 National Parks in England and Wales, and the Broads have recently been given similar status. A Festival of National Parks was held at Chatsworth in September 1987. Speaking at the Festival, the President of the Council for National Parks reminded us of the purpose of the Parks:

"The National Parks are the most beautiful parts of England and Wales. There are many other areas of outstanding natural beauty but none more beautiful. That is why the National Parks were chosen. They are neither State-owned, nor fenced off. They are an inheritance, not an invention. And they are there to be enjoyed.

The National Park Authorites have two principal duties; to protect and enhance the natural beauty of the Parks, and to ensure that the public has the access to enjoy them.

And if they carry out those duties responsibly that will ensure the social and economic well-being of the people who live and work in the National Parks.

The Parks must come first. Wherever competing interests conflict, the Parks are the priority. And there are many threats to their integrity . . . .

To look after the National Parks is the best guarantee of livelihood for the people in the Parks.

What is needed is for the National Park Authorities to have the powers and the money, and the understanding, so that they can fulfil their obligation to our inheritance.

Future generations will have inventions which we cannot even dream of, but with our help they will also have the National Parks that we know and love.

If we look after the Parks, the future will look after itself." [1]

The Peak National Park

1.3 The Peak District National Park was set up in 1951. It was the first National Park in England and Wales to be designated, under the provisions of the National Parks and Access to the Countryside Act of 1949 ('the 1949 Act'). It is of interest historically to read the Hobhouse report on the Peak District — reprinted at appendix 3. It has provided protection for a remarkable landscape and the provision of recreational opportunities for tens of millions of people. It is recognised as a leader in the management of protected areas; and is still the only National Park in this country to hold a Council of Europe Diploma for such work, a distinction which it has held since 1966. Its location in the midst of the towns and cities of the North and Midlands is shown on map 1.1.

1.4 What is it that makes this beautiful area so special? There are at least four elements:

(a) The *distinctive beauty* of the Park, which is largely unspoilt. This is a result of a subtle blend of natural forces (soil, climate, topography) and human activities, which have for the most part responded to and harmonised with these natural forces. Three examples illustrate this:

(i) The settlements are often in sheltered hollows and are largely built from local stone.

(ii) The vegetation cover of the Park is often self-sown, influenced by grazing and simple farming methods.

(iii) Field boundaries are constructed of stone found in the locality and thus mirror the underlying rocks.

(b) The *building development* which, until the mid 19th century, almost always fitted into the traditional character of the area in a generally subtle way, absorbing the inheritance from the past and reinterpreting it to meet the needs of the moment. For example the textile and other mills of the early 19th century were often located on sites of earlier corn mills, exploiting existing sources of water power. They were built of local stone and they blend into the settlements or landscapes of which they form part. The coming of the railways broke down this constraint, and other materials became cheaper to use. The introduction of non-local materials and the adoption of modern non-local design were factors prompting the public concern which led to National Park designation. Happily, there is now increased emphasis on the use of materials and designs which reflect the tradition of the area.

(c) The geographical position of the Peak District at the *south end of the Pennine uplands*, means that it is surrounded on three sides by more fertile lowlands and often by dense urban development. The historical features, the wildlife and the culture of the area display a distinctive mixture of upland and lowland, northern and southern features.

(d) The character of the Park which is *more than just visual*. The sounds, smells and the general 'atmosphere' perceived by all five senses are important. 'A sense of tranquillity, of escape from urbanisation and contact with nature' were the words used in the Sandford Report[2] to describe some of these other qualities. In the Peak District there are additional qualities of wilderness and a sense of adventure (nowhere more pronounced than on the high moors) and a sense of history, tradition and contact with the past (as can be sensed in some of the prehistoric stone circles or in the less altered villages). Such features also provide an opportunity for modern man to 'discover his soul' by contact with nature or with history. Such environments provide an important ingredient in the quality of life, not only for the local communities, but also for the many millions of people for whom outdoor recreation or 'visiting the countryside' is a major leisure activity.

1.5 The character of the Park, which National Park designation was intended to conserve, thus embraces a unique wildlife, a distinctive cultural tradition, a cultural history stretching back to the Stone Age and a landscape reflecting all these features. These are based on human activities in harmony with natural conditions. There is also great variation from place to place. The contrast between the 'Dark Peak' of the north (based on gritstone rock formations) and the 'White Peak' of the south (based on limestone) is well known. It is for these areas that we have the responsibility to help manage and provide recreational opportunities for millions of visitors each year.

---

1 Brian Redhead, addressing the invited guests to the Festival.
2 'The Report of the National Park Policies Review Committee': (The Sandford Report) HMSO: 1974.

The National Park Authority

1.6 Since its inception the Park has been administered by a Planning Board, with members appointed partly by the Secretary of State for the Environment and partly by the many local authorities whose areas fall partly within the Park. Following the Local Government Act 1972, the Board was reconstituted as the Peak Park Joint Planning Board in 1974. Under Schedule 17 of that Act, the Board is required to prepare a National Park Plan, setting out management policies for the protection and enhancement of the Park's landscape and providing for the enjoyment of the Park by the public.

The National Park Plan, 1978

1.7 The first National Park Plan was produced, following public consultation, in March 1978. Its form was based on advisory notes forming the Annex to Department of Environment Circular 65/74. But its content was much influenced by two other events of the intervening period. These were:

(a) Publication in 1974 of the 'Report of the National Park Policies Review Committee' (commonly known as the Sandford Report); followed in 1976 by Department of the Environment Circular 4/76, which endorsed many of the Sandford Report recommendations, including the requirement to give priority to conservation over recreation where these purposes conflict and cannot be reconciled. These documents broadened the view of the issues involved in the management of National Parks. In particular, they emphasised the inter-relationship between the *three main duties of National Park authorities* — namely to protect and enhance the natural beauty, to provide for public enjoyment, and to have regard to the social and economic well-being of those who live and work in the National Parks.

(b) Publication in 1976 of the Structure Plan for the National Park, produced by the Board in its role as a planning authority. This Plan was approved in 1979 and sets out policies and proposals relating mainly to those activities which can be controlled under the Town and Country Planning Acts, and to the social and economic needs of local communities. It will continue to be the main government approved basis for land use decisions in the Park. Chapter 6 of the Structure Plan reviews the main purposes of the Park by reference to the 1949 Act, Circular 4/76 and to four alternative 'strategies' which had been the subject of the Structure Plan consultation process. It adopts a 'preferred strategy' whose aims are reprinted below:

"The Preferred Strategy . . . the conservation approach

(i) To protect and improve the natural qualities of the Park.

(ii) To protect the traditional, historic and cultural qualities which make up the distinctive character of the Park.

(iii) To promote the continuing development of a healthy and efficient farming and forestry industry in a way which respects the character and qualities of the area and as one of the main means of conserving that character.

(iv) To ensure that visitors to the Park are able to appreciate and understand its character and qualities and to use but not abuse them.

(v) To maintain or create balanced communities and to provide for local needs in a way compatible with the character and qualities of the area.

(vi) To ensure that any developments resulting from national and regional demands which will adversely affect the character of the Park are permitted only if there are no comparable and acceptable alternatives available elsewhere and where the impact on the Park can be satisfactorily controlled.''

This approach is the basis for the three main sub-divisions of this Plan — a Conservation Strategy (i, ii and iii), a Recreation Strategy (iv), and a Rural Development Strategy (v and vi).

1.8 So, the National Park Plan — when published in 1978 — was stated to be complementary to the Structure Plan published two years earlier; and it took into account the broadened view of the Sandford Report and Circular 4/76. Its focus was on policies for *management* of the National Park, in order to achieve purposes of conservation and recreation. It did not dwell on the needs and interests of local communities within the Park, since these had been covered in the Structure Plan. But it made plain that those needs and interests had been borne in mind throughout the preparation of the Plan; and that the Board would involve local interests closely in developing detailed proposals to implement the Plan.

1.9 The other key emphasis in the 1978 Plan was *partnership* with the very wide range of organisations and individuals, public and private, who own land within the Park or have responsibility for aspects of its life or management. The Board was, and is, very conscious that its own land ownership covers only a small fraction of the Park, and that its expenditure is only a small though significant element in the resources flowing into the management of the Peak National Park. For that reason, it sought the approval of many other organisations for the Plan, and has gained their active collaboration in implementing it. Appendix 2 lists the organisations which were consulted on or participated in the preparation of the 1988 Plan (see also paragraphs **1.28-1.33** below).

1.10 Closely related to the principle of partnership is the availability of resources. The Board appreciates that most of the Park is privately owned; and that private owners have to earn their living in a commercial world. Constraints on private forestry enterprises can reduce the income from timber production; constraints on farming policies can reduce farm incomes. Since 1978, landowners, farmers and others have been encouraged to adopt management practices which may not be in their best or most obvious short-term financial interest, without some form of incentive or compensation. These have developed over the years so that in 1988 the Board and the Ministry of Agriculture (MAFF) have devised a series of financial grants — both capital and annual — to provide positive incentives to farmers and others to co-operate in this partnership.

Approach to the First Review of the National Park Plan

1.11 The Board is obliged, under the Local Government Act 1972, to review the National Park Plan after a period of five years. The Plan has served well since 1978, and many of the programmes set out in it have been implemented. The time is now ripe not only to set a new agenda for action within

Map 1.1
Context of National Park

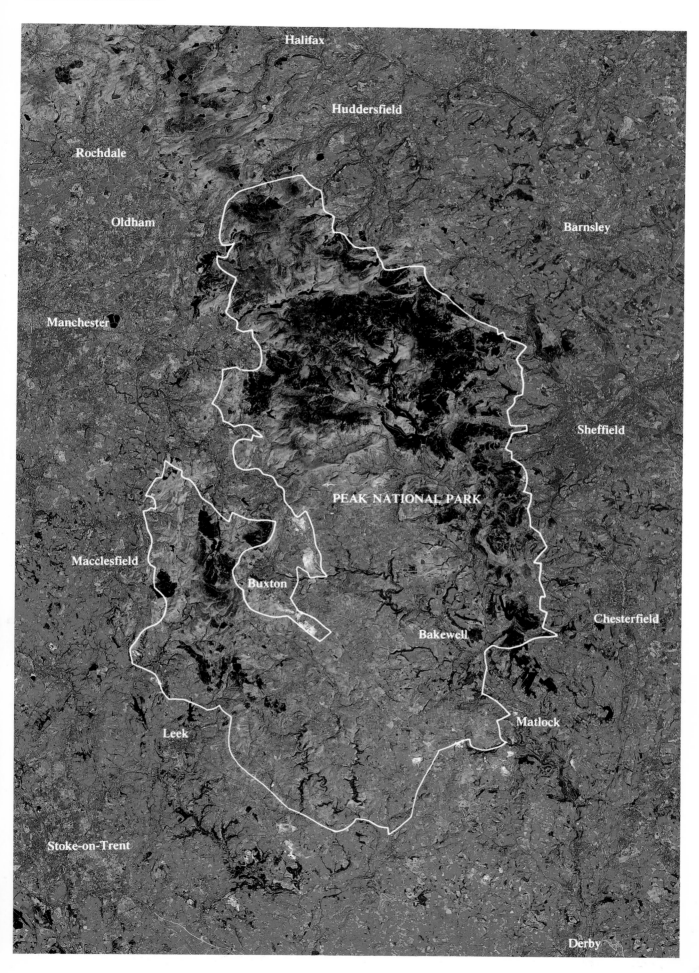

established policies, but also to review and extend the policies themselves to reflect changes in circumstances, ideas, legislation and administration.

Changes in circumstances and ideas

1.12 Environmental awareness The last decade has seen a sharp rise in public and political awareness of the impact of human activity upon the environment. This impact is wide-ranging, from pollution of seas to nuclear fall-out, from desertification to loss of hedgerows, from the effects of acid rain to the destruction of field monuments. This awareness is reflected both in general policy, for example the World Conservation Strategy and its United Kingdom counterpart; and in a more sharply-stated concern for the well-being of the environment in areas (like this National Park) which already have a measure of protection. These Strategies stress the urgency of integrating environmental conservation into all aspects of modern life, and highlight the importance of wildlife to people's spiritual amd mental well-being. The World Conservation Strategy and the UK response to it also emphasise the importance of the wise use of renewable and non-renewable resources and the incorporation of resource conservation into the whole fabric of society. This obliges us to look in more detail than before at the state of our wildlife and natural habitats, our field monuments and historic landscapes, and other features which make up the heritage of the National Park.

1.13 Changes in recreation Surveys undertaken by the Countryside Commission have shown the high and growing popularity of countryside recreation among the British people. In particular, they show the growing interest in walking, cycling, scenic driving, horse riding and other pursuits which take people through the countryside at large, rather than staying in specific places such as country parks. The Peak District has long been used for these kinds of activity, with people using our extensive network of minor roads, footpaths and other routes. We have to ensure, yet more effectively, that our resources are well matched to such activity, on the ground. We also have to consider the needs of relatively new activities, such as mountain biking or hang-gliding.

1.14 Changes in the economy The last decade has seen radical changes in national, regional and local economies, which we have to recognise in policy-making. The loss of jobs in primary industries; the growth of unemployment; the concern of government and of local authorities to boost local economies through manufacturing or service industries; the interest in the potential for growth offered by tourism — these factors are bound to influence the attitude of organisations beyond and within the Park. They sharply underline the Board's duty to have regard to the social and economic well-being of those who live and work in the Park. The importance of this role is more clearly realised in this Plan than in 1978. The Structure Plan is the senior document for the Board's social and economic responsibility.

1.15 Growing interest in integrated action The other main change in ideas has been the growing interest in integrated action. By this we mean ways of tackling things which link up many purposes, partners or sources of money; which bring the local authorities, statutory bodies and local people closer together. The Board has long been a champion of partnership, and has benefited greatly from working with other bodies, for example through the Area Management Studies. The last decade has seen the successful extension of this basic idea into many examples of integrated action — the Rural Development Programmes in Derbyshire and Staffordshire; the Integrated Rural Development project; the joint approach by many bodies to farming and conservation within the Park; the joint working on Tourism; and other initiatives. Increasingly such integrated action allows the purposes of conservation, recreation and rural development to be achieved together or to support each other. These initiatives are described in this Review, with proposals for further application of the idea of integrated action.

Changes in legislation, administration and national policy since 1978

1.16 The Wildlife and Countryside Act 1981, and its amending Act of 1985, extended the duties and powers of National Park and other authorities including Water Authorities, MAFF and the Forestry Commission towards the positive protection of wildlife species and habitats and certain other aspects of heritage. These Acts, plus other changes in agricultural policy such as the farm grant notification process and more recently the designation of an Environmentally Sensitive Area in the North Peak, have much increased the Board's ability to influence the land managememt activity of farmers in the Park.

1.17 The Minerals Act 1981 has placed on the Board a duty to undertake a review of all existing mineral sites in the Park. The Board must then decide whether the planning conditions relating to each of them should be tightened to ensure greater environmental protection.

1.18 The abolition in 1986 of the **Metropolitan County Councils**, with consequential effects on the constitution of the Board[3], has brought us into closer partnership with the Metropolitan District Councils of Barnsley, Kirklees, Oldham and Sheffield.

1.19 The Government instructed the **Water Authorities** in 1985 to consider disposal of lands or properties which were surplus to operational requirements. In 1986 the Government announced proposals for privatisation of the Water Authorities. It is likely that this will begin in 1989. Three Water Authorities (North West, Severn Trent, Yorkshire) between them own 15% of the land within the Park. These prospective changes could therefore have major implications for future management, particularly as regards concessionary footpaths, permissive access to wander at will, access to crags, the intensity of grazing and responsibility to further the interests of nature conservation. Efforts will continue to ensure that recreation and conservation interests are furthered either by the Water Authorities prior to disposal or by their successors, and by transfer of the existing provisions in the relevant legislation.

1.20 In 1984, consultants were appointed by Government to carry out a review of the Economic Efficiency of National Parks. This was followed by the introduction in 1985 of new procedures for handling the bids which National Park

---

3 The constituent councils of the Board are now three shire counties (Derbyshire, Cheshire and Staffordshire), five shire districts (Derbyshire Dales, High Peak, Macclesfield, North East Derbyshire and Staffordshire Moorlands) and four metropolitan districts (Barnsley, Kirklees, Oldham and Sheffield).

Authorities make to government for each year's award of **National Park Supplementary Grant.** These procedures now include the production each year of 'Functional Strategies'. which set out the programmes which each National Park Authority wishes to pursue over the following three years. Since these programmes embrace the detailed timetabling which might otherwise fall within the National Park Plan, this Plan does not need to contain such timetabling. The content of this Plan, on the other hand, *relates to the Functional Strategy heads.*

1.21 The process of preparing functional strategies, and of reviewing National Park Plans, has been much assisted by **advice from the Countryside Commission.** Regular discussion between the Commission and the ten National Park authorities has led to growing emphasis upon issues which did not figure heavily in the 1978 Plan, and which now merit greater prominence. They include (for example) historic landscapes, the built environment, and the social and economic needs of the Park communities.

1.22 The National Parks Awareness Campaign was launched in 1986 by the Countryside Commission, the ten National Park Authorities, the Broads Authority and the Council for National Parks. This Campaign has helped to increase public and political awareness of the Parks. It has contributed, together with the review of economic efficiency mentioned earlier, to the Government's decisions in each of the three years 1986 to 1988 to increase markedly the National Park Supplementary Grant, which is the prime source of the authorities' expenditure. This increase has enabled the Board to move into some new areas of activity which are reflected in this Review. On the occasion of the Festival of National Parks at Chatsworth in September 1987, 24 of our main partners made a declaration or statement of commitment to the National Parks[4]. We welcome this strong acknowledgement of the place of National Parks in their activities.

1.23 Employment Training in the Environment During the main round of preparation of this plan there were many schemes operating in the Park under the Manpower Services Commission (MSC). The Community Programme (CP) in particular had grown, from its origins in earlier schemes which began after 1978, to provide at least 80 man-years of work per year within the Board's influence, and more in the influence of other agencies such as the National Trust whilst this Plan was being completed in 1988, the CP Scheme was closed. In October 1988 as this Plan was adopted, the Government's Employment Training (ET) Scheme (which replaced CP) had failed to gain the support of the local authority Trade Unions. As a result, the Board was unable at that time to take part in the new scheme. Thus, many man-years of work and training in the environment, on which growing reliance had been placed, could not then continue. The MSC also then became the Training Agency. References to the MSC, CP and ET in this Plan are thus complicated by this rapid series of developments.

1.24 Conclusion These changes in circumstances, ideas, legislation and administration all need to be reflected in the National Park Plan. This Plan embraces these changes, but also reaffirms those lasting values of landscape and recreation which animated the designation of the National Park and which it is the Board's duty to protect for generations ahead. Like the earlier version of the National Park Plan, it is complementary to the Structure Plan, whose policies for land use and development are not altered by this Review but will

themselves be subject to review in the period up to 1991. This final version has been considerably amended following a major programme of public consultation (described in Appendices 1 and 2)

Format of the Plan

1.25 Scope This Plan is similar in scope of subjects to the 1978 Plan. In response to the changes described above, it has a greater emphasis in particular upon:

   — A list of priorities for action **1.36-1.38.**

   — Farming (Chapter 4)

   — Nature Conservation (Chapter 6)

   — Cultural Heritage and Towns, Villages and Buildings (Chapters 8 and 9)

   — Rural Development — meeting the social and economic needs of those who live or work in the Park (Chapters 20 and 21).

It takes a different approach to Ways and Means i.e. the resources and techniques by which the policies of the Plan are to be implemented, including partnership and integrated action (Chapter 23).

1.26 Sequence The sequence of chapters is similar to that of the 1978 Plan, with five main sections:

   — Conservation — Chapters 2 to 9

   — Recreation — Chapters 10 to 19

   — Rural Development — Chapters 20 to 22

   — Ways and Means — Chapter 23

   — Area Summaries — Chapters 24 to 47.

The 23 Area Summaries include one each for the 22 areas into which the Park is (for this purpose) divided, and one for the area centred on Buxton, which is almost surrounded by the Park. The Summaries set out the ways in which key relevant policies apply to those locations. They also refer to land outside the National Park where necessary, as in the case of joint studies with neighbouring authorities.

1.27 Content In each chapter, we summarise the relevant policies of the 1978 Plan and of other documents; state what has been achieved to implement those policies; outline the changes which have to be taken into account in the Review; and put forward the objectives to be pursued and the new draft policies. These policies are underlined at the end of each chapter, or of each section within a chapter. In the area summaries the style and format is a little different: in particular, no 'objective' is separately stated for each area.

Consultation and partnership

1.28 A key element in each chapter, as in the 1978 Plan, is the statement — after each policy — of *the main bodies who have power and responsibility to put the policy into effect.* The Board has obtained, as it did in 1978, the approval and active support of these organisations in framing and implementing these policies. A key purpose in the consultation on the Plan was to secure the agreement of these organisations to the

---

4 'Declarations of Commitment to the National Parks' published by Countryside Commission (CCP 247 1987).

proposals for collaborative action which are implied in each policy. The named organisations only remain in this final Plan with their agreement.

1.29 We have been asked by a number of consultees to re-emphasise this *Partnership*. The very success of the implementation of the Plan depends upon large numbers of partners. Only with their active agreement and participation will this Plan be implemented. It should be emphasised that most local government powers are with the Counties (e.g. Education, Highway, Social Services) and the Districts (e.g. Housing, Environmental Health). The 4 Metropolitan Districts are all-purpose local authorities. Thus there is a complex interrelationship between the Board, the Counties and the Districts. Many other organisations are involved in topics which lie outside local government powers and duties.

1.30 It is especially important to appreciate the local authorities' role when considering the third part of the plan — the Strategy for Rural Development. We can best emphasise this by quoting from the response by High Peak Borough Council to the Draft Plan:

"The Board is often dependent on others to achieve its widely supported objectives. The areas in which this is particularly important are many, but from this Council's point of view they would include not only responsibilities in the Park i.e. public sector housing, tourism and economic development/promotion, environmental health services, some highway functions etc., but also, and perhaps more importantly, those outside the Park, e.g. planning policies which seek to provide some of the things which are inappropriate to the National Park, certain employment provisions, alternative recreation facilities and an acceptance that the quality of the environment outside the Park, whilst very important, does not have the same intrinsic limitations or qualities."

1.31 This emphasis upon the interrelationship with the adjoining area cannot be stressed too much. We have discussed, especially with the District Councils, the relative roles of areas inside and outside the Park. We shall continue to explore and develop this relationship, particularly in the context of local employment and tourism marketing.

1.32 Before the 1978 Plan the Rural Land Management Executive Group (RLMEG) was established. This is a group of representative officers of the key organisations which are crucial to the implementation of land management policies including the Country Landowners' Association, the Ministry of Agriculture, the Nature Conservancy Council, the Forestry Commission, the National Farmers' Union, the Timber Growers' Organisation and the Board. English Heritage joined the Group in 1986. RLMEG has again taken a key role in the preparation of this Plan.

1.33 This approach to consultation, through specialist forums or meetings, has been extended. We now have many of them, including those engaged in farming, tourism, wildlife conservation, cultural heritage, footpath users and housing providers. There are regular meetings between representatives of the Board and of the shire district councils, the metropolitan district councils and the county councils. We will give as much time as we can to these means of co-operative management.

1.34 Facts and figures There has been no comprehensive review or resurvey of statistics or facts specifically for this

Review, but some information is new since the 1978 Plan. The Structure Plan Report of Survey[5] and the Additional Survey Report[6] contain our main database with lists and quantities of the Park's natural and man-made resources, such as the number of caves of scientific and recreational value. The 1981 Census has provided population statistics. Continuous traffic counting has been maintained.

1.35 A cordon interview survey of visitors leaving the Park was carried out in 1986/87. A report of this survey was published in Spring 1988 to coincide with the public and formal consultation on the Plan. A summary of some results of the survey are printed in Appendix 4. Major ecological and archaeological surveys are in progress. The Tourist Boards and the Ministry of Agriculture have provided data on recreation, tourist accommodation and agriculture. Surveys of derelict land and an initial review of mineral sites have been carried out. Other sources of information are referred to as necessary elsewhere in this Plan.

Priorities for Action: The Strategies in Practice

1.36 This is a long, complex and integrated document. A number of consultees felt that it may be helpful to give an *indication of strategy*. They felt that this should be set out near the beginning. This would then set the scene for the detailed content of the Plan.

1.37 We therefore set out below a broad statement of 17 main priorities for action over the next 5 or more years, drawn from the wide range of policies stated in this document. The Board, working with its partners, proposes to pursue these main priorities with vigour. We intend not only to protect the qualities of the National Park, but actually to enhance those qualities and to increase the well-being of those who live and work in it, or who visit it.

These priorities appear in the order of the following chapters and are not in order of importance.

	Main policies referred to:
1. Effective and sensitive conservation of the distinctive character of the different parts of the Park, noting the major distinction between the Natural Zone, the Rural Zone and the Settlements	2.20-2.21
2. Completion of the Section 3 Map, and bringing into place effective measures to secure the protection and management of the characteristic qualities of main types of land embraced by that Map	2.22 3.23-3.29 3.37-3.42 3.49-3.53 3.62-3.69 3.88
3. Sustaining the well-being of agriculture, consistent with conservation of the scenic, natural and historic features of the Park landscape and as the main means of securing that conservation. Of major importance in this regard are the use of the Farm Grant	4.23-4.24

5 Structure Plan Report of Survey 1974 and Report of Survey: Supplement (undated).
6 Additional Survey Report July 1977.

Notification system, AFSDO, the   **4.32-4.35**
Linked Advice Network and the Farm   **4.43-4.47**
Conservation Scheme   **4.55-4.57**

4. Securing the protection and sound
management of existing woodlands,
and encouraging appropriate creation of
new woodlands   **5.25-5.29**

5. Securing the protection of wildlife   **6.23-6.28**
habitats and significant species, both in   **6.35-6.36**
Nature Reserves and other designated   **6.46-6.48**
areas and throughout the Park   **6.61-6.63**
    6.73-6.77
    6.83-6.85

6. Review of planning consents
covering mineral sites, followed by
negotiations to secure appropriate
treatment of sites   **7.39**

7. Securing the protection of ancient
monuments, historic sites and other
features of the cultural heritage of the   **8.20-8.26**
Park   **8.35-8.40**

8. Securing the conservation and
enhancement of the settlements and
historic buildings in the Park, in a
manner which also serves the well-
being of the local community and the   **9.31-9.34**
strength of the local economy   **9.47-9.53**

9. The continued effective provision,
and where appropriate extension, of
facilities for public access and
enjoyment within the Park, consistent
with the conservation of the Park and
with the interests of its inhabitants,
within guidelines provided by   **10.17-10.21**
Recreational Zoning, the principle of   **10.28-10.31**
carrying capacity, the framework of   **Chapters 14-16**
Area Management Schemes   **Chapters 24-47**

10. Raising the whole standard of
maintenance, signposting and public
information on the rights of way
network in the Park   **11.30-11.41**

11. Sustaining, and where appropriate
extending, public access to open
country   **12.26-12.30**

12. Providing, and extending where
appropriate, facilities for specialist
recreational activities compatible with
the character of the Park and taking
account of the interests of its inhabitants   **Chapter 13**

13. Encouraging provision of
accommodation and other services for
staying visitors in or near the Park, in
the context of well-judged tourism
programmes, in a manner consistent
with the character of the Park and taking
account of the interests of its inhabitants   **Chapter 17**

14. Providing, and progressively
enriching, services of information,
interpretation and education for
residents of and visitors to the Park   **Chapter 18**

15. Providing an effective and versatile
Ranger Service within the Park   **19.13-19.14**

16. Encouraging contributions by
volunteers to the conservation of the
Park and other aspects of its
management   **19.27-19.31**

17. Contributing to the well-being of
those who live or work in the Park, by
means of the Rural Development   **20.16-20.20**
Programme; actions relating to   **21.15-21.17**
housing, employment or services; or   **21.29**
other action   **21.38-21.39**

1.38 These priorities are similar in scope to the 23 topics which were described in the consultation booklet (see Appendix 1) and reflect responses in the returned questionnaires.

Programme, 'Functional Strategies' and Budget

1.39 The action proposed or implied by the Board in this Plan exceeds the current trend of an annual 10% increase in the Board's budget. The same may be true for some of the Board's partners. The Plan does not contain a time-tabled programme for action into the late 1990s. Such a programme could well be shaken by unforeseen events, and much will depend on the resources available to the Board and its partners. Moreover, the Board is now required to submit each year to government, in support of its bid for grant, a statement of 'Functional Strategies' which outlines a programme for its own expenditure over the next 3 years. We believe that financial programmes are best handled in this way, not in the National Park Plan. The Functional Strategies will be linked to this Plan by annual monitoring and by a computerised budget system.

Introduction

2.1 The National Parks are identified as the most extensive beautiful areas of England and Wales. The 1949 Act defines the conservation purpose — 'natural beauty' — as including not just scenic beauty but also the geological and ecological qualities of the locality. The reports commissioned by Government[7] which led to the 1949 Act also laid great stress upon the historic components of landscape. They recorded the fact that the beauty of the proposed Parks had been enriched by human activity, especially farming. National Park designation was intended to safeguard this heritage.

2.2 National Park designation was also intended to make available the resources of the Park for public enjoyment. There has occasionally been doubt about the kind of experience visitors seek when visiting the Peak District. The 1986/7 Visitor Survey shows that it is the qualities of beauty and wildness, a rich wildlife and a sense of contact with the past that are sought by the great majority of visitors. The 'unspoilt' and 'uncommercialised' nature of the Park is particularly valued.

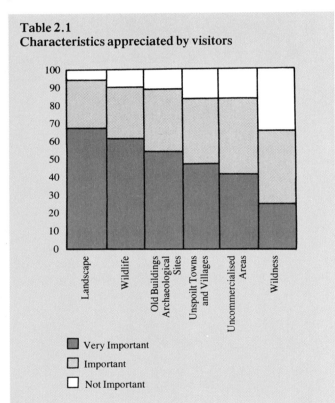

**Table 2.1
Characteristics appreciated by visitors**

Legend:
- ■ Very Important
- ▫ Important
- □ Not Important

2.3 The analysis of the Park landscape carried out for the Structure Plan in 1974 recognised the links between geology, topography, vegetation patterns and human activities. Since then, more has been learnt about the history and wildlife of the Park. This Review therefore contains more detail on subjects like archaeology and nature conservation.

2.4 Paragraphs 1.4 and 1.5 describe the four main elements which distinguish the Peak National Park:

(a) its landscape beauty, arising from the interaction between natural forces and human activity.

(b) its attractive settlements and buildings.

(c) its position at the south end of the Pennines, surrounded by fertile lowlands and the Midland and Northern industrial towns and cities.

(d) its tranquillity, wildness, nature and history, perceived by all human senses.

2.5 The character and qualities of the Peak National Park depend not just on the individual contribution of these particular elements, but also the combination of distinctive elements and the way in which they vary from place to place. Maintaining the distinctive 'Peak District' character of the Park is a challenging concept, but one that runs right to the heart of the National Park concept. It is what visitors seek and what local communities take pride in. Yet the Peak District is a working landscape, shaped by farming and forestry activities. It is also home for a substantial number of people working in and around the Park. Making the Conservation Strategy relevant to the local community is of crucial importance.

2.6 The remainder of this chapter describes the three conservation policy zones which were established in the Structure Plan and the 1978 Plan; describes the special areas, some of which has specific statutory protection; introduces the five main landscape types; and records the legislation introduced by Section 3 of the Wildlife and Countryside (Amendment) Act 1985 to give further status to some landscape types. The policy at the end of the chapter sets out the main elements to the Conservation Strategy for the Park and the overriding policy for the three zones.

The Natural and Rural Zones and Settlements

2.7 The 1978 Plan defined three zones, in each of which a distinct stance was to be taken on the balance between natural forces and human development. These are defined as follows:

(a) **The 'Natural Zone'** consists of those areas where the vegetation is almost entirely self-sown, with only minor modification by human activities. There are few buildings or obvious signs of human influence such as field boundaries. The clearest example is the moorlands of the Dark Peak. The Natural Zone areas are not truly 'natural' since human influence (even if only in the form of grazing livestock) has considerably shaped the environment. However, they are the nearest thing to wilderness in the Park, and probably in England. Natural qualities must predominate in future management.

(b) **The 'Rural Zone'** consists of the enclosed farmland and plantation woodlands and the scattered farmsteads and field barns. In this zone, the hand of man is much more obvious. Field boundaries form a dense network and the trees are normally managed as even-aged timber crops. The degree of man's influence varies from place to place (e.g. some woods contain a high proportion of native trees). In the Rural Zone, the maintenance of distinctive local characteristics (for example the use of stone walls for field boundaries or maintenance of the fields which are rich in wild flowers) is the key to conservation policy.

(c) **The Settlements** — hamlets, villages and two towns. A typical larger village will have houses, shops, school, pub, chapel, church and some industrial buildings. Most will be built of local stone. Each settlement has its own distinctive

---

7 The Dower and Hobhouse Reports of 1945 and 1947 respectively. The description of the nature and vulnerability of the Peak District in the Hobhouse report is reprinted at Appendix 3, with an introduction describing its relationship to the continuing development of policy and practice.

Map 2.1
Natural/Rural Zone

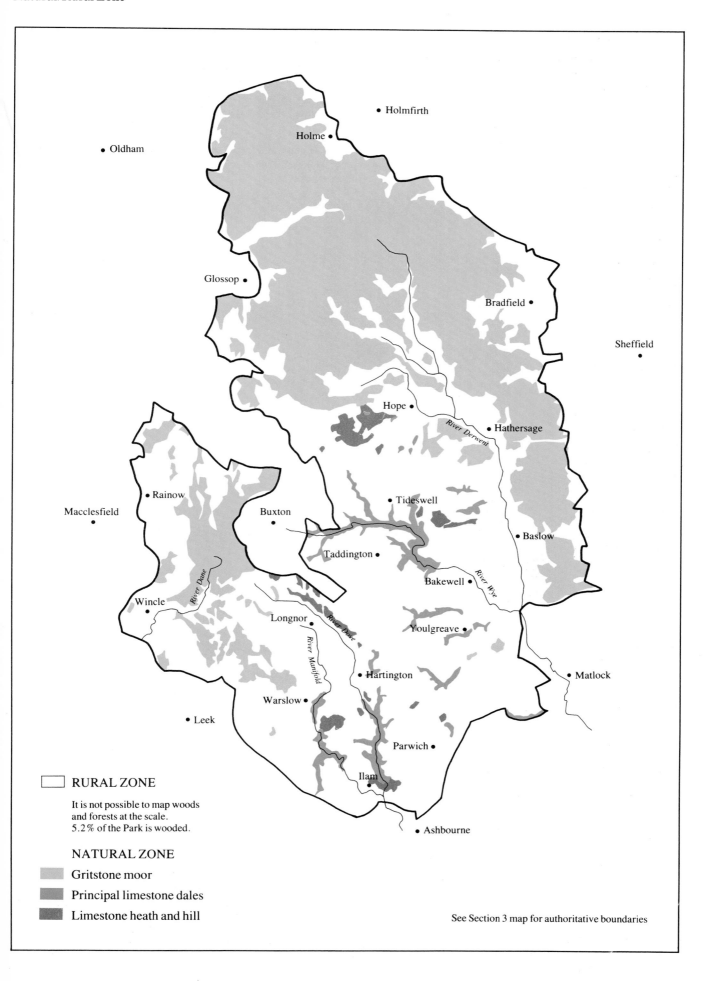

RURAL ZONE

It is not possible to map woods
and forests at the scale.
5.2% of the Park is wooded.

NATURAL ZONE

Gritstone moor

Principal limestone dales

Limestone heath and hill

See Section 3 map for authoritative boundaries

character, and conservation policy aims to maintain that character. Changes to each settlement should both respect National Park purposes, and meet the needs of its resident community.

The Natural and Rural Zones are shown in broad diagrammatic form on Map. 2.1. The Settlements are too small to show on this scale of map.

2.8 Management policies for the various types of land in the Natural and Rural Zones follow in Chapter 3. These contain basic policies for their conservation and enhancement. Policies which relate to the various activities, and which show how these land management policies are to be achieved, follow in Chapters 4 to 9.

2.9 The 1978 Plan set out policies to deal with shifts of land between the Natural Zone and the Rural Zone (for example, by afforestation or agricultural improvement). These policies need to be recast in the light of experience, particularly now that there is a new duty to define certain areas on a Section 3 Map (see **2.16-2.18** and **2.22** below). This sets out a priority for retaining the wild, semi-natural characteristics of areas on the Map. The relevant new policies are in Chapter 3.

Areas Needing Special Attention

2.10 The 1978 Plan recognised that within the three broad zones, there would be specific areas which needed particularly careful attention if their distinctive contribution to the character of the Park was to be maintained.

2.11 Some of these special areas have statutory definitions and protection set out in Acts of Parliament, such as:

— Conservation Areas — parts of the settlements which are of special historic or architectural quality (Section 277 of the Town and Country Planning Act 1971).

— Ancient Monuments — features of exceptional archaeological interest (Section 61 of the Ancient Monuments and Archaeological Areas Act 1979).

— Sites of Special Scientific Interest — areas with an exceptional nature conservation interest (Section 28 of the Wildlife and Countryside Act 1981, as amended in 1985).

2.12 Other special areas do not have statutory protection, but make their own distinctive contribution to the character of the Park. Examples are:

— Flower Rich Fields — those fields particularly rich in variety or number of wild flowers and herbs because of the particular way in which they have been farmed.

— Historic Landscapes — those areas where a particular phase (or phases) of the human use of the land in the past can be seen especially well.

2.13 'Special Area' policies are stated in the remainder of this Plan in the appropriate chapters (for example, Sites of Special Scientific Interest are dealt with in Chapter 6 — Nature Conservation).

Landscape Types

2.14 A typical panoramic view of the landscape contains a mixture of all three zones defined above (Natural, Rural and Settlement). For example a shale valley contains villages on the valley floor, farmland on the valley slopes and moorland on the open hilltops. The division of the Park into 'White Peak' (based on limestone) and 'Dark Peak' (based on gritstone) is particularly clear. Within both the Dark Peak and the White Peak, distinctive landscape types can be identified. The 1978 Plan identified five basic landscape types based broadly on combinations of land form, geology and vegetation pattern.

(a) **Gritstone Plateaux** These high plateaux are mainly moorland and rarely have settlements.

(b) **Gritstone Valleys and Slopes** This is predominantly enclosed farmland with farmsteads and settlements on the valley floor. The tops of the valley sides will often be moorland.

(c) **Valleys with Reservoirs** These are also gritstone valleys, with water areas on the valley floor. They tend to have a fairly high proportion of woodland; relatively little farmland; and few or no settlements.

(d) **Limestone Plateau** This is gently undulating farmland with limestone walls, copses of broadleaved trees and nucleated villages. Some high land will often be rough grazing or, less commonly, heathland.

(e) **Limestone Dales** These are steeply cut valleys and gorges with varying combinations of rock outcrops and scree, broadleaved woodland and scrub, open grassland and, occasionally on the dale bottom, enclosed farmland. Some dales have streams or rivers while others are 'dry' (having no stream except in prolonged wet weather).

2.15 Specific policies are not developed for these landscape types, as it is usually the components within them (the moors or the farmland for example) that best lend themselves to policy definition. An understanding of landscape types and their subdivisions helps to define the specific local circumstance when policies have to be applied (e.g. limestone field walls are such a dominant element on the limestone plateau that the use of any other boundary type needs strong justification). Where relevant in the rest of this Plan, stress has been given to the application of particular policies within particular landscape types.

The Section 3 Conservation Map

2.16 Section 3 of the Wildlife and Countryside (Amendment) Act 1985 lays an obligation on the Board to map certain areas of the Park which are 'particularly important to conserve' and to use guidelines published by the Countryside Commission. The Act requires that the Section 3 Map should include mountain, moor, heath, down, cliff and woodland. The Map was adopted in October 1988 and the Board will publish it in 1989. This will replace the Section 43 (Moor and Heath) Map, which was produced under the provisions of the Wildlife and Countryside Act 1981 and did not include woodland. The policies which relate to the Map are defined in Chapter 3 of this Plan and can be found in the following sections:

(a) Moorland — (**3.2-3.29**)

(b) Limestone Heaths and Limestone Hills — (**3.43-3.53**)

(c) Woodlands — (**3.70-3.88**)

2.17 The Commission's Guidelines acknowledge that policies similar to those defined for the land types covered by the Section 3 Map will often be relevant for other land types. In this National Park, the same type of policies that the

William Clough, in the Natural Zone . . . the nearest thing to wilderness in the Park.

Commission recommend certainly apply to at least one further category of land — the Limestone Dales. In the 1978 Plan, the basic conservation distinction was between the areas defined as Natural Zone and Rural Zone. This distinction has proved to be well accepted by other agencies and useful in practice. It is therefore proposed to keep the zoning policies in this Plan. The Section 3 Map will define in detail where the relevant policies in this Plan will apply. Except for woodlands the Limestone Dales are not mapped under Section 3 because the Countryside Commission does not consider that they come within the scope of the Act. For convenience of users of this Plan (because similar policies apply to them) they are shown on one map which thus becomes the Natural Zone and Section 3 Conservation Map. There will be a cross reference to the appropriate policies in this Plan.

2.18 The Guidelines for the Section 3 Map require the mapping of woodlands. Some of these woodlands fall within the Natural Zone while others are in the Rural Zone. Different policies will apply to the various types of woodland shown on the Map. Cross-reference will be given on the Map to the relevant sections of this Plan. The Section 3 woodland policies are found in the following sections:

(a) Shale-grit semi-natural woodlands — (3.31-3.42)

(b) Limestone Dales — (3.54-3.69)

(c) Trees Woods and Forests (3.70-3.88)

Objective
2.19 To maintain and enhance the particular qualities of the Park by careful recognition of the particular elements (and combinations of elements) that give each part of the area its distinctive National Park qualities.

Policies
2.20 All policies in this Plan relate to the primary purpose of National Park designation — the conservation of the distinctive character of the different parts of the Park — and are set in the context of the Structure Plan policy 8.25. Specific conservation policies will be developed in the rest of this Plan, and each will involve one or more of four main elements:

(i) The use of management techniques to maintain and enhance the distinctive character of different parts of the Park or different elements of the Park environment.

(ii) The sympathetic design and siting of new developments or changes in management practice to respect the distinctive character of the Park.

(iii) The development of measures to protect areas of special character or importance.

(iv) The removal (or mitigation of the impact) of features or elements which spoil the landscape of the different parts of the Park.

2.21 The distinctive characteristics of the three Zones (see 2.7) with their varying degrees of human and natural influences will be maintained as follows (subject to detailed policies in later Chapters):

(i) In the Natural Zone there will be a general presumption against obvious new man-made features and wild semi-natural conditions will be enhanced (See also Structure Plan policy 8.25).

(ii) In the Rural Zone, development and management of agriculture or forestry should respect and enhance

traditional Peak District characteristics. Other new development will generally be restricted to the settlments (SP 8.25).

(iii) In the Settlements, the particular character of each place will be identified, and efforts made to retail the best of the old while accepting new development which is in harmony with the character of the settlement. (Policies 2.20-2.21: Peak Board, RLMEG agencies, Constituent Councils).

2.22 The areas to which the policies for Moorland, Limestone Heaths and Hills, Woodlands and Limestone Dales relate will be detailed on the 'Natural Zone and Section 3 Map' which will be published in 1989 and reviewed as necessary (Peak Board).

Pollution and Disturbance

2.23 Pollution — of air, water or earth — is a major concern in the National Park, where a high quality natural environment is the primary objective. Air can be polluted by noise, dust, smoke or gases. Sources of pollution exist outside the Park (for example, industry, military aircraft, power stations) and inside the Park (for example, mineral extraction, manufacturing industry, road traffic, visitor activities, sewage and the generation of waste materials).

2.24 In the 1978 Plan, the generation of limestone dust by quarrying and processing was the main perceived concern. The second concern was with military aircraft training flights. Although relatively few in number then and now, low passes by high powered aircraft are very disturbing to both people and livestock.

2.25 Structure Plan policy 8.55 is to resist or control new development which would generate unacceptable levels of pollution, and to liaise with the pollution-controlling authorities. In 1988, these are the Health and Safety Executive, the Environmental Health departments of the District Councils and the Water Authorities.

2.26 Air pollution Since 1978, the number of quarries generating dust or noise (such as the limestone quarries and their processing plants) or toxic waste (such as the fluorspar industry) has declined. The Alkali Inspectorate and the limestone quarrying industry have together achieved substantial progress. The industry is still inherently noisy and dusty but less so than it was. Pollution has been a substantial factor in planning refusals (such as Topley Pike quarry) or planning approvals (such as Milldam Mine, with many pollution and waste control conditions). The pollution emitted by industrial processes in and around the Park is primarily a matter for the pollution-controlling authorities. Relatively high levels of lead in air-borne dust can occur in some former lead mining areas.

2.27 Traffic noise and fumes still affect both open countryside and, more acutely and chronically, villages where heavy cross-Park traffic passes through village streets. This subject is dealt with in the Structure Plan and the Transport Study. Noisy motor sports and intensive clay pigeon shooting are undesirable in the Park. There is a limited amount of low-flying by military aircraft.

2.28 'Acid Rain' has been recognised as a serious concern both worldwide and in this National Park. Oxides of sulphur and nitrogen are emitted from factories around the Park, dissolve in atmospheric water and deposit in the Park as dilute acids. This acidity affects mosses and lichens, trees, water quality, invertebrates and possibly higher orders of animals and plants. It is a contributory factor in moorland erosion, and in the erosion of natural stone masonry, including ancient monuments and historic buildings. The Board supports efforts to reduce air pollution particularly those recently announced to reduce the amount of sulphur in power station flue gases. The processes currently under consideration fall into two main types. One of these uses much more limestone than the other, and produces large quantities of gypsum, whilst the other produces sulphuric acid. There is more likely to be a use for the acid than for the gypsum. The CEGB's announcement that National Park sources of limestone will not be used is welcome. However, the use of the relatively scarce sources of purer limestone must, sooner or later, have a knock-on effect resulting in greater pressure on National Park sources (see **22.4-22.8**). The Board therefore hopes that the process with the lowest consumption of primary resources and the least generation of waste for disposal will be used wherever practicable. Research into air pollution is taking place in Manchester University.

2.29 Water pollution The purity of rivers in the Park is of importance to wildlife, recreation and for livestock and human consumption. Great vigilance and high standards should be maintained. Several Acts of Parliament set out the powers and duties of agencies and businesses with regard to water pollution. Pollution can arise from sewage works, industrial processes, silage and other farm effluents, and chemical fertilizers — particularly nitrates. Potential

pollution from certain agricultural operations may be included as part of a current review of the Control of Pollution Act.

Objective

2.30 To maintain and raise standards of purity of earth, air and water throughout the Park.

Policy

2.31 Development will be strictly controlled and other agencies will be encouraged to take measures to reduce and control pollution in the context of the relevant legislation and of the following paragraphs and policies in this Plan:

(a) the privatisation of water authorities (**1.19**)

(b) moorland erosion (**3.5 (b), 3.25**)

(c) environmentally sensitive farming (**3.96, 4.23, 4.40** and **4.45**)

(d) wetlands, marshes and rivers (**6.54**)

(e) mosses, ferns and lichens (**6.71**)

(f) the care of ancient monuments (**8.10**)

(g) the approach to noisy recreation (**10.8, 13.65-75, 13.106**)

(h) the selective encouragement of rural industries (**21.29**)

(i) mineral extraction, waste disposal, traffic and military activities (**22.30-22.33**) (Peak Board)

3 LANDSCAPE CONSERVATION AND LAND MANAGEMENT

Introduction

3.1 The 1978 Plan classified the land of the Park into 3 zones (see **2.7** and Map 2.1). It identified four types of land within the Natural Zone and two types of land in the Rural Zone. Policies for all six types of land are reviewed in this Chapter as follows:

- (a) Gritstone Moorland
  (Paragraphs **3.2-3.30**)

- (b) Shale-grit Semi-natural Woodland
  (Paragraphs **3.31-3.42**)

- (c) Limestone Heaths and Rough Grazings —
  now termed 'Limestone Hills'
  (Paragraphs **3.43-3.53**)

- (d) Limestone Dales
  (Paragraphs **3.54-3.69**)

} **Natural Zone**

- (e) Trees, Woods and Forests
  (Paragraphs **3.70-3.88**)

- (f) Enclosed Farmland
  (Paragraphs **3.89-3.99**)

} **Rural Zone**

Gritstone Moorland (Natural Zone)

3.2 The characteristic appearance of the moorlands is the result of periodic burning and regular grazing. The primary economic interests in the moors are grouse shooting and sheep farming. However other interests have strongly influenced the management of the moors. Water supply interests have regulated the use of many moors for many years and limited the type and intensity of farming activity. Conservation interests are becoming increasingly important as the National Trust and, more recently, the Peak Board, have acquired moorland areas. Large areas of moorland are designated as Sites of Special Scientific Interest. The interests of water supply management and conservation are generally consistent with grazing or grouse shooting, which depend on the traditional management carried out by farmers or gamekeepers. The recreation interest is primarily walking, and is dealt with in Chapter 12 (**12.1-12.30**) and Chapter 13 (**13.29-13.40**).

3.3 The 1978 Plan expressed concern at the possible adverse effects of high grazing levels. Heather moors are ecologically and visually more interesting than the grasslands that succeed them under high grazing pressure. The disappearance of heather also adversely affects grouse shooting interests, as heather forms both the preferred nesting site for red grouse and a major source of their food. Experimental work carried out since 1978 has confirmed that the vegetation cover on the moors of the Peak National Park is largely a matter of choice in management. Heather moors become grass moors when grazing levels are increased. Most grass moors could become heather moors by changing the management regime, provided that a source of heather seed is available to enable the heather to recolonise.

3.4 The 1978 Plan expressed concern at the erosion evident in many moorland areas and proposed a study to examine the

Noe Stool, a natural rock formation in the 'gritstone moorlands' — country for hardy walkers.

extent of the problem, its causes and the possible remedies. This study was set up in 1979 by a steering group with representatives of 12 different organisations (see **23.32**) with an interest in the management of the moors.

3.5 In 1981, a Phase 1 report was produced. This showed that erosion was a more serious problem on many moors than had previously been believed. It also showed that vegetation cover on the Peak District Moors had changed considerably during this century, with areas of heather decreasing and bracken increasing. The Phase 1 report concluded that there was no single simple cause, but rather a complex combination of factors that varied from place to place over time. The five factors identified were:

(a) The harsh climate (which can remove vegetation damaged by other agencies or can inhibit recolonisation of areas made bare by other factors)

(b) Atmospheric pollution (Sphagnum moss, the original peat-forming vegetation, is now virtually absent from Peak District Moors due to the high levels of pollution from 'smoke-stack' industries. Whilst sulphur fallout is less now, it is probably still too great for Sphagnum moss to recolonise) (see **6.71**)

(c) Trampling by people (which is the obvious direct cause of erosion on well-used footpaths, but its effect is exacerbated by the fragile nature of the ground and the severe climate)

(d) Accidental fires (which can be traced as the initial cause of several large bare areas)

(e) Grazing pressure (which seems to act mainly by inhibiting recolonisation of areas made bare by other factors).

3.6 The consequences of the current levels of erosion were also quantified. Some 8% of the moors are either substantially or partly bare of vegetation and a large additional area shows signs of incipient erosion. Grazing values are diminished, grouse numbers reduced and general wildlife interest deteriorates. Reservoirs with moorland catchment have been losing, on average, 1% of their storage capacity every 10 years due to silt and peat washed from the eroding moors.

3.7 In 1980, the Joint Study set up a series of experimental vegetation trials in a variety of locations typical of the varied circumstances of the Peak District Moors. These trials were designed to test whether or not the deterioration so far experienced was reversible. By 1983 the experiments were showing that, even in the harshest localities, extensive areas of bare ground would again support typical moorland vegetation using relatively simple techniques. Temporary removal of grazing was necessary to achieve the best results, but adequate results could be achieved in the milder areas with modest grazing levels. These results led to the establishment of larger scale trials, one using standard agricultural machinery and the other depending on a major input of volunteer labour.

3.8 The Steering Group agreed in 1987 that its terms of reference should be widened to embrace other moorland management issues, and be refocussed to provide a source of practical advice aimed at improving moorland management techniques. It is being retitled the 'Moorland Management Project'.

3.9 In spring 1980, a series of major fires gave an opportunity to study the effects of such fires and to improve the arrangements for fire prevention and fire control. Arrangements to close the moors at times of high fire risk have since been changed to introduce quicker procedures. Liaison between fire brigades, the Ranger Service, landowners and land managers has been improved. The 1980 fires were shown however to be not typical of the fires which initiate major erosion. They occurred in spring and burned lightly and quickly. The vegetation cover was not completely destroyed and the fire did not penetrate deep into the peat. The moor had the following summer to start recovery before the onset of tougher conditions in winter. Consequently the land affected has now largely recovered. The fires which do cause the damage seem to occur mainly in late summer, to burn intensively and deep into the peat and thereby destroy the vegetation and much of the seed bank held in the soil. Fortunately, there have been few fires of this type since 1976. Hopefully the improved preventative measures and fire fighting methods will reduce the area affected when fires occur in future.

3.10 In 1986, the Integrated Rural Development Project (see **23.26-23.29**) extended into a third trial area in two typical moorland parishes. 5 of the 9 eligible farmers were willing to participate in an experimental system of public funding designed to reward management work for conservation as well as food production. Additional jobs have been created and improved standards of moorland management should result.

3.11 Since 1978 the work done has helped to explain the dynamics of moorland change and has demonstrated that the different interests of farming, grouse management, conservation and recreation can be compatible with one another. There is a recognition that it is now possible to reverse the many years of deterioration in ways that will benefit all interests. In the 1978 Plan the priority was to investigate the extent and causes of deterioration and to identify contrasting priorities for different moorland vegetation types. It is now recognised that vegetation cover is largely a matter to be influenced by management. It is not inevitable that the existing situation has to be tolerated, rather new measures need to be introduced to produce the desired vegetation cover. It is therefore important to set new policies and priorities. These are, firstly, establishing mechanisms for improving management based on harmonising the different moorland interests and, secondly, encouraging new management techniques. It is no longer appropriate to have totally different approaches for the different existing moorland types. Modest adjustments to general techniques are needed to meet the specific circumstances of individual areas.

3.12 In 1988, the Ministry of Agriculture designated the northern Peak District Moors, together with the associated farms, as an 'Environmentally Sensitive Area' (ESA). One of the aims of the ESA (see Map 3.1) is to encourage management of the moors in ways which enhance their conservation values through appropriate management. The ESA will in particular encourage appropriate stocking levels on the moors, aim to improve standards of shepherding and encourage improvements to the vegetation cover. The use of fences to subdivide the moors is prohibited in the ESA prescriptions, although temporary fencing where revegetation work is in progress is accepted.

3.13 On those moors where the owners and managers have decided not to participate in the ESA (or for those moors which lie outside the ESA boundary), efforts will be made to achieve these objectives through the Farm Grant Notification procedures and the Farm Conservation Scheme (see Chapter 4) and by using the Moorland Management Project. The general policies which apply to all moorland areas are defined below.

3.14 Most of the present day moorland of the Peak District has never been enclosed and significantly 'improved' for agriculture. However there are many areas that have been moorland in the past but which are now enclosed, improved farmland. There are also some areas which are currently moorland but which were, at one time, enclosed and improved farm land and have reverted since to moorland. The 1978 Plan distinguished between 'core moorland areas' that had never been enclosed and significantly improved, and 'marginal areas' where land had been both farmland and moorland at various times in the past two hundred years or so, depending on the fortunes of the local farming industry. Policies to protect 'core' moorland were agreed, with a strong presumption against agricultural improvement or afforestation. For the 'marginal' areas, the 1978 plan envisaged the possibilities of carefully designed and managed change by a process of consultation.

3.15 When the Section 43 Map was produced (see 2.16), this required a somewhat different approach. The Map included all areas of moorland where this forms a significant landscape feature. Policies relating to the Section 43 Map were agreed by the Rural and Management Executive Group and revised in 1985. These policies indicated a 'strong presumption in favour of conserving the existing semi-natural vegetation' but accepted that there would be four circumstances where substantial change to the current vegetation might be appropriate:

(a) Regeneration of semi-natural woodland and plantations (where these have been included on the map because of the difficulties of excluding small woods from the map, or because of their moorland component) or the establishment of new small plantations.

(b) Scrub clearance.

(c) Bracken clearance.

(d) In exceptional cases, acceptance of agricultural improvement 'of enclosed land on the Map where it can be shown that over-grazing on moorland could not reasonably otherwise be relieved'.

3.16 Such management changes are most likely to be proposed in the 'marginal areas' of moorland as defined in the 1978 Plan. The 1978 Policy on core moorland remains valid and this, together with the Section 43 Policy statement has formed the basis for the policy statements in this Plan. These policies will be applied to the moorland areas defined on the Section 3 Conservation Map which will replace the Section 43 Map (see 2.16-2.18).

3.17 The Section 3 Map will identify the major areas of open moorland in the Park, defining the boundary where the moorland edge is at present (i.e. the Natural Zone boundary). Defining this boundary can be difficult but the intention has been to include those areas of moorland vegetation where there is a feeling of wildness together with contiguous land with a high proportion of moorland vegetation. It therefore includes both 'core' moorland and all the 'marginal areas' that are currently moorland.

3.18 Some areas of moorland vegetation will be excluded from the Section 3 Map because they are:

(a) Small scattered areas mixed in with enclosed farmland, or

(b) Enclosed rough grazing, usually on the edge of open moors, which only includes a small moorland vegetation component. In most cases, these areas are managed as part of enclosed farmland.

Policies for those smaller areas of moorland vegetation not shown on the Section 3 Map will be as defined in the Enclosed Farmland paragraphs, (3.89-3.99).

3.19 The two major land management changes that are likely to be proposed on the marginal areas within the Section 3 Map are agricultural improvement and afforestation.

3.20 Agricultural improvements in areas designated on the Section 3 Map are only likely to be agreed on marginal moorland. They will only be agreed where these improvements are associated with a change in management for the adjacent moorland which will have the effect of reducing the grazing pressure and encouraging the growth of a richer moorland vegetation. Careful siting and design will be appropriate.

3.21 The Section 43 Map policy referred to the possibility of establishing new small woods. Any substantial woodland planting is likely to be in the 'marginal areas'. It is most unlikely that large afforestation schemes similar to those which have occurred in the past (e.g. in the Goyt Valley) would be appropriate, but more modest plantations or the encouragement of semi-natural woodland (see 3.31-3.42) might be (e.g. in cloughs or on steep middle valley slopes). Some could be mixed plantations (especially if other woodlands in the vicinity are of that character), while others could aim to create woodlands similar in character to the shale-grit semi-natural woods (see 3.31). Similar policies to those applying to afforestation in the rural zone will therefore apply (see 3.84 in particular), although there will be a presumption that the land should remain in its existing management. The environmental effects of planting will be carefully assessed for its landscape, wildlife and archaeological impact. If planting were agreed, then it is likely that the area will be deleted from the Section 3 Map moorland category and put into the Section 3 woodland category once the plantation had become established.

Objective
3.22 To maintain or introduce techniques of moorland management that improve the conservation values of the moors by appropriate adjustment to grazing practice and grouse moor management.

Policies
3.23 The Natural Zone policy (see 2.21) applies to this type of land. In particular, subdivision of the moors by new boundaries will not be accepted unless these are temporary measures linked to revegetation work.

3.24 Management regimes will be encouraged which maintain or create well vegetated moors of benefit to an appropriate mixture of agriculture, grouse shooting, water supply, wildlife, landscape conservation and recreation by:

Map 3.1
North Peak Environmentally Sensitive Area

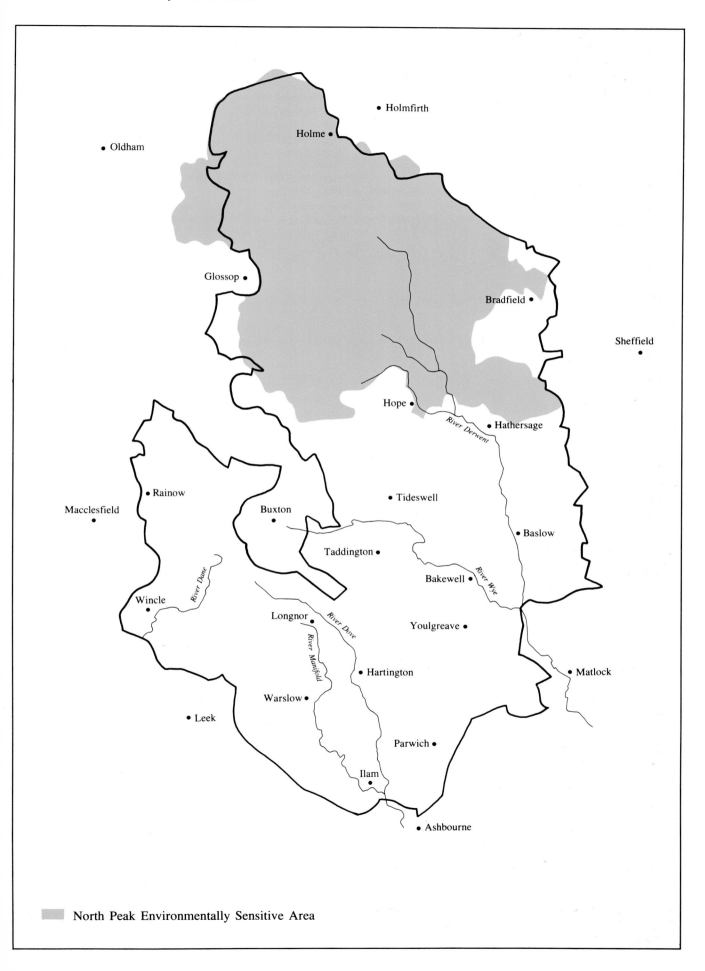

North Peak Environmentally Sensitive Area

(i) Special management incentives under an Environmentally Sensitive Area (ESA) designation (MAFF).

(ii) The development and promotion of a Farm Conservation Scheme (see 4.57) (Peak Board and RLMEG agencies).

(iii) Appropriate adjustments to tenancies, grazing and shooting licences by the relevant landlords when opportunities arise (Water Authorities, National Trust, Peak Board, CLA).

3.25 A Moorland Management Project will be chaired by the Ministry of Agriculture, linked to the ESA scheme and designed to provide advice based on practical research, showing how the objectives of improved moorland management can be put into effect (MAFF and other Steering Group members).

3.26 There will be a strong presumption in favour of conserving the existing semi-natural vegetation in the Section 3 moorland areas. Scrub control will be appropriate in some cases (but see also policies for shale-grit semi-natural woodlands — 3.37-3.42). Bracken control may also be needed (subject to the provision of the local code of practice — see 3.99). (RLMEG agencies)

3.27 In exceptional circumstances, agricultural improvement of land which is currently moorland but which has at some time been enclosed and significantly improved (the marginal areas — see 3.19-3.21) may be accepted provided that:

(a) it has no adverse effect on features of special importance,

(b) it is linked to management changes on adjacent open moorland that would enable livestock numbers to be reduced and encourage a rich moorland vegetation to develop and

(c) it can be sited and designed in a way appropriate to the character of the area. (RLMEG agencies).

3.28 All afforestation[8] proposals will be assessed for their environmental impact (see 3.21). Agreed schemes will generally be of modest scale, located on 'marginal areas' (see 3.14). Individual afforestation schemes will be carefully considered in relation to the character of the area and will be carefully considered in relation to the character of the area and will be sited and designed to be of a scale, shape and species composition appropriate to that character. (RLMEG agencies).

3.29 Agricultural improvement or afforestation should only be contemplated on 'core' moorland areas (see 3.14) in circumstances where it can be jointly agreed by the four relevant public agencies that such changes would be beneficial to the area. Afforestation is most unlikely to be agreed in the 'core' moorlands unless it is aimed at creating woodlands similar in character to semi-natural woodlands (see 3.21). (Forestry Commission, Ministry of Agriculture, Nature Conservancy Council & Peak Board).

3.30 Other policies of particular relevance to the gritstone moors are those related to shale-grit semi-natural woodlands (3.38), Bracken Control (3.99), Moorland boundaries (3.97 and 3.98) and Habitat Conservation (6.63).

Shale-Grit Semi-Natural Woodlands (Natural Zone)

3.31 Semi-natural[9] woodland is generally considered to be woodland having a tree and shrub layer composed of species native to the site (i.e. species that occur naturally in the Peak District, not those introduced by man). In the Park most of the semi-natural woodlands are remnants of the former native tree woodlands and are classified as Ancient[10] Semi-Natural Woodland. Oak, Birch and Rowan predominate in the shale-grit area of the Park. In addition, Secondary[11] woodland, usually of the same species, is gradually establishing itself on neglected pastures or open moorland in a few locations. Most of these shale-grit semi-natural woodlands occur on steeply sloping land of limited value to agriculture — which is why they are woodland. They are also of historical importance in that they demonstrate the former natural vegetation cover of most of the gritstone areas of the Park.

3.32 In the 1978 Plan, the importance of these woodlands was only just beginning to be recognised. The localities of the

---

8 'Afforestation' is defined in this Plan as the planting of trees on land where there is no tree cover at present, and does *not* carry the popular implication of blanket conifer planting.
9 Semi-natural woodlands consist of trees which have established themselves on site naturally from seed, or of coppice regrowth from trees which are themselves natural seedlings.
10 Ancient Semi-natural woodland is a classification used by NCC in its Draft Inventories of Ancient Woodland. Ancient Woodland sites are defined as those which have borne woodland since at least 1600 AD.
11 The term 'Secondary woodland' is used in this Plan to describe semi-natural woodland that is establishing itself on open land (or has done so since 1600 AD).

Padley Gorge, a delightful sheltered walk in the 'shale grit semi-natural woodlands'.

woodlands were only broadly known. Since then a series of studies has identified the locations of most of these woods. This has been followed in some cases by action on site. Usually the action most needed is to enclose the wood against livestock grazing. Such grazing inhibits natural regeneration and is the reason why so many of the ancient semi-natural woodlands appear to be more like a scattering of trees.

3.33 Action since 1978 to secure the regeneration of such woodland has been taken by a number of organisations. Notable examples are:

(a) Enclosure of part of the Black Clough woodlands in Longdendale under the terms of an NCC Management Agreement.

(b) Enclosure of a number of woods in the Upper Derwent by the National Trust, Severn Trent Water Authority and Derbyshire Wildlife Trust.

(c) Enclosure of Padley Gorge (one of the best examples of an ancient semi-natural oak woodland in the Park) by the National Trust.

(d) Acquisition of a number of woods by the Board (e.g. as part of the Eastern Moors Estate (see 35.6 and at Hayfield).

(e) Enclosure of the large open woodland area at Rollick Stones in Longdendale by the Board in conjunction with North West Water.

Action has also been taken that will, in time, lead to the establishment of new woodlands of a similar type. Planting of native species in cloughs and on steep valley sides has been carried out in the Wessenden Valley, at Shining Clough in Longdendale and on the National Trust's Kinder Estate.

3.34 The 1978 Plan was concerned to encourage management for conservation purposes as the 'normal aim', and to provide qualified circumstances in which livestock grazing or conversion to woodland of higher timber quality might be accepted. Since then it has generally been accepted that semi-natural gritstone woods (particularly ancient woods) are such a rare resource that regeneration work is desirable to ensure their perpetuation. (In some circumstances natural regeneration[12] would be the preferred means of achieving this). Grazing should only be accepted in the short term and conversion to more productive woodland is now unlikely to be accepted. Conservation agencies have demonstrated both the will and the ability to establish effective management aimed at natural regeneration, and have established completely new woodlands that will in time develop a natural character. There are however some locations where secondary semi-natural woodlands are beginning to develop as 'scrub' on moorland or other areas of land that are important to retain as open ground. Scrub control in such circumstances is desirable (see 3.26). Conversely development of secondary semi-natural woodlands on land that is currently moorland may be desirable for special nature conservation reasons. (This certainly applies in parts of the south west moors.)

3.35 Existing semi-natural gritstone woods, including areas which still have a woodland flora even though the tree cover may be very sparse, will be shown on the Section 3 Conservation Map. Other areas that are developing into such woods will be added to the Map on review.

Objective

3.36 To secure effective management of all shale-grit semi-natural woodlands aimed at maintaining and enhancing their semi-natural characteristics, and to establish new woods that will develop a natural character.

Policies

3.37 The Natural Zone Policy (see 2.21) applies to this type of land.

3.38 The aim for management of the shale-grit semi-natural woodland is its perpetuation, by excluding grazing and encouraging regeneration. (Where a boundary is needed, policies 3.97 and 3.98 apply). Planting of appropriate native tree species should only be accepted in ancient semi-natural woodland where tree cover is particularly sparse and where natural regeneration will not be effective. In secondary woodland, planting of appropriate native[13] tree species would normally be accepted (Peak Board, NCC, County Nature Conservation Trusts, National Trust, Forestry Commission).

3.39 Conversion of semi-natural shale-grit woodlands to primarily timber production woodlands will be resisted (Forestry Commission)

3.40 Periodic grazing of semi-natural shale-grit woods may be accepted in the short term if long term regeneration of the woodland is not adversely affected and if such grazing is compatible with other conservation objectives (Peak Board, NCC, County Nature Conservation Trusts, National Trust, Forestry Commission).

3.41 All the Ancient semi-natural woodland and the secondary woodland which it is considered important to conserve will be included on the Section 3 Conservation Map (Peak Board).

3.42 New areas of woodland using appropriate native[13] tree species may be established in cloughs or on steep slopes where this does not conflict with other conservation interests (see also 3.28) (National Trust, Water Authorities and RLMEG agencies).

Limestone Heaths and Hills (Natural Zones)

3.43 The 1978 Plan identified areas of open semi-natural grassland, not improved for agriculture, which in places contain a heathland type of vegetation. They display an immense variety of species mixtures from the purely calcareous grasslands through to the heaths. Different areas contain different mixtures of lime-loving and lime-hating plants depending on soil type and depth, agricultural management and many other factors.

3.44 The grasslands generally occur on thin soils on steep slopes where the soil is relatively alkaline and grazing has produced a characteristic flower rich grassland. They tend to occur on steep hillsides and hilltops and form a landscape very similar to the downs of southern England. They are usually enclosed by field boundaries but are distinctly different from the normal enclosed land as the enclosures are very large. 'Limestone hills' thus have an open, wild

---

12 Natural regeneration is the process by which seed from existing trees in the locality germinate and the resulting seedlings develop into mature trees.
13 For definition of 'native' see 3.31.

character (for example, High Wheeldon, Treak Cliff, Roystone Rocks, Eldon Hill).

3.45 On flatter areas, continued leaching has produced more acid soils which support a heathland vegetation. Where grazing is limited, this will develop into a rich vegetation dominated by heather and other ericaceous[14] shrubs. Such heaths were characteristic of the limestone plateau 200 years ago before the Parliamentary enclosures and associated intensification of agriculture. The more extensive areas of limestone heaths which are now found in very few locations (for example, Bradwell Moor and Longstone Moor) are therefore of wildlife or landscape importance, and of considerable historic importance as the last remains of a formerly very common landscape. The limestone heaths are one of the rarer semi-natural habitats and are under considerable risk from changes in agricultural management. They are often accessible to agricultural machinery and even if not ploughable can be improved for food production by fertiliser application or other techniques. Increases in grazing pressure can also reduce the variety of flowers and herbs and, in particular, can eliminate the ericaceous shrubs.

3.46 Since the 1978 Plan a detailed survey of the limestone heaths has been undertaken, together with a basic survey of the limestone hills. A SSSI is being declared by NCC on Longstone Moor (the largest area of Limestone Heath remaining). The Peak Board has concluded Management Agreements on other areas of Limestone Heath. In total 118 of the 148 ha of Limestone Heath are protected by SSSI designation or by Management Agreement. Management Agreements or other measures to influence the management of other areas will be an important priority. Thus since 1978 the rarity of limestone heaths has been documented and appropriate action initiated. The emphasis is switching from trying to establish a programme of action to maintaining and building on the existing programme of work in collaboration with owners and land managers.

3.47 The major areas of limestone heath are shown on the Section 3 Map because they contain moorland species. The limestone hills are on the Map because of their downland character. Similar habitats also occur in the limestone dales (see **3.54-3.69**). Other smaller areas occur in the enclosed farmland. Relevant policies for these fragments of enclosed semi-natural limestone habitats are therefore in **3.96** below.

Objective
3.48 To maintain the remaining areas of limestone heath and open limestone hills as important landscape and historic features of great ecological interest, and to improve management for nature conservation values.

Policies
3.49 The Natural Zone policy (see 2.21) applies to this type of land.

3.50 The areas of limestone heath and the limestone hills with an open wild character will be included as two separate notations on the Section 3 Map. Where field boundaries are necessary (e.g. around the perimeter of the Section 3 Map areas) policies 3.97 and 3.98 will apply. (Peak Board).

3.51 Intensification of agricultural use and afforestation on the limestone hills and limestone heaths will be resisted. Improvements in management by defining appropriate levels of livestock grazing for conservation benefits will be

secured through the SSSI provisions or by other means (e.g. the Farm Conservation Scheme — 4.57) (NCC and Peak Board).

3.52 The Limestone Heaths will be priorities for protection by Management Agreements and similar action because of the rarity of this type of land. (Peak Board, NCC).

3.53 Scrub incursion on the limestone heaths will be resisted by introducing appropriate management. On the limestone hills, scrub incursion can be managed to improve the range of habitat types, but the characteristic smooth outlines of the hills should be maintained.

A curiosity-heather hates lime, but acid soils have built up in the "limestone heaths and hills".

Limestone Dales (Natural Zone)

3.54 The limestone dales are among the most beautiful landscapes of the Park. They are of international importance for wildlife conservation. Many of the dales are already managed by conservation bodies or are SSSIs. Extensive grazing is the main agricultural use in most dales, although there are a few improved fields. Most of the woodlands are semi-natural. Some are managed for timber production. Some dales have streams or rivers, while others are 'dry' (no flowing water except in prolonged wet weather).

3.55 Scrub has spread through many of the limestone dales during the last century, probably because of a reduction of traditional sheep grazing. Some scrub has been there for centuries, and is rich in species. Hazel scrub in particular is very rich in associated plants and animals. However, in many dales, hawthorn scrub and secondary woodland threatens to cover some areas of the landscape, changing the scenery and often masking the splendid natural sculpture of rock bluffs and screes, and eliminating the grassland. The dale grasslands contain the widest variety of plant species found in the Park. These areas are irreplaceable and scrub is a major problem when it is encroaching into them. With different soil depths, slopes, water content and aspect, many dales contain an immense diversity of wildlife. The succession of flowers adds to the scenic interest. A study of scrub incursion in the Limestone Dales has been initiated. It indicates that scrub control should concentrate on maintaining areas of herb-rich grassland and keeping well-loved rock features open to view.

3.56 The 1978 Plan gave priority to establishing effective management of the dales. The aim was to maintain the

---

14 Ericaceous: plants of the order Ericales (Heather, bilberry, etc.).

mixture of grassland, scrub and woodland which varies from dale to dale. Policies aimed to enhance natural qualities by encouraging natural regeneration of the woodlands and introducing conservation-orientated management. Since 1978 a considerable area of the dales has been brought into management by the National Trust, County Nature Conservation Trusts and the Nature Conservancy Council.

3.57 Action along the lines agreed in 1978 has concentrated on the need for:

(a) definition of Management Plans for the more important dales

(b) scrub cutting and other tree felling to limit scrub incursion and to open up rock features

(c) maintenance of sheep grazing of the grasslands by the use of Management Agreements which define stocking rates, type of stock and time of grazing (or grazing licences on NCC managed land)

(d) improved control of livestock management (with many stone walls rebuilt)

(e) removal of sycamore to retain the character of the native ash woodlands.

3.58 The 1978 policies remain broadly relevant and only minor changes are made in this Plan reflecting operating experience and the increased emphasis on conservation management. The increased scale of conservation management of the dales should make the achievement of policies easier in future.

3.59 The agricultural use of the limestone area has changed considerably over the past century, with more dairy cattle and fewer sheep. Traditionally, sheep were kept in the dales, and the resulting pattern of grazing did much to sustain the flower-rich grasslands and to control scrub incursion. Following milk quotas, many farmers are turning again to sheep and beef. However the use made of the dales needs careful regulation. Too many animals or grazing in the wrong place or at the wrong time of year would be very damaging. The limestone dales are farmed in conjunction with the enclosed fields of the limestone plateau. The plateau landscape itself contains many landscape features that depend on appropriate farming practice (e.g. stone walled field boundaries, flower rich fields, small woods). The White Peak, based on the limestone dales could therefore be ideally suited to the establishment of a further 'Environmentally Sensitive Area' (see **4.19**) or the use of other methods which ensure an appropriate type and intensity of agricultural use.

3.60 The woodlands of the limestone dales will be included on the Section 3 Map. Some of the semi-natural woodlands in the limestone dales are of ancient origin, while others are secondary woodlands. In a few cases plantations have been established on Ancient Woodland sites, but they may retain the ground flora associated with ancient woodland if appropriate tree species were planted. The remaining areas of the dales (scrub and grasslands) will be indicated on the same Map but in a different notation (see **2.18**). Thus the integrity of the dales as distinctive landscape units should be plain to see from the Map. As the Map is reviewed, further areas may be added to the woodland category in those cases where scrub gradually develops into woodland. Only recognisable woodland will be included on the Section 3 Map.

A dynamic mixture of river and rock, scree and scrub, grassland and woodland. Water-cum-Jolly Dale, one of many limestone dales.

Objective

3.61 To ensure the maintenance of the distinctive mix of semi-natural habitats in the limestone dales by appropriate conservation orientated management.

Policies

3.62 The Natural Zone policy (see **2.21**) applies to this type of land.

3.63 Existing management plans for the various limestone dales will be maintained and new plans developed. These will show how the maintenance of the distinctive mixture of grassland, woodland, scrub, rock outcrops and scree will be maintained to enhance their landscape, wildlife and geological interest. Action outline in **3.57** will continue to be taken. (County Nature Conservation Trusts, NCC, Peak Board).

3.64 The natural regeneration of the ancient semi-natural woodlands will be encouraged. In some areas, complete exclusion of grazing livestock and careful management of visitor access will be needed. Where possible secondary[15] semi-natural[15] woodlands should be managed in the same way. The possibilities for conversion to more commercially productive woodland will be limited due to access and slope problems, but will usually be undesirable even where favourable circumstances exist. (NCC, Peak Board, Forestry Commision).

3.65 There is very little scope for afforestation by planting in the limestone dales. The limited areas of commercially productive woodland will be managed so as to maintain, and where possible enhance, their wildlife value and natural character (Forestry Commission, Peak Board, NCC).

3.66 Scrub control will be undertaken where necessary to maintain important open grasslands and views of important rock features. Some scrub of wildlife importance will be maintained and perpetuated by rotational cutting. Other areas of dense scrub will be encouraged to develop into semi-natural woodland (NCC, County Nature Conservation Trusts, Peak Board, National Trust).

3.67 Efforts will be made to ensure that the grassland areas of particular wildlife or scenic importance are regularly grazed, the scrub removed, and existing limestone walls

15 For definitions see footnote to paragraph 3.31.

Another classic scene, in the rural zone. Trees, woods and forests and the walls around them do not look after themselves.

are refurbished to permit control of livestock. Some new walls or fences may be necessary in some areas. The few areas of enclosed improved land in the dales should continue to be used as part of this management system. Where boundary work is necessary, policies 3.97 and 3.98 will apply (NCC, National Trust, County Nature Conservation Trusts, Peak Board).

3.68 There will be an examination of the means by which an appropriate agricultural management regime of an 'environmentally sensitive' type might be introduced for the limestone dales and related farmland plateau. (MAFF, Peak Board, NCC).

3.69 The woodlands of the limestone dales will be recorded on the Section 3 Map. The boundaries of the dales will also be shown, but in a separate notation (see 2.18) (Peak Board).

Trees, Woods and Forests (Rural Zone)

3.70 Trees, woodlands and forests make a contribution to the character of the Peak District out of proportion to their surface area, which over the Park as a whole is about 5%. As well as providing landscape, wildlife and recreational benefits, they offer employment and raw materials for local businesses. In many cases, timber production was the main reason for their establishment.

3.71 There are three broad types of tree cover in the Park. The largest wooded areas are the conifer forests of the shale-grit valleys, often planted around the margins of reservoirs.

By contrast the woodlands associated with the enclosed farmland are smaller and usually broadleaved or mixed broadleaved and conifer. Especially notable are the woods of the limestone plateau which are small, scattered plantations of beech, sycamore, ash and elm. Semi-natural woodland is mainly confined to the limestone dales and the higher and steeper slopes of the shale-grit valleys (see 3.60 and 3.31-3.35 above).

3.72 The 1978 Plan encouraged continued development of woodland management in ways that contribute to the conservation objectives of the Park. Close liaison was proposed between the Peak Board, the Forestry Commission and all other interested parties. The broadleaved character of the small woods on the limestone plateau, compared to the larger conifer and mixed conifer/broadleaved woodlands on the gritstone, was recognised. Policies aimed to maintain the small woodland character of parts of the Park, especially the limestone plateau, by promoting Forestry Commission grant schemes; through acquisition by the Peak Board; by developing grant and management schemes to be introduced by the Peak Board; and by co-ordinating the grant schemes of other bodies. The 1978 Plan provided guidelines for the management of semi-natural woodland and identified circumstances in which large-scale afforestation might be acceptable. The 1978 Plan also stated that the Peak Board would make particular efforts to maintain and establish single trees and groups of trees in villages, where such tree features were of historic importance and in association with recreational developments. This work has been carried out as part of the village work described in Chapter 9 and the area management plans described in Chapters 24-47.

3.73 The policies established in the 1978 Plan remain relevant. The main changes have been in the methods used to encourage appropriate woodland management and the improved consultation arrangements introduced by the Forestry Commission. These include the development of new national grant schemes to encourage broadleaved woodland establishment and management, especially on farms. These developments in methods are recorded in Chapter 4, while this section concentrates on land management policies for forest, woodland and trees. Policies for the semi-natural woodlands are set out in paragraphs 3.37-3.42 and 3.62-3.69. As the land management policies for the other tree and woodland areas have scarcely changed since 1978 they are repeated virtually verbatim below.

3.74 **Larger Woods and Forests** The management of the larger predominantly conifer woods is almost always based on timber production as a primary objective. However management is increasingly paying regard to National Park interests by measures such as:

(a) The adjustment of plantation boundaries to avoid breaking open moorland skylines.

(b) Amending the boundaries of plantations or compartments[16] to produce shapes that fit the natural contours (and modify the harsh rectilinear appearance of early plantations).

(c) The introduction of a proportion of broadleaved species, especially alongside rights of way and streams.

(d) Careful design of clear felling areas to minimise abrupt changes in the landscape.

(e) Where a plantation is important for rare wildlife species (e.g. Goshawk or Red Squirrel), land management needs to take this into account. Where some disturbance is inevitable, this should be carefully timed.

3.75 There has been controversy in other National Parks and other upland areas about new large-scale afforestation schemes. There have been few such problems in the Peak District, where consultation has ensured that afforestation schemes which have proceeded were acceptable. Schemes which were not acceptable to the Board have not proceeded, despite the absence of legal controls on afforestation, thanks to the co-operation of the owners or managers. Most of the extensive conifer forests are managed by the Forestry Commission or the Water Authorities. There is only one private forestry company scheme in the Park, established in the early 1970s at Gib Tor (see also 5.9).

3.76 The 1978 Plan concluded that further large scale coniferous afforestation would be unlikely to be appropriate in the Park other than in certain shale-grit valleys. The agreed 1978 policy is repeated with only minor changes below (3.84).

3.77 **Small Woods** A characteristic feature of much of the Peak District is the scatter of small individual woods which break up the dominant land use of enclosed farmland. These woods are mainly plantations, originally established by the large estates for a combination of motives (game, shelter, beauty, timber or use of land damaged by mineral working). With the decrease in the proportion of land owned by the estates and the increase in costs of small-scale woodland management, few of these woods are in active management. Some such woods have been acquired by the Board (see 23.10). To improve the incentives to owners of such woods, the Board, the Ministry of Agriculture and the Forestry

Commission have introduced special grant schemes, particularly aimed at small woods on farms (see 4.49, 5.7 and 5.13).

3.78 Some small woods, especially those owned by the Peak Board, have been managed under a selection system (i.e. small areas are felled and replanted at regular intervals to give a varied aged structure to the woods). However such a system is very expensive and can only really be justified where the particular wood is of exceptional landscape importance. In cases where there are many small individual woods in a landscape, it will usually be more economic to clear-fell and replant each wood in turn, while ensuring that there is a balance of young, medium age and mature woods in the area. When the woodland is larger, dividing it into compartments and dealing with the different compartments at different times is likely to be appropriate, to ensure that the woodland as a whole always has a significant element of mature trees.

Objective
3.79 To maintain the distinctive woodland character of the different parts of the Park, and to improve standards of management to ensure that woodlands make an increased contribution to conservation objectives.

Policies
3.80 The Rural Zone policy applies to this type of land (see 2.21).

3.81 The basic character of the woodlands of the Park should be maintained, with broadleaved species predominating on the limestone area (in some cases conifer 'nurses' are necessary to help broadleaved trees become established) and mixed broadleaved and conifer woodlands on the grit and shale-grit areas. An increase in the proportion of broadleaved species used in the shale-grit areas will be encouraged (see also 3.86) (Peak Board, Ministry of Agriculture, Forestry Commission).

3.82 As with field boundaries (see 3.97-3.98), the use of local stone or hedges as woodland boundaries will be encouraged. This should provide adequate stockproofing, but the use of rabbit sleeves or tree shelters will be necessary while young trees are becoming established. Rabbit fences should not be used to replace walls for woodland boundaries, although such fences may be necessary on a temporary basis for large areas of young trees (Peak Board, Ministry of Agriculture, Forestry Commission).

3.83 When management plans for existing extensive woodland areas are revised, the opportunity will be taken to improve plantation or compartment outlines, to introduce a greater proportion of broadleaved species where appropriate and to improve the wildlife, scenic and recreational values of the area (see 3.74). Care will also be taken in the design of felling areas so as to minimise the inevitable short term change in the landscape (Forestry Commission, Peak Board).

3.84 There are some areas of poor farmland of limited wildlife value that might be suitable for quite extensive afforestation. Such planting should be designed carefully to retain better farmland in agricultural use, provide shelter benefits, avoid sites of particular wildlife or historic

---

16 Compartment: a sub-division within a woodland defined for management purposes. Typically one compartment will be different from its neighbours in its species composition or age or both.

'Enclosed farmland' consisting of lanes, small irregular fields and outlying farmsteads. It is managed by 2,000 farm businesses.

importance, and integrate into the landscape character of the area. Such large-scale planting should generally be limited to shale-grit valleys already associated with coniferous woodland or around the fringes of reservoirs (NB Policies for the moorland areas apply to many areas that might be suitable for afforestation — see 3.23-3.29) (Forestry Commission, Peak Board).

3.85 Small-scale woodland planting integrated with farmland will be encouraged throughout the Rural Zone, subject to wildlife and archaeological conservation interests, with an emphasis on encouraging the restocking of existing mature woodlands. There will be particular emphasis on the limestone plateau area, where most mature but unmanaged woodlands are situated (Peak Board, Ministry of Agriculture, Forestry Commission).

3.86 The policies on shale-grit semi-natural woodlands, and on plantations and semi-natural woodlands in the limestone dales, set out in 3.37-3.42 and 3.62-3.69 above, will be applied (Forestry Commission, Peak Board).

3.87 Efforts to maintain and establish single trees and groups of trees will be concentrated on:

(a) Villages and their settings (see 9.31)

(b) Landscapes of historic importance where trees are an important element (e.g. parklands 9.54-9.61)

(c) New developments, to help to integrate buildings into the landscape (larger scale developments may need woodland scale planting)

(d) In ancient parklands and wood pasture (see 6.59).

Appropriate use of Farm Grant Notifications, AFSDO (see 4.38) and planning conditions will be a major means of encouraging such work (Peak Board).

3.88 The broadleaved and mixed plantation woodlands of the Park will be defined on the Section 3 Map (see 2.16-2.18). A few conifer woods where landscape considerations are the primary consideration will also be included on the Section 3 Map, but only where there is specific agreement that the woods will be managed in this way. Where felling of such woodlands on the Section 3 Map is needed, then policies 3.81-3.83 and the considerations set out in 3.74 will be applied. (Peak Board, Forestry Commission).

Enclosed Farmland (Rural Zone)

3.89 Some 50% of the area of the Park is occupied by enclosed farmland. This section sets out the policies for this land type. The operation of the various mechanisms by which these policies can be implemented are set out in Chapter 4. The enclosed farmland of the Park is almost entirely grassland although in a few areas arable crops are grown. The enclosed grasslands have often been 'improved' to increase their agricultural productivity but it is in the 'unimproved' grassland that much of the wildlife interest of the farmland is found. Such fields have not been subject to fertiliser application or herbicide use on any significant scale. Such grasslands are often rich in colourful flowers which make a special contribution to the landscape during Spring and Summer.

3.90 For many visitors, it is the almost universal use of stone walls for field boundaries that sets the Peak District apart from the surrounding lowlands (70% of visitors thought that landscape was a very important reason for their visit[17]). Some walls are particularly striking landscape features, for example the 'strip fields' around many villages (see 8.17c) or the boundary wall between enclosed land and moorland. As the Park is a mainly livestock area with small farms, small fields have often been retained, with walls and (in some areas) hedges retained to a greater density than is commonly the case in the rest of England. The Countryside Commission's Upland Landscapes Study showed a clear trend towards larger fields and the replacement of stone walls and hedges by post and wire fences. For many years, field enlargements and the replacement of traditional boundaries was common, often resulting from the grant schemes offered by the Ministry of Agriculture. Since the 1978 Plan, the Ministry has ceased to grant aid removal of field boundaries and has introduced extra grant-aid for construction or renewal of boundaries in traditional materials.

3.91 The Farm Grant Notification Scheme (see 4.36) has given the Peak Board an opportunity to influence the management of enclosed farmland. Farmers are encouraged to retain 'unimproved' fields and to concentrate their efforts on maximising the use of already improved or partly improved land. This approach balances the need for conservation of important wildlife and landscape features with the need to ensure the continuation of a viable local farming industry which is essential for social, economic and environmental reasons. Farmers are also encouraged to maintain existing field boundaries (where necessary with the addition of one or two top-wires to prevent sheep jumping the wall) in preference to replacing walls or hedges by post and wire fences. To assist in defining where different types of field boundary work are appropriate, RLMEG has agreed a local 'Code of Practice' which is summarised in 3.97 and 3.98 below. Most farmers willingly accept modifications to their original proposals, to bring work into line with the Code. Management Agreements with financial compensation are only necessary where 'improvement' of fields is the farmer's only real alternative to increase agricultural income, but where such improvement would damage significant wildlife or archaeological conservation interest (see 4.43).

3.92 Changes in the Ministry of Agriculture grant schemes and the introduction of positive conservation incentives — such as the Farm Conservation Scheme (see 4.48) and the Environmentally Sensitive Area concept (see 4.19) — are changing the climate of farming opinion. They mean that conservation of flower-rich fields and maintenance of traditional field boundaries are becoming objectives for farm management as well as food production. While in 1978 food production and environmental conservation might have been competing claims on the management of farmland, they are now seen to be potential partners. The aim in the next few years is to make this partnership a reality, with farmers taking as much pride in the wildlife of their fields and the condition of their field boundaries as in the milk yields of their cows. This will have the added benefit of increasing the attraction of the area to staying visitors either on the farm or in the village. Maintaining the distinctive Peak District environment is of increasing importance in the lives of the wider local community as a contribution to the general 'quality of life'.

3.93 Encroachment of bracken onto steeper fields in the gritstone area has been a particular concern of farmers. Bracken has also encroached onto many moorland areas. Bracken spreads rapidly and is difficult to control. It is of no agricultural value (indeed it can be harmful to grazing livestock) and can often replace important grassland or moorland habitats. In some cases, however, eradication of bracken can create problems of soil erosion or can cause wildlife losses if, for example, the dense cover is important for more sensitive animals. The chemicals used for bracken control can also affect other ferns: where these are of wildlife importance, special care needs to be taken. A local 'Code of Practice' for bracken control has been agreed by the relevant local organisations through RLMEG.

Objective
3.94 To encourage effective agricultural management of enclosed farmland, while ensuring that farmers and owners give increased attention to the management of their land for environmental conservation.

Policies
3.95 The Rural Zone policy (see 2.21) applies to this type of land.

3.96 The management of 'unimproved land' to maintain or increase its wildlife and scenic values will be encouraged by developing the approaches of the Environmentally Sensitive Area and Farm Conservation Scheme (see Chapter 4). Where agricultural improvement is needed, efforts will be made to ensure that this is directed to the unimproved land of least environmental value. Land of high agricultural value should be maintained in good productive condition wherever possible (RLMEG agencies).

3.97 Management of existing traditional field boundaries will be encouraged by a variety of methods, including developing the approaches of the Environmentally Sensitive Area and Farm Conservation Scheme. Where major field boundary work is needed, the use of traditional materials will be encouraged, particularly by renewing existing boundaries (RLMEG agencies).

3.98 The use of netting or post and wire fences parallel to existing drystone walls will be discouraged. The use of one or two strands of 'jump wire' to existing boundaries will be encouraged, provided no other netting or wiring is used and provided walls are maintained in good condition. Where no existing boundary can be renewed and a new boundary is essential, walling or hedging will be used as appropriate wherever possible. Only where it is agreed that high costs make this impossible will fencing be used. The Local Code of Practice on which this policy and policy 3.97 is based will be used in discussions on all field boundary proposals and will be reviewed as necessary (RLMEG agencies).

3.99 The eradication of bracken will be favoured where there has been relatively recent invasion or where conditions have not favoured bracken domination, provided that this does not otherwise conflict with landscape or wildlife interests and in accordance with the agreed local Code of Practice (RLMEG agencies).

---

17 Appendix 4 contains a brief summary of the Visitor Survey.

4 FARMING

Introduction

4.1 The landscape of most of the National Park has been created to varying extents by farming activities. Although much of the inherent attraction of the National Park is due to the natural landform and vegetation, farming and its resulting features (field boundaries, farmsteads and barns) have reflected and in many ways accentuated the ecology and landforms. Thus the highest land is open moorland, the steeper slopes are rough grazing and the dense network of stone walls form the enclosed landscapes of the shale valley bottoms and the limestone plateau.

4.2 The type of agriculture also reflects the physical conditions. Half of the Park is enclosed farmland in which grassland predominates. Rough grazing dominates the remainder. Especially on the sheep farms of the north, the balance between rough grazing and enclosed 'in bye' land is a constraint on the farm enterprise. Dairying still dominates the lower lying land and the limestone area, but the effect of milk quotas (which were intoduced in 1984 to limit, and then to reduce, milk production) has been to encourage many dairy farmers to diversify into livestock enterprises (beef and especially sheep). Grouse management is an important element in the management of many moorland areas, although it is rarely the farmer who is the manager of the grouse. Most commonly the sheep are managed on a grazing licence system, and the moorland management rests with the landlord or the shooting tenant.

4.3 All the Park is a 'Less Favoured Area' under European Economic Community (EEC) regulations. This means that special Ministry of Agriculture financial assistance is available to farmers. Two forms of assistance are especially important:

— the Hill Livestock Compensatory Allowances, paid per head of breeding ewe or suckler cow

— preferential rates of grant for certain types of capital investment.

4.4 Many landowners and farmers have been sympathetic to conservation and have managed their land with conservation in mind. However this was often achieved in a piece-meal way and almost despite the then prevailing climate of public policy. When the 1978 Plan was written, the ability of the Peak Board and other conservation interests to influence agricultural management was very limited. Conservation priorities had to be identified; and great reliance was placed on voluntary discussion, initiated by farmers and owners, to incorporate conservation requirements into farming practice. National agricultural policy was addressed almost singlemindedly to food production, as it had been for over forty years. Conservation policies had to operate within the constraints of the food production priority.

4.5 Things have changed over the past ten years, and it seems certain that further changes will occur in the near future. The two most fundamental changes in recent years have been:

— the change in agricultural policy, whereby the achievement of conservation objectives is increasingly an element in agricultural grant schemes. Conservation and food production are no longer necessarily competitors but are starting to become partners in a more broadly based land management policy

— the direct involvement of conservation organisations in influencing management practice in detail on individual farms.

4.6 The Current Position Since the 1978 Plan, farming has changed considerably. Up to the mid 1980s agricultural output from the Park steadily increased, especially in sheep production. The number of farms remained stable while the numbers employed in agriculture appears to have increased. This is remarkable, for the national pattern since the 1940s and the local pattern until the 1970s has been for increased production to be accompanied by a decrease in the number of farms, an increase in their average size and a fall in the number of people employed in farming. The recent local trend can be seen in Ministry of Agriculture statistics reproduced in Table 4.1 below. Several points may be noted:

(a) While the number of farms has been broadly stable, there has been a marked change in the size of farms. There has been an increase in the number of large farms (over 80 ha) and of small farms (less than 20 ha) while there are fewer medium-sized farms.

(b) The number of dairy farms has fallen, while livestock farms and part-time farms have increased in number. However 'part-time farms' are classified by the amount of

Land which has been improved over the years has less conservation value.

theoretical employment they generate. The Ministry of Agriculture calculate 'standard man days' of the labour requirements for the type of land and numbers of stock. In practice many 'part-time' farms provide the sole income for the farmer and are often worked on a full-time basis.

(c) The numbers of cattle are broadly stable, but there has been a very large increase in the number of sheep.

(d) The statistics in tables 4.1-4.3 cannot be easily compared with data in the 1974 Report of Survey or the 1978 Plan. Those figures were from the 1971 agricultural census and prepared on a different basis. For example, a number of parishes are split by the Park boundary. The earlier data were compiled by dividing the statistics for the 'split parishes' pro rata for the proportion of land inside and outside the Park. The figures in these tables use the figures for whole parishes and are therefore exaggerations of the data for the Park alone.

CHANGES IN FARMING 1977-86

Table 4.1
Changes in number and size of farms 1977-86

Size in ha:	1977 number	%	1986 number	%	Change
Less than 10	140	6.3	166	7.4	+26
10-19	517	23.1	535	23.8	+18
20-39	672	30.0	613	27.3	−59
40-59	413	18.5	394	17.5	−19
60-79	203	9.1	199	8.8	− 4
80-89	110	4.9	132	5.9	+22
100-149	100	4.5	107	4.8	+ 7
150+	83	3.7	103	4.6	+10
Total	**2,238**		**2,249**		**+11**

Table 4.2
Changes in farm types 1977-86

Farm type	1977 number	%	1988 number	%	Change
Dairy	796	35.6	731	32.5	−65
Livestock	255	11.4	290	12.9	+35
Pigs/poultry	28	1.2	29	1.3	+ 1
Arable	6	0.3	12	0.5	+ 6
Horticulture/ fruit	13	0.6	17	0.8	+ 4
Mixed	11	0.5	12	0.5	+ 1
Part time	1,129	50.4	1,158	51.5	+29
Total	**2,238**		**2,249**		**+11**

Table 4.3
Changes in livestock number 1977-86

	1977	1986	Change
Dairy cows	43,718	44,344	+626
Beef cows	13,457	12,598	−859
Other cattle	77,652	76,961	−691
Breeding ewes	123,735	194,446	+70,711
Other sheep	134,454	222,793	+88,339

4.7 These statistics, which compare the position at the start and end of a ten year period, do not seem to support the general feeling that farming has recently entered a period of fundamental change, not just in the Peak District but throughout the United Kingdom and indeed the rest of the EEC. This change is being brought about by the sheer success of the industry in responding to Government exhortations for more than 40 years to produce more food, more efficiently. The result of this process has been the generation of surpluses in many foodstuffs. Because of EEC policy, this surplus food is bought at above world prices by an EEC 'intervention' system which provides a guaranteed market for most agricultural products. This means that the surplus food has to be stored (at a cost to the EEC) and eventually disposed of, often at further cost again. Most commentators believe that this agricultural policy needs fundamental reform. The crucial questions are likely to be when, what form any replacement policy might take.

4.8 While the number of farms has remained broadly the same and the stock numbers have increased, the profitability of farms has declined between 1977 and 1987. On a national basis the income of Hill and Upland Livestock Farms has declined by more than one third during this period, with most of this decline being between 1982-1987. The picture for dairying is similar. A high proportion of farmers (one third in 1983) have a source of earned income apart from the family farm[18].

4.9 Any changes in EEC and National Policies for agriculture will need to balance the food production requirements with the social and economic consequences of any changes, and with the environmental side-effects which any change in agricultural practice is bound to create. The first signs of the general direction of future policy can be seen in action taken in the last few years:

(a) The introduction of milk quotas which limit the amount of production the EEC will support financially and which impose penalties on any production above this level.

(b) The encouragement of farmers to 'diversify' into new forms of economic activity ancillary to farming. Special government grants have been available since 1985 to farmers in the less favoured areas to assist them in setting up new enterprises. On 1st January 1988 the Ministry of Agriculture introduced the Farm Diversification Grant Scheme for new business enterprises on farms (see also **4.25-4.35**).

(c) Woodlands are seen to be an alternative enterprise that will also have the effect of taking out of agricultural use and thereby reducing agricultural production. Again special grants are being introduced to help farmers move into new woodland enterprises (see Chapter 5).

(d) The introduction of Environmentally Sensitive Areas (ESAs) which encourage farmers to manage their land in a traditional way with the aim of conserving the environment. It is hoped that food production in the ESAs will be stabilised (see **4.19** below).

(e) The initiation of a debate on 'set aside'—deliberately taking land out of agricultural use to reduce food production. According to some commentators an area equivalent to the whole of the ten National Parks could be

---

18 All figures from 'Farm Incomes in the United Kingdom' 1987 edition, HMSO.

Perhaps the most intensive event in the farmer's year. There are now more sheep than ever before.

taken out of agricultural use completely and there would still be a problem of surplus production at the turn of the century. This is one of the reasons behind a more liberal attitude to building development on agricultural land introduced in 1986. Government has however made it clear that there is no change in policies in National Parks where strict control of building is essential for environmental reasons. In July 1988 following EEC legislation, the Ministry of Agriculture launched a Set-Aside Scheme. This voluntary scheme is designed for arable farmers willing to take at least 20% of their land out of production.

4.10 Changes of this sort have complex, and in some cases potentially serious, implications for the landscape and other features of the National Park. There are three possible ways in which the position might change over the next few years:

(a) Substantial areas might be taken out of agricultural use altogether with uncertainty as to the replacement use. In January 1988 the Government published a consultation paper which envisaged taking land at present used for beef or cereal production out of agricultural production. A cereal Set Aside Scheme was subsequently introduced (see 4.9(e)). Set aside cereal land cannot be put to 'green fallow' — i.e. it cannot be used for livestock production. The Government is now examining the more complex issue of 'extensification'; proposals affecting both the cereal and livestock sectors may be forthcoming. The use of nitrates is also being examined.

(b) Farmers may wish to turn to activities that are not necessarily compatible with National Park interests in order to maintain their incomes (for example dealing in scrap metal, industrial uses in remote areas, high intensity recreation use). Issues of this kind are already arising in planning applications. The introduction of the Farm Diversification Grant Scheme and the Set Aside Scheme may prompt pressure for new enterprises on farms.

(c) Farmers might be encouraged to earn a substantial part of their income from environmental management. The ESA approach is a first step in this direction.

4.11 A key way forward is to build on the ESA approach and on techniques learnt in the experimental Integrated Rural Development (IRD) Project (23.26) and initiated in the Farm Conservation Scheme (4.48). The aim would be to encourage farmers to secure new supplementary sources of income from business enterprises that contribute directly to National Park

conservation, such as stone wall contracting, woodland management, moorland management, building renovation. Such activities can generate employment and new sources of income from conservation work. These kind of incentives for appropriate land management work could be allied to other forms of non-agricultural employment, such as farm tourism enterprises or small workshops, but only of a type and scale appropriate to the National Park.

4.12 The IRD work has shown that the rural economy and rural employment can be improved while actually benefiting environmental interests. MAFF, the National Farmers' Union, the Country Landowners' Association, the Peak Board and many other organisations have been partners in this work and it is this form of partnership which should be the key to future initiatives. This envisages a completely different relationship between food production and environmental conservation. Instead of conservation being a constraint on agriculture to be sparingly, sometimes reluctantly accommodated, it becomes an integral part of farming activity. This is quite a different relationship and one that was only hinted at in the 1978 Plan.

4.13 This chapter therefore sets out to examine how the situation has changed since 1978 and to set general directions for future policy. Policies for different types of land are set out in chapter 3. The remainder of this chapter sets out future policy and the means by which it may be implemented. It is divided into the following sections:

— Future directions for agricultural policy (4.14-4.35)

— Farm diversification (4.25-4.35)

— Farm Grant Notifications and the Agriculture and Forestry Special Development Order (4.36-4.47)

As in the 1978 Plan, these policies have been developed with the Rural Land Management Executive Group (RLMEG).

Future Directions for Agricultural Policy

4.14 In 1978 it was accepted that there would be a continuing need for food production to increase. The 1978 Plan sought to minimise the problems this might have for conservation interests, for example by defining special areas as 'Historic Landscapes' or 'Herb Rich Meadows'. Farmers were encouraged to have regard to the character of the Park in their food production activities, for example by the maintenance of stone walls. Special incentives to encourage environmental management were thought worth considering, but not envisaged on the scale now possible. Management Agreements were thought to be a useful means of encouraging farmers to maintain important environmental features in special circumstances.

4.15 In 1978 the conservation agencies only had formal influence over a few aspects of agricultural activity, mainly farm buildings. The 1978 Plan therefore set out general principles and hoped that farmers would follow them, influenced by Ministry of Agriculture advisers. In 1980 a new administrative procedure was introduced by the Government, which obliged farmers and owners who intended to carry out work on which they would claim Ministry of Agriculture grant to first obtain the agreement of the Peak Board (throughout the Park) and the Nature Conservancy Council (in Sites of Special Scientific Interest).

Thus, for the first time, conservation agencies were able to influence farming activities of all kinds by direct negotiation.

4.16 In 1978 the Peak Board had already begun to explore the use of Management Agreements to encourage the management of particular areas of land for conservation objectives. The NCC had made use of these Agreements for nature conservation purposes for many years. The ability of the Park Board to apply Management Agreements was improved by the Wildlife and Countryside Act 1981. This Act also modified the way in which the Peak Board could apply Farm Grant Notification procedures. It introduced an obligation to offer a Management Agreement where discussions on a Notification failed to be resolved amicably and the Ministry of Agriculture agreed that the work should not go ahead. This form of Management Agreement involves a payment to the farmer, based on a calculation of the difference in profits the land would yield with or without the work originally proposed. The 1981 Act also introduced new arrangements for Sites of Special Scientific Interest, whereby consultation is required with NCC on any work which might damage the interest of the site.

4.17 The nature of the Ministry of Agriculture grant schemes in 1980 was that they were aimed primarily at increasing food production. Conservation agencies were therefore seeking to modify proposals that were frequently contrary to conservation objectives. Since 1980, the Ministry have gradually changed their grant schemes so that environmental management is encouraged more directly and the more obviously environmentally damaging work is no longer eligible for grant aid. For example in 1980 there was a 50% grant for new field boundaries of any type in the Less Favoured Areas. As a result most boundary notifications were for new fences. In 1987 there is a differential rate of grant between new walls (60%) and new fences (30%): top wires to well maintained existing walls are eligible for the 60% rate of grant. In the early 1980s the trend was for walls to be neglected and be replaced by fences. In 1987 the trend is to rebuild walls or to retain existing walls and top-wire them. Government grant is thus now more in harmony with conservation aims.

4.18 Between 1982 and 1988 the Integrated Rural Development (IRD) project (**23.26**) showed that many farmers would willingly work towards conservation objectives, given simple incentives to maintain existing features like stone walls and flower-rich fields (**6.57**). By encouraging routine maintenance, there is less need for much more costly capital investment later ('a stitch in time saves nine'). The lessons of this approach are being incorporated into a new Farm Conservation Scheme (see **4.48**).

4.19 In 1988 the Government designated the North Peak as an ESA (see also **3.12**). The ESA system falls part way between the Capital Grant Incentive system, the Management Agreement method and the IRD approach. It encourages routine management of conservation features by means of a 5 year Agreement linked to a special grant system and also encourages capital investment of an appropriate type. It prohibits damaging work as part of the Agreement. The detailed way in which the ESA system works is likely to develop with experience.

4.20 In 1987 the Countryside Commission announced[19] That it would press for the the introduction, in the next 5 years, of a completely new agricultural policy regime in the National Parks — a regime that would combine food production and environmental conservation in a single policy applicable to the whole of the land in the Parks.

4.21 In 1978 the achievement of conservation objectives could only be secured when it was compatible with food production. Conservation agencies had very little opportunity to influence farming practice. In 1987 the position is dramatically different and it seems quite possible that environmental managemant will become an increasingly important justification for all government policies for agriculture in the National Parks.

Objective

4.22 To encourage gradual change in the role of agriculture to become increasingly aimed at both food production and environmental management and to create new economic and employment opportunities for farmers in this joint role.

Policies

4.23 Policies for the development and extension of 'Environmentally Sensitive' agriculture regimes will be applied (MAFF, Peak Board, other RLMEG agencies).

4.24 The possibilities will be pursued of establishing a new agricultural policy covering the whole of the National Park in which farmers will be encouraged to manage their land for joint purposes of environmental conservation and food production (Countryside Commission, Peak Board, MAFF).

Farm Diversification

4.25 An element in the developing agricultural policy described above has been the encouragement of farmers to 'diversify' — to obtain an increasing proportion of their income from activities other than food production. This has at least four main elements:

(a) The new businesses must be compatible with National Park interests.

(b) The farmers should have the necessary skills to engage successfully in new enterprises.

(c) The farmers should be able to obtain the advice needed to ensure that they choose the most appropriate new enterprises.

(d) The opportunity should be taken to encourage farmers to take on a wide variety of financially rewarding conservation work.

4.26 In March 1987 the Government published a policy statement 'Farming and Rural Enterprise', outlining a variety of approaches to farm diversification. The main widely-canvassed types of diversification are:

(a) Workshops for craft and farm-related and clean, light industry.

(b) Tourism (see **17.50**).

(c) Woodland industries (see **5.29**).

All three of these may have their place in certain circumstances, but all three require farmers to have (or acquire) skills other than farming. All involve capital investments with uncertain returns and all depend to some extent on the right location for success. Simple diversification

---

19 'National Parks : Our Manifesto for the Next Five Years', CCP237, 1987.

related to the existing skills of the farmer or the existing buildings on the farm has often been successful. The establishment of the Peak and Moorlands Farm Holidays (PMFH) Group and the camping barns scheme are examples of this (see Chapter 17). This suggests that the best approach might be to seek new business opportunities in activities much more closely related to agricultural skills, which require little new capital investment. There is a tremendous amount of work needed in conservation management and farmers have already proved very adept at this. For example, stone wall contracting has grown considerably in recent years and there is a great deal of scope for other work of this type.

4.27 A further possible diversification is the processing of food on the farm for sale 'at the farm gate' or for wholesaling. The sale of local food products in village shops and catering businesses in the Park could be encouraged, strengthening the producer/retailer links (see **21.29**). In 1988, MAFF introduced its new Farm Diversification Grant Scheme, (see **17.13**).

4.28 Through its development control powers and established Structure Plan policies, the Peak Board is able to assess farm diversification proposals and resist those of a scale, type or location inappropriate to National Park conservation. The IRD project has shown that new economic and employment opportunities of many different types can be created that positively contribute to conservation objectives, for example, by finding new uses acceptable for redundant traditional buildings (see **23.26-23.29**).

4.29 In 1986, the Ministry of Agriculture announced a Farm and Countryside Initiative aimed at encouraging people to learn countryside skills through a Manpower Services Commission Training Scheme (MSC). The method chosen was to use groups of unskilled youngsters working in mobile groups under the supervision of an hitherto unemployed supervisor. There should be an opportunity to train youngsters within the more effective working relationship of a small business. This would have the added benefit of providing an additional source of labour to help that business to prosper.

4.30 The RLMEG agencies all feel that this approach, based on mobile gangs, is not well-conceived. The mobile gangs are likely to take work away from local businesses. It would be much better to place trainees in small numbers with existing businesses. This would provide better training; enable the business to take on more work, and to be more competitive by having reduced labour costs; and produce a better standard of finished work. There are some signs in the new Employment Training Scheme that representations made on these lines may be having some effect (but see **1.23**).

Objective
4.31 To encourage diversification of business and employment opportunities related to agriculture but in ways that contribute to, and do not conflict with, the conservation of the distinctive character and qualities of the different parts of the Park.

Policies
4.32 Grant aid will be provided to encourage various new rural enterprises on farms linked to agricultural activity such as drystone walling, woodland management, food and timber processing and building construction, but only of a scale, type and in a location appropriate to other National Park policies (especially the Structure Plan).

Appropriate assistance will be given to marketing such enterprises (MAFF, RDC, Tourist Boards, Peak Board).

4.33 Continuing and consistent application of Structure Plan policies will be used to oppose diversification proposals which, by virtue of their type, scale or location, are incompatible with National Park policies (Peak Board).

4.34 Encouragement will be given for training to enable new enterprises to be set up or for new employment opportunities to be sought, particularly in skills which contribute directly to National Park objectives (see **4.32**) (RDC, Agricultural Training Board, Training Agency).

4.35 Ways in which training initiatives might also benefit local businesses will continue to be explored and appropriate action taken (Ministry of Agriculture, Peak Board, Training Commission).

Farm Grant Notifications (FGNs) and the Agriculture and Forestry Special Development Order (AFSDO).

4.36 In 1980 the Ministry of Agriculture introduced new procedures whereby the Board (and NCC inside SSSIs) have to be consulted by farmers intending to carry out work for which they intend to claim grant. This gives an opportunity to 'modify' (by agreement with the farmer) the investment work so that conservation interests can be safeguarded or enhanced. The decision on whether or not grant should be paid remains a matter for the Ministry, but every opportunity is used to reach agreement rather than to have to seek a Ministry ruling by recording an 'objection'. Since the Wildlife and Countryside Act 1981 an objection upheld by the Ministry automatically triggers the need for the Peak Board to offer a Management Agreement with compensation (see **4.16**). In these cases, where a farmer's proposals can not be modified by agreement, because of a fundamental incompatibility with conservation objectives, negotiation towards a voluntary Management Agreement is offered and if it is accepted by the farmer no objection is registered. It is worth pointing out how much willingness there is among farmers to agree (without financial compensation) to modify their original proposals to meet conservation objectives. It is also interesting that very few formal objections were registered and even fewer resulted in the need for the Minister to make a determination. In recent years 30% of notifications have been 'modified' in this way (table 4.4). The 1981 Act also changed the arrangements in SSSIs and the duties and role of the NCC but the position in relation to Management Agreements is broadly similar (see also **4.16** above).

4.37 In 1985 the Ministry of Agriculture changed its grant scheme to introduce an Agricultural Improvement Scheme (AIS). As noted in **4.17** above this encouraged work of environmental benefit. Many items of work that could cause environmental damage (e.g. moorland 'improvement') were deleted from the list of grant-aided investments. The AIS also required farmers to agree the work with both the conservation authorities and with the Ministry before carrying out the work. The new AIS therefore largely eliminates the problem of retrospective notification. (Between 1980 and 1985 the farmer could do the work and then seek grant; such 'retrospective' claims had to be evaluated by the conservation

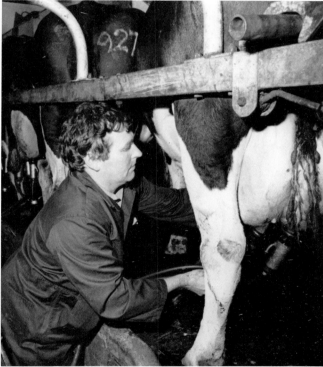

There is growing support for 'environmentally friendly farming' — a return
to a closer unity of the purposes of food production and care for our
landscape, wildlife and cultural heritage — for all to enjoy.

authorities but in some cases 'unable to approve' had to be recorded as it was impossible to know whether or not the work had damaged conservation interests). The outcome of the 3849 notifications made to the Peak Board between October 1980 and March 1988 is recorded in Table 4.4 below.

4.38 In November 1986, the Government introduced a new procedure to replace the Landscape Areas Special Development Order that had operated in parts of the Park since before the Park was designated. This new Town and Country Planning (Agriculture and Forestry Development in National Parks etc.) Special Development Order 1986 (AFSDO) extended farm building controls throughout the National Park. Anyone intending to construct, extend or alter a farm building or a farm road must notify the Peak Board first. Work must not be started until agreement is reached. Buildings or roads required for forestry, open silage clamps or storage areas, feed hoppers and slurry stores fall within the scope of the regulations. The Board has combined the administration of AFSDO with the administration of farm grant notifications. Table 4.5 shows the numbers of AFSDO notifications processed since November 1986. Again there is a large number of agreed modifications, and in this case no formal objections.

4.39 The Peak Board has produced a 'Farm Building Design Guide' in consultation with other RLMEG organisations to set standards for farm building work. Among its recommendations are:

(a) The use of dark coloured roof cladding (normally dark brown in the gritstone area and dark slate blue in the limestone area).

(b) The planting of belts of broadleaved trees to help the buildings to fit into the landscape.

(c) Use of stone walls to enclose related stockyards and similar features.

4.40 Waste disposal facilities are also frequently notified under Farm Grant or AFSDO procedures. Attempts are made to ensure that waste disposal techniques minimise adverse effects on important habitat and do not cause pollution of water courses. Water Authority approval is also required for such grant aided installations and for other agricultural proposal that may affect water quality. Extensions to the powers of the Water Authorities under the Control of Pollution Act also seem likely, which will influence farming practice whether or not grant aid is being sought.

4.41 There has been concern that two of the changes introduced in 1985 — cessation of grant-aid for certain kinds of work, and lower rates of grant for some other items — might mean that conservation authorities may no longer be notified of all work. In other National Parks there have been cases in which farmers, being refused grant, nonetheless proceeded with the work. To meet this concern the Government circulated proposals for a new 'Landscape Conservation Order' in 1987. In principle, this would provide conservation authorities with the ultimate response to agricultural change, a power of last resort to prevent works going ahead. Although the proposed Order was strongly welcomed in principle by conservation authorities, there was much criticism of the detail in the proposals, particularly on mechanisms for notifying the proposed work. In September 1988 the Government announced that it would not make Landscape Conservation Order regulations; this decision was a surprise and a disappointment to conservation bodies.

Objective
4.42 To use all formal application and notification procedures to influence agricultural practices to make them as compatible as possible with conservation interests.

Policies
4.43 Farm Grant Notifications and AFSDO procedures will continue to be the basis for negotiating changes to agricultural proposals so that they meet National Park objectives in line with policies in this Plan. Most adjustment will be sought by modification in agreement with the farmer, but when agreement to the work cannot be reached in any form, Management Agreements (or other financial incentives to maintain the conservation interest) will be considered (Peak Board, MAFF).

4.44 Where new roads or buildings are proposed for agriculture or forestry purposes, careful consideration will be given to their siting, scale, design, colour and materials. Structure Plan policies, the Farm Building Design Guide and the policies in this Plan will be the basis for determining planning applications, AFSDO and AIS notifications (Peak Board, MAFF).

4.45 Proposals for storage and disposal of farm waste products will be influenced to avoid damage to vegetation

Table 4.4
Farm Grant Notifications: October 1980 to March 1988

Number of Notifications	Agreed as Notified	Modifications Agreed	Withdrawn	Management Agreement Sought	Unable to Approve (Retrospective)	Objections	In Hand
3,849	2,715	875	90	39	13	24	93

Table 4.5
AFSDO Notifications: November 1986 to March 1988

Number of Notifications	Agreed as Notified	Modifications Agreed	Withdrawn	Refused	Planning Permission Needed	In Hand
331	103	191	7	0	7	23

of National Park importance or contamination of water courses, and to take account of siting and design considerations as set out in 4.44 (Peak Board, MAFF, Water Authorities).

4.46 Where grant aid is not sought for farm investments, farmers will be encouraged to consult conservation authorities with their proposals, to ensure that conservation interests can be taken into account before work goes ahead (MAFF, NFU, CLA, FWAG,[20] Peak Board).

4.47 Government will be requested to honour its original commitment to introduce a new Landscape Conservation Order procedure to deal with those rare circumstances where voluntary agreements cannot be reached on farm or forestry investment proposals (Peak Board).

The Farm Conservation Scheme

4.48 The roles of the Ministry of Agriculture and the Forestry Commission have changed in recent years in that they increasingly give advice on conservation work. Farming and Wildlife Advisory Groups (FWAGs) have also been established since 1978, based on Counties; and the Peak Board have offered financial assistance to the various County FWAGs operating in the Park. With so many different organisations giving conservation advice, it was agreed in 1986 to set up a 'Linked Advice Network' which would involve all the advisers from all relevant organisations agreeing on:

(a) Exchange of information on each other's operations.

(b) Joint promotion of the respective services they offer — a leaflet has been produced and joint displays are provided at local shows.

(c) A mechanism by which the needs of a particular farm can be identified and then met by the appropriate combination of advice and financial assistance.

4.49 As so much conservation work on farms can be assisted by grants, the organisations involved in the network have gone on to examine ways in which their grant schemes can be linked together. The result of this has been an examination of the various types of desirable conservation-orientated farm management work and the identification of the appropriate source of grant aid. Most such grant schemes are operated by national agencies, but they do not always meet the specific needs of the National Park. The Peak Board has therefore amended its own grant schemes, which increasingly overlapped with national schemes as they changed to become more conservation related. A new Peak Board Farm Conservation Scheme is being gradually introduced which 'fills in the gaps' in the national schemes or provides particular supplementary assistance to help achieve the full range of National Park benefits, for example, stone walling around a wood established under a Forestry Commission scheme.

4.50 As a direct response to a proposal contained in the Farm Conservation Scheme, the Government announced in September 1988 that National Park Authorities have the discretion to pay grants to 'top-up' Ministry of Agriculture grants for certain environmentally beneficial works. This welcome decision will help to further the 'linked conservation' approach of the Farm Conservation Scheme.

4.51 Changes in Ministry grant schemes now make it much easier for new farming investment to be made which positively contributes to National Park conservation. However, what is frequently needed is the continued management of existing features. Existing Ministry grant schemes make no provision to assist in routine maintenance (with the exception of the new ESA — see **4.19**). Yet experience with the Farm Grant Notifications shows that most farmers are very willing to maintain features of National Park importance. Modest financial assistance for management will almost certainly result in an expansion of management effort. Thus other mechanisms are needed to encourage more effort on routine management for conservation benefit. These are likely to be well received and acted on, and in the long run may save money that would otherwise be needed for capital investments.

4.52 Three different approaches have been used since the 1978 Plan to encourage such management:

(a) In the few cases where agreement could not be reached on a modification to a Farm Grant Notification which, had it gone ahead, would have resulted in the loss of important wildlife landscape or archaeological features, Management Agreements have been used. In these cases the Financial Guidelines published by the Government are followed. By June 1988 a total of 23 such Agreements had been concluded and 21 others were under negotiation.

(b) Other Voluntary Management Agreements have been concluded or are under negotiation to ensure appropriate management where the Peak Board or NCC have taken the initiative. In such cases the financial guidelines are rarely appropriate because the farmer is only seeking management assistance and had no intention of damaging the feature by new work. 25 such Agreements had been concluded by June 1988, mostly for woodlands, and a number of others were under negotiation, including a notable scheme for the Chelmorton Historic Landscape (see **8.17-8.18**).

(c) The integrated Rural Development Project introduced a simpler form of management payments for conservation work, notably the maintenance of stone walls, flower-rich fields, woodlands and moorland.

4.53 To encourage routine management of field boundaries, flower-rich fields and other features of conservation importance, there are specific elements of the Farm Conservation Scheme which provide annual payments in return for continued appropriate management.

4.54 The Farm Conservation Scheme and the various grant schemes operated by other public agencies therefore provide grants for capital investments and incentives for annual maintenance for a wide variety of conservation work on the farm. The aim is to encourage farmers to direct their energy into appropriate management of the National Park environment, and to create business opportunities for the many skills that can help to achieve this.

Objective
4.55 To ensure that the various organisations advising farmers and landowners work together as effectively as possible and jointly promote work on farms that is consistent with the policies in this Plan.

---

20 Farming & Wildlife Advisory Groups — see **4.48**.

Care of field walls is a major element in the farm conservation scheme run by the Board with MAFF and others.

Policies

4.56 The Linked Advice Network will be maintained to ensure efficient co-ordination of grants and advice to farmers and landowners. This network will ensure close working links with the staff of all organisations with agriculture-related duties. The network will be supported by the preparation of a handbook on sources of grants and advice, which will be regularly updated (RLMEG agencies and other organisations in the Linked Advice Network).

4.57 The Peak Board's Farm Conservation Scheme will be used to provide grants and other help to encourage conservation on farmland, in a manner which complements the support from other agencies. This scheme will be modified as necessary to avoid overlap with national schemes and to address aspects of conservation interest not covered by other agencies (Peak Board).

4.58 Policies on farm woodlands set out in paragraphs 3.80 - 3.88 will be applied (see also policies on shale-grit semi-natural woodlands and limestone dale woodlands at 3.37 -3.42 and 3.62 - 3.69 respectively). (RLMEG agencies)

Introduction

5.1 Trees, woods and forests make a major contribution to the landscape of the National Park. These include the crucial specimen trees in a village setting, trees randomly spaced in hedgerows and along field boundary walls, small woodlands in enclosed farmlands, larger woodlands in the dales and shale-grit valleys and coniferous plantations in reservoir valleys.

5.2 Detailed policies for the management of trees, woods and forests are set out in other chapters in this Plan as follows:

— As part of the landscape conservation and land management (Chapter 3)

    (a) Shale-grit semi-natural woodlands (**3.37-3.42**)

    (b) Limestone dale woodlands (**3.62-3.69**)

    (c) Other trees, woods and forests (**3.80-3.88**)

— As part of farming (Chapter 4)

    (d) Woodland management as part of farm diversification (**4.32**)

    (e) Woodland management as part of the Farm Conservation Scheme (**4.57**)

— Trees in villages (Chapter 9)

    (f) Village management schemes (**9.31**)

5.3 This chapter deals with the co-ordination of the various sources of advice, grant aid, tax incentives and work on the Board's own estate, to encourage the development of a local forestry and forest products economy.

5.4 Just as agriculture is the management of land for food production and other ancillary purposes, so forestry is the management of woodland. There is a strong tradition of a multiple-purpose approach to management. Timber production, wildlife conservation, scenic beauty, shelter for livestock and game for sport may all be primary aims of woodland management, depending on the circumstances. Sometimes the same area is managed to achieve an optimum mix of all these objectives.

5.5 With the gradual depletion of the woodland cover of Great Britain over many centuries, there is not such a strong tradition of forestry in this country as in most other European countries. Many farmers on the Continent are also woodland managers and derive a part of their income from their trees. In the U.K. the institutional arrangements have tended to separate agriculture and forestry into separate ownerships and management responsibilities, with different public agencies supporting each. The Forestry Commission, established in 1919, has tended until very recently to be interested only in large units of land, concentrating on timber production. In recent years, these institutional barriers and single-purpose approaches have begun to be broken down. Forestry is increasingly seen to be complementary to agriculture, to be a justifiable activity of many people, and to be producing a range of public benefits.

The Changing Background of National Policy

5.6 Considerable changes have taken place in national forest policy since 1978. The Forestry Commission's Dedication

Trees and small woodlands make a major contribution to the landscape of the Upper Dove Valley.

Scheme has been closed to new entrants, although existing dedicated woodlands continue to receive Commission assistance. From 1978 afforestation or restocking of existing woods was grant-aided mainly through the Forestry Grant Scheme (FGS). This national scheme marked a move away from annual management grants, which were a feature of the Dedication Scheme, towards a simplified system of planting grants.

5.7 A review of the Forestry Commission's broadleaved policy led to the publication in 1985 of 'Guidelines for the Management of Broadleaved Woodland'. This included the important presumption that broadleaved woods will be maintained as such and that there should be no clearance of such woodland for agriculture. A new Broadleaved Woodland Grant Scheme (BWGS) was introduced to encourage the planting of pure broadleaved woods, or the restocking or natural regeneration of existing woods. There was an encouraging interest in the BWGS in the Park. The BWGS Scheme has been replaced by a new scheme — (see **5.10** below).

5.8 Another welcome development in the protection of trees and woodlands from gradual, piecemeal felling, has been the tightening of felling licence regulations. Only 5 cubic metres of timber, amounting to perhaps 2 or 3 large trees, can now be felled without a licence in any calendar quarter. Only 2 cubic metres can be sold. Consultations with the Peak Board on felling licence applications have been used to ensure appropriate replanting.

Trees should be felled before they are past their best. After selective felling, gaps are replaced and the harvested timber can be converted into more valuable articles.

5.9 The 1988 Budget changed the system of financial support for forestry, by removing commercial forestry from the scope of income tax, and effectively abolishing the Schedule D provisions which had sustained upland private afforestation. In practice this tax relief has little impact in the Peak District with only one significant scheme of this type having been established — at Gib Tor (see **3.75**). The tax changes will probably mean that investment in forestry will no longer be so attractive to top-rate taxpayers. Income from timber sales will continue to be free of income tax, without recourse to the provisions of Schedule B. The Government's aim is to encourage a wider spectrum of people to plant trees and it still has hopes of achieving an annual target of 33,000 ha of afforestation which has previously taken place almost entirely in the uplands. It will be some time before the full impact of the tax changes becomes apparent as the former provisions will apply to woodland owners, in occupation at the time of the 1988 Budget, for a five year transitional period.

5.10 Soon after the Budget the Government announced a new Woodland Grant Scheme (WGS), effectively merging the FGS and BWGS. Levels of planting grants were increased to compensate for the loss of tax incentives, for example the largest increase (to 256% of former levels) applies to conifer planting over 10 ha in extent. It can now be estimated that WGS grants could cover 60-75% of planting and regeneration costs, although this depends very much on the particular circumstances and the amount of fencing or walling needed can be an important factor. The grants will continue to be of limited benefit in aiding the management of a mid-rotation woodland, particularly where the maintenance of boundary walls or the extraction of uneconomic thinnings might be desirable. Such work could also previously be offset against tax. Thus the problem of neglected broadleaved woodlands may well continue despite the presence of grants towards new planting. It was to deal with these issues that the Peak Board became increasingly involved in woodland management on private land (see **5.17**).

5.11 In March 1988 the Secretary of State for the Environment announced that there was to be a presumption against large-scale conifer afforestation in the uplands of England. The application of this policy in the Peak District has yet to be clarified but it is assumed that it applies to the National Park.

5.12 These changes in Government policy have been generally welcomed by the Peak Board. It was felt that the former arrangements were of little benefit to many farmers who owned small woodlands. However, it is recognised that some owners of traditional, mixed estates derived considerable help from income tax concessions in managing their diverse woodland holdings, and that in such cases the change could be detrimental. The Government does, however, recognise this problem and it is possible that new management incentives will be introduced at the end of the transitional period. Any such measures that encouraged sound management by all woodland owners would be welcomed.

5.13 The Government brought in a new Farm Woodlands Scheme on 1st October 1988. This has been prompted by the desire to shift land out of food production in order to reduce agricultural surpluses (see **4.9**). The Government recognised that the existing planting grants were not sufficient to encourage farmers to plant trees on a substantial scale. The proposals are for a system of annual payments for the first 20-40 years to supplement planting grants available through the WGS. The payments are made for 40 years for broadleaved woodland (with at least 90% oak or beech), 30 years for mixed woodland with more than 50% broadleaved, 20 years for other woodland, and 10 years for coppice. The aim is to achieve 36,000 ha hectares of planting over the first 3 years targeted on arable land and improved grassland. Only 3,000 ha can be in the Less Favoured Areas; thus the impact on the National Park is likely to be modest.

The Local Situation

5.14 Until recently the Forestry Commission was almost entirely concerned with forestry in which timber production was the predominant aim. Because of this the Peak Board has introduced its own policies and mechanisms to encourage 'non-commercial' forestry in the Park.

5.15 The first action taken, mainly in the 1950s, was to define Tree Preservation Orders (TPOs) under the Town and Country Planning Acts. Forty-six such orders were made, covering 312 woods and 49 'areas of trees', totalling approximately 600 ha.

5.16 TPOs do not in themselves encourage woodland management, but were the only means available at the time to ensure that conservation interests were considered in woodland management. Since then the Forestry Commission has agreed to consult the Peak Board on all felling proposals (except silvicultural thinning); on planting schemes on their own land; or where a private owner is seeking WGS or Felling Licence approvals. Because of the changed policies of the Commission, these mechanisms effectively ensure that trees and woods of environmental importance are effectively managed. The need for further TPOs is therefore very limited.

5.17 Recognising the limited value of a TPO, the Board started to acquire (by agreement) woodlands of environmental importance to ensure they were effectively managed. Other areas are leased by the Board or are managed by the Board on behalf of other public agencies. This policy led to the Board managing some 200 ha of woodland by 1977. By 1987 this area had grown to 240 ha of scattered woodlands. A further 240 ha are managed as part of the Board's major estates. Thus 480 ha of woodland are now in Board management.

5.18 It is obviously unlikely that the Peak Board could ever manage directly all the woods of environmental importance. The 1978 Plan recognised this and the (then) limited ability of the national grant schemes to encourage the planting and management of small woodlands. The 1978 Plan therefore proposed the establishment of an additional grant scheme to be run by the Peak Board and designed to complement national schemes.

5.19 In 1978 the Board introduced such a Forestry Grant Scheme, and in the period to 1985 this covered 113 individual schemes with a total area of 53 ha. From 1985 up to 1987 the Board administered a system of Woodland Management Agreements under Section 39 of the Wildlife and Countryside Act 1981 — 22 such agreements were concluded, covering 48 ha of woodland. Thus a total of 101 ha of woodland were brought into effective management by the actions of owners with grant aid from the Peak Board. Other organisations also operate grant schemes, for example Staffordshire Moorlands District Council have their own scheme operating in that area of the Park.

5.20 Since the summer of 1987 the Board has provided assistance with woodland management through its Farm Conservation Scheme. The Board encourages the use of the nationally funded woodland schemes provided by the Forestry Commission and MAFF which have changed considerably in recent years. These now effectively replace many elements of the Park Board's schemes. The Farm Conservation Scheme is designed to 'fill in the gaps' in national schemes or provide supplementary assistance for work of particular environmental importance e.g. walling around woods (see **4.49**).

A Local Forestry Industry

5.21 Management of woodland areas is a very direct way by which the local economy can benefit from National Park purposes and a means by which local jobs can be secured. However, there are few timber merchants in the Park and many jobs in processing the timber of the Park are located several miles from the Park boundary.

5.22 Few small woodland owners have the expertise to manage their woodlands effectively or to know the best markets for their timber. As many individuals own small areas of woodland, the volume of timber made available from any one owner is often inadequate to encourage contractors to offer good prices. There is little effective co-operative marketing of timber in the Park which some observers believe will help the management of small farm woodlands. In recent years several local wood-using businesses have become established, but they often purchase their timber from some distance away.

5.23 There could therefore be a considerable opportunity to encourage more effective woodland management by showing that it could, in the right circumstances, yield some financial return. There is also an opportunity to find ways in which the local economy might benefit from a more active forestry industry. Measures such as co-operative marketing and encouragement of local wood-using businesses would be two obvious possibilities.

Objective
5.24 To encourage the development of a local forestry industry which contributes to the achievement of National Park purposes but which also benefits the local economy.

Policies
5.25 The various Forestry Commission and Ministry of Agriculture grant-aided schemes and applications will continue to take full account of environmental considerations in the design of new planting and in the management of woodland in accordance with the policies in Chapter 3 of this Plan (see 3.37-3.42, 3.62-3.69 and 3.80-3.88) (Forestry Commission, MAFF, Peak Board).

5.26 Liaison and co-ordination between the various sources of funding for small woodlands will be provided through the Linked Advice Network, using where appropriate the national grant schemes and the Peak Board's Farm Conservation Scheme (see 4.48-4.57) (Peak Board, Forestry Commission, MAFF).

5.27 The woodlands managed by the Peak Board will maintain a balance between wildlife, landscape, historic features, recreational use, and the requirements of timber production according to local circumstances and in accordance with the relevant policies in Chapter 3. Advice and encouragement to other woodland owners will be based on the Board's own experience (Peak Board).

5.28 The management of woodland owned by the Forestry Commission and by other public or quasi-public agencies will include environmental considerations. The Peak Board will continue to be consulted on major new acquisitions or revisions of management plans, with the object of reaching agreement on detailed proposals in accordance with the policies in Chapter 3 (Forestry Commission, Water Authorities, Nature Conservancy Council, National Trust).

5.29 The means by which the local forestry industry might help the local economy to benefit from National Park management will be explored including improved advisory services, marketing arrangements, local furniture-making and other crafts (Peak Board, Forestry Commission, Development Commission).

5.30 Policies on the management of different types of existing woodland are set out in other sections of this Plan as follows:

(a) Shale-grit Semi-natural Woodlands (3.37-3.42)

(b) Limestone Dale Woodland (3.62-3.69)

(c) Other Trees, Woods and Forests (3.80-3.88)

5.31 Policies for afforestation are set out in other sections of this Plan as follows:

(a) Moorland policy (3.28)

(b) Limestone Heaths and Limestone Hills (3.51)

(c) Limestone Dales (3.65)

(d) Rural Zone enclosed farmland (3.84-3.85)

6 NATURE CONSERVATION

Introduction

6.1 The wildlife[21] of the Peak District, and its geological and geomorphological features, are an integral part of the area's natural beauty. Their stewardship is one of the main statutory purposes of National Park designation.

6.2 Since the 1978 Plan, public awareness of the problems affecting the natural environment has substantially increased. Chapter 1 describes the international confirmation of this awareness in the form of the World Conservation Strategy and the UK adoption of its principles (see **1.12**). Chapter 2 contains the strategy for conservation and refers to the need to control pollution. This chapter interprets these principles for the wildlife and habitats in the Park.

6.3 There have, in addition been a series of international conventions on wildlife (notably the Berne, Ramsar and Washington Conventions). This increase in 'official' awareness has been paralleled by a huge increase in public support for nature conservation.

6.4 The 1978 Plan aimed to incorporate wildlife conservation considerations into all the land management policies and recreation development proposals. It was a fundamental element in the Natural Zone/Rural Zone policy division (see Chapter 2). Specific wildlife conservation policies for special areas were identified, notably for Sites of Special Scientific Interest (SSSIs) and National Nature Reserves. Special protection for 'herb rich meadows' was also proposed.

6.5 Since 1978 not only has the concern for wildlife increased, so too has the knowledge of the wildlife resources of the Park and the ability and willingness of many different organisations to make their contribution to wildlife conservation. The Peak Board now convenes an annual wildlife liaison meeting with all statutory and voluntary wildlife conservation organisations with an interest in the Park to discuss programmes of work.

6.6 Wild plants and animals do not occur in isolation. Each species depends on the particular set of environmental conditions to which it is adapted (its habitat): its survival may be threatened as soon as these conditions are altered or disturbed. The richest habitats for wildlife are often those which have existed for very long periods of time, in some instances hundreds of years. There are probably no truly natural habitats left in the Peak District as human influence has been present for so long. The most important wildlife habitats are therefore called 'semi-natural', for although they

consist of self-sown native species, they have been influenced by low intensity human activity (usually livestock grazing). Most of the important semi-natural habitats — ancient woodlands, old permanent grasslands, moorlands — are virtually impossible to recreate once they have been destroyed.

6.7 The Nature Conservancy Council (NCC) were concerned enough about the continuing nation-wide loss of the most important semi-natural habitats to record in their 1983 Annual Report that 'there is just about enough habitat left to ensure continuity for Britain's wild plants and animals — if it is conserved. The danger is that if it is not wholeheartedly protected now, in ten years time it will be too late'. Five years have passed and habitat loss has continued over this period.

6.8 The Park still supports a greater proportion of surviving semi-natural habitats than most lowland areas. The relative scarcity of these habitats elsewhere means that those in the Park assume a greater importance in a regional and national context. However serious habitat loss has also occurred in the Park.

6.9 Knowledge of the Park's wildlife resources has been greatly improved by a series of surveys, mainly carried out by Manpower Services Commission teams under the guidance of the Board or of the County Trusts. These surveys are still incomplete (see **1.23**), but they were rapidly improving the knowledge of important sites, particularly those surviving in the Rural Zone where there has been the greatest change in land management practice. This is where survey work has been concentrated.

6.10 Probably the most striking change in wildlife habitats since the National Park was designated has been in the grasslands of the enclosed fields. These cover about half the area of the Park (70,000 ha). 83% of the 28,403 ha of grassland so far surveyed by Board sponsored surveys has no special wildlife interest, whilst detailed surveys of two representative areas totalling 2,450 ha have shown that only 4% of fields now support more than 35 species of typical grassland plants.

6.11 The reason for this, which has been well documented by NCC on a national level, is that farmers have been encouraged by successive governments to adopt modern farming techniques, in order to improve agricultural productivity. These techniques include the use of chemical fertilizers, herbicides, ploughing, re-seeding and silage production, which all favour the growth of a limited number of vigorous grasses at the expense of wild flowers and less vigorous grasses. A typical 'improved' field might support 10 plant species, whereas a traditional 'unimproved' pasture might support up to 70.

6.12 Since the 1978 Plan, there have been greatly increased opportunities for the Board and NCC to influence agricultural practices, mainly through Farm Grant Notification procedures (see Chapter 4). To make the most of these opportunities, it is important to know where the most important habitats are and how important each particular area is.

6.13 The remainder of this chapter is divided into six sections:

Lathkill National Nature Reserve — Conservation through designation, from National Nature Reserves to local agreements, in the wider countryside.

---

21 In this Plan 'wildlife' means the whole of the native fauna and flora of the Park.

(a) Division of Responsibilities for Wildlife Conservation (6.14-6.28).

(b) Habitat Surveys (6.29-6.36).

(c) Habitat Conservation (6.37-6.48).

(d) Individual Habitat Management (6.49-6.63).

(e) Species Protection (6.64-6.77).

(f) Geology and Geomorphology (6.78-6.85).

Division of Responsibilities

6.14 The NCC is the lead government body for nature conservation in Great Britain. It is responsible for establishing a network of protected National Nature Reserves (NNRs), owned or managed directly by NCC; and for other Sites of Special Scientific Interest (SSSIs) whose owners and occupiers must consult NCC on most land management changes or on development proposals. It also has special responsibilities for the protection of rare or endangered species and the promotion of nature conservation by providing expert advice and grant aid. The NCC also commissions and carries out research into ecology and related issues.

6.15 Within this National Park, the area of land now owned or managed by NCC is 238 ha and the SSSIs have increased in number to 54, covering 20,385 ha — about 15% of the Park. The NCC is in the process of revising its schedule of SSSIs, and re-notifying the owners under the provisions of the Wildlife and Countryside Act 1981. Map 6.1 shows SSSIs as at 1988.

6.16 In 1978, the Peak Board largely relied on the NCC to provide wildlife conservation advice. Although the resources available to NCC have increased since 1978, they have found it increasingly difficult to provide a general advisory service for the Park as a whole. The Peak Board therefore now employs its own ecologists. The Board tends to concentrate its efforts in nature conservation on the protection of the best sites that have not been designated by the NCC, and on the protection of wildlife in the wider countryside. Moreover, wildlife conservation is an important ingredient in the management of the Board's estates and was among the main reasons why the land was acquired by the Board.

6.17 The NCC retains a general responsibility for wildlife conservation in the Park and there is therefore a potential overlap in activity. While in recent years NCC's efforts have concentrated on SSSI and NNR work, they will be increasingly involved in other areas of the Park such as the Environmentally Sensitive Area (4.19) and Ancient Woodlands (6.59).

6.18 Considerable advice and assistance has been made available to the Board and NCC from the many voluntary organisations concerned with different aspects of nature conservation in the Park. The help and co-operation of the County Nature Conservation Trusts, and the Royal Society for the Protection of Birds (RSPB) has been particularly valuable. The most active organisations and individuals have formed the Peak Park Wildlife Advisory Group (PPWAG), a group which is not linked to the Board but which advises on various wildlife issues in the Park generally. PPWAG members are invited to an annual wildlife liaison meeting (see 6.5).

6.19 With so many interested organisations and individuals involved, it is important to avoid duplication of effort and to ensure firstly that data collected are made readily available and secondly that expertise is concentrated where it can be most effective. Such information and expertise is crucial when making decisions, for example on planning applications, Farm Grant Notifications or on farm plans in the Environmentally Sensitive Area. Different statutory organisations are involved in making these decisions. These agencies and the land managers they advise need to know quickly where to turn for objective information and professional advice. Without well-founded knowledge, wildlife sites of importance can be (and have been) lost. Proposals for simplifying data storage and retrieval are set out below (6.29-6.36).

6.20 The roles of the Peak Board and NCC are fairly clear and defined by law. The particular role other organisations can play in wildlife conservation was clarified during consultation on the draft plan. Some suggestions, based on current practice, are set out in the rest of this chapter.

6.21 With so many organisations involved, there is value in having a clear and agreed programme of work, in which each knows what the others are doing. The existing wildlife liaison meetings go some way to achieving this. An agreed 'Programme of Action' would help to direct resources to where they would be most effective.

Objective
6.22 To clarify responsibilities of the statutory wildlife conservation organisations and to enlist the help of voluntary organisations to minimise duplication and maximise effectiveness in working to conserve the wildlife resources of the Park.

Policies
6.23 Nature reserves will be gradually extended so that the best wildlife sites are managed primarily for wildlife conservation. A current priority is the limestone dales but other important habitats will be considered for nature reserve status (NCC, County Nature Conservation Trusts, National Trust, County and District Councils[22]).

6.24 SSSIs will continue to be notified to owners and land managers and the wildlife conservation interest of these sites will be protected by the use of SSSI procedures (NCC).

6.25 The management of land outside NNRs and SSSIs should respect and wherever possible enhance wildlife conservation interests, particularly in areas of semi-natural habitat. Farmers and landowners will be encouraged to take full account of those interests in their management decisions (see Chapter 4) (RLMEG agencies and other organisations in the Linked Advice Network — see 4.56).

6.26 Close liaison will be maintained between the Peak Board and the NCC to monitor their respective roles in nature conservation (Peak Board, NCC).

6.27 It is anticipated that the voluntary wildlife organisations will continue to contribute to wildlife conservation primarily through the acquisition and management of nature reserves and by making

---

22 The Peak Board does not have the legal power to designate statutory National or Local Nature Reserves but much work by the Board is equivalent to work carried out in them (see **6.39** & **6.41** below).

information available to the proposed Peak District Biological Records System (see 6.36 & 6.74) (County Nature Conservation Trusts, RSPB).

6.28 A forum of the major nature conservation organisations will be formed as a Wildlife Executive Group, convened by the Peak Board. Its aim will be to produce an agreed Wildlife Conservation Programme, identifying priorities and establishing how and where each organisation can best contribute to wildlife conservation in the Park. The annual liaison meeting will be maintained to ensure general agreement on the programme and progress in implementing it (see 6.18) (Peak Board).

Habitat Surveys

6.29 Within the SSSIs and NNRs, the NCC have established their own systems for recording wildlife interest. Their systems are largely based on paper records in maps and written reports.

6.30 Outside the SSSIs and NNRs the Peak Board, with the assistance of Derbyshire Rural Community Council and other organisations acting as agents for MSC has carried out a basic habitat survey covering most of the Park. This Phase 1 survey identifies the type of habitat and whether or not a site may have some wildlife interest. The Phase 1 sites are mapped, and the records have been partly computerised. Detailed surveys (Phase 2) are needed to clarify the precise wildlife characteristics and relative value of the Phase 1 sites. This Phase 2 work is still at an early stage, though the limestone heaths have been covered (see 3.43-3.53).

6.31 Since 1983, 28,403 ha of grassland outside the SSSIs and NNRs have been surveyed in phase one. The results are summarised in Table 6.1 below.

6.32 In addition to surveys commissioned by the NCC and Peak Board, Nature Conservation Trusts, Universities, local societies, other organisations and individuals collect data on wildlife in various parts of the Park. These different surveys often use different systems for recording and storing data, which can make it extremely difficult to pull together all the data for a given site. A further problem is that much information is recorded on a county or 'vice county' basis whereas NCC or Peak Board need to evaluate the data on a National Park basis. There is increasing need for an agreed standardised system for storing, updating and analysing records of species and sites in the Park, in order:

(a) To know how to respond to a proposed change in management in a particular area and to advise on how the land would be best managed for wildlife conservation.

(b) To prepare programmes of action to ensure that the best sites are identified and appropriate management is secured.

(c) To facilitate long-term monitoring of the wildlife resources of the Park.

6.33 There are over 2,000 site records already in the Peak Board's Phase 1 survey. As Phase 2 progresses, additional data on individual sites will become available. As time passes, new data will become available which can be compared with previous information to examine changes in wildlife characteristics and decide whether action is needed. Most information is needed by NCC and Peak Board, for it is these two statutory organisations who are most often called upon for advice. Currently the information is kept in different

Flower-rich meadow — surveys show that very few grasslands remain which support valuable flora. We identify and seek to conserve what is left.

**Table 6.1
Grassland Surveys in Part of the National Park[a]
(December 1987)**

	Area (ha) of surveyed area	Percentage
Unimproved grassland justifying detailed (Phase 2) surveys (i.e. may have high wildlife interest)[b]	4,654	16.4
Unimproved and semi-improved grass-land not justifying Phase 2 surveys (i.e. known to have only limited wildlife interest)	1,122	3.9
Improved grassland with negligible wildlife interest	22,454	79.1
Wetland and Marsh in enclosed fields.	173	0.6
Total	**28,403**	**100**

(a) Surveys of the White Peak, Glossop, Hayfield and Bradfield areas concentrating on enclosed farmland. Surveys carried out by MSC teams.
(b) Where detailed (Phase 2) surveys have been carried out, a quarter of the land surveyed has proved to be of high wildlife value.

forms in different locations. Definitions, storage methods and access systems need to be co-ordinated and linked. Ideally improvements to data storage systems adopted in the Park and in areas adjacent to the Park should be compatible with each other and with national systems so that the Park's wildlife resources can be analysed in a wider context.

Objective
6.34 To ensure that accurate, comprehensive, comparable and up-to-date records of important wildlife sites, including records of habitats and species, are available quickly and easily.

6.35 A basic (Phase 1) habitat survey of the Park will be completed as quickly as possible. Detailed (Phase 2) coverage will be provided as soon as possible, with priority being given to the rarest or most severely threatened habitats including flower-rich grasslands, wetlands and ancient woodlands (Peak Board, NCC).

6.36 Discussions will be initiated with the aim of setting up a single Peak District Biological Records system, using standard recording methods, to make data available quickly on a comparable basis to all contributing organisations (see also 6.74) (Peak Board, County Councils, NCC, County Nature Conservation Trusts, local museums, National Biological Records Centre, National Federation for Biological Recording).

Habitat Conservation

6.37 Many of the important wildlife sites have some form of protection. The Derbyshire Dales National Nature Reserve and 54 SSSIs cover in all 20,852 ha or 15% of the Park (see Map 6.1). The NCC is in the process of revising its schedule of SSSIs. Once a site is notified to the owner and occupier of the land, they are obliged to consult the NCC on any work which could potentially damage the site (see 4.16). The NCC is able to influence such work either by using a voluntary management agreement (in most cases) or, in extreme cases, it may apply to the Secretary of State for the Environment for a Nature Conservation Order. This procedure was introduced in the Wildlife and Countryside Act 1981. Policies in the 1978 Plan laid stress on the voluntary notification of such work. This has been encouraged by the NFU and CLA. To some extent this voluntary informal arrangement has been made redundant by the 1981 Act, at least for SSSIs.

6.38 SSSI designation is intended to safeguard sites of national or international importance. This designation may not, however, secure the ideal management for nature conservation when used in isolation, and it may be necessary to offer a Management Agreement, or to lease or purchase the land. Not all areas known to be of SSSI quality have yet been notified: as survey work proceeds, new areas worthy of SSSI status will probably be found.

6.39 The Peak Board now owns 5,410 ha of land on the Eastern Moors, North Lees, the Roaches and the Warslow Moors. Of this total, approximately 3,480 ha is of high wildlife value, indeed much of this land is also designated as SSSI. Management Plans have been produced, or are being produced, for each of the main estates. These plans aim to safeguard key wildlife areas and integrate wildlife · conservation with other aspects of estate management (see Chapter 23).

6.40 Whilst sites of recognised international or national importance should be safeguarded by SSSI or NNR designation, it is also essential to safeguard the full range and diversity of all characteristic habitats occurring in the Park by other means. The most important sites in a National Park context will therefore be treated together with SSSIs and NNRs as 'key sites' and appropriate means of safeguarding them will be actively pursued.

6.41 In accordance with this philosophy, the Board has so far concentrated its efforts on providing protection for the best wildlife sites that have not been and are not likely to be notified as SSSIs. The Board has negotiated 21 Management Agreements over 230 ha of land where wildlife conservation is one of the objectives. Management agreement negotiations are in progress (March 1988) for a further 91 ha. Section 21 of the 1949 Act provides the power to designate Local Nature Reserves (LNRs), but this can only be exercised by County and District Councils. Circular 4/76 recommends that it be delegated to National Park Authorities in National Parks. Designation as a Local Nature Reserve may increase the public awareness of a site, help to obtain grant aid from NCC and other sources and also gives the ability to create bye-laws. As yet no Local Nature Reserves have been designated in the Park.

6.42 County Nature Conservation Trusts manage 232 ha of land in the Park, as non-statutory nature reserves. There are 18 sites held on a variety of bases ranging from direct ownership to various forms of licence. Many are SSSIs or other key sites. Financial assistance has been made available from the Peak Board and NCC to support site acquisition and other work carried out by the Trusts.

6.43 Up to the present time, most work on wildlife conservation has been 'reactive' — dealing with a farmer's proposals to change the management of land, mainly through Farm Grant Notifications. The prevention of damaging work or the designation of important sites will, on their own, achieve little. Increasingly it is intended to move to positively encouraging appropriate management of important wildlife sites, partly by financial incentives. Such management is necessary because most habitats of importance have been created in part by human activity and need continuing management of a similar type if their wildlife value is to be retained. Such an approach can also be extended to promoting the creation of new wildlife habitats typical of the area. The Integrated Rural Development Project and similar schemes elsewhere have proved the value of this positive approach. It applies equally to other conservation interests (e.g. archaeological conservation). To establish an integrated approach to positive management for conservation purposes, a Farm Conservation Scheme has been introduced (see 4.48-4.56).

6.44 This change in philosophy aims to encourage landowners and farmers to regard environmental management as an integral part of their normal land management and to positively improve wildlife interest, not merely protect what currently exists. Wildlife conservation is no longer confined to the NNRs and SSSIs and other key sites, although this must remain the priority, but becomes part of the management of the Park as a whole. The North Peak Environmentally Sensitive Area will be a further move in this direction of a positive approach to nature conservation, encouraging farmers with land both inside and outside SSSIs to manage their land for a combination of food production and conservation, both maintaining existing features and creating new wildlife habitats.

Objective
6.45 To identify and safeguard key sites for wildlife conservation representing the best and most typical habitats of the Peak District, and to encourage positive management of all land in the Park to maintain and enhance its wildlife value.

Policies
6.46 The nationally and locally important wildlife sites will be identified as 'key sites' so as to protect the full range of habitats, communities and species occurring in the Park

Map 6.1
Sites of Special Scientific Interest

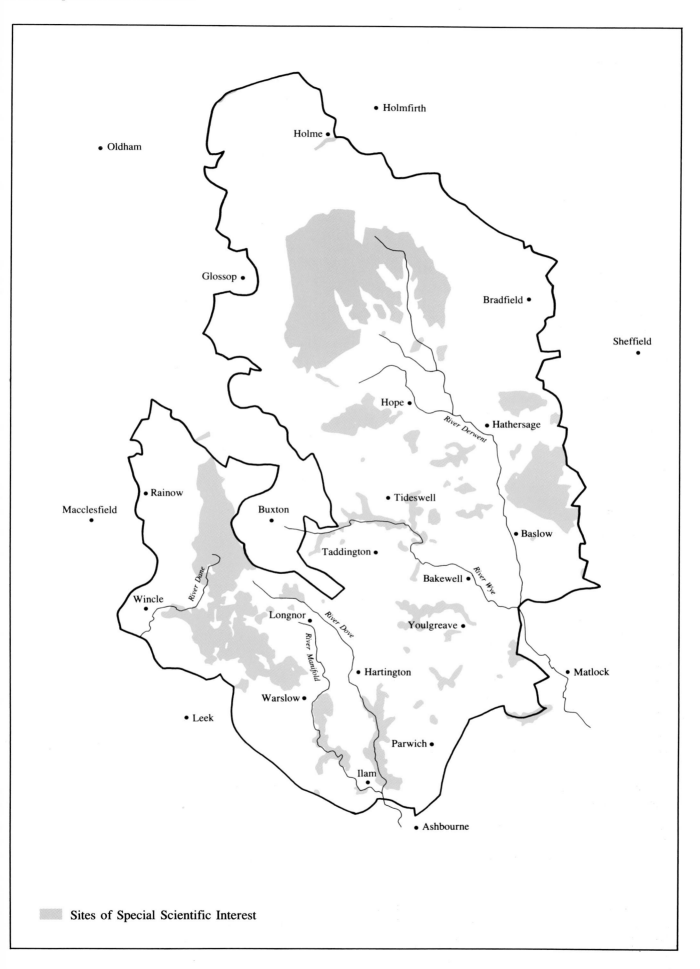

Sites of Special Scientific Interest

(see 6.40). Special priority will be given to those habitats which are already known to be rare, for example, limestone heaths, flower-rich grasslands and ancient semi-natural woodlands. Protection will be achieved by appropriate designations, negotiation of Management Agreements, use of the Farm Conservation Scheme, negotiated site purchase, or other forms of nature reserve agreement, as appropriate (Peak Board, NCC, County Nature Conservation Trusts, National Trust, RSPB).

6.47 The establishment of Nature Reserves will be encouraged as one means of achieving 'key site' protection (County and District Councils, NCC, Peak Board, County Nature Conservation Trusts).

6.48 A programme of measures will be pursued through the Wildlife Conservation Programme (see 6.28) and through the Linked Advice Network (see 4.56) to protect and encourage the full range of wildlife species, communities and habitats which occur in the Park. Particular priorities will include:-

(a) encouragement to landowners, farmers and others to incorporate nature conservation as an integral part of all forms of countryside management (Peak Board, NCC).

(b) informing landowners, where appropriate, about the wildlife interest of their land (this being often all that is needed to encourage interest in its conservation) (Peak Board, NCC).

(c) providing advice, financial incentives and practical assistance to encourage the management of land for nature conservation, including the creation of new wildlife habitats, particularly through the Farm Conservation Scheme (see 4.57) (Peak Board, NCC, MAFF, Forestry Commission).

(d) modifying farm and forestry grant proposals to ensure protection or improvement of wildlife values and where necessary offering Management Agreements or other grants in order to achieve this (see 4.43) (Peak Board, MAFF).

(e) the management of important wildlife habitats by the statutory conservation bodies (Peak Board, NCC).

(f) providing financial or other assistance to other organisations wishing to acquire and manage 'key sites' for conservation management (Peak Board, NCC, County Nature Conservation Trusts).

(g) encouraging local community groups to take an active interest in the conservation of their local wildlife (Peak Board, NCC, Rural Community Councils, County Nature Conservation Trusts).

(h) identifying priorities for interpretation as part of the Interpretation Programme (see 18.36d) (Peak Board, NCC, County Nature Conservation Trusts).

Individual Habitat Management

6.49 The overall importance of habitat management is outlined above. Specific policies for most of the important habitats of the Park are covered in other chapters. This section summarises the important wildlife conservation issues related to the main habitats of the Park, and provides an index to where detailed policies can be found in other parts of this Plan.

Moorlands support a unique wildlife. Controlled heather burning is part of skilful management.

Cottongrass dominates large areas of wet moorland, which are the habitat for birds such as Golden Plover and Dunlin.

6.50 Moorlands demonstrate the complexity of management issues better than most other habitats. They support a wide range of different land uses (sheep grazing, grouse shooting, recreation, water catchment), which are not always compatible with each other or with the needs of important moorland wildlife species and communities. Although there is much information on moorland management practices, the exact nature of the interaction of these activities and their associated forms of management on wildlife have, in many instances, still to be researched.

6.51 The moorlands also face problems of large scale erosion, accidental fires and the spread of bracken (see 3.99). In an attempt to resolve some of these problems, the Board is currently supporting a major new Peak District Moorland Management Project (see 3.2-3.30). Research is in hand to establish the effects of recreation on moorland bird species (see 12.21).

6.52 Limestone Dales support a complex of important habitats each of which has different management requirements. Scrub invasion of irreplaceable grassland (amongst the most beautiful and species-rich in Britain) is a particularly urgent problem (see **3.54-3.69**).

6.53 Limestone Heaths and Limestone Hills These are usually extensive areas of open shrub and grassland habitats, commonly containing a mixture of lime-loving and lime hating plants — a rare combination (see **3.43-3.53**). Changes in agricultural practices have dramatically reduced the area of this type of land.

6.54 Wetlands, Marshes, Rivers and Water areas Many wetlands have been lost over the years due to drainage schemes. Water quality generally has been affected by 'acid rain' caused by industrial activities (see **2.28**) but its consequences in the Park are only just beginning to be researched. Its effects in the limestone area are not believed to have been serious to date. Otherwise rivers and water courses are not seriously affected by pollution associated with specific industrial activities. The Water Authorities monitor water quality and have taken action where pollution incidents have occurred (see **2.29** and **4.40**).

6.55 Farm ponds are less useful to farmers now that piped water is available. A survey of a sample area of the limestone plateau showed that half the ponds shown on the most recent Ordnance Survey Map no longer exist. Others are affected by fertiliser run-off or slurry effluent which greatly affect their wildlife value (see **4.40** and **4.45**). In recent years, dredging has safeguarded a number of ponds (e.g. Heathcote Mere) and farmers have become interested in creating new ponds (a notable award-winning project is at Barn Farm, Birchover). Grant aid is available for such work from various organisations including the Ministry of Agriculture and the Peak Board (see **7.26**).

6.56 River engineering works are not common in the Park but care needs to be taken with such schemes to protect and further wildlife interests. Codes of Conservation Practice have been introduced, notably by Severn Trent Water Authority. Wetland and water habitats are generally important for wildlife. They give a major ingredient to the variety of Peak District habitats including, in many cases, a rich flora; some (for example the limestone streams) are of national or international importance. They provide habitats for nationally or locally rare species like the Great Crested Newt, or the Common Sandpiper. They can provide sources of food for many species and stop-over points for migrating birds like waders. Wetland wildlife is under pressure from recreational activity.

6.57 Flower-rich fields (including the 'herb-rich meadows' of the 1978 Plan) are becoming increasingly rare. They are extremely vulnerable to changes in agricultural management. The use of appropriate traditional, usually low intensity, methods of management of these sites will be encouraged to secure their survival (see **3.96** and **6.48**d). Road verges and green lanes can provide some of the best examples of flower-rich grasslands in the Rural Zone, and special care should be taken in their management (see **7.44**b).

6.58 Lead rakes support vegetation which has managed to colonise toxic waste, and are of great scientific interest. Being on old lead workings, they are often also sites of great historic interest. On the whole, these sites have mellowed into the surrounding landscape, but the distinctive flora of those which are not tree-covered calls for special management (see also **7.41**).

6.59 Semi-natural woods are relatively scarce in the Park, and most of them now suffer from a lack of active management. Ancient semi-natural woodlands are of special importance (see **3.31**). The absence of enclosure means that many are subject to frequent grazing and thus have very poor ground flora, little or no shrub layer and no natural regeneration (see **3.38-3.42 & 3.64**). 'Wood Pasture' is a special form of ancient woodland in which old trees, set in (usually) unimproved grassland of deer parks have been retained as remnants of a former woodland. Such trees are also important for their invertebrates and lichens.

Objectives

6.60 To ensure appropriate management of the full range of habitats present in the Peak District.

Policies

6.61 The main survey, research and management requirements of the full range of Peak District habitats will be defined. Collated relevant information will be published in the most appropriate form and made available for habitat management. (Peak Board, NCC).

6.62 Research into the most appropriate management techniques for the different habitats of the Park will continue to be supported. (Peak Board, NCC).

6.63 Action will be taken to safeguard the richness and variety of the typical Peak District habitats by the most appropriate agency (Peak Board, NCC).

Species Protection

6.64 The measures aimed at conserving wildlife habitats should ensure the conservation of most species. However, some species face problems additional to those posed by habitat change. These apply particularly to the very small remnant populations and those species affected by illegal activities such as collecting or disturbance. These require additional protection. Moreover, some species are at the edge of their natural range. Upland species are mixed with lowland species, and plants which are typical of wet western Britain occur in conjunction with species from the drier east. This unique blend of species is of great importance.

6.65 The Wildlife and Countryside Act 1981 gave legal protection to many species not previously protected (for example, all species of bat). Badgers are specially protected under the Badgers Act 1973 and the Wildlife and Countryside (Amendment) Act 1985. EEC Directive 79/409 requires special measures to be taken to ensure the conservation of certain bird species, including several found in the Park. By means of site purchase and management agreements, the Board has protected several sites for rare or local species, for example Black Grouse.

6.66 Mammals Although badgers are still widespread, illegal badger digging and baiting continues to be a serious problem in certain areas of the Park. The small naturalised population of Red Deer in the Park is subject to considerable pressure from poaching and is sensitive to disturbance. Eight species of bats occur in the Park. They are at risk from the destruction or disturbance of their roost sites, loss of still suitable feeding areas, and timber treatment with chemicals lethal to bats. A few small remnant populations of Red Squirrel still survive in the Park. Otters were last regularly recorded in the 1950's and are now probably extinct in the Park, but might become re-established if appropriate habitats can be secured.

Black grouse need a complex habitat — special steps are being taken to safeguard the surviving Peak District population.

6.67 Birds The Peak District moorlands and rough grazings provide a valuable refuge for a range of upland bird species. The populations of breeding and roosting waders and raptors are particularly important. The Park supports the most south-easterly viable breeding population of Golden Plover in Britain, one of the few upland winter roosts for Hen Harrier in England, and about one third of the total British breeding population of Goshawks. Nevertheless, the future prospects for some species — Black Grouse, Peregrine and Merlin — remain tenuous. Illegal disturbance and theft continue to affect nest sites of several species of rare birds of prey. Large areas of the Park, including much moorland, have not yet been systematically surveyed for breeding and roosting birds.

6.68 Reptiles and Amphibians With its fairly cold and wet climate the Park has very few sites which contain important populations of reptiles. Amphibians — frogs, toads and newts — are still quite common. Because of catastrophic decline elsewhere, sites of importance for reptiles and amphibians in the Park should be conserved. These are mainly wetland sites (see **6.54** above).

6.69 Invertebrates Knowledge of invertebrates in the Peak District is still extremely patchy. The Invertebrate Sites Register (maintained by the NCC) indicates that much more survey work needs to be done before the importance of the Park can be established.

6.70 Plants The Park supports a number of locally or nationally rare plant species. Many of these have specific habitat requirements and may be very sensitive to small changes in their environment. For instance, several of the rarer moorland species, such as Butterwort, which occur in bogs and marshes, are particularly susceptible to damage through drainage or trampling. The Park's flora is also particularly interesting because of the large numbers of species which occur here, either at the extreme North or South limits of their range. Some other species, such as Mountain Pansy, although not rare, are particularly characteristic of the Park.

6.71 Mosses, ferns and lichen The Park also contains some relatively rare mosses, ferns and lichens. Almost certainly the Park was much richer in mosses and lichens before the Industrial Revolution and the effects of atmospheric pollution. Pollution control measures may improve the flora of the Park in due course. The Board supports in principle all efforts to reduce industrial air pollution (see **2.28** and **2.31**).

Objective
6.72 To ensure the conservation of the full range of species that make up the characteristic flora and fauna of the Park and to take special measures to ensure the survival of species which are most at risk.

Policies
6.73 Efforts to monitor rare, localised and especially characteristic species within the Park will be supported, and ways sought to ensure that key sites for these species are not damaged, destroyed or subjected to excessive disturbance (Peak Board, NCC, County Nature Conservation Trusts, RSPB).

6.74 A confidential register of sites for rare and local species in the Park will be established as a separate element of the Biological Records System (see 6.36), available only to certain authorised users (Peak Board, NCC).

6.75 The creation and management of suitable habitats for rare, localised and especially characteristic species will be encouraged, where appropriate (Peak Board, NCC, County Nature Conservation Trusts, RSPB).

6.76 Steps will be taken to make the public aware of species protection legislation and to discourage and prevent illegal activities against protected species in the Park (for example, egg stealing, badger digging and baiting, destruction of bat roosts). Where appropriate, legal action will be encouraged and publicity given to prosecutions (NCC, Peak Board, Police, RSPCA, NFU, CLA, County Nature Conservation Trusts, Bat Groups, Badger Protection Groups, RSPB).

6.77 Specialist groups and individuals concerned with the study and protection of wildlife species in the Park, will be encouraged, supported and where appropriate funded for particular activities (for example, surveys) which would lead to significant benefits for species conservation in the Park (Peak Board, NCC).

Geology and Geomorphology

6.78 Geological features and processes such as earth movements and folding, rock deposition and formation, and subsequent weathering can be demonstrated particularly well throughout the Park. Karst[23] landforms, natural landslips and cave systems are among the special geological features in the Park of national importance. In addition, there are sites of special significance, including places where particular minerals outcrop, or which contain the 'type' location for particular rock strata, or provide good examples of erosion features, fossil beds or soil formation processes.

6.79 The NCC is currently re-notifying nationally important geological sites as SSSIs under the Wildlife and Countryside Act 1981 (see Map 6.1). The occupier is obliged to notify the NCC of any 'potentially damaging operation' affecting the SSSI (see 6.37). Some SSSIs have both wildlife and geological interest. Site management will need to respect both interests. For example, limited clearance of semi-natural woodland has been accepted in Dovedale as a means of opening the limestone features to view.

6.80 There is no comprehensive list of sites of regional or local importance within the Park as a whole. Some are recorded on a county basis under the National Scheme for Geological Site Documentation — for example, coverage within the Sheffield City Council area is good. As with wildlife conservation, the aim should be to identify and conserve a full range of key sites representing the main geological features of the Park.

6.81 The conservation of SSSIs should be ensured by the operation of the Wildlife and Countryside Act 1981 and the development control process. There is a threat to several geological sites from over-collecting of specimens. More could be done to suggest suitable sites for study by students of different levels and to discourage collecting.

Objective
6.82 To identify, protect and manage sites of geological importance as an integral part of the character of the Park.

Badgers are protected by law, but sadly there is still digging and baiting. Prosecutions are encouraged.

Policies
6.83 Features of national geological interest will be notified as SSSIs and appropriate conservation action initiated. Where necessary, steps will be taken to ensure that any proposed operations or management changes take into account the national significance of the site (NCC, Peak Board).

6.84 A list of the other 'key sites' of interest (i.e. those of regional and local importance) will be compiled so that their conservation value can be assessed. Steps will be taken to protect them in the same way that wildlife sites are identified, protected and managed (see especially 6.36 and 6.46 above) (Peak Board, Geological recording centres, Derbyshire Caving Association).

6.85 The educational use of suitable geological sites will be encouraged, taking into account rarity, vulnerability to damage, access and willingness of landowners. Collecting will generally be discouraged and the Geological Association's Code for Geological Fieldwork will be promoted (Peak Board, NCC, Education Authorities).

---

23 Karst : limestone country shaped largely by water erosion with thin soils and underground drainage.

7 OTHER LAND MANAGEMENT

Introduction

7.1 Most of the National Park is cared for as an integral part of farming and forestry businesses or of estate and moorland management. General policies are set out in Chapters 2 to 6. This chapter deals with a remaining series of specific issues which affect the whole of the Park (for example, litter services), or specific parts of it (for example, common land).

7.2 The Structure Plan pledges the Board to remove or reduce eyesores, and the 1978 Plan contained policies for derelict land, public service installations, enhancement schemes and mineshaft protection.

7.3 This chapter deals with the following topics:

(a) Derelict Land (7.5-7.16)

(b) Public Utility Installations (7.17-7.24)

(c) Enhancement projects (7.25-7.30)

(d) Mineral sites and mine shafts (7.31-7.41)

(e) Roadside verges (7.42-7.47)

(f) Litter collection (7.48-7.58)

(g) Common Land (7.59-7.63)

7.4 Most of the work in these fields falls to public agencies to initiate, and they provide most of the money. Contracts are let to private businesses, many of which are based in or near to the Peak District, and which employ local people and use local services. Great investment of labour is made by conservation volunteers, managed by the Board's Ranger Service and other bodies (see Chapter 19).

The relevance of pollution to the management of land is described in Chapter 2 (2.23-2.31).

Derelict Land

7.5 Derelict land is defined by the Department of the Environment as 'land so damaged by industrial or other development that it is incapable of beneficial use without treatment'. In the Park, this definition applies mainly to abandoned quarries, associated tips, and redundant railways. The 1978 Plan referred to the Board's duty to review and co-ordinate action on derelict land, and outlined specific proposals. These included proposals for the Buxton to Matlock railway(including abandoned stations and quarries), and abandoned quarries near Hartington and on the Meltham and Bradwell Moors.

7.6 The legal powers for derelict land treatment are found in Section 89 of the 1949 Act as amended by the Derelict Land Act, 1982. Grant for such work can be made available from the Department of the Environment (DoE). DoE Circular 28/85 made it clear (for the first time) that the Board is eligible for 100% grant on relevant expenditure. The County and District Councils have concurrent powers under this Act. The private and voluntary sectors can seek 80% grant aid from the Government.

7.7 The Peak Board and the local councils have reclaimed many areas. Notable examples since the 1978 Plan are:

(a) **Calton Hill Quarry, Taddington (1979)** — an extensive scheme by Derbyshire County Council restored tipping areas to agriculture, and screened a rubbish tip

which can later become a touring caravan site. An important geological SSSI was retained as part of the scheme.

(b) **Railways** — 31.5 miles of old railways were converted by the Board and Derbyshire County Council into the Tissington and High Peak Trails in the late 1960s and early 1970s and recorded in the 1978 Plan. Since then the Peak Board acquired 4 sections of the Buxton-Matlock line in 1980 with a dowry of £154,000 from British Rail to assist with essential repairs. Nine miles are now in use as the Monsal Trail. Action at former station sites has resulted in new small factories and a car park at Bakewell. At Millers Dale, a car park, ranger briefing centre and toilets have been provided, lime kilns restored and old concrete platforms removed. There are SSSIs of both geological and biological importance along the Monsal Trail. There is a proposal to re-establish a railway between Buxton and Matlock by Peak Rail, whilst still allowing it to be used as a Trail. (see **16.8** and **38.23**)

(c) **Meltham Moor tip** — the reclamation of a waste tip to farmland was carried out at Royd Edge by the former West Yorkshire County Council, followed by fencing and tree planting by the Board with help from the farmer and the local Civic Society.

(d) **Green Lane Pits, Middleton by Youlgreave** — dumped tyres, wire burning and tipping created an eyesore around a geological SSSI, which included an attractive pond and rich limestone flora. Derelict Land Grant paid for the purchase by the Board. Restoration works, retaining important features, were completed in 1987.

7.8 The Board has continued to carry out derelict land survey work and to co-ordinate the Derelict Land Survey return made to the DoE for the Park by its liaison with the County and District Councils. The last full re-surveys were in 1982 and in 1988. The 1982 survey revealed 142 sites (235 ha.) of derelict land. Some had revegetated naturally with trees, grasses and herbs and no treatment was needed. However 63 sites (110 ha.) justified action. The 1988 Derelict Land Survey review revealed 23 sites amounting to 20.7 hectares had been reclaimed since the 1982 survey. It indicated that 139 sites (299.5 ha) of derelict land remain, of which 30 sites (124.3 ha) justified action. Thus, despite some progress with reclamation, there is a net growth in derelict land in the National Park.

7.9 The programme set out in the 1978 Plan has largely been acted upon, with the following exceptions:

(a) Quarries alongside the Monsal Trail are now considered to be of conservation value and do not require treatment.

(b) Hartshead quarry near Hartington was deemed by the House of Lords not to have been 'abandoned', and thus can legally be re-opened as quarry without any new planning permission being needed. The mineral owners have not used the permission, so neither the mineral not the recreational value of the site has been realised.

(c) Action at Dirtlow Rake near Castleton was delayed, but is now in progress and should be completed in 1989.

7.10 Other areas have become derelict since the 1982 survey — for example the Woodhead railway. The 1988 survey has provided an opportunity to re-assess the extent of dereliction

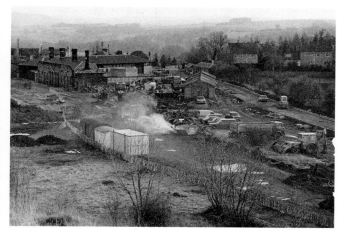

The railway closed, and these tenants moved onto Bakewell Station yard . . .

. . . it now looks better, and employs more people. The railway land is also still available, should Peak Rail re-open the line.

and priorities for action. It has not yet been discussed. Meanwhile, the following possibilities can be listed as obvious candidates for early action:

(a) **Mam Tor** A mile long section of the main A road has collapsed beyond repair. Landscaping, car park provision, interpretation, farm access and a bridleway are proposed, retaining the most spectacular sections of collapsed road as a monument to nature's power (the area is also part of an SSSI).

(b) **Ashford Road Tip, Bakewell** This old tip site is now redundant as a tip. Surveys have been carried out and proposals have been drawn up for landscape reclamation and industrial development so that either the private or public sectors can claim grant (see **38.18**).

(c) **Woodhead Railway** 19 miles of railway closed in the early 1980s. The land is now in the process of being acquired for new uses. The options for future use are dealt with in the relevant area summaries (Chapter 27 and 30).

7.11 As recorded in 7.6 above, 100% government grants are available on the eligible costs of local authority schemes, and 80% for the private sector. The Government's priorities for DoE grant aided work are set out in Circular 28/85. This gives highest priority to schemes leading to private sector commercial, industrial or residential development. Lower priority is given to environmental improvement or the creation of agricultural land. It is this lower priority work that is the most appropriate treatment for most derelict land in the Park. Grant for such schemes, if available, is for basic work leading to the equivalent of a 'green field site'. Other essential elements to create a new landscape appropriate to the Park (for example walling and tree planting) are expensive and regrettably are not normally eligible for derelict land grants. Some sites have a high wildlife, geological or archaeological value and reclamation schemes need to respect these interests (see Chapters 6 and 8). Some sites earmarked for reclamation would have commercial value as workshop, caravan site, farming or similar directly profitable end uses.

7.12 On most sites, however, major new economic uses for reclaimed land are impossible or undesirable. But an enhanced landscape is indirectly of economic importance — good landscape attracts recreational investment and 'footloose' industries both to the villages of the Park and to areas adjacent to the Park. DoE grant has been made available in recent years for such landscape enhancement work (e.g. at

Millers Dale Station and Dirtlow Rake — see **7.7b** and **7.9c**), and it is hoped that grants will continue to be paid for schemes which are not directly profitable.

Objective
7.13 To minimise the area of derelict land by taking action to bring the derelict areas in to new uses appropriate to the National Park.

Policies
7.14 The survey and programme of derelict land treatment within the National Park will continue to be reviewed and co-ordinated (Peak Board, District and County Councils).

7.15 Derelict land improvement schemes will continue to aim at integrating the land back into its landscape setting, and treating it in such a way as to make it available for new use approppriate to the character of the area. Care will continue to be taken to safeguard areas and features of archaeological, geological or wildlife interest (Peak Board, District and County Councils).

7.16 DoE funds will be sought for derelict land treatment even when there is no obvious direct economic benefit. The DoE will be asked to amend the regulations to allow work to be carried out to meet wider National Park objectives (see 7.11 & 7.34) (Peak Board).

Public Utility Installations

7.17 Structure Plan policies encourage the development and improvement of community and public utility services within the Park, provided they respect the character of the area. However, the 1978 Plan identified types of public service installations which can adversely affect the character and qualities of the Park . These include overhead electricity and telephone lines, aerials and transmitter masts, water and gas supply pipelines, pumping stations and sewage works. The Peak Board is normally consulted about the siting and design of utilities, either because of statutory requirements, or through voluntary arrangements. Public bodies are under a duty to consider the impact of new installations on the National Parks. Existing liaison arrangements generally work well. A point of particular concern has been the increased pressure for radio masts, from a range of public and and private bodies. Careful examination is needed to be sure that a site in the Park is really necessary and whether or not new users can share existing masts.

Natural forces at Mam Tor have closed a principal road. We hope to repair the eyesore and use the site for education and recreation.

7.18 Action has been taken to reduce the impact of many existing public utilities. There has been welcome co-operation between Electricity Boards, British Telecom and the Peak Board in many Village Conservation Areas to share costs of undergrounding the most offensive overhead lines (see **9.13**). In the rural areas, the Board has negotiated modifications to proposals for new and reconstructed lines in the interests of landscape conservation (in some cases offering grant-aid to help meet the additional costs involved). Action has been limited to a few miles of undergrounding, with very limited expenditure by the Board since 1977. Area studies with Water Authorities have resulted in much positive action, for example the removal of 3 miles of roadside concrete post and wire fencing at Ladybower.

7.19 Further undergrounding of lines in Conservation Areas is proposed (see **9.30**). In the rest of the Park, existing surveys of overhead lines need reviewing to establish priorities for undergrounding. Ministry of Agriculture grants of 30% are available to help install electricity supplies in farms. There may also be occasions when the Board can grant aid work needed for environmental reasons (see **4.57**).

7.20 In the case of underground utilities — electricity, water supply, gas and sewerage — there should be an ecological and archaeological survey prior to underground route decisions and an appropriate archaeological record made during the installation.

Objective
7.21 To reduce the impact of any necessary public utility services on the Park by treatment of existing installations and by appropriate siting and design of any new installations.

Policies
7.22 Public and private utility agencies will continue to minimise the impact of existing and proposed installations on landscape, ecological and archaeological interests in liaison with the Peak Board (see also 7.17 and 7.20 above) (Water Authorities, District Councils, Electricity Boards, British Telecom).

7.23 Overhead electricity and telephone lines and other installations such as substations will be reviewed, and a more ambitious programme will be devised to encourage the undergrounding of existing or new overhead lines (see also 22.30) (Peak Board, Electricity Boards, British Telecom).

7.24 Joint studies and working with Water Authorities in reservoir catchment areas will continue to identify and improve the appearance of existing installations (Peak Board, Water Authorities).

Enhancement Projects

7.25 Some uses of land spoil the appearance of the Park even though the area may not be officially 'derelict' (see **7.5**). The 1978 Plan proposed to carry out surveys and to achieve action by voluntary agreements with owners and occupiers. The legal powers include Discontinuance Orders, Modification Orders and Waste Land Notices under the Town and Country Planning Act 1971. There are other areas where positive improvements can be encouraged.

7.26 A grant-aid scheme for Landscape Enhancement was introduced in 1978 by the Peak Board. It provides for work such as small scale landscape improvements, tree planting, pond restoration and village green improvements. Grants are discretionary, and may cover up to 80% of eligible costs. Such grants by the Board have helped small projects, for example restoration of a mill leat at Fenny Bentley, tree planting at Black Hole Mine, Eyam, and restoration of the Mere at Heathcote. In response to a village-led initiative, the village green at Grindon has been improved, a pond constructed and trees planted. The grant-aid scheme has thus enabled a wide variety of work to be encouraged or supported where a landowner, parish council or company can take responsibility and pride in the project.

7.27 The Landscape Enhancement grant-aid scheme will be reviewed, given the changes in grants and assistance available from national bodies and constituent authorities, and with the advent of the Farm Conservation Scheme (see **4.48-4.57**). However, any new arrangements will need to ensure eligibility for similar schemes to those already implemented and possibly broadened to enable wildlife and historic conservation schemes to be undertaken.

Objective
7.28 To promote enhancement projects to encourage a widely-based pride and interest in the heritage of the Park.

Policy
7.29 Surveys of the Park will continue to be surveyed to identify inappropriate uses and potential enhancement, with the aim of achieving voluntary agreements for action with owners and occupiers. Compulsory powers will only be used in the last resort (Peak Board, Parish Councils).

7.30 A grant scheme will be maintained to assist voluntary action to benefit the landscape, wildlife and cultural heritage features of the Park (Peak Board).

Mineral Sites and Mineshafts

7.31 There has been a minerals industry in the Peak District from Roman times (lead) to the present day (hard rock, vein minerals and other materials). Following the Town and Country Planning Act of 1947, planning consent was needed to continue workings or to open new mineral sites. There is a substantial legacy of mineral sites — nearly 400 were listed in the most recent (1985) survey of sites in the Park, which have had planning consent for mineral working. Most of these are no longer active and some need treatment to bring them to a satisfactory condition. There is some overlap with the derelict land survey (see **7.5-7.15**). A further minerals survey is in hand in 1988/89.

7.32 Most sites which are covered by modern planning permissions have conditions requiring restoration or landscaping. These can normally be enforced through the use of development control powers. The recent appointment of extra Minerals and Enforcement staff at the Peak Board should help to ensure that active mineral sites are progressively restored. Some permissions granted many years ago did not, however, contain such conditions. The new powers provided by the Minerals Act of 1981 will enable the Board to carry out a 'Review' of such mineral permissions. It will then be possible to negotiate with the relevant owners and operators in order to amend conditions where necessary and improve restoration or landscaping. This will need careful design as some sites have significant wildlife, geological, historic or recreational features which must be safeguarded, particularly climbing and caving interests. Recent work on 'restoration blasting' (DoE/Peter Gagen) will be taken into account. Carrying out a scheme may involve the payment of compensation in certain cases, the extent of the financial compensation being related to the cost of the work involved. No date has yet been set for the start of the 'Review', but compensation provision may be needed from 1989/90 onwards.

7.33 There are thousands of abandoned mineshafts in the Peak District, following lead, copper or coal mining activity. Mineshafts sometimes have geological interest, for example as the habitat for bats. Some occur near footpaths and in areas of particular recreation importance. Shafts themselves can give opportunities for caving. Shafts and areas of mining activity nearby are sometimes of historic significance. Capping, grilles and access arrangements can be provided. Similar opportunities and issues arise in the case of abandoned quarries which can have wildlife, historic and recreational value (especially for climbing).

There are thousands of mineshafts. Those which are a danger to the public are capped, but access is allowed for special interests.

7.34 The main responsibility for work on mineshafts rests with land and mineral owners including British Coal. Much work has been done by the County Councils to reduce dangers associated with such shafts. The District Councils also have a role, as Environmental Health Authorities, for unprotected shafts which are clearly a health hazard. Since the 1978 Plan, British Coal has done significant capping in the Axe Edge area and Derbyshire County Council has been active in co-ordinating survey work and action in signing and capping shafts. A County Council Liaison Committee meets annually. In the Park, action has chiefly related to former lead mines in the Castleton and Winster areas and on Bonsall Moor. The Peak Board helps to fund schemes where special additional work is needed because of the historic, wildlife or recreational value of shafts or their immediate surroundings. Such work only currently qualifies for Derelict Land grant where it is part of a larger scheme. It would be helpful if grants were more generally available for there are large numbers of potentially dangerous shafts (see also **7.11**).

7.35 There remain many unprotected shafts, and the programme of action is therefore continuing, at least in Derbyshire. A 'Mind that Mine' leaflet has been produced by Derbyshire County Council, and warning signs erected on footpaths crossing areas with many shafts for example, along the Limestone Way. Protection work and controlled access arrangements under the auspicies of the Derbyshire Caving Association may be carried out at Black Marble Mine, Ashford, within a woodland owned by the Board.

7.36 There is much industrial archaeological interest in the history of the quarrying and mining industries, particularly in the Derbyshire part of the Park. Two principal organisations are actively developing educational, interpretive and recreational values. The Council for the National Stone Centre proposes a major visitor centre at Wirksworth and recognises the potential for 'satellite' sites or other links with the National Park. The Peak District Mines Historical Society (PDMHS) is longer-established, with a main centre in Matlock Bath, a field centre at Magpie Mine, Sheldon, and with a number of other sites under its care and maintenance.

Objective

7.37 To achieve appropriate treatment of all mineral sites and mineshafts.

Policies

7.38 A survey of mineral sites will be carried out for the Department of the Environment in 1988 (Peak Board).

7.39 A Review of planning consents covering mineral sites is being carried out in accordance with the provisions of the Minerals Act 1981. Negotiations will then commence with owners and operators to secure improved landscaping and appropriate treatment of sites (Peak Board, British Aggregate Construction Material Industries (BACMI).

7.40 A continuing programme of mineshaft protection will aim to safeguard the public, while recognising the historic, wildlife and recreational value of the shafts and the character of the locality (County Councils, Peak Board, District Councils, British Coal, NCC, PDMHS).

7.41 Where mineral features (e.g. quarry faces, plant, shafts) or surface vegetation (see **6.58**) is of particular historic, ecological or recreational importance or form part of such sites, the Peak Board will undertake or assist protection and interpretive work (Peak Board, County Councils, BACMI, National Stone Centre, PDMHS).

Roadside Verges

7.42 Over 95% of visits to the Park are by road. 40% of visits are by people who drive around or are on a sightseeing visit. Kerbs, verges, boundaries and signs form the foreground of the landscape viewed in this way. Verges are a major land area in the Park and often form (or could be managed to form) important wildlife habitats. (Road signs are dealt with in Chapter 15).

7.43 The 1978 Plan proposed that the Board would work with the Highway Authorities the NCC and others to agree a code of practice for the management of verges. Ad hoc arrangements have been made, but the only formal code to have been agreed so far is with Derbyshire County Council. There are now 8 Highway Authorities in the Park. Roadside walls are generally the responsibility of landowners. Where the walls support the highway, the Highway Authorities almost always accept responsibility for maintenance. In some cases, other walls may also be the responsibility of the Highway Authority.

7.44 Road verges and roadside walls in the Park are generally in good order, but in some areas there is scope for significant management improvement. There is a case for seeking an agreed code of practice with all the highway authorities, the Rural Land Management Executive Group (RLMEG) and others to ensure that the view from the road is given the priority indicated by its significance to the travelling public. The following issues should be given attention, subject throughout to the prime importance of road safety:

(a) The existing or potential use of the verge for walking, riding or cycling and the need for any surfacing or other work to provide for such uses.

(b) Methods and timing of verge maintenance to ensure the widest and most attractive range of herbs and flowers.

(c) Priorities for the repair and maintenance of roadside walls, hedges and other boundaries both ensuring appropriate standards of work in character with the area and allocating responsibility between Highway Authorities, landowners and others.

(d) The design and location of road signing and other highway furniture.

(e) The use of the least damaging methods of snow clearance.

(f) The careful location and screening of roadside salt and grit stores.

If the importance of landscape is measured by the number of people seeing it close to, then roadside verges are a most important asset.

(g) Design of kerbing and drainage systems.

(h) Standards of reinstatement where services are needed in verges (see **7.17-7.24**).

(i) Use of road verges for temporary storage of materials or equipment.

(j) The retention or reinstatement of roadside heritage features (e.g. mileposts and tollgates).

7.45 There are difficulties in making much progress on such issues when all the Highway Authorities believe that they have inadequate funds for routine road maintenance work, which they regard as of higher priority. Nonetheless they are normally willing to consider specific needs if extra costs are not significant. In some cases other agencies may be able to help with roadside work. For example Staffordshire Moorlands District Council worked with an MSC scheme on improving stone walls on the Buxton to Leek road.

Objective
7.46 To ensure that road verges and boundaries are maintained in a condition which contributes to National Park values.

Policy
7.47 Discussions will continue with the aim of increasing the priority given to the care of roadside verges and boundaries. The wildlife value of verges will be included in the interpretive programme (see **18.33**). A Code of Practice will be sought with the relevant authorities (Peak Board, NCC, Highway Authorities).

Litter Collection Service

7.48 The main responsibility for litter collection rests with the District Councils. The County Councils fund and manage waste disposal sites. There is only one major waste disposal site in the Park (at Calton Hill): this will soon be full. Waste disposal will thereafter take place mostly at sites outside the Park (see **22.9**). The Metropolitan District Councils exercise both collection and disposal functions. In recent years, the Peak Board has volunteered to assist with litter collection in the countryside, where the local councils are not accustomed or well placed to operate.

7.49 Since 1979 the Board's full time litter collection service has dealt with litter at the Board's own campsites, Hagg Farm Hostel, some of the Board's own car parks, informal and formal lay-bys and at known places where unauthorised dumping takes place. This has been achieved by one full time employee, with a vehicle. About 300 sites are visited on a regular basis, some weekly, some at longer intervals or in response to specific known incidences of unauthorised dumping. Litter drives take place at the discretion of the Ranger Service in areas or along routes where litter has been noticed to be a growing problem. These activities give rise to the collection and removal to Council tips of about 15,000 bags of refuse and 50 tons of associated material each year. The Peak Board's litter collection service covers about 60% of the geographical area of the Park, the principal exceptions being areas north of the A.57 and east of the Derwent reservoir chain. At present in the remaining 40% of the Park, the Ranger Service does as much as possible to control litter, but much more needs to be done.

It is a pleasure to picture 'chief womble' Malcolm Padley, following his receipt of the British Empire Medal, here at work in a litter blackspot.

7.50 The 1978 Plan set out a series of objectives for litter collection and management to reduce litter problems. These have been followed to varying extents by the various agencies involved, but a clearer framework for co-operation may be needed.

7.51 At selected sites, litter bins have been removed and the public encouraged to take their litter home. In general terms, success has been achieved in significantly reducing the amount of litter at these sites. However, the choice of sites needs to be carefully made and progress monitored. 'No Litter' signs need to be designed and sited with care. Often they are unnecessary and sometimes they are a bigger eyesore than the litter they hope to prevent.

7.52 The problem of litter shows no signs of abating and may be increasing. The possible consequences of recent policy changes by Derbyshire County Council are giving rise to concern. The County Council, seeking revenue savings, have replaced the former service in which skips stood unsupervised at skip sites to be collected weekly, with short visits by manned skips or lorries. This may lead to more unauthorised dumping on the fringes of some settlements, which would increase the burden on the District Councils and on the Board's existing services. The situation is being monitored.

Objective
7.53 To minimise problems of litter in the Park.

Policies
7.54 Every opportunity will be taken to encourage the public to 'take nothing but photographs, leave nothing but footprints' (Peak Board, Keep Britain Tidy Group).

7.55 A litter collection and disposal service will continue to be provided by the District and/or County Councils. The Peak Board will continue to complement the local councils' efforts with a countryside litter collection service and will seek to extend this to the rest of the Park as resources permit. A co-ordinated policy will be sought (District Councils, County Councils, Peak Board).

7.56 Periodic litter drives will be carried out where necessary (Peak Board).

7.57 In most remote picnic sites and lay-bys, no litter bins will be provided. Where necessary and appropriate, the public will be encouraged by discreet on-site signs to 'Take Your Litter Home' (Peak Board, County Councils, District Councils).

7.58 Prosecutions of serious litter offences will be encouraged (Peak Board, Police, District Councils)

Common Land

7.59 England and Wales have an historic legacy of common land over which people other than the owners hold long-standing legal rights. Only about one-fifth of common land is legally open to access by the general public. Few commons have any formal management structure. The Law of Property Act 1925 requires the consent of the Secretary of State for the erection of any building or fence or any other work on common land.

7.60 Within the National Park, records held by the 3 County Councils and 4 Metropolitan District Councils indicate that there is very little common land. However, village greens are often common land and are important to the local community as small yet highly significant village features. Opportunities may arise to provide facilities beneficial to both local residents and visitors. An example was the work at Grindon village green, where trees have been planted and a car park, picnic area and pond were provided (see **9.29**).

7.61 The need to safeguard and manage common land is fundamental to the recommendations of the Common Land Forum set up by the Countryside Commission which recently reported to Government. It is intended that the Forum's recommendations should provide the basis for future legislation in the form of a new Commons Act. If accepted, there would be a requirement for the Secretary of State for the Environment to appoint a day from which a general right of public access, 'on foot for quiet enjoyment', would exist to all commons. There would be provision for the initiation of management schemes to be formulated and operated by management associations. It is clearly important that the approach to management of common land should be consistent throughout the National Park. To ensure this, the appropriate County and Metropolitan District Councils (on whom other additional proposed duties related to common land will probably fall) will be asked to enter into liaison arrangements with the Peak Board. The Board will ask to be a relevant authority preparing and implementing Management Plans.

Objective
7.62 To improve the management of common land and to encourage the incorporation of National Park purposes into common land Management Plans.

Policy
7.63 Common land management schemes will be initiated as a means to integrate local community interests and conservation, farming and recreation objectives. (Peak Board, County Councils and Metropolitan District Councils).

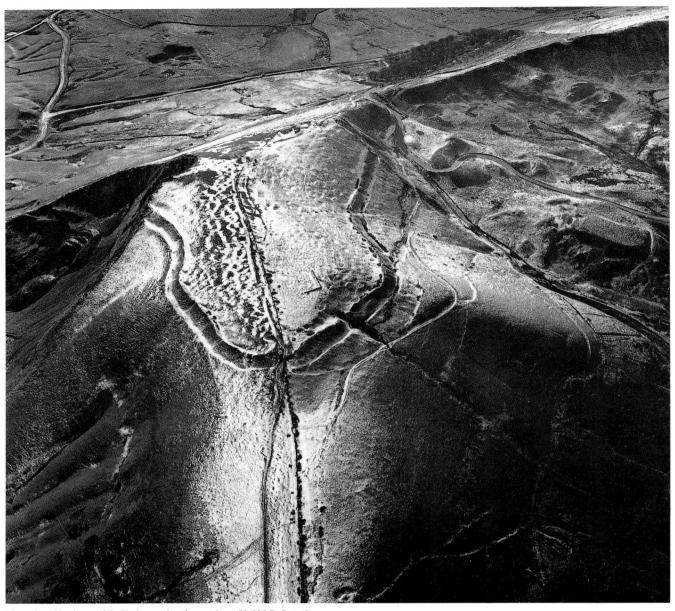

The cultural heritage of the Park stretches from at least 50,000 B.C. to the present day. Many people visit Mam Tor hill fort.

Introduction

8.1 This chapter deals with former human settlement of the Park — the 'cultural heritage' of old village sites, historic landscapes, forts, roadways, burials and other monuments, customs, traditions and legends. Chapter 9 deals with the towns and villages and buildings which are in use today.

8.2 The earliest humans in the Peak District were visiting hunters of the Old Stone Age, tens of thousands of years ago. The only evidence of their presence is the occasional artefact or animal bone, left in caves used as temporary shelter. Successive millennia saw the retreat of the glaciers, the eventual introduction of agriculture and domesticated animals and the building of the first permanent structures like Arbor Low henge and Minninglow chambered round barrow. As human society grew and developed, once-used structures became memorials to earlier society.

8.3 Bronze Age burial mounds pepper the White Peak. Ring-cairns, stone circles and prehistoric settlement sites occur on the gritstone. Hillforts crown the limestone and gritstone heights. Roman roads cross the Park, some of them now underneath modern roads. The conversion to Christianity can be charted between pagan post-Roman burials and the decorated stone crosses of the pre-Conquest period. Peveril Castle records the Norman Conquest of the Peak District. The village of Peak Forest is a reminder of the former Royal Hunting Forest of the medieval kings. Many other villages reflect the strength and longevity of agriculture over a thousand years or more, with different patterns in the village layouts and the shapes of fields reflecting the way in which the village was settled and developed. Many of the grange farms, away from the villages, testify to the agricultural activities of the monastic orders. Quarries and the detritus of the lead mining industry, mills, and former railway lines bear testimony to the area's contribution to the Industrial Revolution.

8.4 The National Park is thus rich in features demonstrating the history of human settlement, cultivation, social and industrial development. Although some have been lost, many sites, monuments and landscapes of great age and diversity have survived without damage from subsequent development, ravaged only by the passage of time. This quality, quantity and variety of historic features is of greatest importance. Each individual feature can be fitted into its historical and geographical context. Compared to most lowland areas the Park still contains sites showing an almost continuous record of past human activity. The protection, conservation and sympathetic management of this culture heritage is a fundamental aim of this Plan.

8.5 Because of the long settlement history and the relatively slow evolution of human activity in the area, the Park still retains a wealth of folk lore and tradition. These traditions have been lost over much of Britain because of rapid changes in the population and the urban way of life of the communities. The slower pace of change in the Peak District means we retain more of these links with the past.

8.6 The distinctive character of the Peak District has led writers, artists and others to portray the life of the area and its landscapes. The Peak can claim literary connections such as Walton and the Brontes and the area is rich in legends and settings for books. There are connections as varied as Arthurian legend and the Alison Uttley children's books. The Park continues to provide the home and/or inspiration for many modern day artists, writers and craftsmen.

8.7 The cultural heritage of the Park is one of the main reasons why visitors come. In the Visitor Survey 1986/87, about 70% of visitors said that 'old buildings and archaeological sites' (as opposed to towns and villages) were an important or very important reason for their visit. This is a significant justification for most of the policies in this chapter. Chapter 18 deals with the interpretation of National Park features and customs. This chapter is divided into four sections:

(a) Sites, Monuments and Historic Landscapes (8.8-8.26)

(b) Archaeological Research, Advice and Intergretation (8.22-8.40)

(c) Customs and Traditions (8.41-8.46)

(d) Legends and Artistic Associations (8.47-8.54)

Sites, Monuments and Historic Landscapes

8.8 There are some 200 Scheduled Ancient Monuments designated by the Department of the Environment (DoE) in the Peak National Park. Of these, 127 are burial mounds, megalithic monuments or ritual/ceremonial sites, 12 are camps, settlements or hut circles in enclosures, and 27 are medieval or later structures. Four sites (Arbor Low, Nine Ladies Stone Circle, Hob Hursts House, and Eyam Moor Barrow and Stone Circle) are in the guardianship of the DoE and managed by the Historic Buildings and Monuments Commission (HBMC) — (also commonly known as English Heritage). All have statutory protection under the Ancient Monuments and Archaeological Areas Act 1979.

8.9 However, the Scheduled Ancient Monuments do not adequately reflect the range of historic features present in the Park. HBMC are about to review the Schedule of Ancient Monuments. This is likely to result in a four-fold increase in the number of Scheduled Monuments (comparable to the increase in Listed Buildings recorded in **9.35**).

Arbor Low is one of 200 scheduled monuments and 5,000 entries in the sites and monuments record.

8.10 Responsibility for the protection and interpretation of scheduled ancient monuments rests with DoE (Scheduled Monument Consent) and HBMC. HBMC seeks to protect ancient monuments through partnership with owners, farmers, other land-users and local authorities, by means of both advice and financial assistance. The 1979 Act brought in stronger restrictions on Scheduled Ancient Monuments and widened the powers of HBMC and Local Authorities enabling them to conclude Management Agreements for important sites. Throughout the country HBMC works closely with local authorities and National Park Authorities in particular have a very important role. There is a clear need to maintain and increase the level of liaison which has been established between HBMC and the archaeologists working in the Park.

8.11 To ensure that there is a record of the known historic sites a 'Sites and Monuments Record' (SMR) has been produced for each county. This lists features which are considered worthy of record, whether or not they have any current protection such as Scheduled Ancient Monument status. The current record for Derbyshire for example was begun in 1982, and there are now some 5,000 entries for the National Park, ranging from caves to medieval stone crosses and 19th century industrial buildings. For many years before this, Parish Councils, organisations and individuals have notified the Board of features of local natural and cultural interest under a 'Peak Park Treasures' scheme. Those 'Treasures' of cultural heritage importance have been incorporated into the SMR (biological 'Treasures' are being transferred to the Biological Records system — see

The dig at Roystone Grange features in a guided walk, and could be introduced to many more people.

6.36). Most of these SMR entries have no statutory protection in their own right. Their conservation is taken into account whenever a proposed change comes to the Board's attention through the development control or farm grant notification processes.

8.12 The system of recording items for inclusion in the SMR is based on field survey work carried out by the Peak Board, by Community Programme teams and from a variety of other sources. Suggestions are received from parish councils and interested individuals. Information on sites is also often available from Museums Services. The importance of such heritage features to the local community can also be expressed in the form of a 'Parish Map', the preparation of which is encouraged by the Rural Community Councils. This has the added benefit of involving local communities in finding out more about their particular area and taking an interest in the conservation of its features.

8.13 In the 1978 Plan it was assumed that the government agencies and County Councils, who have the statutory powers relating to archaeological conservation, would take the main action. The Peak Board also supported local archaeologists and used their work for local planning purposes. In practice, neither the government agencies nor the County Councils have been able to take much action in the Park, although the SMR system is set up and maintained on a County basis.

8.14 In 1986 the Metropolitan County Councils ceased to exist and their functions have passed to other organisations acting through and on behalf of the Metropolitan District Councils.[24] With the growing interest in the history of the

Park, the fragility of many features and the growing need for cultural heritage conservation to be linked into other conservation work, the Peak Board has become increasingly involved in this work. This includes the appointment of its own full-time archaeologist. This chapter illustrates the extent of this involvement, little of which was predicted in the 1978 Plan.

8.15 The various county-based SMRs use different recording systems. The quality and quantity of their records is highly variable. They are based mainly on written and mapped work and represent a Phase 1 survey broadly equivalent to the biological records (see **6.30**). Enhancement programmes are underway to improve the quality of some of the SMR records. This is equivalent to the Phase 2 records for biological purposes. However, the Park is not a priority for many county archaeological services. This means that much SMR enhancement work in the Park is likely, in practice, to be carried out by the Board who will in turn ensure that the SMR authority receives relevant information. Other agencies too will be contributing. Making these records freely available to the Peak Board has been agreed.

8.16 One proposal that was developed in some detail in the 1978 Plan was the concept of 'Historic Landscapes'. These are areas of the Park which demonstrate particularly well, through a variety of features, a particular phase (or phases) of human occupation of the area.

8.17 Since 1978 the Peak Board has looked in some detail at 6 examples of Historic Landscapes:

(a) The Eastern Moors — an extensive upland bronze age landscape.

(b) Chee Tor — a Romano-British settlement and field system.

(c) The Chelmorton field system — a fossilised medieval strip field system.

(d) Cronkstone Grange — a medieval monastic sheep farm.

(e) The Ballidon area — with a series of sites from prehistoric through to the 19th century illustrating the different types of farming activity.

(f) The Winster barns and fields — a relic of the dual economy of lead mining and part-time farming.

8.18 Action on these six landscapes has been taken, with some success. The Eastern Moors and part of the Ballidon landscape (Roystone Grange) have been purchased by the Board, with financial assistance from the National Heritage Memorial Fund, Countryside Commission, NCC and HBMC. Conservation of the other landscapes is progressing slowly through management agreements (with Inheritance Tax exemption where relevant), grant aid and conservation assistance in kind. Action on the Winster barns and fields is slower, due to the difficult and costly conservation work on barns which often have no obvious economic use. A number of other sites merit similar action to define and conserve further 'Historic Landscapes'.

Objective

8.19 To identify, record, research, conserve and manage by whatever appropriate means, heritage features and artefacts

---

24 The South Yorkshire Archaeological Unit, the West Yorkshire Archaeological Service and the Greater Manchester Archaeological Unit.

which provide evidence for, and illustrations of, human occupation and use of the National Park from the earliest times to the present.

Policies

8.20 The number and range of sites with statutory protection will be reviewed as part of HBMC's Monument Protection Programme in close liaison with the Peak Board and the various SMRs covering the National Park. Ways to widen the scope and nature of partnership between HBMC and the Peak Board will be investigated, especially in the positive management of monuments (HBMC, Peak Board).

8.21 Sites and Monuments Records (SMRs) will be maintained and extended for the various parts of the National Park by the County Councils and Metropolitan District Councils with contributions from the Peak Board and others interested in archaeological conservation. Access to the SMRs will be made freely available to the Peak Board who will make extensive use of them to ensure the conservation of sites and monuments wherever possible (County Councils, Metropolitan Archaeological Services, Peak Board, Museums Services).

8.22 Enhancement programmes to improve the quality and quantity of data on the various SMRs will be discussed with the relevant authorities (Peak Board).

Protection and positive management of the cultural heritage features in the National Park will be sought. The development control and farm grant notification systems will be used to achieve this. Where appropriate, the Farm Conservation Scheme will be used (see 4.48-4.57), voluntary management agreements will be sought or other options considered (Peak Board).

8.24 The Board will continue to seek delegated powers from the relevant authorities under the Ancient Monuments and Archaeological Areas Act 1979, to ensure it has the full range of powers available to secure appropriate conservation action. The Board will use these powers, if agreed, to develop a grant-aid scheme for archaeological work (Peak Board, County Councils, Metropolitan District Councils).

8.25 Local individuals and organisations will continue to be invited to record cultural heritage features of interest. Suitable features will be forwarded for inclusion in the Sites and Monuments Record (see 8.21). Conservation action may be initiated, possibly as part of a village management schemes (see 9.18-9.23) (Peak Board, Rural Community Councils).

8.26 Measures to protect the characteristic features identified in the existing Historic Landscapes will continue to be applied or sought (see 8.16). Further Historic Landscapes will be identified and appropriate conservation work initiated (Peak Board).

Archaeological Research, Advice and Interpretation

8.27 Every effort is made to conserve the wide variety of sites, monuments and landscapes of cultural importance as explained above. Damage to Scheduled Ancient Monuments is an offence without Scheduled Monument consent but the protection available to other SMR sites is very limited. In some cases it is inevitable that archaeological sites will be lost through new development. In such cases archaeological investigations can be organised to record the site before it is destroyed. The Trent & Peak Archaeological Trust is the body mainly concerned with such work in the Peak District. Other organisations include the Universities of Sheffield and Keele, HBMC and the Royal Commission on Historic Monuments.

8.28 Other organisations and individuals also undertake archaeological research employing a range of techniques to make a record of cultural heritage features. Such work, particularly when linked to the SMRs of the constituent local authorities (see **8.11**-**8.13** above) provides valuable data for the management of the Park's heritage. In recognition of this, the Peak Board has made small grants available to further archaeological research in the Park particularly when the information collected can be added to the SMR as part of an enhancement programme (see **8.15**).

8.29 One device that can be very useful in archaeological research is the metal detector. However, many people who use metal detectors are not trained archaeologists and can, by digging out a find, destroy much of the other archaeological evidence which would help an archaeologist piece together a comprehensive record. The Peak Board, in common with most authorities with an interest in archaeology, discourages the use of metal detectors except within a properly controlled archaeological research project under the supervision of a trained archaeologist. Advice to this effect has been given to landowners and farmers in the Park by courtesy of the Ministry of Agriculture, NFU and CLA.

8.30 The 1978 Plan envisaged that archaeological research work would be carried out under the sponsorship of the Ancient Monuments Inspectorate of the DoE, mainly using organisations such as the North Derbyshire Archaeological Committee (which subsequently became a Private Trust and has since ceased to exist, its role now being performed by the Trent & Peak Archaeological Trust). In the event the scale of the need for archaeological information and the attendant problems in providing it, has led to quite different arrangements evolving. Some work is now assisted by grant aid from HBMC. Frequently MSC Community Programme teams and volunteers have been used for fieldwork. This has often been organised through the archaeological staff and the Peak Board also (since 1987) employs a full-time archaeologist. Co-ordination between the Peak Board and other local authorities is concentrating on the Board organising most field work in the Park and the constituent authorities[25] recording it in their SMRs (see **8.13** and **8.15** above).

8.31 To maintain links with the various interests concerned with archaeological work, the Peak Board and Derbyshire County Council supported the establishment in 1982 of the Derbyshire Archaeological Advisory Committee (DAAC), which is now the principal advisory body. The Committee has produced a report 'Archaeology in Derbyshire: Research Potential' and has been invited to produce a more specific theme-related report with suggested priorities for action.

8.32 The Park falls within the collecting areas of a number of museum services — principally Derbyshire County Museum Service, Sheffield City Museums and Stoke on Trent

---

25 In this context 'constituent authorities' means the County Councils and Metropolitan District Councils with parts of their area within the National Park (see also **8.14**).

Museum. Other museums with Peak District material include Manchester, Bolton, Doncaster, Derby City and the British Museum. They all hold collections of artefacts and information relevant to the understanding of the heritage of the National Park. Although artefacts are usually the property of the owner of the land where they are found, a museum is the safest repository for such heritage material unless it can be conserved and subsequently displayed on site and thus seen in its proper context. It is hoped that discussions with the various museums will lead to agreement as to which museum is the most appropriate in any given circumstance with provision for local special events or displays.

8.33 One of the purposes of archaeological work is to provide information so that the public can appreciate the history of the Park. Public awareness and enjoyment of the cultural heritage is increased by interpretation, for example simple plaques on site (e.g. Pilsbury Castle, Bamford Tollgates), and publications such as the Royston Grange Trail. This Trail is a waymarked footpath route through part of an Historic Landscape in Ballidon parish (see 8.17e) with information boards at intervals. A booklet guides visitors round the trail and explains the various historic features that can be seen. Because of the action taken to safeguard the main historic features at Roystone Grange there is a major opportunity for a project in partnership with Sheffield University (who have been involved throughout in the work at Roystone Grange and who organised much of the work at this site). Chapter 18 describes the Board's interpretation and education objectives in which cultural heritage is expected to play a growing and major part.

Objective
8.34 To discover as much as possible about the cultural heritage features of the Park and to use the information gained to secure appropriate conservation and enhance public enjoyment.

Policies
8.35 Guidance and advice will be sought from the Derbyshire Archaeological Advisory Committee and other organisations and individuals. The aim is to prepare a series of Cultural Heritage Action Programmes for different areas or themes, defining the work to be done and the role of each participant (DAAC, Peak Board, HBMC, Constituent Authorities).

8.36 The possibilities of establishing a fund for long-term research into elements of the Park's heritage, and for the enhanced public understanding of that cultural heritage, will be explored (Peak Board, DAAC, Constituent Authorities).

8.37 Where damage occurs to heritage features, appropriate steps will be initiated to prevent further damage and to agree and implement conservation measures (see also 8.23) (Peak Board, HBMC).

8.38 When on-site physical preservation of a heritage feature is not practicable, an appropriate record will be made wherever possible. Financial support will be provided for this work and publication ensured where appropriate (Peak Board, Constituent Authorities, HBMC).

8.39 In general, the more robust artefacts are best left on site where they can be seen in context (e.g. mileposts). Where this is not possible or desirable, artefacts should be deposited with an appropriate museum, or where this cannot be achieved, be properly curated within private collections. Records of collections should be lodged with the appropriate museum and Sites and Monuments Record (see 8.21). The collecting policies of the various museums will be co-ordinated so that artefacts can be kept in the most appropriate place for their conservation and interpretation to the public (Peak Board, Museums, Constituent Authorities).

8.40 The use of metal detectors should be limited to archaeological research programmes co-ordinated by professional archaeologists linked to the overall agreed research programme for the Park. Advice to this effect will continue to be given to owners and land managers (Peak Board, MAFF, NFU, CLA).

Customs and Traditions

8.41 The Park has an unusual variety and wealth of customs and traditions. Some are well known to the general public, for example well dressing: others are of greatest significance to particular groups of people, for example the Alport Castles Love Feast, a non-conformist religious event linked to the historic persecution of non-conformists. Many of these customs and traditions are linked to specific features, for example wells or barns. Others are just traditional to the area and not tied to any specific feature, for example the Winster Gallops, a local Morris dance.

8.42 These customs and traditions have evolved in the area because of the particular local circumstances and are kept going by local people as part of their way of life. There is a growing interest in folklore and increasing pride in local traditions. Public authorities should foster these customs and traditions by helping in whatever way the local community think is appropriate, for example, by including well dressings in the Calendar of Events. The Peak Board has assisted the maintenance of sites linked to customs, for example village wells. To avoid the danger that local traditions become trivialised or commercialised, all such assistance must be at the request of the community; and all work should continue to be organised by the villagers as a truly living local tradition.

8.43 In some cases old customs and traditions have died out, although they remain in living memory. There is some interest in reviving such traditions while these memories remain. Recording such events is closely linked to recording bygone ways of doing things, for example old agricultural practices. This can sometimes generate what in effect are 'new traditions'. For example, at Ashford there is now an annual ceremonial sheep wash in the river during well dressing week: this revives what used to be a regular farming practice, now overtaken by new agricultural techniques. Work in Village Conservation Areas (see 9.8-9.14) has frequently revived memories of what a particular building was used for, who owned it and how the job was done. Old photographs are produced and 'tales my grandparents told me' are recalled. There is urgent need to record oral history before memories fade and the oldest generation dies. Such records can be used in a variety of ways for example to help communities take a pride in their old buildings or to provide information for visitors.

Objective
8.44 To help and encourage local communities to maintain their customs and traditions and to record information about former ways of life.

Policies
8.45 Assistance for local customs and traditions will

The Longnor silver band plays at village functions, indoors and out.

Farmers now use a sheep dip, but the annual ceremonial sheep washing continues at Ashford.

continue to be provided at the request of the local community, so that the events can continue to be purely a relfection of local pride (Rural Community Councils, Peak Board, County Associations of Parish or Local Councils).

8.46 Efforts will be made to systematically record old customs, songs, traditions and elements of bygone ways of life (by means such as tape recordings, old photographs and copies of documents) and to make these records available for local community and other use. The ways in which this might best be done in partnership with local communities will be explored (Rural Community Councils, Peak Board, Museums Service, District Councils, County Associations of Parish or Local Councils).

Legends and Artistic Associations

8.47 In a fairly wild but long settled area, it is not surprising that stories and legends abound. 'Sir Gawain and the Green Knight' is a medieval poem about one of King Arthur's Knights, possibly set in the Back Forest area of North Staffordshire. The eastern side of the Peak District was traditionally part of Robin Hood's territory and his name recurs in many local place names: the alleged grave of his lieutenant, Little John, is in Hathersage Churchyard.

8.48 Artists and writers have drawn their inspiration from the area. 'Jane Eyre' by Charlotte Bronte is set in the Park. The author of the much loved 1960s television series 'Upstairs Downstairs' based his stories on the Legh family of Lyme Hall. The 'Compleat Angler' is related to Dovedale; North Lees Hall is 'Thornfield Hall' and Hathersage is the 'Morton' of Jane Eyre. Knowing of these connections can add to the interest of visits to these places. Maintaining the high-quality distinctive environment also gives a source of inspiration for current and future generations of artists and craftsmen (for example several nationally-known photographers and many local craftsmen and artists use or live in the Park).

8.49 To explore the ways in which the relationship between art and the National Park might develop, the DoE recently appointed an 'Artist in Residence' to each of the ten Parks. The Peak Board provided accommodation and other help to its appointed Artist, whose work on 'sheep-places' has been exhibited nationally.

8.50 Obviously the legends and associations of the Peak District give an added source of local pride to local people. For example even the humble Bakewell Pudding — a gastronomic work of art — is probably consumed in greater quantities per head of population in Bakewell than anywhere else and is 'required eating' or a souvenir present for any visitor. Local People are proud of its 'invention' in their town. This and other legends and associations give added character to the Park and a source of wonder and enjoyment to local people and visitors alike. They are also of course a major benefit to the tourist economy (a pudding not made in Bakewell doesn't look or taste the same!).

8.51 The special qualities of other local foods and other basic crafts can also enhance the experience of a visit to the Park. Local producer-retailer links can be developed.

Objective
8.52 To maintain records of the landscapes and features of the Park which have provided the links to local legends and the inspiration for books and other works of art.

Policies
8.53 The means by which to record legends, literary and artistic associations will be sought — for example, important sites could be notified and recorded in a system similar to or within the existing SMRs (Peak Board, Regional Arts Councils).

8.54 The Artists in Residence scheme will be reviewed and further proposals brought forward to strengthen the links between art and the National Park (Department of the Environment, Peak Board, Countryside Commission).

Introduction

9.1 The towns and villages of the Park form a third zone in land management policy (see **2.7**). The buildings and the spaces around them form the most obviously man-made environment in the Park. The appearance of each settlement often reflects its natural setting. Local materials have been used and sheltered sites have been favoured, not just in villages but in all buiding work. Simple and robust building put up by local people, using local materials to suit local conditions, have produced buildings which fit into their setting and contribute to the character of the Park.

9.2 The settlements of the Park contribute to its environmental character. But they are also the places where most of the Park's 38,000 people live and the focus of much of the Park's economic and environmental objectives should be a key element in policies. If the character of the 'built environment' is to be conserved, this can only be achieved by the actions of the people who live and work in the Park. Recent work has shown that conservation can contribute to the quality of life of local residents (for example, at Longnor and Tideswell) in many different ways and can help, not hinder, the local economy.

9.3 In addition to the settlements, there are other areas where the hand of man is dominant — individual buildings and formal gardens. This chapter is divided into three sections:

    (a) Towns and Villages (**9.4-9.34**).

    (b) Historic Buildings (**9.35-9.53**).

    (c) Historic Parks and Gardens (**9.54 -9.61**).

Towns and Villages

9.4 The Park has more than 100 towns, villages and hamlets. They reflect the local building traditions, the history of man's settlement in the Park and the life and work of its inhabitants. Maintaining the distinctive unspoilt character which is apparent in most of the settlements of the Park is a high conservation priority. Improving the environmental qualities of the settlements is a key element in this Plan.

9.5 The settlements have developed to reflect the social and economic needs of the population as this has changed over time. In the 20th century, modern demands mean that the settlements have inevitably changed, for example to accommodate motor vehicles.

9.6 Established policies are based on conserving the best of the heritage of the past and guiding new development. The framework for this is provided by settlement policies in the Structure Plan. These seek to ensure that genuine local needs for housing, jobs or services are met, but to concentrate most development in certain key towns and villages to ensure the continuation of viable communities (see Chapters 20-22).

9.7 Settlement policies have tried to maintain a balance between social and economic needs and environmental considerations. There are two main threads to settlement policy:

    (a) The identification and sympathetic management of the best existing features in a village (for example the buildings and open spaces) and the elimination of features that spoil the character of the place.

Castleton is one of nearly thirty Conservation Area villages. Special effort is made to protect its character.

(b) Careful 'managed change' to ensure that new needs are met by finding new uses for existing buildings or by new development which fits in with the character of each settlement.

9.8 The development of work in the settlements In the early years following National Park designation, village work concentrated on the control of new development. A Building Design Guide, prepared in the mid 1970s and revised in 1987, analysed the building traditions of the Park and suggested ways in which those traditions can be reinterpreted to meet modern needs. This Guide has helped to improve the quality of new development in the last 10 years and in particular has reduced the amount of bad design.

9.9 Since 1976, efforts have been made to encourage the protection and enhancement of the important features of the most attractive settlements. These features include the buildings but also the spaces between buildings, the trees, and 'street furniture' such as lamp posts and seats. Conservation Areas have been designated and enhancement work has begun using powers under the Town and Country Planning Acts. A programme of Conservation Area work was set out in the 1978 Plan.

9.10 A Conservation Area is designated so as to give clear recognition of the special architectural or historical character of the area. It includes the historic core of the village and can extend to include the landscape setting of the village. Conservation Area designation provides encouragement to all to respect the special character of the defined area. The evidence shows that this works. Many public agencies have higher standards for environmental work within designated Conservation Areas. Designation provides the basis for enhancement schemes agreed with the local communities and implemented in partnership with them. The Board is also able to give grants towards the costs of repairs of important, but non-listed buildings, within a Conservation Area (see **9.39**). Currently, the Peak Board has a budget of £65,000 each year to carry out or encourage such works.

9.11 Conservation Area designation also provides a modest extension of the Board's powers, as owners must seek permission to demolish most buildings within them (whether listed or not) and must notify the Board of proposals to cut down, lop or top most trees. This extension of legal powers is not, however, the main reason for designation. Indeed since the first Conservation Area was designated in 1976, agreement has always been reached on the work necessary on trees and buildings.

Trees, seats and paving now complement the attractive stone houses around the Square in Eyam.

9.12 28 Conservation Areas had been designated by September 1988 (see Table 9.1). Enhancement schemes have been agreed for all but one of the Conservation Areas and most schemes have been wholly or partly implemented. Work carried out has included removal of overhead wires, paving, and planting of trees and shrubs.

Table 9.1
Conservation areas designated 1976-1988

(In each case, the designated area covers that part of the town or village which is judged to be of historic or architectural importance).

Alport	1982	Ilam	1977
Alstonefield	1979	Langsett	1977
Ashford	1981	Litton	1987
Bakewell	1980	Longnor	1977
Beeley	1988	Monyash	1981
Bradfield	1981	Parwich	1986
Bradwell	1976	Pott Shrigley	1979
Butterton	1986	Ravensdale	1987
Castleton	1976	Rowsley	1987
Cressbrook	1986	Stoney Middleton	1987
Eyam	1981	Tideswell	1981
Hartington	1977	Upper Midhope	1977
Hathersage	1981	Winster	1981
Holme	1981	Youlgreave	1982

9.13 Increasing emphasis has been placed on joint funding and working within the Conservation Areas. This both makes the Board's funds go further and helps to promote commitment from the local community, the District and County Councils and other public bodies, which is vital if conservation is to succeed in the long term. It is now established practice that overhead wire removal projects are funded half by the Board and half by the Electricity Boards and/or British Telecom; and that local communities currently make at least a 10% contribution to other improvements. Building repair grants require the major part of total costs to be met by the owners or occupiers of the buildings.

9.14 Enhancement schemes have been widened progressively in recent years to include an element of land use planning. By agreement with the community, several schemes have indicated both those sites which were not suitable for development and those where development would be beneficial in physical terms. This has provided a useful indicative basis for dealing with subsequent planning applications and ensuring that any necessary new development is integrated into the fabric of the village.

9.15 In a few villages, a wider variety of work has resulted from the Integrated Rural Development Project (IRD), the Rural Development Programmes, the Community Action in the Rural Environment scheme (CARE) in Barnsley Metropolitan Borough, and Derbyshire Dales District Council's General Improvement Area schemes. Where these initiatives have been taken, the work in the villages has incorporated a broader spectrum of environmental improvement work linked to community and economic development work. These projects are more fully described in Chapter 23.

9.16 Recent advice from Government, through the Countryside Commission, has pointed towards increased emphasis upon the protection and enhancement of the built environment in the National Parks. It is also intended to encourage other initiatives which assist the social and economic well-being of those who live in the Parks. An integrated approach to the creation of social and economic and environmental improvements is advocated.

9.17 Experimental work in the IRD project has shown that social and economic and environmental objectives can all be combined to created benefits much greater than could be realised by the separate and single-minded pursuit of each. A more detailed account of IRD work and how its lessons might be applied in future work in the Park is set out in paragraphs 23.23-29.

Village Management Schemes

9.18 Because many different organisations need to work together in the more ambitious village management programmes, it is likely that moving into a fully-fledged integrated approach to village work will be a gradual process. The intention is to adopt a broader concept of Village Management Schemes in all village work. However, the content and detail will vary according to the village.

9.19 In all cases it is likely that Conservation Area designation will be an integral part of the programme of work, identifying those parts of the settlement of particular architectural or historic interest. In many cases the Village Management Scheme will consist of little more than the definition of the Conservation Area, combined with a plan indicating where physical improvements might take place (both inside and outside the Conservation Area boundary). It is likely that funds for environmental improvement will be concentrated on Conservation Areas.

9.20 In a settlement which seems to need a broader-based programme of work, and particularly where change is taking place, the Village Management Scheme would often incorporate a broader range of work. For example it might indicate:

(a) Sites where new buildings would be desirable or undesirable.

(b) Opportunities to generate new community or business activities (e.g. a play area or a new business in a disused building).

9.21 The Village Management Scheme will therefore indicate the types of physical developments that could take place in the village. However, the needs of a village may not always have physical implicataions. Helping a business to expand or encouraging the formation of a mother-and-toddler group does not necessarily involve changing the appearance of the village, but it can change the spirit of the place. The IRD project assisted an enormous range of activities generated by three different communities. Few new buildings were needed, but the environments have been tangibly improved, there are many new jobs and both community life and the local economy has benefitted. This kind of approach needs to draw in a very wide range of public agencies. At present it is envisaged that further Village Management Schemes of this type, aimed at simultaneous improvement to the social, economic and environmental qualities of a settlement will concentrate on a few places of special need. These localities are likely to pay regard to the Rural Development Programmes (see 23.24).

This local landmark in Hathersage was restored by the Parish Council with advice and grant from the Board.

9.22 Village Management Schemes will be worked out with the communities concerned. They will be general indications of opportunities that could be followed up, not definitive proposals. Such detailed proposals would then need to be produced and planning consent sought where relevant. The Village Management Schemes would give a general brief for the type of development that best meets the particular combination of social, economic and environmental needs.

9.23 The Village Management Schemes should be followed by action. This will often involve many different organisations. The Village Management Scheme should be of a form and to a level of detail that both meets the needs and possibilities of each place and can be quickly translated into programmes of action. Village Management Schemes will need to be periodically amended to meet new needs and possibilities.

9.24 A key principle must be to make environmental conservation work relevant to the local community and to link it into social and economic needs. Three examples illustrate how this might be achieved:

(a) A new use for a prominent unused building may both save a local landmark and provide jobs for local people or a much-needed social facility.

(b) A well-placed new car park may both reduce unsightly on-street parking and enhance the trade of a local inn or other business.

(c) A new playground with grass, trees and new stone walls may both tidy up a waste piece of ground and enhance the lives of village children.

9.25 The corollary of this is that social and economic needs should be met in ways which can enhance the environment of the village and sited and designed deliberately to achieve this. This will require careful thought and an examination of various options to get the best results. Time and care will be well spent, for work in villages will have and impact for many generations ahead.

9.26 The choice of villages and the form of the Village Management Scheme will need careful consideration. Four considerations are particularly relevant:

(a) The character of each village.

(b) The needs and opportunities in each place.

(c) The interest of the local community.

(d) The willingness of other agencies to participate.

9.27 The interplay of these four considerations varies and it is not intended to produce a rigid programme of Village Management Schemes in this Plan. The villages which are likely to be considered first for such schemes are those where there is no Conservation Area, but where there seems to be a need or potential for social, economic or environmental action – Bamford, Great Longstone, Hope, Taddington, Warslow, Wetton.

9.28 Those settlements where Conservation Areas have already been defined and where major follow-up work is still needed include Bakewell, Bradwell, Castleton, Cressbrook, Hathersage, Hartington, Langsett, Litton, Parwich, Rowsley, Stoney Middleton, Tideswell, and Youlgreave.

9.29 Many other settlements may deserve attention, in response to opportunities and the interest shown by the local community and subject to the considerations in paragraph 9.26. Recent examples include individual schemes at Grindon, Rainow and Middleton by Youlgreave, where there was an opportunity to respond to local enthusiasm for specific environmental improvement projects. In Tideswell, a parish council employee helps keep the village trim – a sort of 'lengthsman' in the old tradition. Such arrangements could add to the care provided by the District Councils – the possibility of extending this practice to other villages will be explored. The work of such a parish-based employee could also take in local footpaths (see 11.21).

Objective
9.30 To maintain and enhance the special environmental qualities of Peak District settlements and to simultaneously improve, wherever possible, the well being of the local community and the strength of the local economy.

Policies
9.31 An expanded programme of work will be initiated in the settlements of the Park based on the concept of Village Management Schemes, selected as set out in 9.26 and 9.27. These will be of different types depending on the needs and opportunities of each village. Efforts will be made to integrate social, economic and environmental objectives in linked programmes of work. Environmental imporovement will be concentrated mainly in Conservation Areas. All such work will be developed in consultation with the communities concerned and will seek to involve, as partners, the relevant other public agencies.

9.32 Work in the Conservation Areas already designated will continue. General priorities for further village work will be the settlements listed in 9.27, 9.31 and 9.32: (Peak Board, Electricity Boards, British Telecom, Highway Authorities, Rural Development Commission, Parish and District Councils, Rural Community Councils, RDC).

9.33 In all village work, the opportunity will be taken to encourage local communities to continue to express pride in their heritage and their environment. Local people will be involved in all aspects of the work (Peak Board, Rural Community Councils).

9.34 The Building Design Guide will assist the design and siting of new buildings in the villages and will be used, together with Structure Plan policies, for development control purposes (Peak Board).

Historic Buildings

9.35 Vernacular and traditional buildings are an important part of the character of the Peak District. The most interesting of such buildings are 'listed' by the Department of the Environment as buildings of architectural or historic interest. A recent national resurvey has increased the number of listed buildings in the Park from 800 to over 2,000. This is expected to reach 2,250 by the time the resurvey is complete in 1988. However, the resurvey is not succeeding in identifying all buildings worthy of protection. There remains the occasional need to get a building listed urgently ('spot listed'). Once a building is listed, the Peak Board make a photographic record, together with notes on its appearance and condition.

Each year, the owners of over fifty historic buildings receive grants to help repair them in authentic materials. This building is in Litton.

9.36 There are many other buildings and structures of cultural interest, demonstrating the social history of the area. Some of these are Scheduled Ancient Monuments. Others, such as the barns at Winster associated with the lead mining history of the area, have no statutory protection. The importance of conserving the historic element of the built environment will be pursued through the Sites and Monuments Record (see **8.11**)

9.37 The 1978 Plan recognised the importance of conserving important individual buildings. The main features of the policies adopted were:

(a) Provision of grant aid for repairs.

(b) Negotiation with owners of disused buildings to agree suitable restoration or conversion schemes.

(c) Where new uses of buildings were appropriate, these uses should meet local community needs wherever possible, especially in villages.

9.38 The increase in the number of listed buildings has increased the Board's workload. 'Listed Building Consent' is needed for work which will change the appearance of a listed building. Listing has increased public awareness of the need for historic building management: this has led to more enquiries, requests for advice and help with repairs, and a greater interest in the conversion of redundant buildings.

9.39 Some 60 to 70 historic buildings a year receive grant under the Board's Historic Building Grant Scheme for repair and restoration. The Scheme covers listed buildings throughout the Park and important non-listed buildings in Conservation Areas. The budget for this is around £60,000 per year, but is inadequate: funds are exhausted well before the end of each financial year. Over recent years, demand for grants has increased significantly because there are more listed buildings, because the cost of repairs in traditional materials is growing faster than the rate of inflation, and because of the reduction in District Council Housing Act grants which covered certain structural work. Some limited extra money has been made available by the Historic Buildings and Monuments Commission (HBMC) through the establishment of schemes under Section 10 of the Town & Country Planning (Amendment) Act 1972. To date this has applied only to the centre of the Eyam and Bakewell Conservation Areas, where the Board's normal grants are supplemented by 25% grants from HBMC. Other very similar national schemes — 'town schemes' — also exist but, despite requests, have not to date been made available by HBMC in the Park.

9.40 The rate of Board grant is periodically adjusted in the light of experience, and in 1988 varied from 25% for stone slate roofing to 15% or 20% for other work. The grants can be increased (up to a maximum of double the normal rate) in special circumstances of financial hardship, or to encourage necessary but expensive restoration work. In order that funds can be used to maximum effect, there is also a normal limit of £2,000 grant per application. County and District Councils within the Park have concurrent powers with the Board to award historic building grants, although few in practice operate their schemes in the Park.

9.41 The Peak Board provides a general advisory service to owners of listed buildings. Grants often follow earlier advice about repair and restoration. Normally such advice is specific to the items of work, but for more seriously threatened historic buildings, a comprehensive approach may be needed. Feasibility studies have been prepared to encourage the rescue of redundant or poorly used and maintained historic buildings. The Board has worked with the Derbyshire Historic Buildings Trust (DHBT) to devise such studies. The DHBT has produced important studies for Burton Closes, Bakewell; Cressbrook Mill; and Newhaven House Farm. The Board has produced studies for the Feoffee's property in High Bradfield; Pictor Hall at Green Fairfield and has recently begun other studies for several properties, including Townhead Farm, Flagg.

9.42 In 1987 a new private charity was formed called the Peak Park Trust. This Trust has the general aim of improving environmental, social and economic conditions in the National Park. It has decided to concentrate initially on finding new uses for historic buildings, acting in a similar way to the historic buildings trusts. The Trust's assistance has been sought in relation to the restoration and conversion of Langsett Barn, and it is intended that other historic buildings at risk will be helped.

9.43 A 'Buildings at Risk' service has been introduced and lists of buildings for sale or lease are now publicised by the Board. The difficulty with a problem building may often be an owner who is reluctant either to repair (even with the offer of grant) or to sell. Time and effort is often needed to encourage such owners to act. The feasibility studies referred to above are useful in persuading reluctant owners that their buildings can have a viable future.

9.44 The Board does have a power, under the Town and Country Planning Act 1971, to require a reluctant owner to carry out repairs to listed buildings. The Board can even carry out the work and recharge the costs to the owner. These powers have only been used in a few cases, as a last resort, after long periods of unsuccessful negotiation and when the building is in poor condition.

9.45 A list of 'Other Redundant Buildings' has also been prepared. These buildings are not listed but, despite their lower individual merit, they may contribute to an important landscape or townscape, or may provide an opportunity to meet a social or economic need as an alternative to a new building. A nationwide survey of farm barns is also in progress. The re-use of 'Buildings at Risk' will take priority wherever there is a choice. The 'Other Redundant Buildings' list and its use in the assessment of the use of resources will be reviewed.

Objective

9.46 To ensure the conservation of buildings of architectural or historic interest and to encourage the re-use of neglected buildings of local importance.

Policies

9.47 Detailed records of all the listed buildings within the Park will be maintained. Every building will be inspected at least once every five years to record its condition. This will include making a photographic survey of all changed exterior elevations and, in the case of Grade I and Grade II buildings, of important interior features as well. The link to the Sites and Monuments Record system will be maintained and developed (See 9.36) (Peak Board).

9.48 Owners of historic buildings will be offered advice on repair and maintenance. Leaflets on the general repair and maintenance of historic buildings will be kept up to date (Peak Board).

9.49 The main source of grant aid for the repair of Grade I and Grade II listed buildings will continue to be HBMC. Listed buildings and important non-listed buildings in Conservation Areas will continue to be eligible for grants for their repair and restoration from the Peak Board (see 9.39) (HBMC, Peak Board).

9.50 Section 10 and other special arrangements such as 'town schemes' by which national grants can be made available to supplement local grant schemes will continue to be sought (Peak Board, HBMC).

9.51 County and District Councils will be asked to continue or to start to give grants in the Park for historic building repair work in order to increase the amount of work carried out. The Peak Board will seek to co-ordinate policies for the use of the various local authority grant schemes (County Councils, District Councils, Peak Board).

9.52 Where owners are unable or unwilling to carry out adequate repairs, the sale or lease of such buildings to others who can maintain them will be encouraged or other appropriate measures will be taken. A register of 'Buildings at Risk' will be kept to help market such threatened buildings. In a limited number of cases where the appropriate re-use of a redundant or under-used listed building is not obvious, feasibility studies to examine suitable new uses within the context of Structure Plan policies will be produced or commissioned (Peak Board, Building Preservation Trusts).

9.53 The 'Other Redundant Buildings' register will be reviewed. Policies will be reviewed and means sought to safeguard locally important but unlisted buildings (Peak Board).

Historic Parks and Gardens

9.54 Interest in the conservation of historic parks and gardens in the Park is quite new. But they form an important ingredient in the character of various parts of the Park and show a special element of the relationship between man and nature.

9.55 An historic garden will almost always be associated with an important building which may be listed as having historic or architectural interest. The listing may cover significant garden features such as terraces and statues. But just as a village consists of more than its buildings, there is growing awareness that a garden too must be looked at as a whole. The same applies to the Parks which surrounded many notable country houses, often deliberately landscaped for aesthetic effect. Some old parks also contain important wildlife habitats, in particular long established lawns and old trees which may be the remnants of ancient woodlands, as at Chatsworth. Historic gardens and parklands can also contain features from various points in time; for example medieval ridge and furrow cultivation may underlie 18th century parks, and it is often the story of the area over time that is important.

9.56 Since December 1984, county registers have been issued by HBMC showing parks and gardens of national importance. Three parks or gardens in the Park are included — Chatsworth House, Haddon Hall, and Lyme Park. There are others of less importance nationally, but which are significant features of the National Park. The grounds of Cressbrook Hall, for example, were laid out by the Victorian garden designer Edward Kemp and appear in his book 'How to Lay out a Garden' of 1858.

9.57 There is no established practice of statutory protection for gardens in their entirety. Listed building legislation is only for structures, not total landscapes. Conservation Area legislation might however be appropriate and at least one garden, at Ilam Hall, is partly within an existing Conservation Area. Management Agreements are another possible way forward. The first priority is to draw up a list of the more important historic parks and gardens. Methods of conservation can then be worked out for each one.

Objective
9.58 To identify all parks and gardens of special character or historic interest and to assist in their conservation.

Policies
9.59 An initial list of historic parks and gardens of the Park will be produced; incorporating the HBMC register of parks or gardens of national importance (Peak Board).

9.60 Steps for the protection and conservation of the more important historic parks and gardens will be examined (Peak Board).

9.61 Where needed, advice will be made available to owners of such parks and gardens for their maintenance and restoration (Peak Board, HBMC).

Historic parks and gardens need to be conserved as well as their houses. This old photograph shows Thornbridge Hall in its prime.

Walking is the most popular informal recreation in the Peak District. It has a long history . . .

Introduction

10.1 The second statutory duty of National Park Authorities under the 1949 Act, is to promote the enjoyment of the area by the public. 'Enjoyment' is specifically linked to opportunities for open air recreation. Subsequent Government advice, following the Sandford Report, made clear that wherever there is a conflict, this duty is secondary to that of conserving and enhancing the natural beauty of the area (para. 4, circular 4/76).

10.2 The Structure Plan and the 1978 Plan state basic policies for the development of recreational opportunities in the Park. In summary, these aim to enable visitors to appreciate, use and understand the character and qualities of the different parts of the National Park, whilst ensuring that these attributes are maintained for the benefit of further generations. This is essential if the National Park landscape is to be maintained as the principal recreation resource. The 1986/87 Visitor Survey established that, of those interviewed, 66% think that distinctive landscapes, 60% think that uncommercialised areas and 42% think that the presence of wildlife are very important (see table 2.1 Chapter 2).

10.3 This chapter establishes a fundamental objective and general policy for recreation management in the Park. The first part of the chapter examines the different types of visitor activity.

10.4 The second part of the chapter re-endorses the five recreation zones of the 1978 Plan. The measurement of capacity is extended by a proposal to measure the physical

. . . large numbers now enjoy some beauty spots, such as Dovedale, for long walks, short walks, picnics and riverside play. Too many . . .?

capacity of roads and accommodation, to assess current levels of use and thus assess the carrying capacity of an area. This system has not yet been proven in practice in the Park and may prove useful only in a limited number or type of applications.

10.5 Balanced judgements will then be made in the light of conservation values (Chapters 2 to 9), in the application of the policies and proposals for recreation, access, and visitor services (Chapters 10 to 19) and in the different areas of the Park (Chapters 24-47).

Objectives

10.6 To ensure that visitors to the Park are able to appreciate and understand its character and qualities, and to use but not abuse them in their recreational activities. To ensure that, wherever possible, recreational development contributes to conservation objectives. To ensure that such recreation uses are compatible with conservation objectives and policies. To consider the social and economic benefits which can arise for the Park's resident community from the reception of visitors.

Policy

10.7 Only those recreational opportunities appropriate to the physical resources, character and capacity of the different parts of the Park will be encouraged. Recreational activities for which the resources exist only or mainly within the Park will be particularly acceptable. Every effort will be made to ensure that recreation facilities are provided and activities take place in a manner consistent with the conservation of the natural and man-made beauty of the Park and its wildlife (Peak Board).

Visitor Activities

10.8 The Structure Plan identifies three broad types of recreation activity — informal recreation, active recreation and staying visitors. These categories remain relevant. Three specific policies were developed in the Structure Plan and the 1978 Plan to meet the needs of these different types of visitor. These have been re-stated below, and updated for changes in demands since 1978. A more comprehensive list of activities is included under active recreation (**10.6**(b)).

(a) Informal recreation and low key activity is to be encouraged. Where it is necessary, in accordance with carefully designed management schemes, there will be an increase in appropriate recreational facilities and use in areas which can accommodate it, but a reduction of use in sensitive or overloaded areas. Informal recreation includes (for example), nature study, motoring[26] for pleasure on highways and byways (which the disabled particularly value), short strolls and picnics. These all depend on attractive surroundings and visitor attractions but need only relatively simple facilities such as car parks and toilets.

(b) Active recreation is classified into five categories by reference to their impact on the environment and the degree to which the special resources of the Park are used. These five categories start with those which are most acceptable and end with those which should generally be excluded from the National Park.

(i) Activities using nationally scarce but locally plentiful resources, for example climbing, caving, trout fishing, fell walking and nature study. These will normally be encouraged with careful management.

(ii) Traditional country activities, for example walking, cycling, horse riding, grouse and rough shooting, fishing and camping. These can normally be accommodated with careful management.

(iii) More formal activities needing special facilities, for example canoeing, sailing, rowing, sub aqua, gliding, hang gliding, ballooning, orienteering, mountain biking,[27] informal winter sports, sponsored walks and rides. These can normally be accommodated where there is a legal right of way or owners' permission, but are less likely to be acceptable in quieter, more remote areas. In

the case of sponsored walks, rides and similar events organisers will be encouraged to consider whether alternative sites exist outside the Park.

(iv) Formal activities of a disruptive or intrusive nature, but using the Park's resources, for example moto-cross and scrambling, rallying, off-road (cross country) motoring, power boating, water ski-ing, target and intensive clay pigeon shooting and golf courses. These are generally inappropriate. They will only be accepted in exceptional cases and will be strictly controlled.

(v) Major formal or intrusive events not requiring National Park resources or setting, for example Pop festivals and motor racing. These will generally be excluded, except where they relate to local customs and events such as agricultural shows and carnivals and traditional use of village playing fields.

Most of these recreational activities are dealt with in Chapter 11 (Rights of Way), and in Chapter 13 (Active Recreation).

(c) Overnight stays by visitors are to be carefully encouraged, in order to gain the benefits of an environmentally sensitive tourist industry as described in **10.15**.

10.9 Since 1978, a variety of work has been carried out to clarify and implement policies for staying visitors. The Caravan Study, for example, outlines policies aimed at careful control of touring caravans, encouragement for lightweight camping and opposition to static caravans. The economic benefits of staying visitors to the local community are greater than those of the day visitor by a factor of over three to one (Visitor Survey 1986/7). Catering for staying visitors and their needs has developed since the 1978 Plan into a more clearly defined local tourist industry. Government and other agencies are offering greater encouragement for the construction of buildings for holiday accommodation and facilities.

10.10 The Structure Plan and the 1978 Plan recognised the vital role of recreation areas — existing and proposed — on the periphery of the Peak District. They envisaged that provision for many of the physical needs of tourism, and for those activities less appropriate to the National Park, would be accommodated where possible outside the Park. The role of towns such as Buxton and Matlock and of country parks and similar facilities, was stressed. The Board will continue to rely upon the constituent and surrounding District Councils to develop their own tourist industries both inside and particularly outside the National Park to the benefit of their own economies and, in the case of more intensive tourist development, relieving pressure on the Park.

10.11 The Board hopes that a wide range and increasing number of people can enjoy the recreational resources of the Park, but consistent with overriding conservation constraints. Thus the Structure Plan and the 1978 Plan include policies, for example, for developing public transport services, providing for disabled visitors and for youth and school groups.

---

26 'Motoring' in this Plan refers to travel by two, three or four wheeled vehicles powered by internal combustion engines.
27 'Mountain bikes' are pedal cycles of especially rugged construction which can be physically used on rough tracks or other rough terrain.

10.12 The recreation strategy outlined in the Structure Plan and the 1978 Plan has had general support, to the extent that some of the least appropriate uses are now seldom proposed. Similarly, proposals for improving appropriate recreational facilities and opportunities have come forward. Since 1978, the Board has been involved in many joint schemes with both the public and private sectors. For example, the Upper Derwent Study resulted in improved access for walking and cyling; cycle hire; restrictions on car access, with a bus service; better car parks; a new information centre, a joint Ranger service and many landscape improvements. This and many other recreational schemes are reported in the Area Summaries (Chapters 24-47).

10.13 Most of the policies and work programmes put forward in the 1978 Plan have been successfully translated into achievement on the ground. In a few cases, action has been limited because of legal problems, major conflicts between interest groups or lack of finance. This Plan restates existing policies and examines the topics where difficulties have arisen, such as access to open country, caving, canoeing and traffic management. Solutions are sought.

10.14 A continuing growth in demand for countryside leisure is shown by the Countryside Commission's national recreation surveys and the Board's own recent surveys of visitors to the Park. These also indicate a greater spread of demand over the whole year, an increase in staying visitor numbers and substantially increased spending by staying visitors. The surveys in 1971/2 showed about 16 million visits to the Park in a year. The 1986/7 survey is not directly comparable. It shows 18½ million visits to the Park in that year of which about 2 million are staying visitors. Further research should be carried out to clarify the numbers and characteristics and particularly of visitor trends to help to draw predictions for the future.

10.15 Tourism There has been a major growth of interest in and acknowledgement of the economic benefits of tourism (earning money by providing for the needs of those who seek recreation in the area). Since the 1978 Plan, the Board has committed resources to the selective promotion of tourist businesses, directed particularly at staying visitors, at the least developed areas of the Park and at existing businesses such as farms and village inns. The development of tourism is welcome within the Park, subject always to the Board's primary duty of conservation. Some work has been carried out that was not identified in the 1978 Plan, such as the Integrated Rural Development Project and the beginning of joint working on tourism (see Chapter 17). Both encouraged the local community to provide for and gain from visitors' use of resources or businesses. Further development on these lines is anticipated, and can best be expressed strategically as a commitment to an increase in the percentage of staying visitors. The partners to the Rural Development Programme have accepted the recommendations of the Tourism Action Plan (reported at **17.9**) and are now seeking ways to implement it.

Objectives
10.16 To ensure that recreational activities that have particular need to use the special qualities and resources of the Park receive preferential treatment over other recreation users. To ensure that local economic benefits of recreation and tourist activity are maximised, but only to the extent that they are compatible with conservation objectives and with other community interests. To achieve a more even spread of

these economic benefits throughout the year, and an increase in the percentage of visitors who stay one night or more.

Policies
10.17 Recreation management will be used to attract people to areas which lend themselves to visitor activity of particular types, to deflect visitor activity away from particularly sensitive areas and to encourage development where appropriate in the areas surrounding the Park. (Peak Board, County and District Councils, Tourist Boards and Associations).

10.18 Wherever practicable, partnership with other organisations, particularly user groups will be sought in the development of recreation facilities. The area management schemes and the Tourism Action Plan (see 17.9) provide a basis for this partnership. (Peak Board, Tourist Boards, Sports Councils, County and District Councils, Water Authorities).

10.19 The development and promotion of the recreational resources of the Park will be carefully controlled to relate to the character and capacity of the Park and to those activities which are appropriate (as set out in paragraph 10.8). Other recreation agencies will be encouraged to adopt a similar stance, through joint working (Peak Board, County and District Councils, Tourist Boards).

10.20 The Park's residents will be encouraged to take part in the development of recreation and tourism, and to share the facilities provided (Peak Board, Rural Development Commission, Rural Community Councils, County and District Councils).

10.21 Development control powers and other methods will be used to prevent inappropriate development, to direct development to the right location and to help develop the right type, scale and detailed design of any recreational facility. Policies in the Structure Plan are particularly relevant (Peak Board).

Recreation Zones and Carrying Capacity

10.22 The Structure Plan introduced the concept of 'carrying capacity', defining it as the 'maximum intensity of recreation use that could physically be accepted' in different parts of the Park. It made clear that maximum levels of use are not necessarily desirable and that lower levels would be appropriate in many cases. The 1978 Plan applied the carrying capacity concept in a recreation zoning policy. This policy is still valid and form the basis of this Plan – but we seek to carry the recreation zoning still further by assessing carrying capacity against current levels of use and by using survey information and local knowledge.

10.23 In approving the Structure Plan, the Secretary of State recommended that the zoning and carrying capacity concepts should be carried further in the 1978 Plan, and be reflected as a land use policy in the first review of the Structure Plan.

10.24 The zoning policy developed in the 1978 Plan identified areas which were, in general, likely to be appropriate for various types and intensities of recreational use and for different scales of provision of recreation facilities. Five zones were defined, with Zone I being the area least capable of intensive recreation use and Zone V being most suitable for such use. The zones are illustrated on Map

Map 10.1
Recreation Zoning

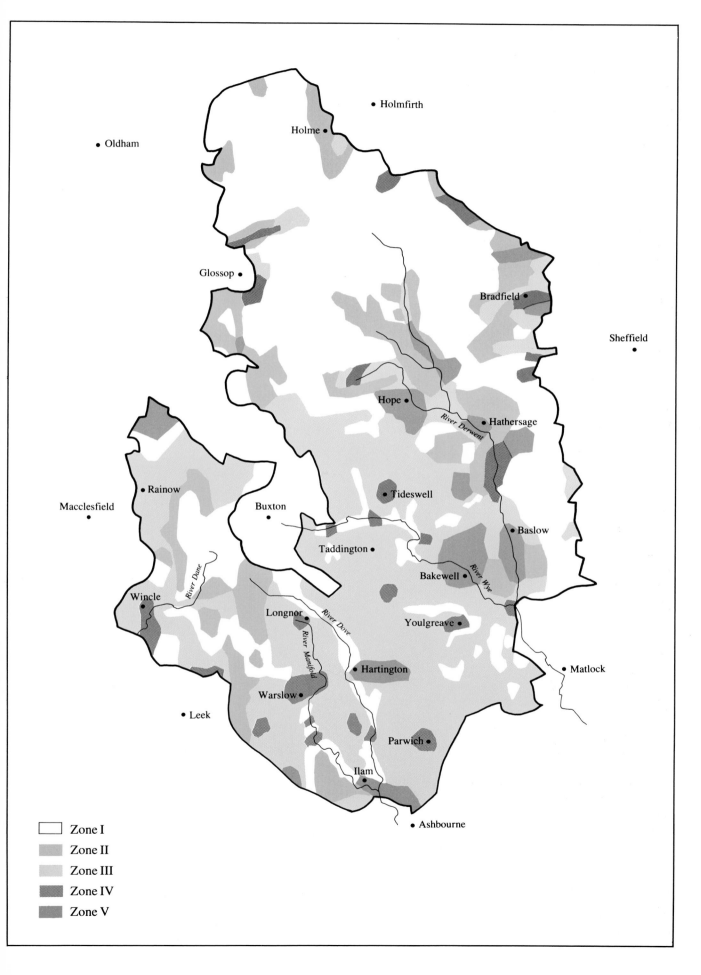

- Holmfirth
- Holme
- Oldham
- Glossop
- Bradfield
- Sheffield
- Hope
- Hathersage
- *River Derwent*
- Rainow
- Tideswell
- Macclesfield
- Buxton
- Baslow
- Taddington
- *River Dane*
- Bakewell
- *River Wye*
- Wincle
- Longnor
- *River Dove*
- Youlgreave
- *River Manifold*
- Matlock
- Hartington
- Warslow
- Leek
- Parwich
- Ilam
- Ashbourne

Zone I
Zone II
Zone III
Zone IV
Zone V

10.1 accompanying this chapter. The following points are relevant when referring to the five zones:

(a) They are based on a combination of landscape character and land use patterns.

(b) They are a basis for area management plans, which apply the zoning policies in the light of detailed study of local conditions. (Much work has been done on this basis since the 1978 Plan).

(c) The representation of an area as a particular zone is based on the type and scale of activity and facility appropriate to it, irrespective of whether or not such use is already made of the area. It does not represent a presumption in favour of additional facilities.

10.25 Carrying capacity can be assessed by reference to three key factors:

(a) **The special characteristics** of the area including its landscape, wildlife, cultural heritage, and architectural values.

(b) **The physical capacity** of the roads, public paths, car parks, public transport and visitor accommodation. These can each be given a value based upon their ability to accommodate visitors.

(c) **Current levels of use** measured by specific surveys of car parking, vehicular traffic, pedestrians, visitor interviews and occupancy. Many of these have been carried out by the Peak Board, in the context of individual proposals and in area management work.

10.26 Assessment of spare capacity By considering zoning policy combined with the various elements of carrying capacity, it may be possible to identify whether or not an area has spare capacity. This can be supplemented by skilled observation of the over-or under-use of the area in question, including the 'feel' of the area. 'Skilled observers' include representatives of local communities, rangers, tourism and conservation specialists. These assessments will be made both in judging individual proposals, and in area management work. It should be emphasised that this will be experimental work, and is yet to be proved in practice.

Objective
10.27 The objectives of the following policies are the same as those set out in paragraph **10.16** above.

Policies
10.28 Proposals for the promotion, provision, constraint or removal of recreational facilities and services will be assessed in the light of the Board's conservation duty and whichever of the five recreational zones they lie within:- (see Map 10.1)

Zone I
Wild areas with a general absence of obvious human influence. Access will normally be on foot although there are routes with rights of way for riding and cycling. The main recreation facilities will be footpaths and wildlife hides (or other similar provisions essential for the use of the area) which cannot be provided in the other zones nearby (Zone I coincides generally with the Natural Zone — see chapter 2).

Zone II
Remoter areas of farmland and plantation woodland with generally poor vehicular access. Recreation facilities will be linked to the use of the Zone I areas as well as any particular use of Zone II itself for low impact recreation. Thus back pack campsites, hostels and farmhouse accommodation might be provided as well as walking, riding and cycling routes.

Zone III
The majority of the Park with its network of roads, tracks and paths, set within landscape of farmland, woodland and small settlements. Recreation facilities of modest scale will be provided or welcomed, such as small car parks linked to features of interest and small farm-based caravan sites, as well as facilities linked to riding, walking and cycling.

Zone IV
Specific localities which are particularly suited to a modest scale of recreation use. Such areas will often provide car parks and picnic sites linked to informal recreation use or provide particular concentrations of facilities for overnight accommodation (e.g. larger settlements).

Zone V
Associated with the highest intensities of recreation use and the major visitor facilities. The locations are likely to be in more robust landscape settings capable of absorbing such uses (e.g. parkland, reservoir margin woodland). The major car parks, information centres, caravan sites and similar facilities will be accommodated here. (Peak Board, Tourist Boards and Associations, Local Authorities).

10.29 Where specific proposals for recreation development arise from policies or programmes in the later chapters in this Plan (particularly Chapters 13, 14) they will be determined against the carrying capacity of the area, assessed in the manner set out in paragraphs **10.24** to **10.26** above. This will conclude with an overall, balanced judgement, including the conservation values set out in Chapter 2 to 9 of this Plan (Peak Board).

10.30 Where possible and worthwhile, overall carrying capacities will be estimated, (see paragraphs **10.25** and **10.26**) for the areas of the Park described in Chapters 24-47, to give a broad indication of the scope for further development or constraint (Peak Board).

The zoning and carrying capacity policies of this Plan will be reflected in the first Review of the Structure Plan (Peak Board, Department of the Environment).

Introduction

11.1 The primary responsibility for the public path[28] network rests with the 7 highway authorities — Derbyshire, Cheshire and Staffordshire County Councils, plus the Metropolitan District Councils of Barnsley, Kirklees, Oldham and Sheffield. They can and do delegate some of their powers to other authorities, e.g. district and parish councils. The powers and duties of highway authorities to keep under continuous review the definitive public rights of way network cannot be delegated but, in the case of maintenance, delegation can be sought.

11.2 In addition to the public path network, there are many unclassified county roads and there are roads used as public paths (RUPPS). The Highway Authorities have a duty under the Wildlife & Countryside Act 1981 to re-classify RUPPS according to evidence to use as either a by-way open to all traffic, a bridleway, or a footpath. Re-classification as a footpath is extremely unlikely following a legal test case.

11.3 The Board has not formally sought delegation agreements from the highway authorities. In many cases it has established mutually beneficial working arrangements on public path maintenance and other public path procedures but much remains to be done. The Board obtains grant from Derbyshire, Staffordshire and Cheshire County Councils for path maintenance work. It prefers the highway authorities to retain their legal duties in this matter, with the Board acting either in a supportive role, or as agent for the Councils.

11.4 An exception is the Pennine Way, which is a designated long distance footpath. This is the responsibility of the Countryside Commission, which has delegated its powers to the Board for the Derbyshire section of the Way. A Project Officer has been appointed and a review of the Pennine Way, its maintenance and improvement is underway at the time of writing (1988), seeking methods to control erosion without losing its wild country qualities.

11.5 The public path network in the Park was created largely for workaday purposes. Now, it represents a major recreational resource. Conflicts have arisen in the past from this change in use. Even today, some farmers still resent the assumption by visitors that the path from their neighbour's farm to the village is there for the public pleasure of townsfolk. At the other extreme, some involved in countryside recreation would like to see a presumption in favour of access throughout the countryside. They claim that this would 'spread the load' and avoid the concentration of use (and conflict) into small 'hot spots'. It is in the interests of all concerned to find a happy compromise between these two extremes — to improve the existing network, add to it where possible, and to make conflict a thing of the past.

11.6 This chapter describes the provisions of the 1978 Plan, the extent of the public path network, the work done to date, and the main prospects for the future.

The 1978 Plan

11.7 The 1978 Plan recognised that walking is the most popular recreational activity in the Park, ranging from short strolls to lengthy expeditions. The 1986/7 Visitor Survey showed that 22% of all visits involved a walk of more than 2 miles and 7% of visits a short stroll. Policies to be followed envisaged close co-operation with highway authorities and landowners in the definition, signing and encouragement of use of the basic network of paths. New link routes to features of interest were proposed by the use of concession paths.

Proposals for horseriding establishments were to be considered in the light of the availability of suitable bridleways. Information was to be provided on cycling, horseriding and walking, and holidays based on these activities were to be encouraged.

Work to date

11.8 The number of paths available to visitors and local people has been increased since 1978 by the creation of public paths in various parts of the National Park. 25 legal paths of varying lengths have been created by the Board, particularly on routes to access land. In addition, 40 concession paths have been created by the Board, for example the Monsal Trail. Concession paths have also been provided on land owned by the Water Authorities, the National Trust and the Forestry Commission and many private landowners. Routes for disabled people have been created where appropriate.

11.9 In addition to the maintenance and improvement work carried out by the highway authorities and their district and parish council agents, the Board has also carried out path maintenance, stile, gate and bridge building, waymarking and signing, in order to encourage public use and to reduce trespass and inadvertent damage. Finance from Highway Authorities, the MSC Community programme and joint working arrangements, particularly with Water Authorities, has trebled the amount of maintenance and improvement work done since 1980. Of particular note is the major

---

28 'Public path' is used throughout this Plan as shorthand for various types of public rights of way: footpaths, bridleways, roads used as public paths and long distance footpaths.

The Pennine Way is our most special public path. As a long distance footpath, it has its own project team.

programme of path repair and improvement in Dovedale. Rangers and volunteer groups such as the British Trust for Conservation Volunteers have been trained to organise and undertake path maintenance work. In Derbyshire, Staffordshire and Sheffield City, some parish councils receive grant aid from the highway authority to undertake minor works of maintenance to public paths. Societies, such as the Peak & Northern Footpaths were involved in provision of signs and maintenance of paths before the National Park was designated and continue to make a major contribution.

11.10 Various special long and medium distance public paths or routes have been created or improved. These are of three main types: The Pennine Way (see **11.4**); the trails created on former railway trackbeds; and the routes, such as the Limestone Way, 'created' as ways or trails by means of way-marking a variety of existing public paths. The converted railways — the Tissington and High Peak Trails and the Monsal Trail — have been more successful. The land is almost entirely in one ownership, is hard-surfaced, traffic-free, wide and well-fenced from neighbouring land. They can take heavy use with few problems of erosion or trespass. Where routes cross the Park boundary, specific liaison with the adjoining district or county council footpath officers is needed.

11.11 The way-marked trails by contrast cannot easily take such heavy use. They consist of a variety of paths some of which may be narrow, soft or poorly defined. They rely on the effectiveness of the way-marking and written guides. Problems of erosion or difficulties for neighbouring land managers can arise. If they are promoted too much, they can be over-used.

11.12 With the co-operation of other agencies such as the rambling organisations and the British Horse Society, 16 walking, riding and cycling publications have been produced, and much advice given to private authors of similar publications. Unfortunately, private authors do not always seek advice and this can cause difficulties through trespass, damage and the overuse of sensitive areas. Other authorities, notably the county and district councils, also produce public path guides and leaflets.

11.13 The 3,510 definitive paths in the National Park were surveyed by the Board's Ranger Service in 1985/6. These surveys are to be regularly updated. The surveys found that there were 2,200 missing statutory roadside signs. (The highway authorities have a legal duty to sign public paths where they leave the road). In addition there were 1,400 obstructions, 90 missing or poorly repaired bridges, and 150 sections of path so overgrown as to be impassable. This major backlog of essential repair of the existing network is currently being tackled by the combined efforts of the highway authorities, the Board, district councils and voluntary agencies. The priority which the highway authorities can place on paths in the Park will be influenced by their countywide responsibilities.

11.14 The Board has powers under the Planning and Highways Acts for diversion, creation and stopping-up of public rights of way. These powers have been used to re-route paths to accommodate approved development such as quarries or new houses, and to avoid farmyards where conditions underfoot are poor and paths are difficult to follow. The new routes must provide an 'equally commodious' alternative. The highway authorities and district councils have also used Highways Act powers in the

Park, but to a lesser extent. Annual meetings now take place between the Board and representatives of footpath user groups. Similar meetings take place with the British Horse Society to discuss bridleway issues.

11.15 The Board offers advice to landowners, voluntary bodies and individuals on all types of matters affecting the public path network, on maintenance practice and liabilities.

Priorities and policies

11.16 It is proposed to continue much of the work currently in hand and to take up the challenge, offered in the Countryside Commission's review of recreation 'Enjoying the Countryside', to improve greatly the condition and extent of the public path network. Paths need to be well signed and maitained, free from obstruction or danger. People need to be confident of walking for recreation without conflict with other users, animals which may be dangerous, landowners or occupiers. The needs of the less agile members of public must be considered. Bridleways in particular need to be designed to avoid undue erosion and conflict with other users. The Countryside Commission recommends that local authorities should devote far more resources to public paths, that highway authorities should recognise their statutory obligations, and that all local authorities should look at paths from a recreation viewpoint, as part of an overall strategy.

11.17 In many areas around the Park this advice is already being followed, for example Derbyshire's Recreational Paths Project, where there may be direct assistance with public paths in the Park. The Countryside Commission is investigating the possibilities of more long distance routes for walking and riding across the Park, both north-south and east-west. Derbyshire County Council is interested in building on initiatives such as the Goyt Valley Way, the Shires Way and extension of the High Peak Trail.

11.18 Unclassified county roads and RUPPS have been referred to in 11.1. Some are surfaced with tarmacadam, others are little more than rough tracks. They are used by walkers, horse riders and cyclists and to some extent by motor vehicles. In some cases, these routes form vital links in the footpath and bridleway network. 'Green lanes' are a feature of the landscape of considerable recreational potential. Most are public paths. Some are private accommodation roads, but may have been created by or for public use. There is scope for managing the foot, horse, bicycle and vehicular use of these routes either in area management schemes (see Chapters 24-47), or as individual parts of the network which are being specially developed.

11.19 In considering proposals for new medium or long distance paths into, across and within the Park, the Board will expect robust surfaces, clear definition, a commitment to maintenance and reasonable regard for adjoining land managers interests. Routes already established will be monitored, with a view to improvements or route adjustments. If problems cannot be solved, future promotion will be discouraged.

11.20 The present effort being applied to paths in the National Park is patchy and lacks co-ordination in many cases. A major initiative is taking place throughout the country as a result of the widespread recognition of the recreational importance of the public path network both locally and regionally (see **11.16**). It is vitally important that in the National Park all authorities pull together to take advantage of this impetus and the resources which will flow from it. Means should therefore be sought for improving the co-ordination and allocation of those resources between the various authorities and user organisations concerned, particularly now that the former MSC community programme may not be easily replaced in the new Employment Training schemes. The means are set out in the policies at the end of this Chapter.

11.21 During the life of this Plan, it may prove appropriate to investigate whether the highway or recreation authorities, or MAFF, might pay farmers to carry out footpath work. Footpath user organisations might themselves consider a shift of effort from vigilance to positive action. Paragraph **9.29** mentions the possibility of parish councils employing local maintenance workers.

11.22 Within the National Park, commitment to the maintenance of the whole of the public path network is required by all authorities and agencies concerned with its well-being and promotion. This needs to be given higher priority by all concerned. Realistically however, resources will always be limited and must be applied where they are most needed. It is therefore proposed that the allocation of resources for the maintenance and development of the network should pay regard to the following types of path:

1. Arterial routes which carry high volumes of use, such as the Pennine Way, the trails, the main path through Dovedale, the advertised medium distance routes and the long-distance routes proposed by the Countryside Commission.

2. Network routes which carry medium to high volumes of recreational use, or which have been or are to be developed and improved by the Board, local councils, a user organisation or others in order to increase their use.

3. Local routes which carry medium to low volumes of use, with fewer links to the network.

11.23 This approach should be applied not only to definitive routes, but also to concessionary paths, unclassified county roads and the known 'de facto' paths which may become public rights of way at review stage.

11.24 In considering priorities, routing and design, the impact of public paths on wildlife and heritage features should be taken into account. In the event of an irreconcilable conflict between recreational needs and an important habitat, species or feature, the conservation interest should normally take precedence.

11.25 In the meantime, the functional approach set out in paragraphs **11.21-11.23** does not detract from the statutory duty of the highway authority for basic maintenance or removal of obstructions. The system is designed to enable the Board and its partners to plan their resources, but not in a rigid way. There must also be a response to changing circumstances. Individual problems must be met, and opportunities taken on a pragmatic basis. It is envisaged that the creation of this hierarchy of routes will be the first step towards a programme of ongoing maintenance and improvement works for footpaths and bridleways, including the creation of new walking and riding circuits backed by selective publicity and promotion and related to visitor car parks, public transport stops and horseriding or trekking centres.

11.26 Reviews of definitive rights of way have not made the progress many users would like to see. Highway authorities would need to give greater resources to these reviews, in order to achieve the priority proposed by the Countryside Commission. Secondly, there can be time lag of many years between the definition (or alteration) of a public path and its appearance on an Ordnance Survey sheet. More frequent revision of OS sheets will be sought and consideration will be given to the printing of amendment slips to be distributed with maps on sale or made available in information centres and to user associations.

11.27 Many miles of walking and riding routes in the National Park are not definitive rights of way, but exist by express concession of a public or private landowner (such as the Water Authorities or the Peak Board), or by unchallenged de facto use. Some of these concessionary paths might not have been offered if it were the policy or practice of the particular highway or planning authority to convert concessionary routes to definitive paths. A blanket policy to this effect would similarly discourage some landowners from volunteering further concessions. Furthermore, public path creation orders cost staff time and money to carry out and can involve compensation. However, there are some paths which, either because of their overriding importance, or as a protection against a future change of ownership, should be converted to public paths preferably by agreement or, in the last resort, by order.

11.28 This chapter has dealt with the public paths network for walking and riding. Another major user of parts of the network is cycling which is dealt with at Chapter 14 (visitor facilities) in the context of cycle hire centres.

Objective

11.29 To maintain and increase opportunities for visitors, and residents to walk and ride in the National Park and to resolve, so far as possible, any conflicts that occur between different users, and between users, landowners, occupiers and conservation interests.

Policies

11.30 The public path network will be assessed in the light of paragraph **11.22**. A programme of maintenance, improvement and promotional works will be prepared. This should take account of conservation interests, the safety of users, the needs of disabled people and should be related to the carrying capacity[29] of the area.

11.31 Resources will be sought to clear the backlog of maintenance on the existing network of public paths in accordance with the programme.

11.32 Regular surveys will take place to update information on the condition and use of all public paths and other routes used for walking, riding and cycling.

11.33 Ways to fill gaps or extend the public path network will be sought, preferably by creating new public paths or by negotiating concessionary paths.

---

29 Carrying capacity — see paragraphs **10.25**, **10.26**, **10.30** for definition and policy.

11.34 Where appropriate (see 11.27) the conversion of concessionary routes to definitive public paths will be sought and will be implemented on the Board's own land.

11.35 Selective traffic management will be examined so as to reduce conflicts between various users, to minimise environmental damage and, as appropriate, to reduce vehicular traffic on minor roads which link public paths.

11.36 When assessing new developments especially mineral workings, the Board will seek to ensure the continuation of existing public paths or their temporary diversion and ultimate reinstatement or the creation of a new route.

11.37 The maintenance of the Pennine Way will be improved in the light of the current project which is supported by the Countryside Commission.

11.38 The trails on former railway track beds will be maintained and enhanced.

11.39 The publicity and maintenance given to other unofficial long distance paths will be reviewed in the light of the proposed categories of recreational paths and of experience in use.

11.40 Faster progress with definitive map reviews and more rapid updating of public path maps will be sought.

11.41 The public paths advisory service for the public, landowners, occupiers, authors and other interests will be maintained. (Policies 11.30-11.41 variously: Peak Board, County, District and Parish Councils, NFU, CLA, Members of the Annual Footpaths Meeting, Ordnance Survey).

Much of the local footpath network is also of high quality, such as the Roman Way at Redmires.

Introduction

12.1 The demand for the freedom to roam unhindered on foot over open moorland was a major force in the growth of the National Park Movement in England and Wales. The Peak District was one of the main areas of controversy, and the scene of mass trespasses on Kinder in 1932.

12.2 This demand for access led to a specific part of the National Parks Act of 1949 being devoted to 'Access to Open Country'. Local Planning and National Park Authorities have the powers to make Access Agreements (or, if necessary, Access Orders) in order to enable the public to gain access to 'wander-at-will' in 'open country'. This was defined in that Act as 'mountain, moor, heath, down, cliff, or foreshore'. This definition of 'open country' was extended by the Countryside Act 1968 to include woodlands, rivers and river banks. This definition includes open water areas through which rivers flow. Thus the reservoirs in the Peak District are also strictly speaking 'open country'.

12.3 In 1952, the Board prepared a map identifying the extent of 'open country' in the Peak District, as defined under the 1949 Act. That Act also required the Board to take account of two particular factors before seeking to make Agreements or Orders:

(a) The extent to which access is already available on a particular area.

(b) The extent of need for further access to be made available.

12.4 In the light of those two factors, the Board negotiated Agreements to secure wander-at-will access to areas of moorland which were not open to the public and where there was a plain need. Negotiations did not proceed on other areas of moorland to which there was already access in some form. Nor did negotiations commence on areas which were unlikely to be particularly popular for recreation.

12.5 Between 1953 and 1970, the Board concluded 19 Access Agreements with a total area of 76 square miles, mainly on the Northern Moors which had been the focus of controversy in the 1930's and including the whole of the Kinder and Bleaklow plateaux. These Agreements provide for public access, on a wander-at-will basis, to specified areas of moorland; payment of compensation by the Board to the owners for the impact of visitors on land management; the provision of a Ranger Service; and the closure of the moors on shooting days. Most of these Access Agreements are secure until 1993 when they terminate. The Board's aim will be to renegotiate these Agreements taking them well into the 21st century. Map 12.1 shows the areas concerned.

12.6 Having met the main needs for access to open country, the Board's efforts then focussed upon other opportunities to improve public enjoyment of the Park. During the 1960's and 1970's there was substantial investment in the conversion of redundant railway lines to walking and riding routes. Visitor movement by car, foot or cycle was improved, e.g. in the White Peak 'Routes for People' scheme. Cycle hire schemes were opened, car parks were provided and special facilities were developed for the disabled. In these ways, the Board's limited funds were used to develop a wide variety of

Open country on a busy day — the anniversary walk on Kinder, to celebrate the outcome of the 1932 trespass.

recreation opportunities, appropriate to the resources of the Park. This was seen as providing the greatest benefit for the greatest number of people.

12.7 During the 1970s, concern was expressed by wildlife organisations and sporting interests about the possible effect of wander-at-will access to open country on biological conservation interests. It was particularly feared that the decline in population of certain moorland and waterside birds and other fauna might be caused in whole or in part by human disturbance. Proof of cause and effect is very difficult to establish in such matters. However it was plain that the Board would not be acting responsibly in negotiating further open country Access Agreements for those areas of highest wildlife value, if there was a risk that this interest would be harmed. This is because wildlife value, once lost, is either very difficult or impossible to re-establish.

12.8 The 1978 Plan therefore sought to achieve a balance between recreation and conservation interests. The policies stated then remain relevant, and are repeated in a modified form at the end of this chapter. In summary, they sought to:

(a) Maintain existing Agreements.

(b) Seek new Agreements, with the main priority upon those areas which offer a challenge to navigation on foot across wild country.

(c) Provide only limited access to areas of the highest wildlife importance.

12.9 There was also growing concern in the 1970s that moorland areas were beginning to be used for a wider variety of activities. Motor cycling across open moors was a particular problem, causing erosion as well as disturbance to others whose enjoyment of the moors depends on contact with nature, peace and quiet. Increasing use by horse-riders, orienteers and sponsored walks was also a cause of concern. The 1978 Plan aimed at maintaining the moors as areas for access on foot only and generally limiting other uses to public rights of way. This policy is still relevant and is repeated below.

12.10 The 1978 Plan also contained policies to minimise the impact of obvious manmade features in open country areas. This took the form of resisting any new manmade features, like fences, buildings or transmitter masts; trying to find ways of mitigating such developments as might prove to be necessary, for example highway improvements for road safety reasons; and seeking ways to eliminate or modify such features as currently exist. Policies to achieve the same purposes are repeated in this Plan.

12.11 **Developments since 1978** The Board has taken increasing action to try to balance conservation and recreation interests in important open country areas. Two examples illustrate the approach adopted in the 1978 Plan:

(a) In Dovedale, there are no Access Agreements even though most of the land is 'open country'. Instead the Dovedale Plan, now largely implemented, concentrated on channelling car parking into unobtrusive locations on the edge of the Dale with good footpath links to the Dale, but avoiding the main wildlife habitats (see Chapter 46 for further detail).

(b) On the Roaches and Eastern Moors Estates, both acquired by the Board since 1978, there are areas of open country access and wildlife sanctuary areas. The access areas are along the ridge walks and cliff edges which are the

places which most people naturally use. The wildlife sanctuary areas are the remoter areas, often of dense moorland vegetation, not particularly favoured by visitors but providing perfect habitats for a wide variety of both typical and rare plants and animals.

12.12 In other ways, public access to open country has been improved since 1978. Access improvements have been achieved as part of Area Management Plans. These involve other agencies in agreeing the content of the Plans and often in implementation, for example public access to reservoir margins is now often provided by the Water Authorities. Elsewhere in the Park, similar comprehensive management plans which allow for public access are being developed and implemented by the National Trust for their properties and by other agencies with whom the Board has consultative arrangements.

12.13 Ramblers' organisations began in the 1980s to renew their requests for the negotiation of further access agreements on the lines established in the 1950s. In response to this, the Board decided to open negotiations for additional Access Agreements on certain areas of moorland. The theoretical scope for these agreements is a total area of about 80 square miles (see table 12.1 below). Between 1982 and 1986, the Board approached seven of the owners of the remaining main blocks of moorland. Of these seven, two welcomed discussion in principle; four agreed to discussions, but a satisfactory conclusion is not yet in sight; and one refused to consider any access additional to existing defined public rights of way. Negotiations for new Access Agreements have focussed on the two positive responses, but at October 1988 had not been concluded.

12.14 **The Current Situation** The position in mid-1988 is therefore that public access has been secured through access agreements on 76 square miles of moorland. On a further 19 square miles of moorland, mainly owned by the Board itself or by the National Trust or local authorities, public access is either welcomed or not opposed, even though not covered by Access Agreements. The potential for conflict between recreation and conservation interests remains acute. Indeed as wildlife habitats generally have declined and as other recreation activities become popular (for example mountain biking, see **13.36**), the need for a careful approach becomes even more necessary now than it was in 1978.

12.15 The combined total of 95 square miles of existing 'access land' represents just over half of the total area of main moorland blocks, but only about a third of the total area of 'open country', in the Park — as shown on Table 12.1 below:

12.16 The total of 275 square miles of 'open country' includes, in addition to the main moorland blocks:

(a) Other areas of moorland, small or scattered, which even if open to the public would in practice be very little used in most cases.

(b) Areas of woodland, river, river banks, reservoirs and reservoir margins which were brought into the definition of open country by the Countryside Act 1968. Access to such lands is needed in some places not only for purposes of walking, but also for access for particular recreational activities (see **13.76-13.100**).

(c) Further areas of open land, for example limestone dales and limestone heaths, which usually have a high wildlife conservation value and where conventional Access

Map 12.1
Access to Moorland

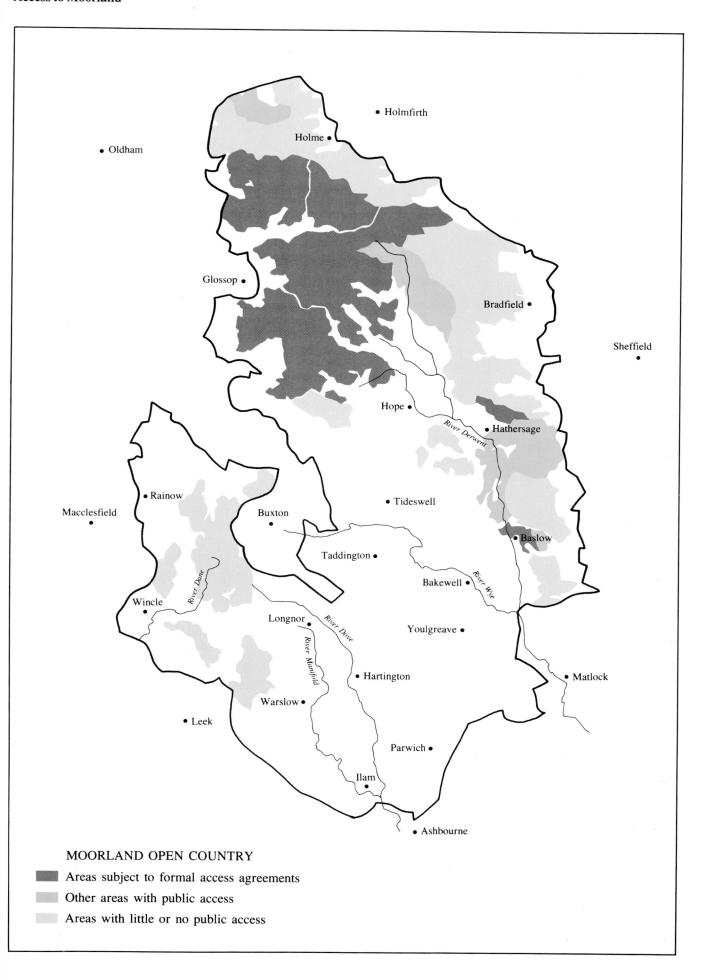

MOORLAND OPEN COUNTRY

Areas subject to formal access agreements

Other areas with public access

Areas with little or no public access

Agreements will only rarely be the most appropriate method of balancing conservation and recreation.

Table 12.1
Access to Open Country

Estimated Area in square miles of:-

	Main Moorland Blocks	Other Open Country	Total = all Open Country
Areas subject to formal access agreements	76	—	76
Other areas with public access	19	—	19
Total area with access	95	—	95
Areas with little or no access	80	100	180
Total Area	**175**	**100**	**275**

12.17 The Board's view remains that the deed for general public access on a wander-at-will basis for walking is still related to the main moorland blocks. It is generally agreed by all parties involved that the existing Access Agreements work well, subject to a need to review the byelaws and their enforcement. This is assisted by a close working relationship between the Peak Park Moorland Owners and Tenants Association (PPMOTA) and the Board, and by the annual liaison meeting between the Board and Ramblers groups. The public have become accustomed to their freedom to wander-at-will, yet generally respect both the landowners' needs and those of nature conservation.

Directions for Future Policy
(see also **3.2 -3.25**).

12.18 A balance has to be struck between access and conservation. Of the moorlands which are not now accessible, some have high value as wildlife habitats. The NCC, and naturalists' organisations, have urged the Board to be cautious in extending public access into such areas, particularly where rare and timid species of birds, animals or reptiles are present. The Board must give priority to important conservation interests where they are, or might be, at risk. The same priority extends to important cultural heritage sites which may be vulnerable to extensive public access (e.g. due to trampling). The Board will not pursue additional access where it is satisfied that there is or might be an irreconcilable conflict with important conservation interests (see DoE Circular 4/76).

12.19 It is important to be clear which wildlife species are at risk from human disturbance and in what circumstances. To this end the Board and NCC have commissioned research as referred to in **6.51**. This will hopefully enable the Board's judgements on the balance that must be struck between conservation and recreation to be progressively better informed.

12.20 In negotiations on possible future Access Agreements, moorland owners have expressed the view that increased public access on a wander-at-will basis could make grazing management more difficult and expensive; increases fire risks; and could reduce grouse bags. The Board notes these fears, but has pointed out that these are fundamentally economic issues. The compensation paid under the terms of the Access Agreement is intended to defray any such economic losses. Evidence is not conclusive as to whether public access conflicts with the needs of grouse. Research has been carried out by Picozzi, (NCC 1970) into the effect on grouse and by P.C. & D.W. Yalden (1987) into the effect on other moorland birds. Evidence will be examined further, and where appropriate, future negotiations will reflect the agreed findings.

12.21 It may be that areas important for wildlife or archaeological conservation will coincide with areas important for grazing or grouse moor management. Thus although the Board and the moorland owner may have different reasons for wishing to exclude a particular area from an Access Agreement the practical result may be the same. Areas of particular importance for livestock management might also be regarded as 'excepted land' under the provisions of Section 60(5) of the 1949 Act if they are important for reasons other than rough grazing. In such cases the land would not be open to public access.

12.22 Against this background, the Board continues to be committed in principle to sustaining wander-at-will access wherever it has been secured; and to extending such access onto further parts of the main morland blocks where consistent with conservation interests. As was the case when the main existing Access Agreements were originally concluded, there remains a lot of land where there is little need for an Access Agreement because access is already tolerated, or there is little evidence that the area would be used by more than a very small number of people. Some areas of permissive access, however, may be vulnerable to changes in land ownership such as the privatisation of the Water industry and should be specially assessed. Access Agreements are expensive, and Access Orders could be very time-consuming and labour-intensive. The Board has only limited staff-time and funds and many other demands for these resources. Thus effort will continue to be directed primarily into Access Agreements, and the use of Orders must be the last resort.

Objectives
12.23 To sustain wander-at-will access to open country for the general public wherever it has been secured by an Access Agreement or on a permissive basis. To extend access to further areas, minimising impact on landscape and wildlife conservation interests (including grouse) and protecting archaeological sites.

Policies
12.24 Existing Access Agreements will be maintained and negotiations for new Agreements continued or entered into. The main priority will be the extension of the areas providing a challenge to navigation and a wild country experience across tracts of open country, subject to conservation interests. This applies particularly to the Northern Moors and may follow from other Area Management Plans (Peak Board, PPMOTA).

12.25 Other ways of securing improvements in public access to open country will be investigated and appropriate agreements negotiated. Where important conservation interests are or might be at risk, this might involve allowing public access only to the areas most attractive for

Open country, on Derwent Edge — a walker experiences 'quiet enjoyment'.
More access areas would be appreciated.

recreation and of least value to conservation. This
approach might involve close-season agreements at times
and/or in places when sensitive wildlife is at greatest risk
(Peak Board, Nature Conservancy Council, English
Heritage).

12.26 Priority will be given to negotiations on areas where
permissive or de facto access may be at risk through
prospective changes in ownership (Peak Board).

12.27 Activities relying on access on foot and self-reliance
will be encouraged in access areas. The co-operation of

owners and tenants will be sought, to generally discourage
other recreation activities except on appropriate rights of
way (Peak Board, PPMOTA).

12.28 Agreements will be negotiated for access to other
types of land and water included in the definition of open
country in the Countryside Act 1981 (see 12.16) (Peak
Board).

13 ACTIVE RECREATION

Introduction

13.1 This chapter deals with all major forms of recreation which are particularly popular, or for which a demand exists because of the special resources of the Park. Active recreation requires specific resources — rocks to climb, good quality water in which to fish, clearly defined paths, edges to fly from, open horizons, remoteness and clean air — qualities which now have high rarity value in industrial Britain. Maps 13.1 and 13.2 give an overall impression of the location of recreational sites in the Park. Access to open country is dealt with in Chapter 12.

13.2 Policies in the Structure Plan and the 1978 Plan were geared to reconciling any potential conflicts between different types of recreation and the environment. Pursuits more closely related to the resource characteristics of the area were to be favoured (see Chapter 10).

13.3 The Recreation Strategy of the 1978 Plan has been widely supported. Some notable achievements have been made in improving outlets for active recreation. The acquisition of climbing areas such as the Roaches and Eastern Edges, sailing on Torside, and creation of additional recreation routes have been achieved through area management plans (Chapters 24 to 47) or through estate purchase (see **23.10**). However, some studies and proposals such as those for caving and canoeing have not made much headway. The 1978 Plan envisaged monitoring the extent of active recreation pursuits and the problems caused. This has not been comprehensively achieved, though ad hoc observations have been made on various topics by the Ranger Service and others. Some councils, for example the Staffordshire Moorlands District Council, have appointed a Sports Development Officer.

13.4 New sports, or variations on old sports, continue to come forward. Most people expect there to be a continued general growth in demand for active recreation. The criteria set out in Chapter 10 will form the basis for the many judgements which will arise as the competition for resources in space and time becomes progressively more intense.

13.5 This Chapter reviews the following activities, and reflects reviews of policies currently being undertaken by Regional Councils for Sport and Recreation in consultation with the various user associations:

(a) Caving (**13.6-13.11**)

(b) Climbing (**13.12-13.18**)

(c) Hang Gliding and gliding (**13.19-13.28**)

(d) Horse riding, cycling and walking (**13.29-13.40**)

(e) Orienteering (**13.41-13.45**)

(f) Sponsored Walks and Events (**13.46-13.53**)

(g) Winter Sports (**13.54-13.59**)

(h) Playing Fields & Play Areas (**13.60-13.64**)

(i) Motor Sports (**13.65-13.75**)

(j) Reservoir Recreation (**13.76-13.89**)

(k) River Recreation (**13.90-13.100**)

(l) Shooting (**13.101-13.106**)

Cycling is 'active recreation' but is also dealt with in conjunction with the provision of cycle hire (visitor facilities, Chapter 14).

Caving

13.6 The survey for the 1978 Plan identified 69 caves and mines of scientific and recreational importance within and close to the Park. Of these, 12 were of national importance, 52 of regional importance and 5 were show caves popular with tourists. Caving is an activity to be encouraged using those nationally scarce resources of which the Park has a reasonable supply. The 1978 Plan explained why some of the resources are not being used for caving, and proposed that Management Agreements should be investigated with other interested parties. There has been little progress with formal agreements perhaps because the relevant legislation places undue responsibility for the safety of visitors on landowners. The Derbyshire Caving Association (DCA) has pressed for action in one specific case (in the Board's ownership) at Black Marble Mine, Ashford where controlled access is being discussed.

13.7 Landowners, mine owners and land managers are often reluctant to allow access, for reasons of safety, often compounded by legal issues. Caves are not 'open country' and thus Access Agreements cannot be negotiated under the 1949 Act. There have been problems of damage to cultural heritage features such as palaeolithic remains or 19th century mining artefacts. Caving can also disturb hibernating bats (see paragraph **6.66**) and damage geological features. Where geological or biological interest is considerable, access might need to be restricted to people specialising in those interests, rather than to allow general access for caving as a sport.

13.8 To overcome these problems the DCA has negotiated agreements with some owners to allow access to cave systems subject to various conditions. However, in some cases owners have still been unwilling to allow access. Thus some cave systems of national significance are at present closed to cavers. A recent change in law has clarified that owners are not responsible for injury caused by accidents occurring in natural caves. This should encourage owners to allow more access to caves. Owners are responsible for public safety in man-made voids. Several other initiatives have been taken by the DCA including a regional liaison system with the NCC, membership of the Derbyshire County Council Disused and Abandoned Mines Working Party and in ensuring greater responsibility for conservation amongst instructors and club members.

13.9 Various agencies aim to enable access, where owners agree, to capped mineshafts of importance to cavers by way of a manhole cover or similar means. Caving interests are normally involved in discussing methods of treating mineshafts (see Chapter 7). In other circumstances, the Peak Board negotiates management agreements with both positive and negative covenants. Where the DCA has been unable to reach agreement for access to important cave systems, the Peak Board might be able to negotiate agreements to the satisfaction of owner or tenant and caver, subject to the availability of resources of both Board and user. The DCA or other caving interests should generally continue to take the lead.

Objective

13.10 To increase access to caves for recreation and study, subject to adequate safeguards and protection of interesting features and wildlife.

Policy

13.11 Management agreements will be negotiated for access to caves of national and regional significance. If

Map 13.1
Riding, Cycling and Trails

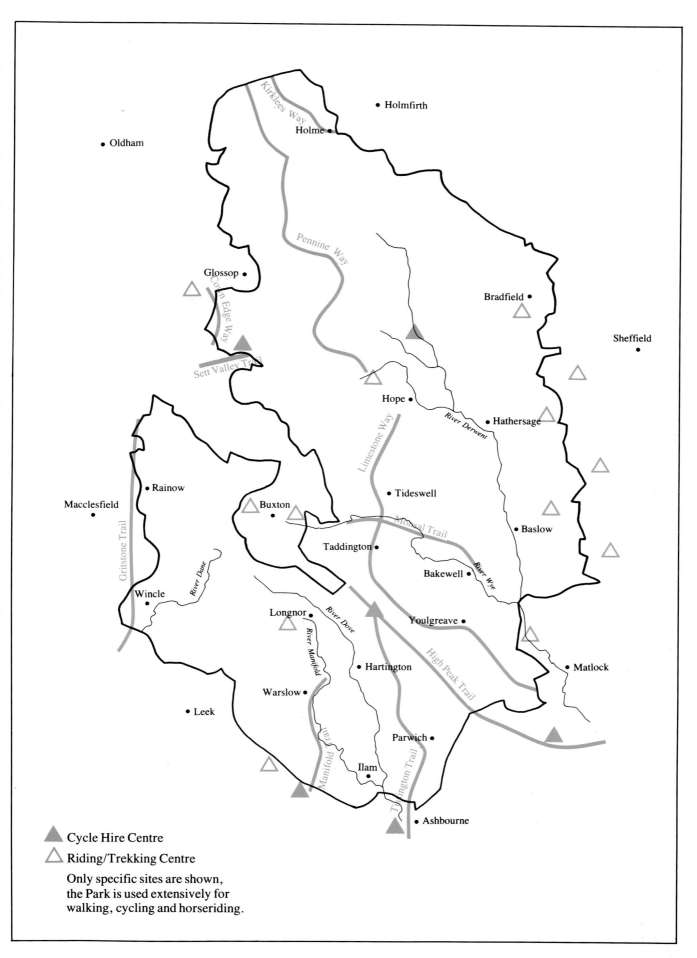

▲ Cycle Hire Centre

△ Riding/Trekking Centre

Only specific sites are shown,
the Park is used extensively for
walking, cycling and horseriding.

70 listed crags are accessible to climbers. In some cases, access is managed to protect wildlife.

successful, a programme will be drawn up for further access, which must consider the conservation interests of each cave (DCA, Sports Council, Peak Board).

Climbing

13.12 The climbing resources of the Park are exceptional both on gritstone edges and in limestone dales. The survey for the 1978 Plan identified 37 crags of national, and 33 of regional, importance for climbing. The Plan stated that climbing was generally to be encouraged, and that most of the important climbing areas had few access problems. There was (and is) some concern about the disturbance of wildlife. As with caving, the scope for concluding additional agreements for climbing, whilst safeguarding wildlife interests, was proposed. Special attention was drawn to Chee Dale, Monks Dale, Cressbrook Dale and the two Deep Dales.

13.13 Access to most of the important climbing areas is secured either through Access Agreement or the tolerance of the landowner. No new access agreements have been made; but land acquisitions made by the Board over the last six years have assured climbing at crags on the Eastern Moors, the Roaches, Hen Cloud and Ramshaw Rocks. However, several landowners in the Park have prohibited access to old quarries because of the problem of accident liability (on man-made features only, under the Health and Safety at Work Act). Few rock faces seem to be barred to climbers, but the extent of any present need for action should be assessed in consultation with the BMC. It may be desirable, for both landowner and climber, to clarify what appears to be an unsatisfactory

situation about liability. The British Mountaineering Council (BMC), whilst influential over its members, obviously cannot guarantee every individual's behaviour and cannot easily influence non-members.

13.14 In several places, important climbing faces are also important wildlife habitats (or potentially so), both botanically and for cliff-nesting birds. With few rock faces not being subject to climbing, naturalists are concerned that some species of bird may leave the area and that other species which are trying to re-establish may find nowhere to nest. Conservation bodies have been asked to suggest cliffs which might be used for nesting by rare birds if disturbance by climbers ceased. They may be reluctant to do so for fear of drawing attention to vulnerable species. If this problem can be overcome, a solution might be on the lines of that adopted at South Stack (Anglesey), where a close season for climbing has been agreed by the BMC during the nesting season. This deserves further investigation, but implementation may not be easy in the Peak District because of the difficulty of supervising climbing on less visible faces.

13.15 At some specific climbing areas problems of car parking, path erosion (as at Hooks Carr below Stanage), litter and excessive use of climbing aids may need specific action such as BMC's recent 'clean up the crags' event. Where consistent with reasonable safety requirements, the use of free climbing techniques is preferable to aided climbing, to conserve the value of cliffs. Sponsored competitive climbing involving advertisements, fixed routes and spectators is potentially disruptive and is likely to be against the interests both of access for climbing and of National Park qualities.

13.16 To increase access for climbing where possible subject to land management and nature conservation interests.

Policies

13.17 The extent of present problems and the scope for negotiating climbing access in management agreements will be reviewed (Peak Board, BMC, Sports Council).

13.18 Existing Access Agreements together with access to land owned by the Board at Stanage Edge, Windgather Rocks, Eastern Moors, Roaches, Hen Cloud and Ramshaw Rocks, will continue to provide both for the protection of wildlife and to enable climbing to take place. Sponsored competitive climbing will be discouraged. (Peak Board, BMC, NCC, Sports Council).

Hang-Gliding, Gliding and Ballooning

13.19 At the time of the 1978 Plan, hang-gliding was a fairly new sport, with 11 sites then in use in the Park. There are now about 14 sites distributed through the centre and south of the Park. There is demand for a variety of launching sites with different slope aspects to give usable areas irrespective of wind direction. The 1978 Plan proposed careful monitoring and liaison with landowners and clubs, and hoped that remoter areas would be avoided. This work has not yet been comprehensively carried out.

13.20 There are two gliding centres in the Park, at Bretton Edge and at Morridge. Both use land based tows to launch the glider, and are subject to planning controls preventing the use of powered aircraft. There have been no proposals for additional centres, and the sport has given rise to few complaints. Hot air balloons are occasionally launched or retrieved in the Park, but there have not been any proposals for a formal base for the sport in the Park. Powered microlight aircraft are open to objection because of disturbance to peace and quiet for people, grazing animals and wildlife, but are not common in the Park.

13.21 The Board has granted licences for hang-gliding on parts of its own land. There is still some concern about parking by participants and spectators, though the earlier 'novelty' attraction is less. Some individuals do not keep to licensed take-off and landing areas. Other sites in Board ownership are not licensed for use, but are used by individuals. This is causing problems, for example disturbance to residents and parking problems at North Lees. Elsewhere, hang-gliding has continued by formal agreement or by the tolerance of owners. Payments are sometimes made as 'landing fees'.

13.22 Agreements not to fly on Sundays (when there are more visitors) have helped at certain sites. In wilder and more remote areas, hang-gliding, with its brightly coloured equipment, and possible conflict with other recreation users and landowners' interests, is still resisted by some owners. It has been specifically excluded from some revised access agreements. However, modern practice is to take off from a small area of robust land and to climb quickly to heights where little disturbance is caused. Hang-gliding will disturb wildlife and sensitive vegetation, if launching and landing areas are not well chosen. Hang-gliding could avoid critical times, such as lambing. The use of land for hang-gliding for more than 28 days in the year is subject to planning control,

and special measures (Article 4 Directions) can be applied to less frequent use where necessary).

13.23 Liaison has improved between landowners and hang-gliding clubs. 'Codes of Practice' can be agreed between landowner and club where necessary. In theory, the clubs can control all individuals since all pilots must be registered and must carry insurance. There seem to be adequate areas for this use within the Peak at present but some extra sites might help spread the load from any over-used sites such as Mam Tor. Substantial further expansion in any of these sports is unlikely to be acceptable.

Objective

13.24 To maintain limited opportunities for non-powered hang-gliding, subject to the overriding requirements to conserve and enhance the natural beauty of the Park.

Policies

13.25 In consultation with landowners and managers, the Board will monitor sites used for hang-gliding, gliding and ballooning as necessary (Peak Board).

13.26 The Board will not license the use of any of its own sites for microlight aircraft, nor will it license sites in the remoter areas of Zone I for any form of hang-gliding use nor in areas managed primarily for nature conservation. The Board will ask other landowners/managers to apply similar policies to their land (Peak Park, CLA, British Hang-Gliding Association, Sports Councils).

13.27 In considering licence applications, the Board will take into account the effects on traffic, parking, nature conservation and other land management issues. Other landowners/managers will be invited to consult the Board on these matters before granting or renewing a licence (Peak Board, Highway Authorities, NCC, CLA, BHGA).

13.28 If circumstances make it necessary, codes of practice will be sought or licence conditions will be strengthened or enforced. Planning controls or Article 4 Directions will be considered to prevent hang-gliding or other aerial sports at specific sites but only as a last resort (Peak Board).

Horseriding, Cycling and Walking

13.29 These active pursuits are together the most popular activities in the National Park, making use of the network of public paths, minor roads and concessionary routes, and in the case of walking only, the freedom to wander-at-will across open country where access agreements or landowners' permission allows. Access to open country is dealt with in Chapter 12.

13.30 Horseriding The 1978 Plan recorded the existence of 18 stables with horses for hire for 'hacking' or 'trekking' in or around the Park; included policies which dealt with the need to take the availability of routes into account before approving more stables; endorsed the British Horse Society's Riding Code; and proposed the production of information on stables and routes.

13.31 Since 1978, there does not seem to have been a major growth in either hacking, trekking or the number of horses for hire at stables. There is no evidence as to whether this is a result of limited opportunity or low demand. Leaflets on riding in the National Park are produced and updated. Chapter 11 deals with Rights of Way and concessionary routes, including bridleways.

A more recent sport, at Mam Tor. Most hang-gliders are now registered and insured, and respect the Park.

13.32 The Sports Council and the British Horse Society believe there is scope for growth, and point out that informal horseriding does not place a heavy demand on the network or require many special facilities. Some specific proposals are in hand (see, for example paragraph **27.11**) and the Countryside Commission have proposed major new long distance bridlepaths which will probably require action through the life of this Plan.

13.33 Cycling is an increasingly popular way of taking exercise and of appreciating the scenic and wildlife qualities of the Park. The 1978 Plan noted the early years of the cycle hire experiment on the Tissington Trail and the use of roads by touring and competitive cyclists.

13.34 Since 1978, there has been a major growth in family leisure cycling. The continued provision of cycle hire centres, signposted cycle route networks and leaflets, and the newer activity of mountain biking (with rapidly growing use of robust 'mountain bikes') is dealt with in paragraphs **14.38-14.49**.

13.35 Cyclists can use both minor roads and bridleways and it is now possible in law to create cycling rights of way (for example, on suitable footpaths) without creating bridleway status. (Cycle Track Act 1984). (Chapter 11 deals with rights of way and concessionary paths).

13.36 Mountain biking on sturdy bikes designed for cross-country riding is growing in popularity. This is an acceptable activity in policy terms, making use of the Park's special resources. These bikes can physically use unsurfaced tracks and are carried, by some users or in some events, cross-country. However, bikes can only be ridden where they have a right of way or landowner's permission. They do not fall within access agreements, and no special physical provisions need to be made. Mountain bikers will be expected to avoid conflict with other path users and avoid physical damage to paths or vegetation. Failure to adopt good practice could lead to exclusion from sensitive routes or areas.

13.37 Walking is the single most popular activity in the National Park, ranging from short strolls by visitors from their cars, to hardy ramblers who walk the full length of the Pennine Way and those who take part in competitive circular walks and marathons. This Plan (as in the 1978 Plan) contains policies for walking in the context of Rights of Way (Chapter 11) and Access to Open Country (Chapter 12).

13.38 Disabled people can readily gain access to selected parts of the public path network or the concessionary routes and trails. Several organisations specialise in enabling the disabled to take part in horse-riding especially, and also cycling and walking.

Objective
13.39 To continue to provide the best possible access to and within the National Park for horse-riding, cycling and walking. To seek to resolve conflicts between these users where they arise, to achieve a fair share of access for each activity. To pay regard to the needs of disabled people.

Policies
13.40 Cycling is an accepted activity (see 10.8b ii) on appropriate routes. Cycle route networks will be improved, waymarked and recommended (Peak Board, Highway Authorities, Sports Councils).

13.41 The growing activity of mountain biking will be monitored. If necessary, a code of practice will be prepared (Peak Board, Sports Councils, Rough Stuff Fellowship).

Policies for horse-riding, cycle hire and walking are as follows:

Chapter 11 — Rights of Way paragraphs 11.29-11.40
Chapter 12 — Access to Open Country paragraphs 12.26-12.30
Chapter 14 — Cycle hire paragraphs 14.45-14.47
Chapter 15 — Traffic Management paragraph 15.20
Chapter 18 — Information and Interpretation paragraphs 18.33(k) and 18.35

Orienteering

13.42 Orienteering has become very popular in Britain over the last 10 years. It requires the use of extensive areas of relatively well-wooded country and occasionally areas of moorland. In 1978, some 11 areas of the Park were used for this activity, and events were generally well run. Additional scope seemed to exist in wooded valleys. Remoter areas of Zone I were not thought generally suitable for this use on a frequent basis. The Board sought consultation by organisers under the auspices of the British Orienteering Federation (BOF). This has largely been achieved by liaison between the Ranger Service and BOF.

13.43 There is no comprehensive evidence to hand, but the sport seems to be growing in the number and size of events. Consultation about events and their careful management has been generally satisfactory, for example, the East Midlands Orienteering Association pay regard to local requirements. Careful attention to parking arrangements, potential trespass and damage continues to be necessary. Great care is needed in selecting courses and dates in avoid damage to conservation interests including archaeological sites, sensitive vegetation or disturbance to wildlife. Co-operation will therefore be sought where necessary to avoid the breeding season for birds (March to July inclusive) and to avoid the use of sites where birds of prey roost in winter. This is already a requirement of events planned in the Upper Derwent area. Some semi-natural habitats such as blanket bogs could be eroded in wet seasons and need to be avoided in planning events.

Objective
13.44 To cater for orienteering in appropriate areas, and at appropriate times, subject to the overriding constraint of conservation of the natural qualities of the area.

Policy
13.45 Organisers of orienteering courses and events will continue to be asked to consult the Peak Board and landowners in good time to resolve organisational problems, and to agree guidelines for routes and the management of events (Sports Councils, Peak Board, CLA, BOF, NCC).

Sponsored Walks, Rides and Other Events

13.46 Since 1978, there has been a marked growth in the number and size of events including sponsored walks and rides, mountain marathons and army training. Some areas, e.g. Upper Derwent Valley, are experiencing considerable demand which poses problems over and above normal visitor activity. Problems can include parking, inadequate sanitary arrangements, disturbance to people, livestock and wildlife, litter and wall damage and the establishment of new de-facto paths. In practice, these events are very difficult to control, and consultation prior to events is very variable — sometimes well in advance and responsive to guidance, sometimes at the

A rider approaches the packhorse bridge below Jacob's Ladder. There is scope for more local and long distance bridleways.

last minute, and sometimes not at all. Favourite venues are within easy reach of cities, in areas where routes have been improved and are clearly set out in leaflets. Specially developed, well advertised trails and routes are also a natural target.

13.47 Walks, rides and events need the Board's consent on the Tissington, High Peak and Monsal Trails and that of Derbyshire County Council on the High Peak Trail outside the Park. Events are not allowed on Sundays between April and the end of September, numbers must not exceed 100 and a fortnight's gap is required between events. Sponsored walks also take place on the Manifold Valley track.

13.48 In the Upper Derwent, guidelines have been produced for the organisers of events. There is liaison between the major landowners and the Board over events, and some success in controlling activity when prior notification is given. The agreement between the Board and the Peak Moorlands Owners and Tenants Association concerning advance notice of events, walkers and army exercises will continue. However, there is no absolute power of control over such events where public routes are being used, and where the Board's own land is not affected.

13.49 Many events are from schools around the National Park, and some may not need the special resources of the area. Many sponsored events could as easily be staged in Country Parks and City Parks which have surfaced routes capable of taking such abnormal wear. Education authorities will continue to be asked to limit the impact of this activity on the Peak District.

13.50 Some of the major mountain marathons have to be arranged secretly months in advance. The Board will seek to be consulted by the organisers on a confidential basis to enable times and places to be chosen with local knowledge.

Objective

13.51 To accept in principle but substantially limit the adverse effects of sponsored walks, rides and events in the National Park.

Policies

13.52 Organisers of sponsored walks, rides and events and mountain marathons planned on the Tissington, High Peak and Monsal Trails and elsewhere on the Board's Estates will continue to require permission. Strict conditions of good behaviour and management should be observed in the interests of other users and of adjoining owners and farmers (Peak Board, Derbyshire CC, Sports Councils, Education Authorities).

13.53 Organisers of events within the National Park will be encouraged to consider whether alternative sites are available outside the National Park. Organisers are urged to co-operate with landowners to agree areas, routes and times, and to provide appropriate supervision, management of participants and reinstatement where necessary (Peak Board, NFU, Sports Councils, County Councils, Metropolitan District Councils).

Winter Sports

13.54 The incidence of winter sports activity is very erratic, being totally dependent on snow or ice. However when snow does settle, considerable numbers of people ski (both downhill and cross-country) and toboggan in several places in the Park. Downhill sports sometimes cause parking and traffic congestion as well as some trespass. The policy in the 1978 Plan was to negotiate agreements for winter sports areas if necessary. No agreements have been made. It nevertheless seems right to adopt a similar policy in this Plan. The Board has dismantled its one ski tow at Edale and has disposed of part of its interest in the site. Cross country ski-ing is more akin to open moorland walking (see Chapter 12).

13.55 As regards local needs, it is worth noting the early success of the Elton Ski Club, which has provided considerable pleasure for local children and parents, and managed 30 ski sessions in 1985/86.

13.56 There has been one proposal to construct an artificial ski slope in the Park and others can be expected. Such development is best located outside the Park in accordance with the Board's policies, which favour only those activities which make use of the natural characteristics of the Park (see **10.7**). Artificial surfaces and ancillary arrangements are likely to be visually intrusive.

Objective

13.57 To encourage the establishment of informal winter sports areas, subject to the overriding need to conserve and enhance the environment of the Park.

Policies

13.58 Should circumstances warrant it, the establishment of informal winter sports areas will be encouraged on suitable sites well related to car parks associated with the better roads of the Park, with management agreements being concluded where necessary (Peak Board, Sports Councils).

Playing Fields and Play Areas

13.60 Playing fields and play areas are largely matters for the Education Authorities or schools where school sites are involved, or for District and Parish Councils in relation to public playing fields and play areas. Bodies such as the Sports Councils, National Playing Fields Association and Rural Community Councils are able to advise and assist where provision is for public use. The East Midlands Sports Council has carried out a survey of playing fields. The 1978 Plan did not make any direct reference, but this Review is giving greater weight to socio-economic matters. In practice, most facilities can be shared between visitors and local people.

13.61 The Board has been involved in efforts to improve such facilities and can offer design help, as it did for the play areas at Monyash and Longnor. School playing fields can be improved to allow combined use by the school, youth club and community. Most Education Authorities now arrange such multiple use of school facilities as part of their expanding programme of community education.

13.62 Many playing field and play area sites would benefit from additional planting for shelter and landscaping reasons, as has been done recently at the playing fields at Lady Manners School, Bakewell by Derbyshire County Council. The Board can assist the Parish Council in the enhancement of play areas, possibly combining them with a picnic area as in Middleton-by-Youlgreave, or with tree planting in playing fields and play areas as in Bradwell. The creation of a community swimming pool at Lady Manners School has been assessed by the District Council; it is considered to be feasible and desirable, but resources are not available at present. Where the effect on the landscape and neighbourliness allow, the installation of carefully designed floodlighting can extend the use of play areas.

Objective
13.63 To increase visitor use of playing fields and play areas wherever possible, in order to maximise their usefulness to the whole community; to enhance their appearance where necessary; and to consider local use when providing visitor facilities.

Policy
13.64 Where appropriate and with the co-operation and agreement of the responsible local authorities, the Board will encourage and assist the multiple use and enhancement of playing fields, play areas, and other sports facilities (Peak Board, District and County Council, Rural Community Council, Sports Councils, Parish Councils).

Motor Sports

13.65 Various forms of motor sports are practised in the Park ranging from informal non-competitive motoring for pleasure using public vehicular routes, to organised competitive events. Informal trail riding activity using low-noise motor cycles driven slowly and sensibly on vehicular rights of way may be reasonable in much of the countryside and can provide access for disabled people. There may however be specially sensitive areas where regulatory action for example Traffic Regulation Orders may be desirable. Problems arise mainly from irresponsible ('cowboy') riders with no respect for the countryside or for those who live, work or use it for quiet enjoyment.

13.66 Formal motoring activities of a potentially disruptive or intrusive type include rallying, motorcross and scrambling, and off road (cross country) motoring. These activities are not generally consistent with the primary conservation role of a National Park. Alternative venues should be sought outside the Park (see 13.70 below). The noise and disturbance conflicts with quiet enjoyment, and causes complaints from other users of the Park and residents.

13.67 Circular 4/76 (paragraphs 51 and 52) states that government policy is generally not to provide for noisy pursuits in National Parks. The 1978 Plan proposed close co-operation with organisers of motor rallies, motor cycle trials and similar events in order to minimise their impact. Monitoring of sites for scrambling and stock car racing was proposed, with a view to bringing them under planning control if necessary.

13.68 Organisers of motor rallies and trials following set routes along public roads are required to obtain RAC approval in consultation with the Peak Board, and police before proceeding with any event involving more than 12 vehicles. These requirements are under the terms of the Motor Vehicle (Competitions and Trials) Regulations, 1969. Landowners' approval is sought before using unfenced minor roads. Co-operation has remained good in relation to advice offered by the Board. No serious problems have arisen, and there have been few complaints. The Land Access and Rights Association (LARA) has offered the Board consultation over Trials and events held under the auspices of its member associations where they do not fall under RAC control. Agreed Codes of Conduct to be followed by all motor sports organisers for such events will be sought.

13.69 Casual use of tracks and paths, particularly by motor cycles and 4-wheel drive vehicles, sometimes irresponsibly, has caused an increase in complaints from other users, landowners and wildlife interests. In some cases this use is perfectly legal on non-classified county roads, even where they are unsurfaced green lanes. Traffic Regulation Orders, or reductions in highway status, can be considered where problems are severe, in consultation with user groups. Such orders are made by Highway Authorities. Previously such action has been taken for example on a route between Kinder Road, Hayfield and Edale.

13.70 Stock car racing has not occurred in the Park. Moto-cross is common in some places and is permitted development in planning law for up to 14 days a year. In particularly bad cases where erosion and disturbance is being caused to a prominent area, and where consultation has failed to produce a solution, the Board is ready to consider use of an Article 4 Direction to bring the activity within planning control. A Direction was successfully served near Monsal Head, and the motor cycling stopped. The East Midlands Regional Council for Sport and Recreation produced a report on off-road motor cycling in 1985. It pointed to the need for a hierarchy of sites with a minimum area of 2 acres for various motor cycling events and activities. The above activities may be able to make use of old quarries without giving rise to objections, and meet local or regional needs, provided there is no special wildlife interest and provided the events are not too large or frequent. Derbyshire Councty Council's site at Victory Quarry, Dove Holes outside the Park, for example, is let to a Club for organising practice and trials.

Reservoir Recreation

13.76 There are 48 reservoirs in the Park greater than 3 ha in area. Access to Open Country can include access to open water areas. In 1978, angling was the most common active recreation on the reservoirs, being permitted on 12, but not significant in many more because the waters were too acid to support fish life. Sailing was confined to 5 reservoirs. Damflask Reservoir was used for rowing.

13.77 The 1978 Plan established the criteria by which additional recreational opportunities should be judged. They are still relevant and are readopted in this Plan (**13.88** below). The 1978 Plan proposed boat fishing and sub aqua at Ladybower, and sailing at Torside, Winscar and Lamaload.

13.78 Use of reservoirs, and related facilities, has been carefully considered in Area Management Studies, by Water Authorities in reviewing water purity, and by Regional Councils for Sport and Recreation in their Strategies. The overall picture has not changed significantly, but certain improvements to recreational use of reservoirs have been achieved, notably sailing at Torside in Longdendale and boat fishing and sub aqua at Ladybower.

13.79 Consideration has also been given to sailing at Winscar, Langsett, Lamaload and Ladybower, but for various reasons has not been achieved. At Winscar the reason was lack of demand, at Langsett there is alternative provision close by at Underbank, and at Lamaload the new predicted draw-down is too great. Ladybower was confirmed as a possible venue for sailing and canoeing in the Upper Derwent Valley Draft Management Plan (1979), use being limited to the southern arm at a suggested site near Ashopton. A sailing club was formed, but planning permission for a clubhouse was refused at two sites other than Ashopton, and appeals to the Minister

were dismissed. No site acceptable to all interests seems to exist but sailing remains acceptable in principle if a suitable site can be found. It has been suggested that Ladybower has potential for a 'canoe trail' (see Chapter 31).

13.80 Additional recreational use of reservoirs is subject to a number of constraints, including conflict with other National Park aims and objectives; the function of the reservoir; the type and efficiency of water treatment works; conflict with other water sports; and the nature of the terrain in the vicinity of the reservoir.

13.81 By application of the Recreation Zoning described at paragraph **10.8** different types of reservoir recreation are generally appropriate from a National Park point of view as follows:

Zone I and II: Angling, Nature Study and Sub-aqua

Zone III: Angling, Nature Study, Sub-aqua and Canoeing

Zone IV: Angling, Nature Study, Sub-aqua, Canoeing, Boat-fishing and possibility Sailing and Rowing

Zone V: Angling, Sub-aqua, Canoeing, Boat-fishing, Sailing and Rowing

13.82 Water skiing and motor boats are unlikely to be acceptable. There are no motor boats on reservoirs in the Park, with the exception of rescue boats at some reservoirs, and limited model boating. However, approval has been given, subject to rigorous conditions, for water-skiing at Bottoms Reservoir near Tintwistle on the fringe of the Park, but a more intensive water sports centre has been rejected.

13.83 It is the duty of the Water Authorities to consider the use of reservoirs for recreation and to protect and enhance nature conservation interests. The Peak Board has good working contacts with these authorities and is involved in local studies on the use of various reservoir areas. (The Board's concern over the possible sale of water authority land and companies is referred to at **1.19**). The interests of water purity must be fully protected and an examination of the possible pollution and necessary preventative and treatment measures will be essential when considering water based activities in particular locations. This will be especially true of sailing, swimming and motor boat use.

13.84 Many of the reservoirs, particularly in the Zone IV and V areas, would be suitable for more than one use. These uses can cause conflicts such as those between angling and canoeing, which can be overcome by various management methods such as the segregation of uses over time and area. However, opportunities for greater recreational use of reservoirs in the Park seems fairly limited. The main opportunities for water recreation may lie outside the Park, as at Rother Valley, and eventually at Carsington.

13.85 The nature of the land in the vicinity of some reservoirs is such that particular sports cannot be accommodated. For example, steeply sloping banks to reservoirs can make it impossible to find suitable sites for storing and launching boats and for parking cars.

13.86 The day to day management of reservoir recreation can most easily be organised by clubs or other organisations who lease property and the use of the water surface from the Water Authority. This is how most sailing is catered for, whilst much angling on reservoirs is on a day-ticket basis. Non-members should not be excluded, so that staying visitors may

Map 13.2
Water Based Recreation

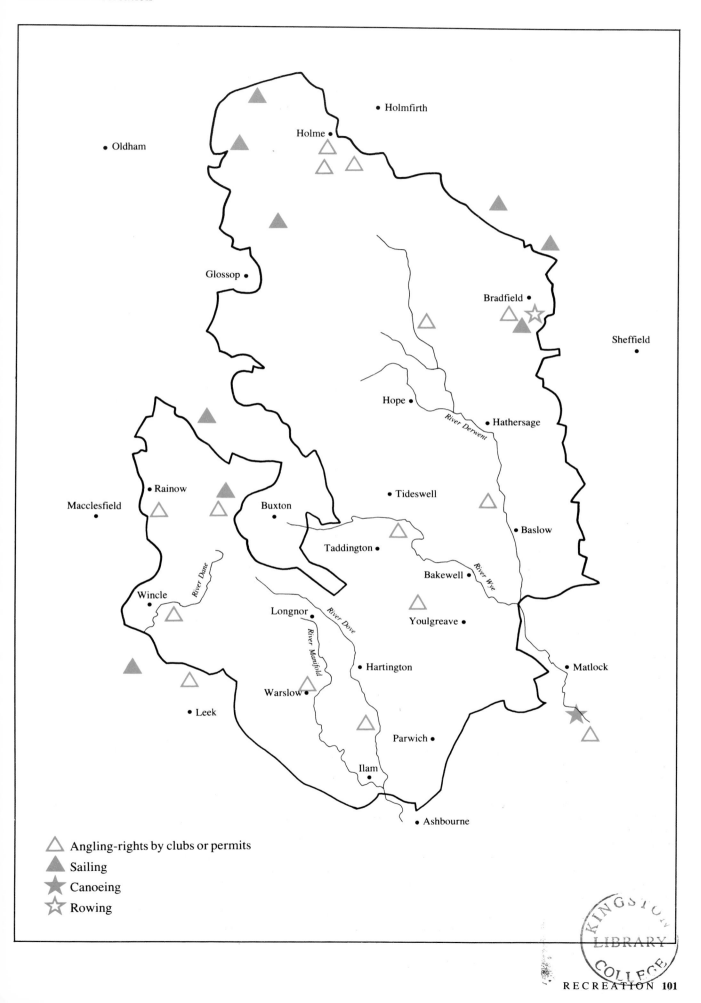

• Holmfirth

• Oldham

Holme •

• Holmfirth

Glossop •

Bradfield •
☆ Rowing star
Sheffield •

Hope •
River Derwent
• Hathersage

• Rainow
Macclesfield •

Buxton •
• Tideswell

Taddington •
• Baslow

Wincle •
River Dane

Longnor •
River Dove
Bakewell •
River Wye

Warslow •
River Manifold
• Hartington
• Matlock

Youlgreave •

• Leek

Parwich •

Ilam •

• Ashbourne

△ Angling-rights by clubs or permits

▲ Sailing

★ Canoeing

☆ Rowing

take part. The Board's objectives and policies will aim to encourage greater public use of reservoirs and their surrounding land.

Objective

13.87 To encourage recreational use of reservoirs and their immediate surroundings, providing suitable arrangements can be made consistent with Water Authority policies, and conservation interests.

Policies

13.88 The creation of additional recreation opportunities at reservoirs will be sought in the light of paragraphs 13.81 and 82 where appropriate in relation to approved Board policies and to the following criteria:

(i) The availability or planned provision of facilities to cater for similar demand outside the Park

(ii) The type of recreation, the recreation zoning and capacity of the area and the value of the particular area for other uses or interests

(iii) Conservation interests

(iv) Water purity considerations

(v) The range of uses possible, the degree to which they are already catered for, the evidence of demand for additional facilities and the possibilities of shared use

(vi) Detailed considerations in relation to any necessary facilities for users or spectators

(Peak Board, Sports Councils, Water Authorities).

13.89 In seeking additional recreation opportunities at reservoirs, full consideration will be given to the use of facilities by the general public (Peak Board, Water Authorities, Sports Councils, Royal Yachting Association).

River Recreation

13.90 The main rivers in the Park are the Derwent, Wye, Dove, Manifold and Dane. Rivers and river banks are 'Open Country' in which Access Agreements can be negotiated (see Chapter 12). They are at present officially used only for angling, and for limited canoeing by recognised youth organisations by agreement with owners. There is some unofficial canoeing, paddling and bathing. The rivers of the Park are generally narrow, shallow and fast-flowing but with no recognised 'white water'. No rights of navigation have been established and they are generally not suited to other forms of recreation. In wildlife and conservation terms, several of the rivers pass through Sites of Special Scientific Interest. There is a need for quiet stretches on rivers with very limited recreational activity, in the interests of wildlife conservation and quiet enjoyment. Water authorities are required under the Control of Pollution Act 1974 to maintain the quality of river waters (see **2.29**).

13.91 In the 1978 Plan, it was proposed that the rivers of the Park should continue to be used primarily for fishing. The scope for negotiating canoeing rights experimentally on selected stretches of rivers was to be investigated.

13.92 **Canoeing** is physically possible on some of the rivers in the Park which are sufficiently wide and deep with few obstructions (e.g. weirs), and which have vehicular access at some points. The rivers Derwent and Wye seem best suited to canoeing. However, riparian owners own the fishing rights to the rivers. Many fishing rights have been sold or leased, and

there are hundreds of different interests involved for individual rivers. There is some risk that canoeing might disturb some river wildlife.

13.93 It was hoped that the opening up of certain rivers for canoeing would be assisted by the introduction by the British Canoe Union (BCU) of a canoe registration scheme; by the classification of rivers and river banks as 'open country' with consequent scope for Access Agreements; and by the ability of the Board to conclude Management Agreements. A special study was prepared by the East Midlands Regional Sports Council from the findings of a working group on which the relevant interests were represented. Access or management agreements could include financial arrangements to compensate for any loss of angling interests. However, Access Agreements can only relate to access for all users and cannot be restricted to a particular group such as British Canoe Union members. From soundings of landowning and fishing interests, it was clear this is not acceptable because of problems of control and supervision. Agreements concluded by the BCU themselves might be more appropriate. They were asked to take the lead, with the Board considering what assistance it might give subsequently. In spite of considerable efforts by various bodies, no progress has yet been made. The BCU's adoption of complete registration and their promotion of awareness among their members of 'canoeing and environment' may improve the chances of agreement.

13.94 **Fishing** The rivers of the Park generally provide excellent opportunities for both coarse and game fishing. Many rivers, particularly in the limestone area, are carefully managed primarily for fishing use and are artificially stocked. There is the strong literary and historic connection with Izaak Walton and Charles Cotton in the Dove Valley. Conditions are now so good that there are some local aspirations to promote the return of salmon to the Derwent. This follows the completion of the artificial canoe slalom course at Holme Pierrepont near Nottingham (which bypasses the sluice gates and allows salmon to reach the Trent and thence into the Derwent). Discussion is proceeding. The return of salmon would be a symbol of purity and of a return to natural conditions prior to the industrial revolution. Rod licence income would increase. The fact of the restoration of water purity and the return of salmon would assist the promotion of recreation and tourism in the area.

13.95 A number of hotels in the Park own the fishing rights of particular stretches of river. In addition, day tickets are issued for certain stretches of the Lathkill, Derwent and Wye. The Peak Board's information sheet on fishing explains to visitors the arrangements for both river and reservoir fishing.

13.96 River banks provide popular existing walking routes and there is potential for negotiating further access. Opportunities for riding and cycling will be more limited. The practice of encouraging access to one river bank whilst restricting access to the opposite bank for wildlife conservation seems to work well (for example, at Dovedale) (see Chapter 12, access to Open Country particularly **12.16**, **12.30**).

Objective

13.97 To achieve greater public access to rivers in the National Park for the traditional recreation of coarse and game fishing; to seek some access for canoeing and to assist the development of recreation and tourism where consistent with the natural qualities of the Park linked to historical and literary traditions.

Reservoirs can be shared amongst users, either by area or by time — or can be reserved for nature study.

Policies

13.98 The traditional river pursuit of angling will continue to be the major recreational use of most stretches of river in the Park (Peak Board, Sports Councils, CLA, Water Authorities).

13.99 Navigation access arrangements for canoes will be sought on suitable stretches of rivers or on reservoirs by negotiation, initially on a trial, time-share basis, subject to the need to safeguard conservation interests (including fish) and to win the approval of landowners (BCU, Sports Councils, Peak Board, Water Authorities, CLA, Angling Clubs).

13.100 Greater public access to rivers and river banks in the Park will be sought, subject to an overriding need to conserve and enhance the natural qualities of the area (Peak Board, Water Authorities, Sports Councils, BCU).

(Moorland recreation is dealt with in Chapter 12 — Access to open country)

Shooting

13.101 The origins of shooting as a traditional countryside pursuit rest partly in the search for food to live. In the Park, shooting takes five main forms:- grouse shooting, which is dealt with in Chapter 12 as part of the access to moorlands issue; clay pigeon shooting; rough shooting; game and sporting shooting; target shooting on ranges; and military training. The 1978 Plan only dealt specifically with grouse shooting.

13.102 There are few formal target shooting ranges in the Park, and new proposals are rare. However, shooting ranges can restrict public enjoyment of the National Park because of the public safety requirements, and the necessary mounds, sheds, targets and flags can be intrusive in the landscape.

Military training is dealt with at paragraphs **22.22-22.28**. This section of this Plan deals with clay pigeon shooting and shooting ranges.

13.103 Since 1978 there has been a significant growth of interest in more organised and intensive clay pigeon shooting events, in which shoots are arranged by clubs or as a business venture. Larger numbers of people attend, more guns are used for longer periods and/or on a greater number of days per year. Several shoots have given rise to objections, on grounds of disturbance to the quiet enjoyment of visitors or residents, and to wildlife. Litter is sometimes left after the event, including brightly-coloured cartridges and clay fragments.

13.104 Over-intensive or over-frequent shooting close to houses, popular recreational areas or sensitive wildlife sites is open to objection in National Park terms, and is included as a disruptive or intrusive activity at paragraph **10.8**(b). Events or site developments which fall within planning control will be assessed within the context of the policies in this Plan. Co-operation will be sought with the organisers of lesser events to minimise their impact. In the last resort, the use of Article 4 directions, which extend normal planning control powers, will be considered.

Objective

13.105 To accept continued low-key clay pigeon shooting as a traditional country pursuit, but to resist the growth of more intensive events or the establishment of additional sites or shooting ranges.

Policies

13.106 All proposals for or development in shooting events or sites will be rigorously monitored. Those which spoil the quiet enjoyment of residents or visitors, or which harm landscape and wildlife interests, will be resisted, including the use of special planning powers in the last resort (Peak Board, Sports Council).

Introduction

14.1 Most visitors to the Peak District take part in informal recreation. For this, they need good access to the Park by public or private transport; convenient parking places, with opportunities to picnic nearby in attractive areas; easy walking routes to features of interest; toilets; refreshments and information.

14.2 The 1978 Plan considered informal recreation and general visitor services against the background of Structure Plan policies and the Recreation Strategy. Informal recreation activities relying on the particular qualities of the National Park were to be catered for, with careful improvements to facilities where the environment and approach routes were appropriate. These policies remain valid and are the basis for policies in this Chapter.

14.3 Much has been achieved since the 1978 Plan both in area management initiatives and individual projects. The 1986/7 Visitor Survey shows that visitors to the Park expect high standards and ready access to facilities and services. The provision of facilities will continue to be based on the ability of an area to absorb additional visitors in accordance with the zoning and capacity policies set out in the recreation strategy in this Plan (Chapter 10) and will be assessed as part of area management plans where these exist (Chapters 24-47). Policies for traffic management, recreational public transport, information centres and other information and interpretation services and active recreation pursuits are found in other Chapters.

14.4 This chapter deals with the following visitor facilities:

   (a) Car Parking (**14.5-14.19**)

   (b) Picnic Areas (**14.20-14.26**)

   (c) Public Toilets and Shelters (**14.27-14.37**)

   (d) Cycling and Cycle Hire (**14.38-14.47**)

   (e) Catering Facilities in the Countryside (**14.48-14.61**)

   (f) (Provision for Disabled and Disadvantaged People (**14.62-14.70**)

Car Parking

14.5 About 90% of visitors to the Peak District arrive by car, and of these 80% will make one or more stops on a village street, in a layby, on the roadside or in car parks. Over 60% of visitors used a car park, and of these over 80% found the car park adequate (Visitor Survey 1986/7). The 1978 Plan set out the responsibilities for providing for car parks, plus

Most visitors come by car. This is the viewpoint at Monsal Head in 1987. A second improvement scheme is to be completed in 1989.

18½ million day visits each year. Visitors of all ages place a heavy demand on many services.

criteria for their siting and design and means of charging to recover a proportion of the costs. These policies have been followed, are still relevant, and are substantially restated in this Plan.

14.6 Table 14.1 below summarises the changes in off-street car parking provision since 1977.

14.7 The total of places for off-road car parking provided by the public authorities is thus about 9,000. The 1986/87 Visitor Survey indicates that about 75,000 cars stop on an average summer Sunday for 10 minutes or more. At a turnover of, say, three per day, there may be 25,000 cars parked at any one time. There is therefore an apparent shortage of places at the busiest times. Some of this is met by

Table 14.1
Changes in Car Parking provision 1977-1987
Source: Board's own surveys

Year	Sites	Car spaces	Coach spaces	Toilets*	Picnic areas	Sites on which:		
						Parking charge is levied	Refreshments are provided	Information is provided
1977	73	5,063	19	43(12)	37	13	40	34
1987	87	8,044	80	50(17)	40	34	43	44

In addition, there are 28 lay-bys provided by the Board, and 104 by other bodies, probably providing more than 1,000 further car parking places.

*Figures in brackets are the number of toilets with facilities for the disabled

private car parks and by harmless informal roadside parking. However, much undesirable parking and pressure remains in Bakewell, Castleton and Hartington, on country lanes and to a lesser extent on farmland. Countryside Commission expectations on outdoor recreation, and national forecasts of car use, both point to increasing need for car parking and associated visitor facilities.

14.8 Several agencies provide or manage car parks and car parking in the Park. District Councils take the prime responsibility for town and village car parks. Highway Authorities are responsible for Traffic Orders to restrain unacceptable on-street parking. The Board has provided most public recreational car parking in the countryside, with assistance from the Countryside Commission. Other public and private landowners are expected to meet needs generated by the use of their own land or property, such as public houses, or a farmer holding an open day.

14.9 Both the Board and the Countryside Commission operate grant schemes to assist others to provide car parks. The Board's scheme provides for up to 75% of approved costs and the Commission's up to 50%. In some cases, both agencies can assist the same project. An example of this approach is at Monsal Head where the agreed contributions are District Council 50%, Board 25%, Countryside Commission 25%.

14.10 Outside villages, the Board or the landowner (such as the Water Authority) normally takes the lead role in providing off-street parking, or the Board grant-aids others, often as part of Area Management schemes.

14.11 The location and size of car parks is crucial to managing the movement of visitors, both for their enjoyment and to ensure that areas are not overused. The policies on location which follow take account of the recreational zones and capacities of the area (Chapter 10) and the level of landscape screening available. The design of car parks is a matter of detailed practice which were set out in the 1978 Plan and are now published separately. The Board sets high standards in its own car parks and seeks similar standards in those in which it is partner, or by use of its development control powers.

14.12 Car Parks are expensive to build. Costs can be met or offset by charging the users or at least providing them with the opportunity to pay. Most District Council car parks use the 'pay and display' system. The Board installs 'honesty boxes'. The National Trust charges where practicable (Ilam Hall) and installs donation boxes at some other car parks.

Objectives
14.13 To provide car parks to enable visitors to enjoy the National Park and alleviate recreational traffic problems, whilst minimising the impact on the environment and local people. To apply high standards to the location, design and maintenance of car parks and associated landscaping, and to charge where practicable. To consider the needs of disabled people at every facility.

Policies
14.14 In villages, the prime responsibility for off-street parking provision rests with District Councils or private operators. The Board, in conjunction with the Countryside Commission, will consider financially assisting the provision of such car parking (District Councils, Countryside Commission, Peak Board).

14.15 In the countryside, the main responsibility for general public car parking rests with the Board, or its partners (sometimes as agreed in Area Management Plans). In conjunction with the Countryside Commission, the Board will consider financially assisting the provision of car parks in the countryside where these are provided by other agencies (Peak Board, Countryside Commission).

14.16 In the selection of sites and capacities for car parks within approved Structure Plan policies, the following factors will be considered:

(a) The character, qualities, recreational zone and capacity of the surrounding areas and the capacities and locations of nearby parking facilities.

(b) The character of the nearby road network, in particular the ease with which access can be gained to the major recreation routes.

(c) The location and popularity of nearby footpaths and other features of interest.

(d) The presence of reasonable screening by landform, trees, shrubs or walls, or other features such as buildings or woodlands so that the parking does not form a conspicuous element in the landscape.

(e) The local economic benefit to trade or disruption to farming.

(f) Any existing problems caused by unauthorised or disorganised parking.

(Peak Board, Highway Authorities).

14.17 Careful consideration will be given to the detailed design and management of all parking areas and in particular to the safety of access to the road network; the needs of disabled people and the materials used in construction (Peak Board, Highway Authorities).

14.18 Proposals for improving existing parking areas will be identified, involving nearby land management interests where appropriate (Peak Board, District Councils, Highway Authorities).

14.19 Charging at car parks in the Park will be continued and extended where appropriate, except where deemed to be uneconomic or at variance with other policies for traffic management in the area (Peak Board, District Councils, RWAs, National Trust, Forestry Commission).

Picnic Areas

14.20 Most picnicking takes place close to the car. The 1978 Plan proposed that opportunities for picnicking in attractive surroundings should be developed as part of local studies, with formal agreements where necessary. On more remote sites which are within or close to car parks, natural features such as rocks or grass banks are considered more appropriate for picnics than tables. Farming and land management interests must be carefully considered.

14.21 Since 1978 picnic areas have been created near the Derwent Dam, at Torside, Trentabank and Digley. 33% of summer-day visitors interviewed in the 1986/7 survey used a picnic area and the great majority of users found them adequate.

14.22 Grant-aid can be offered by the Board to other developers to provide picnic facilities, for example the joint scheme between the Parish Council, Rural Community Council and MSC Community agency at Middleton-by-Youlgreave, using a derelict site.

14.23 As river banks are now classified as 'open country', access or management agreements can be negotiated to increase pedestrian access to river banks both for walking and picnicking.

Objective
14.24 To make picnic facilities available for visitors close to car parks, and in attractive surroundings elsewhere.

Policies
14.25 As part of local studies and initiatives, opportunities for picnicking in attractive surroundings will be provided or supported. This will be especially at car parks and on reservoir margins, river banks and woodlands, provided there is no undue impact on special wildlife interests. The needs of the disabled will be taken into account (Peak Board, Water Authorities, National Trust, Forestry Commission).

14.26 Where necessary, management agreements will be negotiated to provide picnic areas (Peak Board, landowners).

Public Toilets and Shelters

14.27 The Board has powers under the 1949 Act to provide toilets and shelters related to campsites and car parks. Other public agencies (District Councils and Water Authorities) have similar powers, and private firms involved in the recreation business usually provide such facilites for customers. Over 60% of visitors interviewed in the 1986/7 survey used public toilets and most users found them adequate.

14.28 The 1978 Plan suggested circumstances in which the provision of public toilets and/or shelters should be considered in villages, car parks and particular tourist attractions. It also put forward ways of minimising problems and opportunities for joint provision and management. The need to adapt existing facilities and to develop new ones, with disabled persons in mind, was stressed.

14.29 Toilets for the public are difficult to provide in the countryside. Problems include finding sites that do not cause nuisance to nearby residents, finding appropriate locations in visual terms, providing services (especially water supplies), and difficulties in servicing and cleaning the toilets.

14.30 The Board manages 17 toilets. Six are kept open throughout the year, and at a further six only the disabled toilet is kept open through the year. Four are open for the summer period only, because of the cost of servicing and risks of vandalism. A further 34 toilets are managed by others. The Board tries to maintain high standards of repairs, servicing, cleaning and combating vandalism. Facilities in remote and awkward areas, without main services, require a higher management input. The Board tries to engage local people to act as custodians and cleaners of toilets. Some District Councils now let out some work on contract — for example, High Peak BC supplements its normal direct labour routine by a specialist contract 4 times each year.

14.31 Further public toilets may be justified in popular villages, (where it is hoped that the District Councils might take the lead role subject to the availability of resources); at car parks providing for more than 30 or 40 cars; and at certain popular sites which are some distance from parking areas. On reservoir catchment areas, toilet provision may be desirable at lower intensities of use in order to minimise pollution risks.

14.32 The Board offers grant-aid to bodies who provide public toilets catering primarily for visitors, on the same basis as for car parks. The Countryside Commission has also made grant available for toilets in country parks and picnic sites, for example to the Severn Trent Water Authority at Fairholmes. The English Tourist Board can also assist where projects will give significant benefits for tourists, for example at Torside in Longdendale.

14.33 New proposals for toilets are likely to emerge from area studies, village enhancement schemes, and car park proposals. There is agreement to new public toilets linked to re-use of a barn at Langsett as a Visitor Centre, alongside the new Yorkshire Water Authority car park. The Board's Alsop, Hulme End and Mam Nick car parks alongside busy roads may also need toilets. Others are being considered at Woodhead, Monsal Dale, Wildborclough, Grindon and Hayfield. The existing toilets at Dove Stone reservoir should be altered to provide for the disabled.

14.34 The Board has provided shelters on some of the trails and in association with toilets and picnic site developments.

We continue to provide or encourage picnic areas. This one is part of an award-winning scheme in the upper Derwent valley.

Bicycles can now be hired at a dozen centres in and around the Park.

The provision of shelters elsewhere is likely to be very limited, though there may be circumstances, for instance on major waymarked paths, where simple shelter facilities will be judged desirable.

Cycle Hire

14.38 Cycling is growing in popularity as a simple, healthy form of exercise, and as a pleasant way to see the countryside. Cycling is also considered as an active recreation in Chapter 13. The 1978 Plan encouraged cycle hire, which was then at an experimental stage on the Tissington and High Peak Trails.

14.39 The Board's objectives have been to provide a service to the general public by offering cycling in relatively traffic-free conditions. The Board was a pioneer in cycle hire and has expanded the number of outlets and the number of cycles for hire. Waymarked cycle routes have been established, and the 'Routes for People' traffic scheme established recreational routes and reduced commercial traffic on routes better suited to recreational traffic, including cycling (see paragraph **15.4**). This section deals primarily with cycle hire and cycling on the trails.

14.40 In 1976 there were 13,000 hirings from the first centre opened by the Board at Parsley Hay Centre with 50 cycles. In 1980 the number of cycles had grown to about 190 at 2 centres with 23,000 hirings. By 1986 with 4 centres, the number of cycles had risen to 324 with 39,000 hirings. Provision of further cycles increased hirings to 46,000 in 1987. Hirings are very much dependent upon the weather. Special factors, such as the teachers' industrial action in 1986, can drastically reduce party bookings. Since the Board demonstrated the idea, 5 privately owned cycle hire centres have been established in the Park and there are further hire sites on the periphery of the Park operated by both the public and private sectors.

14.41 Cycling can take place on roads, trails and bridleways but normally cannot make use of footpaths. There is only limited scope to improve and extend the cycling network in the Park; but the popularity of the activity and the willingness to pay for the hire of cycles places a high priority on the improvement of cycling opportunities. The main remaining opportunities include unused former railway routes, better surfacing of existing routes and the continued and extended selection and promotion of suitable routes in the public path network.

14.42 The growing popularity of mountain bikes is dealt with in paragraph **13.36**.

14.43 The Board's cycle hire operation has been reviewed, with a view to saving costs and to encouraging more hirings, with the overall aim of breaking even at least on operational costs. Opportunities for additional cycle hire centres may exist in or close to the Park, where areas can absorb recreation activity, and there is a safe network of routes. Wooden buildings may be acceptable while schemes are in experimental stages (say 3 years), but thereafter traditional stone buildings are expected.

Catering Facilities in the Countryside

14.48 Catering is both a vital service to visitors and one of the most direct ways in which local communities can benefit economically from recreation. At the time of the 1978 Plan, it was estimated that 40% of visitors' expenditure was on refreshments.

14.49 The 1986/7 Visitor Survey indicates that in real tems visitor spending has risen overall, and that spending on refreshments has risen from £2.70 per head 1971/2 to £3.62 per head in 1986/7 (1986 prices). Most public catering in the Park is provided by the private sector in its own premises, mainly in the villages and in roadside public houses. The following paragraphs deal with vendors at roadsides, car parks and picnic sites. (Chapter 17 deals with visitor accommodation).

14.50 The policies in the 1978 Plan were to continue licensing mobile vendors at Board-owned sites, and to monitor and act at places where unlicensed vendors caused problems. Local applications for mobile vendor licences and the provision of farmhouse teas were encouraged as supplements to local income.

14.51 Licensing mobile vendors on selected Peak Board car parks has continued successfully, both as a service for visitors and a source of income to help with the upkeep of sites. In 1988, twelve concessions were let and the use of the Tissington refreshment room has continued. Concessions have also been let by other authorities and interests, for example at Fairholmes, Upper Derwent (by the Peak Board for the Water Authority) and at Monsal Head.

14.52 During the summer of 1981, ranger surveys and other observers noted a considerable increase in the number of roadside traders and mobile vendors in the Peak District,

Young visitors enjoying ice cream at Ashford well dressing.

giving rise to objections of highway safety and appearance. In May 1982 the Board agreed a general presumption against mobile vendors in the National Park and enforcement action was agreed where necessary. The retention of mobile vendors at recreational sites with adequate parking, access and screening was agreed, but only where permanent buildings were impractical, undesirable or not available nearby.

14.53 In 1984, following acute problems on the A57 in the area near the Upper Derwent, High Peak Borough Council prohibited trading except at two specified lay-bys. This was the first time such action had been taken in the Park. No special road markings or signs are needed, and the system has worked well, making alternative off-road refreshments available. Where these restrictions have been applied, they seem to be more effective than the use of development control powers.

14.54 Roadside vending near Longshaw remains a problem which may also justify a 'prohibited streets' order. There is scope for other local authorities to control roadside vending under local authority powers, where necessary.

14.55 In addition to public houses, lay-bys and car parks, there is probable still scope for futher provision of catering in the countryside, particularly at farmsteads. Some farms serve teas and other light refreshments as a separate small business or as part of a wider farm tourism business (see Chapter 17).

Objective
14.56 To encourage or provide refreshment facilities in the countryside, where consistent with the planning and management policies of the Board.

Policies
14.57 The conditional licensing of mobile vendors on Board property will continue, where needed, paying regard to the effect on the local economy (Peak Board).

14.58 Other owners of car parks, particularly District Councils and Water Authorities, will be requested to adopt similar licensing arrangements at appropriate sites (District Councils, Water Authorities).

14.59 Appropriately sited and designed permanent buildings will be preferred for busy sites with a long visitor season, where there is no established refreshment trading outlet nearby (Peak Board, other operators).

14.60 The use of the Park by mobile vendors will continue to be monitored. Attempts will be made to persuade vendors causing particular problems to move to other locations. Where roadside vending problems are particularly bad, District Councils will be asked to use their powers to direct vendors to acceptable locations, or enforcement action will be considered (Peak Board, District Councils).

14.61 The provision of simple catering facilities such as farmhouse teas in existing buildings will be encouraged where appropriate (Peak Board, MAFF).

Provision for Disabled and Disadvantaged People

14.62 Disabled people take part in a wide variety of recreational activities, and there are many things that can be done to make their visits to the National Park easier, more enjoyable and rewarding. The 1978 Plan advocated consultation with organisations representing disabled people in the preparation of area management plans; continued provision for them in toilet and information facilities; the encouragement of catering and accommodation establishments to take account of their needs; and the production of a special information leaflet on facilities in the Park for the disabled.

14.63 Since 1978, routes suitable for wheelchairs have been developed in the Upper Derwent and Goyt Valleys, and at Tideswell Dale. Disabled people are exempted from the traffic-free restriction in the Upper Derwent. A special fishing platform has been provided at Ladybower reservoir for disabled anglers. The 'Ringwood Rambler' bus service, which is financially supported by the Board, provides the opportunity for otherwise housebound disabled people to visit some of the finest parts of the Peak. There are reserved parking bays at some car parks, and many toilets include special provision.

14.64 The Board considers the needs of disabled people in its provisions for recreation. Many disabled people, and organisations like the Fieldfare Trust and Derbyshire Centre for Integrated Living, are keen to see an integrated approach and point to quite modest improvements which can help remove obstacles. A new route for wheelchair users onto Baslow Edge has recently been completed. It is proposed to extend the wheelchair route around Dove Stone Reservoir. The Manifold Valley Track is particularly well suited in its surface and gradient for use by disabled people (see **46.12**). Appropriate heavily used paths, with a good surface, especially those from car parks, should (if practicable and with landowner's consent) be made accessible to the disabled by the provision of bridlegates or kissing gates. Where stiles are essential, they should be as convenient as possible for the elderly, the infirm or partially disabled people. Thought will also be given to 'listening and touch trails' for partially sighted people. Tandems are provided at cycle hire centres so that blind people can cycle. Canoeing is popular with certain disabled people. These and many other special efforts will continue.

14.65 Other people are disadvantage either by their language, cultural or ethnic backgrounds, by the location of their home or by extreme poverty.

14.66 Efforts will be made to meet the needs of disadvantaged and disabled people as an integral part of policies and programmes in the Park.

Objectives
14.67 To enable disadvantaged and disabled people to enjoy the countryside and facilities of the National Park, as extensively as possible.

A little extra thought for the needs of disabled people, when planning and providing, is well rewarded later.

Policies
14.68 Provision for disabled people will continue to be included where possible at all new facilities and services, and existing facilities and services will be adapted where practical, including

   (a) Rights of way (11.30)

   (b) Active recreation (13.39, 13.65)

   (c) Visitor facilities (14.17,14.25,14.37)

   (d) Recreational public transport (16.18)

   (e) Information and interpretation (18.33j)

(Peak Board).

14.69 Facilities available for disabled people will continue to be publicised and monitored (Peak Board).

14.70 Field staff will be advised or trained in the special skills needed to assist disabled people (Peak Board).

15 TRAFFIC MANAGEMENT

Introduction

15.1 Road improvements, the selection of routes for different types of traffic, the use and enforcement of traffic regulation orders, and highways signing are the responsibility of the highway authorities and the police, not the Peak Board. Any of these measures, if ill-handled, can spoil the landscape. The priorities of the highway authorities and police are normally the free and safe flow of traffic. Circular 4/76 and the Structure Plan establish that in the National Park, after road safety, environmental quality is the prime criterion in road planning, highway design and traffic management.

15.2 However, traffic management is of fundamental importance to many National Park objectives. 90% of the 18½ million visits to the Park are made by car. The Board has enjoyed extensive co-operation with the relevant authorities, as encouraged by Government (Circular 4/76). The Board and the highway authorities were closely involved in the Peak Park Transport Study (1977-80) which identified traffic problem areas and put forward a priority list of road schemes, chiefly to cater for longer distance and heavy goods traffic. These schemes will be considered in the review of the Structure Plan.

15.3 A comprehensive approach to visitors' movements from home to their National Park destination and back is of benefit to the visitor, to their hosts and to the places they visit. Such an approach needs to consider the origins of visitors; the provision of information at home; the selection of traffic routes; road improvements; public transport; the provision of car parks, scenic routes and other facilities; information on arrival; improvement to the public path network and access to open country; the current distribution of visitor stops in the Park; and the problems and opportunities created.

15.4 A similar though less comprehensive approach was achieved for a limited area of the National Park (between the A6 and the A515) in the 'Routes for People' project. This was implemented between 1973 and 1975 and is still in operation. The project, which relied heavily on investment by the highway authority, included a new link road for heavy traffic; a major village by-pass; weight restriction orders to protect other villages and country lanes; visitor car parks with on-site information; the 'White Peak' 25 mile scenic drive; cycle routes; and way-marking of public paths.

15.5 The principles and practice established in this scheme and others will be the basis of the Board's approach to the management of and provision for visitor traffic in the National Park. It is hoped that other organisations, particularly the highway authorities, will continue to support this general approach. Whilst it is accepted that levels of expenditure are not likely to match those incurred in the 'Routes for People' project, Government has undertaken to assess the tourism benefit of highway improvements choosing priorities.

15.6 This chapter re-endorses the policies in the 1978 Plan for a hierarchy of routes for different types of recreational traffic, the continued use of traffic orders, further traffic management schemes and the development of highway signing for tourist traffic. These policies cross-relate to others, particularly with those for the management of road verges (**7.42-7.47**), rights of way (Chapter 11), access to open country (Chapter 12), the provision of visitor facilities (Chapter 14), recreational public transport (Chapter 16), the provision of information services (Chapter 18) and regional and national needs for cross-park traffic (Chapter 22).

Hierarchy of routes

15.7 The Structure Plan and the 1978 Plan envisaged co-operation between the highway authorities and the Board to relieve congestion arising from visitor traffic; the promotion of a hierarchy or routes onto which the bulk of recreation traffic would be channelled; and the downgrading of cerain minor roads to footpath or bridleway status. The Structure Plan also contains basic policies on highway design standards and traffic management, which are as appropriate to recreation traffic schemes as to others. These policies envisage that environmental quality will be the primary criterion in the planning and management of traffic, subject to road safety requirements (Structure Plan Chapter 11 and Circular 4/76). The policies in the 1978 Plan and the Structure Plan proposed a concentration of recreational traffic and other traffic (especially large vehicles), onto the major road network, backed up by traffic regulation orders or advisory signing. Traffic mainly uses class A and B roads but surveys show considerable use of minor roads by recreational traffic, with associated problems of congestion, parking and erosion of verges. This Review re-adopts the policies on a hierarchy of traffic routes (see **15.18** and Map 15.1).

Traffic Management

15.8 Proposals in the 1978 Plan included traffic management for the Winnats Pass, Millers Dale, Monsal Dale, the Edale Valley and the Manifold Valley and in the towns and villages of Alstonefield, Ashford, Bakewell, Castleton, Edale (Grindsbrook Booth), Hartington, Tissington, Thorpe and Youlgreave.

15.9 Since the 1978 Plan, there has been limited progress. Existing traffic management schemes such as Routes for People, Goyt Valley and the Winnats Pass have been maintained, albeit with significant amendments. Traffic management, including weight restriction orders, traffic bans at weekends and new car parks, have been included in new schemes for the Upper Derwent, and in villages as part of conservation and enhancement programmes, including Eyam and Tideswell. In Milldale, parking restrictions have been introduced without the use of yellow lines, following close consultation between the Board, Staffordshire County Council and the Department of Transport. These are representative of areas where the highway authorities' priorities of free and safe traffic flow coincide with the Board's objectives of environmental improvements. In the light of the current Transport Policies and Programmes which look forward three years, it is unlikely that the highway authorities would be able to justify expending time and resources on schemes that are solely for environmental benefit, but such schemes may be possible within the life of this Plan.

15.10 There is no evidence of a general decrease in recreational traffic in the Park since 1978. Car ownership and recreation trips continue to rise nationwide. The current estimate of 18½ million visits to the National Park each year, based on the 1986/7 Visitor Survey, is of the same order as in 1978 (there are no strictly comparable figures). The Survey indicates that since 1971 there has been a reduction in the number of Sunday visitors to Dovedale and and increase in the number of Sunday visitors to Chatswoth. The most popular areas still include Bakewell, Chatsworth, Dovedale, Hartington, Goyt Valley, Hope Valley, and Upper Derwent (see Map 24.5).

Map 15.1
Traffic Management

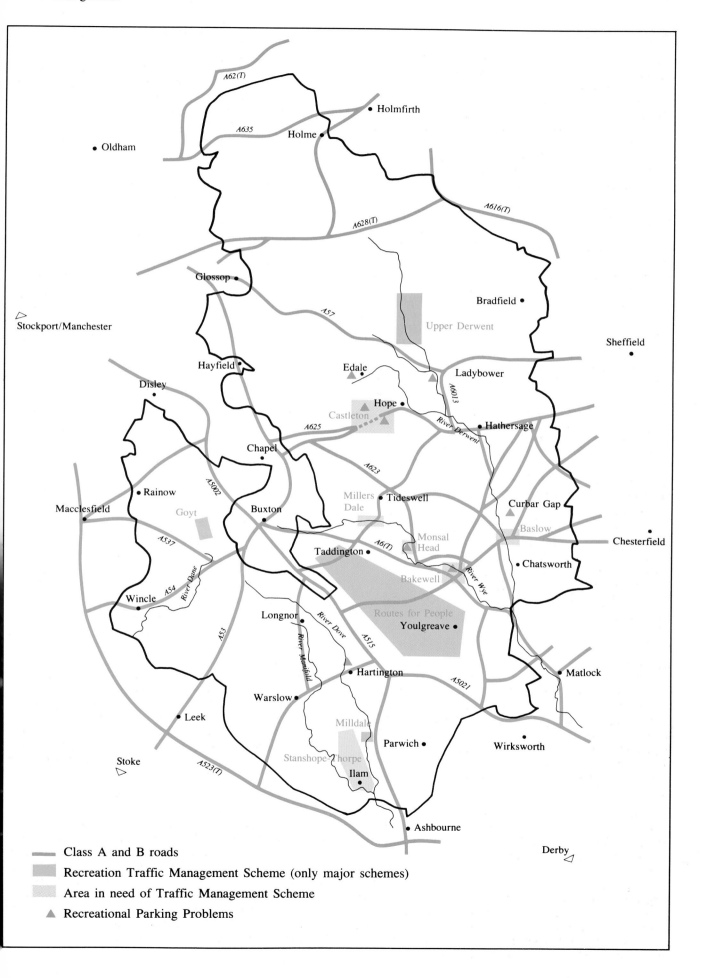

Class A and B roads

Recreation Traffic Management Scheme (only major schemes)

Area in need of Traffic Management Scheme

▲ Recreational Parking Problems

15.11 Further analysis of visitor and car park statistics will assist in judgements on the priorities for traffic management in the various areas of the Park (Chapters 24-47) and the need for other traffic management initiatives on the model of the 'Routes for People' Project. Priorities for traffic management should be considered as part of Village Management Schemes (**9.30**) and of Area Management Schemes (Chapter 24) and may include:

(a) Bakewell, where major changes and congestion in the town demand improved access to and capacity of existing car parks, possibly involving road and bridge construction and the improvement of car parks on the edge of the town

(b) Castleton, where access to parking needs further study (see **34.25**)

(c) The Hope Valley, where the closure of the A625 at Mam Tor has had consequences for Hope, Bradwell and the Winnats Pass which are still not resolved (see **34.19**)

(d) Hartington, where changes to car parking provisions are needed to accommodate a large volume of visitors (see **46.27**).

In these areas, opportunities will be sought to combine environmental improvement with improvement to the free and safe flow of traffic.

15.12 Most traffic management schemes rely mainly upon the driver to obey the various traffic orders limiting vehicle types, access or parking. Effective enforcement is however necessary if traffic management is to be respected by the motorist. This is not an appropriate task for the Board's Ranger Service (see Chapter 19) and police resources are particularly stretched at the busy holiday times when enforcement of recreational traffic orders, should be examined with the highway authorities and the police.

Highway Signs

15.13 The 1978 Plan identified the value of highway signs as a means of discouraging the use of roads unsuited to different types of traffic, and encouraging the use of suitable routes. Signposting can similarly assist in reducing pressure on

overused areas, and in enouraging visitors to go to areas with spare capacity. Government and the Tourist Boards have recently proposed special signposting to help the tourist and tourist businesses, by adopting the white-on-brown signing system.

15.14 The Board has accepted these proposals in principle and has adopted criteria for the assessment, by the highway authorities, of proposals to put up white-on-brown signs. It has also approved a programme for the installation of white-on-brown signs to mark the boundary of the National Park at the points where it is crossed by highways and public paths, which have not already been marked by the stone-built millstone boundary signs. Proposals by adjoining councils or Tourist Boards to sign the National Park specifically as a destination from the surrounding motorway and trunk road network are opposed by the Board. This is because such signing is likely to increase the numbers of day visitors across a broad area, thereby creating greater problems of visitor management than already exist. However, some parts or features of the Peak District are and will be signed by adjoining or constituent authorities.

15.15 The objective and policies which flow from the issues described in this chapter are developed from those agreed in the 1978 Plan. Of necessity, they continue to draw on the resources of the 7 highway authorities and the police within the National Park. It is recognised that these authorities will be asked to devote part of their time to traffic management in the Park, where a strong case can be made.

Objective
15.16 To manage the recreational traffic demands on the Park in a manner which does not damage the environmental quality of the area, and which assists the visitor.

Policy
15.17 In the National Park, environmental quality will be the primary criterion in the planning of road systems, the design of alterations and management of traffic, subject always to the need for road safety (Highway Authorities, Peak Board).

15.18 The highway authorities and the Board will seek to encourage the use of the main road network and deter

This traffic jam often also includes a 38 tonne lorry. Relief roads for Bakewell and other villages are long awaited.

White-on-brown signs can be used to help visitors find their way and to know they have arrived.

large vehicles and heavy volumes of traffic from using roads other than those shown on Map 15.1 (Peak Board, Highway Authorities, A.A.).

15.19 Within the limits of available staff and financial resources, the highway authorities and the Board will jointly devise a programme of traffic management and highway improvement schemes to achieve environmental and safety improvements in settlements or at tourist attractions, and to relieve congestion. Some schemes will affect or be affected by routes outside the Park (Highway Authorities, District Councils, Police and Peak Board).

15.20 The Routes for People scheme will be maintained and improved and measures for the maintenance, extension and enforcement of recreational traffic schemes will be developed (Police, Highway Authorities, District Councils, Peak Board).

15.21 The introduction of white-on-brown signs for recreational attractions will be supported, in the light of the criteria in the current policy note. These criteria will be applied strictly, to keep the number of signs to the minimum necessary to assist visitors and as an aid to traffic management. The National Park should not be signposted from the surrounding motorway and trunk network (Highway Authorities, Peak Board, Tourist Boards, District Councils) (see **17.22**).

15.22 The provision of additional information at car parks will be considered (see **18.33**) (Peak Board, Tourist Boards, A.A.)

On some cross-park roads, it is realistic to plan for very little commercial traffic.

Introduction

16.1 The bodies with chief responsibility for public transport provision within the Park are the County Councils, the Passenger Transport Executives (PTEs), the bus companies and the British Rail. As local planning authority, the Board is concerned with the overall level of public transport provision within the Park, but financially it is only involved as National Park Authority with recreational services. This chapter is solely concerned with recreational public transport, though all the services supported by the Board are available to local residents. Policies for non-recreational services appear in the Structure Plan.

16.2 The Board's current policies on recreational public transport are contained in the Structure Plan and the 1978 Plan. These policies look to:

(a) Encouraging the integration of public transport facilities and the retention of a minimum service network.

(b) Developing recreational services and ensuring that local community needs are taken into account.

(c) Encouraging the use of public transport as an alternative to the private car and as a means of enabling those without cars to enjoy the Park.

16.3 Progress to date These policies have been followed, and the proposals outlined in the 1978 Plan have largely been implemented. The Board's own contribution has been focussed on support for publicity and marketing initiatives; provision of information about services; financial support for recreation services from the surrounding towns/cities into the Park; and services within the Park itself, especially services run as part of a National Park visitor management scheme or local events.

16.4 Recreational bus services in the Park have improved, and now form a wide network, extensively linked through connecting services, marketed both as a whole and through the widespread use of network tickets. Publicity and use was much extended by the Wayfarer project, an all-day multi-service travel ticket sponsored by the Countryside Commission and PTEs, which aided travel on many bus and train routes, Derbyshire County Council introduced a similar ticket, the Day Discoverer, covering the whole of the county and most operators. However, with the exception of the Bakewell Show Park-and-Ride Scheme, no measures have been taken to reduce the severe traffic delays which are experienced by public transport during the summer months at some points.

16.5 The Transport Act 1985 removed the need for licensing individual routes, and divided the bus network into two parts, commercial (i.e. unsubsidised) and tendered (i.e. subsidised). The major public sector operators, the National Bus Company (NBC) and the municipal operators, were restructured. The NBC was split into its constituent companies and privatised; the municipal operators were formed into companies, wholly owned by the local authorities, but with independent financial structure and responsibility. The impact of this radical change will take some time to become apparent, but in early 1988 the services to and within the National Park seem to have survived reasonably well. There has been no reduction in leisure services, nor has the integrated network been greatly affected. However, timetabling and promotion have been made more difficult, and greater public sector intervention is necessary to maintain the marginal and uneconomic recreational and social services.

16.6 Rail Services within and approaching the Park have also been improved. British Rail built a short new line at Hazel Grove, thus allowing Sheffield — Manchester trains to call at Stockport. This permitted the restructuring of the Hope Valley local sevices, which now run through from Sheffield to Manchester mostly via New Mills, but on Sundays also via Stockport, thus restoring a link broken by the Beeching closures in the late 1960s. There has been much new investment in rolling stock and publicity for the local services, including the re-signing of stations on the Hope Valley line. However there is still a need to examine further improvement to the accessibility of the National Park by rail, for example special promotions from Birmingham where a National Park liaison officer has been appointed.

16.7 In 1987 for the first time in many years, a Sunday service was operated on the Glossop branch partly paid for by Derbyshire County Council. Though not in the Park, Glossop is a major entry point to the Peak District, especially for access the Bleaklow and Kinder Scout. Also in 1987, special services operated into Buxton from various points. Some of these are steam-worked and use the Hope Valley line. Others, chartered by Peak Rail Limited, a railway preservation society, run from New Mills or Hazel Grove via Chinley and Peak Dale. A new halt, called Chee Dale, has been opened at Blackwell Mill by Peak Rail. Although the station is just outside the Park, it gives access onto the Monsal Trail in the Park.

16.8 There are now proposals by Peak Rail for re-opening the Buxton-Matlock railway. Much of this line lies within the Park, including the most spectacular structures. Most of the section within the Park is owned by the Board and used as the Monsal Trail. The Board resolved in 1988 to grant outline planning approval as this is clearly a desirable form of recreational public transport — a passport to splendid scenery for many who would not otherwise see it, a generator of voluntary work and permanent jobs, and a boost for tourism. However, there are detrimental features to the proposal, not least its effect on other visitors, wildlife and residents. These issues formed part of the discussions leading up to the decision on the company's outline planning application, in 1988. Within the life of this Plan, the Board will have to decide whether to grant the company detailed planning

Once there was a railway from Buxton to Matlock . . . Peak Rail hope to revive it.

Map 16.1
Sunday Public Transport 1988

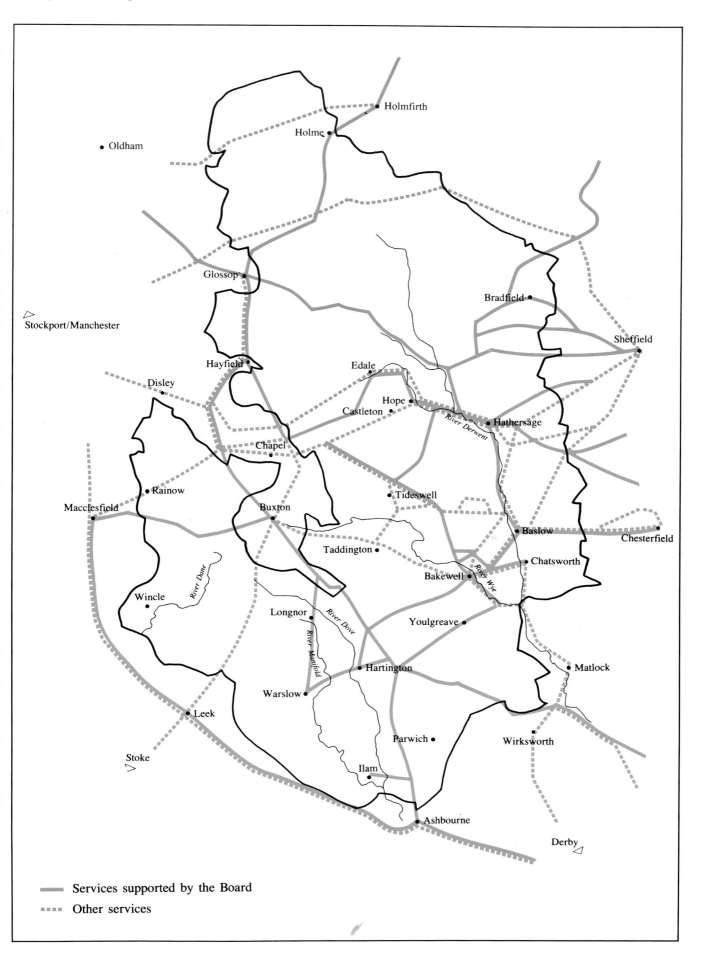

Holmfirth

Holme

Oldham

Glossop

Stockport/Manchester

Hayfield

Disley

Edale

Hope

Castleton

Hathersage

River Derwent

Bradfield

Sheffield

Chapel

Rainow

Macclesfield

Buxton

Tideswell

Baslow

Chesterfield

Taddington

Chatsworth

Bakewell

River Wye

Wincle

River Dane

Longnor

River Dove

Youlgreave

Matlock

Hartington

River Manifold

Warslow

Leek

Parwich

Wirksworth

Stoke

Ilam

Ashbourne

Derby

Services supported by the Board

Other services

approval and, if so, the terms on which it will allow the railway company to use its land.

16.9 The Rural Development Commission has helped set up a network of rural transport advisers with special funding. Their work is focussed on local needs such as community buses or social car schemes. There is little direct connection between these initiatives and recreational activites. The Board assists marginally on social grounds, and in any co-ordination which may arise between social and recreational services.

Approach to future policy

16.10 It is essential to retain a good network of recreational public transport services in the Park, so people can visit the Park without private transport. The Countryside Commission has called for an extension of opportunities for city-dwellers to visit the countryside; the Board supports this policy. In particular the Commission has placed emphasis on the needs of disabled and disadvantaged people (see **14.62-14.69**) The network needs to be better integrated by joint timetabling and ticketing as far as this is possible in a deregulated system.

16.11 Grant-aid to public transport The Board's financial support to specific recreational services — totalling £50,000 in 1987-8 — appears to be essential if a full network of services is to survive in the Park. This support is complementary to the support which County Councils give to tendered services. County Councils and Passenger Transport Authorities (PTAs) have positive policies towards providing services for people in isolated rural areas and for tourism. However, financial pressures are tending to concentrate resources on essential journeys to work, school and shopping services, with Sunday and leisure services being lower priority.

16.12 The Board's work in this field focusses on the National Park as a destination for visitors. It has worked closely with the public transport authorities in and around the Park to decide the services which can be arranged or maintained from city to recreational area. The work cannot be done by either 'end' alone, and joint working should continue. However, the Countryside Commission's proposal to reach a greater cross-section of city dwellers will rest primarily with the city authorities, as the Board has neither the resources nor the expertise to achieve this.

16.13 Map 16.1 shows Sunday public transport services. Those which are supported by the Board, would be at risk of closure if this support were withdrawn. On average, fares cover only one-third of the operating costs of these services, and the Board's support represents an effective subsidy of over £1 per passenger. During the currency of this Plan, efforts should be made to improve patronage, reduce subsidy levels per passenger and persuade the city transport authorities, the Countryside Commission and British Rail to increase their contribution. For example it is no longer easy to get bikes on trains, but a different arrangement of carriages can provide bike storage space on trains with recreational potential.

16.14 Passenger waiting facilities are a vital part of the public transport service. In the main these will continue to be dealt with by District and County Councils, but there may be instances where the Board will need to be involved. The construction of shelters in villages sometimes does not require planning permission, and less expensive shelters can

look out of place in a village setting. Grant-aid is offered to help with the cost of building shelters of traditional design and materials, and as a contribution to community well-being.

16.15 The Wayfarer initiative in the field of recreational public transport publicity and marketing will continue to be supported, especially the network tickets and travel clubs. Distribution of timetable leaflets and other promotional literature will continue: the Board expects to contribute, both financially and in staff time, to these and other public transport marketing ideas.

16.16 When considering proposals for traffic management schemes, the serious delays which are caused to bus services at certain congested places (see **15.8-15.12**) should be taken into account. If possible, public transport should be given priority access to major recreational sites or events, such as the park-and-ride scheme for Bakewell Show.

Objectives
16.17 To support the provision of a reasonably priced and efficient system of public transport to all main recreational areas in the National Park. To ensure that the recreational public transport system is well publicised.

Policies
16.18 The development and recreational use of rail and bus services into and within the Park will be encouraged, both as an alternative to the private car, and to enable disabled and disadvantaged people to visit the National Park (Peak Board, County Councils, PTEs, Bus Companies, District Councils, British Rail, Peak Rail).

16.19 The integration of public transport services within the Park will continue to be encouraged. Local community needs will be considered when routes and timetables are being decided (County Councils, PTEs, Peak Board, District Councils, Bus Companies, British Rail, Peak Rail.

16.20 Grant-aid for public transport services and facilities for recreation purposes, including shelters, will continue to be provided (Peak Board, County Councils, PTEs, Parish & District Councils).

16.21 Publicity and marketing for public transport services will continue to be supported (Peak Board, County Councils, District Councils, PTEs, Bus Companies, British Rail, Peak Rail).

16.22 Serious local delays to bus services will be taken into account when considering proposals for traffic management schemes such as bus lanes and park-and-ride (Peak Board, Highway Authorities).

At least a million visitors a year come to the National Park by public transport.

17 VISITOR ACCOMMODATION AND ATTRACTIONS

Introduction

17.1 The 1986/87 Visitor Survey indicates that staying visitors (as opposed to day visitors) spend over 2 million nights in and around the National Park. Staying visitors spend proportionately much more than day vsitors — £13.50 including accommodation, compared with £3.70, per day. (The relatively low figure of £13.50 is probably explained by the high percentage of campers and caravanners). They thus provide more economic benefit to the area, especially to the place where they stay. This income is the largest single element in the tourist economy of the Park. Figure 17.1 shows the level of use by visitors of different types of accommodation.

17.2 The Structure Plan welcomes the fact that the provision of accommodation for staying visitors can bring farmers an additional source of income. It also favours the conversion of redundant buildings of character, such as farm barns and disused mills, to holiday accommodation. The Structure Plan also contains policies on caravans and camping, including recognition of the growing need to provide for touring caravans, but only where there will be no 'seriously damaging effects on the character of the area'; the provision of temporary peak period sites; and the provision of small 'primitive' sites, catering for only a few tents or caravans at any one time, with minimum facilities consistent with public health.

17.3 The 1978 Plan developed the Structure Plan themes. It encouraged the use of the Park and its surrounding areas by staying visitors. The principles to be followed in this promotion included the need to benefit the local economy; conservation of the particular character and qualities of the various parts of the Park; and encouragement of off-peak and activity holidays. The 1978 Plan also suggested the need for a comprehensive accommodation guide and booking service covering the Peak District as a whole, including the immediate surroundings.

17.4 The 1978 Plan dealt with recreation facilities for staying visitors, and encouraged major facilities in the surrounding town and provision for suitable active pursuits within the Peak District. It suggested that the sources of financial assistance for staying visitor accommodation should be identified and stated that the Board would consider the provision of grant-aid for staying visitor accommodation in order to create extra spaces, help the economy and encourage the re-use of redundant buildings. 12 projects were grant-aided providing 218 bedspaces, but the Board ceased this grant aid when the Tourist Boards began their grant aid scheme.

17.5 In July 1985 the Government report, 'Pleasure, Leisure and Jobs — the Business of Tourism', emphasised the contribution which a vigorous tourism and leisure sector can make to employment across the country and identified a number of 'Action Points'. The report heralded major pressures to convert tourism into jobs.

17.6 As one direct consequence of this government initiative, new types of directional sign for tourist enterprises and small businesses have been devised (see **15.13**). The Board's detailed policies on signing are contained in a signs policy note.

17.7 In the National Park, the 1981 census showed that 45% of the working population is engaged in the service sector.

Many of these jobs are related directly or indirectly to tourism. Employment in leisure and tourism now accounts for over 15% of all jobs in the Park — about half those employed in service industries — and the proportion is rising.

17.8 In the Derbyshire and Staffordshire Rural Development Areas (RDAs), the Board and its partners are tackling problems of unemployment, population loss, declining services and isolation. A wide range of projects has been initiated, including the encouragement of rural and farm tourism as a means of contributing to the ecomony of the area and helping to re-use redundant buildings. An early success of the rural development work was the establishment of the first farm holiday co-operative, the Peak and Moorlands Farm Holidays Group.

17.9 In early 1987, the RDA partners commissioned the East Midlands and Heart of England Tourist Boards to prepare a Tourism Action Programme (TAP) for the areas. The objectives of the TAP were to identify tourism marketing potential and to set out proposals for improving tourism facilities and infrastructure, for stimulating new product development and for effective marketing. All proposals were to be compatible with the environmental constraints of this sensitive area. The TAP was published in late 1987 and formally received and accepted by the sponsoring authorities in 1988. The proposals are set out in an action programme, with indicative costings for each authority within a common strategic framework. It is hoped that it will result in projects being implemented as part of Rural Development Programmes for the period 1989/90 onwards (see **23.25**).

17.10 Some people providing tourist accommodation, including farmers, have expressed concern that the market might reach saturation. To date no evidence has been received of unacceptably low occupancy rates. Farmhouse accommodation is still a small proportion of the total accommodation taken by the Park's visitors.

17.11 The TAP report provides evidence that the share of the market taken by farm, village and countryside based accommodation can be increased further. For example, commercial travellers appear increasingly to seek an alternative to 'standard' hotel accommodation and there is continuing growth of the number of bed nights in camping barns. Until proven otherwise, the Board will assume that accommodation with strong rural qualities can continue to increase its market.

17.12 In 1987 Officers of the Board, the 5 Shire Districts, Cheshire, Derbyshire and Staffordshire County Councils, and the Regional Tourist Boards, initiated a forum to explore and initiate practical ways of joint working on tourism in the Peak District. Potential joint activities include:

(a) A combined accommodation and holiday guide

(b) Central booking service

(c) Joint advertising and marketing initiatives

(d) Expansion of 'Peakland Post', the Board's free newspaper, as a major source of information on the area.

In 1989 a joint accommodation guide, 'Peak District Holidays' is to be published by the East Midlands Tourist Board on behalf of the local authorities. Joint working could develop to embrace the other parts of the National Park and the private sector and could help implement the findings of the TAP in and around the Park.

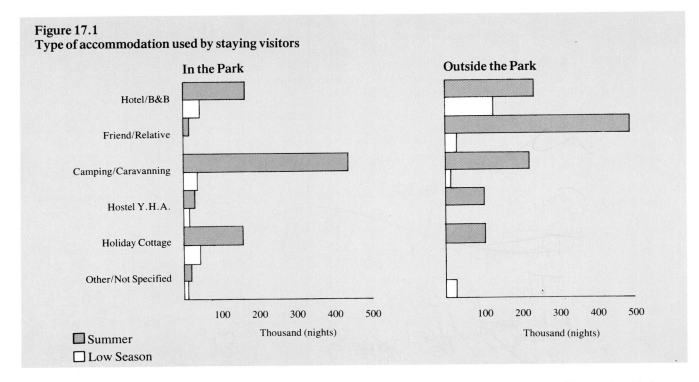

Figure 17.1
Type of accommodation used by staying visitors

In the Park

Outside the Park

Hotel/B&B
Friend/Relative
Camping/Caravanning
Hostel Y.H.A.
Holiday Cottage
Other/Not Specified

100 200 300 400 500

Thousand (nights)

100 200 300 400 500

Thousand (nights)

☐ Summer
☐ Low Season

17.13 In 1986, MAFF introduced grants for tourism projects on farms in the Less Favoured Areas which include all of the Peak District. These are restricted to farms, and are more accessible for smaller projects than those covered by the Tourist Board grants, which have minimum capital investment and demand more thorough justification. In RDAs, the Rural Development Commission offers grants for 25% of the cost of the conversion of redundant buildings to tourist uses (generally excluding accommodation) and operated the 'Accord' scheme of loans for business development. In 1988 MAFF introduced the Farm Diversification Scheme nationwide, providing grant for a range of alternative ventures. It is available to all farmers who derive at least half their income from their agricultural business. In 1988, Government began to review the need for Tourist Board grant-aid. There is some potential overlap between these schemes and the Tourist Boards' grant aid. These three agencies and the Board should therefore co-operate to ensure that each project is supported in the best way, consistent with the relevant policies for the Park.

17.14 The 1978 Plan referred to the visitors need to find 'things to do', additional to the countryside activities considered in Chapter 13. There are many 'attractions' in the National Park for a full and varied holiday. Although secondary to the National Park experience, such activity can be particularly important in encouraging 'off-peak' holidays.

17.15 This chapter deals with the main types of visitor accommodation and attractions as follows:

(a) Hotels, guest houses and inns (**17.23-17.30**).

(b) Camping and Caravanning (**17.31-17.43**).

(c) Self Catering accommodation (**17.44-17.52**).

(d) Farmhouse accommodation (**17.53-17.60**).

(e) Hostels and Residential Field Study Centres (**17.61-17.68**).

(f) Camping barns (**17.69-17.74**).

(g) Visitor attractions (**17.75-17.84**).

17.16 In spite of the increased tempo of the tourism business since the 1978 Plan, the general objective and policy in that document has proved sufficiently robust to remain valid in this Plan.

Objective
17.17 To promote the continued growth of accommodation for staying visitors, and the increased contribution of visitors to the local economy. Such growth should be consistent with the special characteristics of the Park and in direct support of the local economy, the recovery of areas in decline and the use of redundant buildings.

Policies
17.18 Collaboration should continue to secure the selective marketing and development of tourism, in the Park and in the Peak District, between the Board, the Shire County and District Councils, the tourist boards and private sector tourist associations as 'providers' and include the Metropolitan Districts and other agencies as 'users'. (Peak Board, County and District Councils, Tourist Boards, Tourist Associations).

17.19 Subject to the relevant policies in the Structure Plan, the provision of facilities will be supported subject to the application of the following principles:

(a) The conservation of the particular character and qualities of the various parts of the Park as the primary tourist assets of the area.

(b) Prior assessment of the carrying capacity[30] of the area before agreeing new or extended facilities.

(c) The encouragement of the development of accommodation which provides benefit to the local economy.

(d) The encouragement of off-peak holidays to spread the economic benefits and minimise problems of over-use.

---

30 For definition, see **10.25** et seq.

(e) The encouragement of activity holidays which use the National Park's special resources.

(f) The encouragement of the surrounding towns to continue to develop the major centres for large-scale developments and for facilities for visitors.

(g) The use of existing buildings or facilities, sometimes with modest extensions, in preference to new buildings.

(h) A general presumption against the development of new buildings which are out of scale or character with their surroundings.

(Peak Board, Tourist Boards, MAFF, County & District Councils).

17.20 Co-operation between the agencies able to give grant-aid will be sought, to ensure a consistent approach to market assessment, standards and the interpretation of relevant planning and tourism policies (Peak Board, Tourist Boards, MAFF, RDC, County and District Councils).

17.21 Co-operation in the marketing of the Peak District and in the use of information and interpretation services will be encouraged, in particular in relation to a joint accommodation guide and selected accommodation booking services for the National Park and surrounding areas (Peak Board, Tourist Board, County and District Councils).

17.22 The proliferation of unauthorised advertising and directional signs associated with visitor accommodation will be resisted, but favourable consideration will be given to direction signing meeting the criteria in the Board's Signs Policy note (Peak Board, Tourist Boards, County and District Councils, RDC).

Hotels, Guest Houses and Inns

17.23 The policies on this topic in the 1978 Plan stated that new accommodation should generally be in existing buildings. It did not encourage new hotels, except where important buildings are involved or the use is associated with appropriate farm tourism development.

17.24 Since 1978, no new hotels have been built. There has been much extension and refurbishing of accommodation of this type, amounting in some cases to virtual rebuilding. There has also been growth in the bed and breakfast part of the market.

17.25 There are estimated to be 900 bed spaces in hotels and inns in the Park at the time of writing, and many more in the major tourist towns of Buxton, the Matlocks and Ashbourne. The TAP report shows that bedroom occupancy is about 75% in the summer months. This type of visitor accommodation is heavily concentrated in the central swathe of the Park, with little or none in the western and north-eastern sectors. Towns outside the Park may provide the majority of the accommodation, consistent with the recreation strategy (see policy **10.17**).

17.26 Most hotels and inns are reasonably well-known, or advertised or signposted, but some are off the beaten track or in under-used parts of the National Park. In such cases, special promotions might be considered, such as co-operative advertising and activity holiday packages. There are some remaining disused buildings such as old mills which might be used as hotels or inns.

A smile of welcome and of anticipation? Some businesses hope for a greater share of the £75 million spent in the Park each year.

Objective
17.27 To encourage the establishment or improvement of hotels, guest houses and inns especially in areas not already served and where the provision can be made so as to utilise existing under-used or disused buildings or areas.

Policies
17.28 New hotel, guest house or inn accommodation in the Park should be appropriately sited and designed and should normally be related to existing buildings, subject to the recreation strategy policies in Chapter 10 and the Structure Plan. Further development of tourist accommodation outside the Park is encouraged.

17.29 The provision of serviced accommodation in appropriate existing buildings (with modest extension) such as existing pubs or disused buildings will be viewed sympathetically throughout the Park, except in Zone I (see also **17.49-17.52**).

17.30 Improved promotion of existing accommodation will be continued, and grant aid for the provision and improvement of accommodation will respect the Board's policies (Policies **17.28-17.30**: Tourist Boards, Peak Board, District and County Councils).

Camping and Caravanning

17.31 This subject was treated comprehensively in the Structure Plan and in the 1978 Plan. Policies included general site selection criteria; the development of sites outside but within easy reach of the Park; achievement of adequate

18 INFORMATION, INTERPRETATION AND EDUCATION

Introduction

18.1 The Board has long given a high priority to its major ambition to provide the public — visitors and local residents — with opportunities to learn about the Park. Section 86 of the National Parks Act 1949 states that steps should be taken to ensure that people are informed of the extent and means of access to National Parks and the accommodation and facilities available to people wishing to visit the Parks. People need to be able to learn about the history, natural features, flora and fauna of National Parks and the objects of architectural, archaeological and historical interest in them and of opportunities for recreation. Section 12(1) of the Countryside Act 1968 provides for study centres and other facilities for learning about these matters.

18.2 The Board's main achievements in this respect include:

(a) The creation of 7 information 'centres and information points

(b) The establishment of a pioneering and major National Park study centre at Losehill Hall

(c) Wide-ranging publication of books, leaflets and conference reports

(d) On-site information points and information/interpretation boards at villages, car parks and busy places.

(e) An annual tourist newspaper committed to recreational information and a conservation message.

(f) An education and liaison service for youth and school groups.

18.3 This chapter includes proposals for two programme reviews — of interpretation and of education resources and facilities — which will be based on the policies in this Review. The policies and the new programmes may lead to the creation of additional centres, to accommodate either interpretive or information or education objectives or a combination of these. Such objectives should also be married with any other proposal by the Board or its partners to rescue a building or create other facilities.

18.4 This chapter includes sections dealing with:

(a) National Park Identity (**18.5-18.12**)

(b) Information Centres (**18.13-18.25**)

(c) Interpretation (**18.26-18.41**)

(d) Education use of the Park (**18.42-18.58**)

(e) The National Park Study Centre (**18.59-18.72**)

National Park Identity

18.5 Most large organisations recognise the need for a corporate identity, in the form of a single, instantly recognisable symbol and a house style for its literature and products. The National Park is the 'product' with which the public identifies and which the Board and its partners jointly wish to protect, manage and promote. This need was identified in the 1978 Plan. The millstone was recommended as the single, simple symbol required. Its use has been and is accepted by many organisations consulted, and its use was successfully encouraged in many applications to identify the National Park. The millstone symbol, even without words, is now firmly identified in the public mind with the Peak National Park. Commercial companies are using it to sell souvenirs. It has been adopted by the Board as the symbol for the Park and of the Peak Park Joint Planning Board.

18.6 A corporate house style was also established some years ago mainly for signs to the Board's properties, but this has lapsed and different type-faces are used in different applications. It is now proposed to re-establish a new house style. There are many instances in which the Board will publish material either in connection with its own work, or as leader or member of partnerships dealing with National Park affairs. A high standard of co-ordinated graphic design will further reinforce the use of the symbol to establish the unity of work in the Park. This house style would consist of a unified range of type faces, layout, colour and materials.

18.7 The following opportunities will arise for the application of the symbol and house style:

— letterheadings and notices

— the livery of Board vehicles

— all publications

— signs at the Board's properties

— badges worn by field staff

Awareness of National Parks was raised by a campaign, which concluded with the Festival in Chatsworth Park. Efforts to improve the identity of the Park will continue.

Village shopkeepers are a vital part of the information network. Some are contracted to help with tourist information.

- interpretive signs
- village signs
- access points
- exhibitions and presentations
- information centres
- some tourist highway signs
- National Park Boundary signs

18.8 Public relations The work of the Board and the achievement of national park purposes is explained to the public by:

(a) Liaison meetings with the Board's constitutent local authorities

(b) Taking initiatives with and reacting to enquiries from the press, media and publishers

(c) The preparation of press releases

(d) Free factual publications on National Park facilities

(e) Other events, demonstrations and open days to which the public and/or media are invited

(f) Extensive public participation in the preparation of Conservation Area proposals, Area Management Plans, Development Plans and this Review.

(g) A new general booklet 'The National Park and You' on the relationship between the Board's activities and the life and work of the local community, which was delivered to every household just before the public consultation on this Plan.

(h) Other initiatives and activities in information, interpretation and education.

'Public relations' is also an integral part of the wide range of joint actions and consultations described in Chapter 23.

Objective
18.9 To establish a corporate identity for the Park as a product, the Park as a precious resource, and the Park as managed by the Peak Board and its partners.

Policies
18.10 The millstone symbol will be adopted for use by the Board and others, to assist the public to identify with the National Park (Peak Board).

18.11 A co-ordinated house style will be devised and used for all the Board's own publications and signs (Peak Board).

18.12 A good relationship with the public nationally and locally will be sought in all the Board's activities (Peak Board).

Information Centres

18.13 Information Centres play an important part in helping visitors to the Park and carrying out the requirement of Section 86 of the National Parks Act. They are set up and run by the Board; or by other authorities and organisations for example at Lyme Park, Longshaw Estate and Ilam run by the National Trust. The Trust also has unmanned centres in Edale and Milldale. The Board seeks links with the Centres run by

Information centres see more customers each year. Income is also rising and helps pay for their role in interpretation.

other organisations, aiming to explain to visitors the identity of the National Park as a whole and the basic aims of the Board.

18.14 The Board manages four main Information Centres — at Bakewell (run jointly with Derbyshire Dales District Council), Castleton, Edale, and Fairholmes in the Upper Derwent. It also runs a mobile information Centre which visits villages and special events during the summer season. Information Points are open, mainly during summer weekends, at Hartington and Torside in Longdendale.

18.15 The number of visitors to the information centres has increased steadily in recent years, from about 200,000 in 1981 to over 300,000 in 1987. Income from sales at the Centres is also rising steadily, from about £20,000 in 1981 to nearly £69,000 in 1986.

18.16 Information staff answer thousands of telephone enquiries each year and provide additional services such as accommodation booking, the caravan advisory service, daily weather forecasts, talks, videos, and slide shows. The activities of the local community are reflected in the provision of information about accommodation and local events. 25% of visitors use one or more of the various written forms of information distributed by information staff (Visitor Survey 1986/7, see Table 18.1).

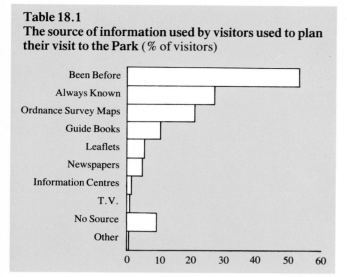

Table 18.1

The source of information used by visitors used to plan their visit to the Park (% of visitors)

18.17 The Board aims to achieve a 'rolling programme' of updating and refurbishing Information Centres and displays. It is intended, staff resources permitting, that the centres which are open all or most of the year should all become Tourist Information Centres (as Bakewell already is), and should provide the services (in particular accommodation booking) which that designation implies.

18.18 A network of information centres should be developed in and around the Park, to provide the basic information needs of visitors where they enter, cross or stop in the National Park in the largest numbers. This network is complementary to that needed for the interpretation of local themes or resources, described in the following part of this chapter. The Board intends to carry out research into where new centres might be needed; to work with and influence other organisations and bodies which also run Information Centres in and around the Peak District; and to continue to provide the back-up services needed. A new centre including an information point is, for example to be developed as part of the use of a barn at Langsett village. The Board intends to look closely at the range of publications and other media provided, to improve the marketing of products and to increase income from such sales. New methods for the distribution of information by electronic means should be adopted as they become suitable for use at information centres.

18.19 Village shops present an opportunity to provide information to the visitor. Shopkeepers are already an informal source of advice. The viability of the village shop can be improved by a contract with the Board to supply National Park information material on a formal basis.

Objective
18.20 To help visitors and local people to find out about the Park, to understand how it works and to respect the place and its people.

Policies
18.21 Information centres at Bakewell, Castleton, Edale and Fairholmes, the mobile information centre and the Hartington and Torside information points will be maintained and improved (Peak Board, District Councils, Tourist Boards).

18.22 Liaison and reciprocal working will be maintained with other agencies providing information centres in and around the Park, to persuade them to assist in distributing National Park information and to distribute their information as appropriate to further policies for the Park and surrounding areas (Peak Board, District Councils, Tourists Boards).

18.23 The sales and marketing of National Park publications and products through information centres will be improved (Peak Board).

18.24 New information centres or information points will be proposed where visitor numbers are high and where information needs have not yet been met (Peak Board).

18.25 Selected village shopkeepers will be invited to contract to carry National Park and tourist information (Peak Board, Peak District Rural Shopkeepers Association, District Councils, Tourist Boards).

Interpretation

18.26 The word 'interpretation' is used in this Plan to embrace action designed to help visitors to arrive at a better understanding of the National Park, and of the features and aspects which create the special landscape of the National Park. In the 1978 Plan, interpretation proposals included interpreting local themes at visitor centres at Bakewell (local history), Magpie Mine (lead mining history), Dovedale (limestone dales), Millers Dale (railway history), North Lees Estate (farming), Chatsworth (farming and forestry), and the history of the water industry (no location). Also proposed were information boards at viewpoints and features; guided walks; publications; talks and lectures; and signs.

18.27 Few of the proposed new interpretive visitor centres have been established, although much work has been done by other agencies such as Peak District Mines Historical Society and Bakewell Historical Society. Some proposals for new Centres have been investigated and deferred on policy or practical grounds. Programmes of illustrated talks and videos take place at Bakewell and Edale Information Centres, and talks are given to a large number of visiting and local groups and organisations. About 60 interpretive boards have been prepared and put up on site and the Visitor Survey shows that these are used by twice as many people as use Information Centres. A good deal of interpretation is carried out through publications, and through displays and other media at InformationCentres. Interpretation is also carried out in other ways, including the use of portable exhibition material and guided walks.

18.28 The scope for interpretation within the Park is great, and lends itself to a wide range of exciting possibilities. Interpretation of aspects of historical and archaeological interest can be carried out through living history events, which try to bring the past to life to make it more enjoyable and understandable. The interpretation of nature conservation interests offers a strong challenge and opportunity, particularly to gain popular respect for sensitive habitats or species and thus improve their chances of survival. The Board's own estates should be interpreted, to lead by example. The full range of opportunities is set out in paragraph **18.31** below. On the other hand trends show that guided walks are beoming less popular. It is no longer necessary for the Board to produce literature covering every aspect of National Park life. In the fields of natural history for example, there are many good privately-published alternatives.

Living history — "t' owd man" describes a lead miner's life at Mandale Mine.

18.29 The need to provide basic information where visitor numbers are high is referred to in the previous section (see **18.18**). The second need is to provide the means to interpret local resources at visitor centres. These should be at a scale appropriate to the resource and the capacity of the site and surrounding area. The projects listed in the 1978 Plan are still relevant, and new proposals will arise, such as interpretation of archaeology at Roystone Grange near Ballidon, and the Bronte story at North Lees.

18.30 Publications should concentrate on those specialist aspects with a strong interpretive or conservation bias and which deal with open-air recreation as part of a visitor management scheme for a specific area. Publications will range from those which are highly popular and can generate income to help support the information service, to those which should be published and distributed free of charge.

18.31 Since the 1978 Plan the Board has worked with other authorities in a number of joint area management studies. One result has been the production of Visitors' Guides for valleys with reservoirs including Dove Stone, Goyt Valley, Macclesfield Forest, Upper Derwent and Upper Longdendale. These guides have been jointly prepared and funded by the authorities involved in the studies.

18.32 The guides are specifically designed to inform people who have already arrived or are considering a visit to the area, to help them appreciate and respect its qualities. They are available free of charge within the area — from an information point, a leaflet dispenser, or a patrolling ranger. They are also available on request from public information places in built-up areas nearby, or from the offices of the authorities which produce them. The guides are not however widely distributed outside the relevant area, so as to avoid increasing the use of areas already under pressure.

18.33 Interpretation Plan A major task is to undertake an overall review of the Board's practice and produce an Interpretation Plan based on the policies contained in this Plan. It will co-ordinate the following elements both of interpretation and information for people of varying backgrounds:

(a) A review of existing publications, and proposals for new ones to fill gaps in the range of subjects covered

(b) Interpretation within the proposals in area plans

(c) A review of guided walks and talks

(d) 'Living History' at selected sites

(e) Further on-site interpretive signs and information boards at villages, car parks, features, resorts, trails and inside libraries, Youth Hostels, conference centres and hotels, but not generally, in more remote countryside (Zones I and II see **10.28**).

(f) Videos on specific topics for loan or sale and for use at information centres

(g) Marketing of publications and souvenirs

(h) A programme for updating existing information centres and points and for creating new ones, with core information and special interpretive material appropriate to each one

(i) Interpretive material at specialist centres or as part of the service at information or study centres

(j) Meeting the needs of disabled and disadvantaged people

(k) The guidance and promotion of acceptable recreational activities.

Objective
18.34 To maintain and increase imaginative ways of interpreting the National Park for the benefit of visitors and local people.

18.35 An Interpretation plan will be prepared and implemented, including the elements listed at **18.33** (Peak Board).

18.36 The policies for interpretation in the 1978 Plan will continue to apply:

(a) To encourage respect for the environmental qualities of the Park

(b) To encourage respect for the social and economic life of the Park — in particular agriculture and forestry interests

(c) To encourage forms of visitor use appropriate to the different parts of the Park

(d) To supply information interpreting the life, landscape and wildlife resources of the Park both for general interest and for specific education purposes. (see **6.48**).

(Peak Board, Tourist Boards, National Trust, HBMC, Museum operators, County and District Councils).

18.37 Priority will be given in the Board's own publications to the interpretation of conservation policy and practice, area management schemes, local recreation opportunities, walks and villages leaflets, and recreational and local community advice (Peak Board).

18.38 Efforts will continue to be made to integrate information about the Park so that the many agencies involved can supply consistent material (Countryside Commission, District and County Councils, Tourist Boards, National Trust, NCC, Water Authorities, Forestry Commission, CLA).

18.39 New interpretive visitor centres will be established on or near sites with special characteristics, in scale with the carrying capacity of the area (Peak Board, Tourist Boards).

18.40 Leaflets which supply simple information or carry a strong National Park message will continue to be prepared and supplied on request free of charge (Peak Board).

18.41 Visitor guides to various areas of the National Park (see Chapters 24-47) will continue to be prepared and issued free of charge. Guides for areas which have reached or exceeded their carrying capacity (see 10.30) will not be distributed widely (Peak Board, District and County Councils).

Educational use of the Park

18.42 Introduction Amongst the earliest advocates of the establishment of National Parks were people keen to further their interest in a wide variety of nature studies, such as the nineteenth century workers' education associations. These bodies, in their modern form, now provide countryside education in the Park as do many other bodies and the country's schools and colleges. Today the Park contains 57 study centres operated by educational, recreational and religious organisations taking advantage of the Park's extensive natural educational resources.

18.43 Heavy use is made of the resources of the Park for education, both by the Board and others. Additional study centres are welcomed provided there is no adverse impact on the Park, and encourages new centres as a use for redundant buildings (see 17.67-17.88). The various users include school groups, youth organisations, adult education and activity/educational holidays.

18.44 This section of this chapter deals with the Board's involvement in the development and co-ordination of the educational use of the Park, mainly through its own Youth and Schools Service. This is based at Losehill Hall which was opened by the Board in 1972 as the first National Park Study Centre in the United Kingdom. The next section deals with the continuing use and operation of the National Park Study Centre itself.

18.45 The 1978 Plan contained policies proposing the continued development of national park studies based at Losehill Hall; short residential courses for the public and day use for students and specialists; promotion of facilities for study at appropriate information centres; links with other centres; and efforts to encourage considerate use of the National Park's natural resources, to respect local residents and businesses and to improve access to sites of special educational interest. A substantial proportion of the Board's resources have been applied to this, and most of these proposals have been carried out or established.

18.46 The Youth and Schools Service offers a wide range of facilities to cater for both the Youth and Schools groups within the Park and the estimated one million visitors who come in such groups to the Park. Liaison is maintained (through meetings, courses and publications) with 'enablers' (advisers, group leaders and teachers). Advice and information is made available through the Youth and Schools

Catch 'em young! River dipping — part of children's environmental education at Losehill Hall.

Liaison Officer and through use of the resource rooms at Bakewell Information Centre and Losehill Hall.

18.47 Recent radical changes in the school curriculum, including the implementation of the GCSE examinations, have placed increasing demands on this service. Reference in examination syllabuses to specific development issues within the Park have resulted in an increasing number of requests for information on these issues.

18.48 The Youth and Schools Service also caters for day visit groups by offering a range of educational programmes including talks, guided walks, farm visits and field work. Since the appointment of a Day Visits Organiser, the number of participants in the Day Visits programme has increased from 8,479 in 1983 to 17,310 in 1987. The anticipated and continued growth of numbers on day visits has been welcome and has given a stimulating breadth to the Board's educational programmes. However, in recent years, the changes in educational use by groups have created a greater demand for staff-intensive activities, especially fieldwork. As this curriculum-led trend continues more expert seasonal and part-time staff are needed.

18.49 Educational bases have been established to cater for these day visit groups at Bakewell and Edale Information Centres; and at Ilam Hall, in co-operation with the National Trust. These bases have the double advantage of providing an educational facility in other areas of the Park, closer to the educational resources in the field, and of reducing pressure for space at Losehill Hall.

18.50 With the growth in the number of educational groups using the National Park, there is a need to formulate an educational programme for the Park to alleviate pressures on over-used and sensitive sites; and to identify alternative sites in accordance with the zoning policy and carrying capacity of different parts of the Park described in Chapter 10. Such a programme will be dependent upon liaison with operators of other field centres and educational user groups in and around the National Park. It will draw on the results of a proposed survey of educational users designed to identify the whereabouts and educational needs of groups visiting or working in the Park. In Derbyshire within the Park, it will also draw upon the Derbyshire Environmental Education Resources Guide. New 'satellite' educational bases will be sought, ranging from simple resource rooms in existing buildings to new independent or shared buildings such as the multiple use proposed at Langsett Barn.

18.51 The Dark Peak is one of only eight areas in England and Wales which is considered to be sufficiently remote to be suitable for use by groups undertaking the Duke of Edinburgh's Gold Award Expedition. All such groups must notify their expedition to the Peak District Expedition Panel. In order to ensure that such groups have up-to-date information, the Board has voluntarily provided secretarial assistance to the Panel since 1968. During this time the numbers of groups visiting the Park has increased substantially. In 1986 over 300 expeditions were notified and a further 32 requested assessment by Panel members. This service is being reviewed with Derbyshire County Council, so as to operate it more effectively.

18.52 The long-term maintenance and development of good relations with the local community in the Park is dependent on a sound presentation of the environmental issues and of the Board's role in conservation. This can be achieved through a structured educational policy for youth and schools within the

National Park, which reinforces the links between the local community and their environment. The Conservation Action Project (CAP) and the Farm Community Link (FCL) are schemes (sponsored by the Board, using MSC funds) which have brought children into contact with farming practice, or enabled them to carry out conservation projects. They have already provided a successful pioneering method involving most of the schools in the National Park. Additional ways of funding and supporting these local projects should be explored.

Objective
18.53 To provide advice and educational facilities for local youth and school groups and many other group visits, in order to ensure wise use of the Park and understanding and care for the countryside, and to minimise conflict with local people.

Policies
18.54 A detailed survey of the existing use of the National Park by educational groups will be undertaken. The survey results will be used to formulate measures designed to alleviate pressure on over-used or sensitive sites and identify alternatives; improve access by negotiation with landowners; and encourage considerate use of the Park's resources in liaison with the operators of other field study centres in and around the Park (Peak Board, Education Authorities, CLA).

18.55 The Youth and Schools Service will continue to respond to the demands of visiting groups, in liaison with constituent and neighbouring education authorities and other organisations concerned with educational opportunities in the National Park, particularly in promoting in-service training courses for group leaders using the Park (Peak Board, Education Authorities).

18.56 The Day Visits Service will be further developed by improving the teaching facilities at Losehill Hall and at centres such as North Lees Hall, Ilam Hall, Langsett and at the Board's Information Centres (Peak Board, National Trust).

18.57 Conservation education projects will be developed for schools within the Park in partnership with other authorities and organisations (Peak Board, Local Education Authorities).

18.58 New 'satellite' education centres will be sought either as independent projects or sharing with interpretive, information or other visitor facilities where resources are underused, or in redundant buildings (Peak Board).

The National Park Study Centre

18.59 Between 1972 and 1987, more than 46,000 people attended 1,725 residential courses at Losehill Hall. The annual programmes cover a wide range of subjects in the natural arts and sciences, from landscape photography to mining history. The residential centre has gained a strong local, regional, national and international reputation.

18.60 Residential courses have developed to meet the demands of three main user groups:

(a) The **General Public** who increasingly seek to study more specialised themes: there has been a growth in demand, particularly from older age groups and groups seeking active recreation.

The education of countryside staff is part of Losehill Hall's nationwide role, supported by the Countryside Commission.

Even younger local children, invited to learn through play — Project Squirrel at Losehill Hall.

(b) **Educational Groups**, a volatile market which has recently decreased, but in which return to former levels or beyond can be expected.

(c) **Countryside Staff** from all over the UK and beyond, among whom there has been a steady growth in demand for training courses.

18.61 Losehill Hall also acts as an important centre for innovation. Pilot courses for new initiatives are run, for example, management training for UK 2000 conservation action supervisors. Conferences, seminars and workshops are organised on topical countryside issues, for example assisting local authority planning staff with the demands of GCSE.

18.62 In response to the need for a co-ordinated programme of training for the Board's own staff and for other countryside officers, the Board appointed a full-time Training Officer in 1987, based at Losehill Hall. An expansion of the existing programme of residential training courses for countryside staff is also planned, in consultation with national and regional bodies such as the Countryside Commission and constituent local authorities.

18.63 A barn in the grounds of Losehill Hall has been converted to provide simple overnight accommodation and a central booking service is provided at the Hall, as part of the camping barns project (see **17.69-17.74**).

Objective
18.64 To promote conservation education and training programmes on National Park themes for visitors, local people and countryside staff; to influence visiting groups to use the National Park wisely as an educational resource; and to maximise learning, understanding and enjoyment.

Policies
18.65 A comprehensive programme of conservation education and training will be maintained and developed including residential courses and conferences and day visits, in liaison with youth, school and local community groups (Peak Board).

18.66 Residential courses will be continued and revised through innovation and a greater emphasis will be given to the provision of training courses, issue-based studies for educational groups, and active conservation-orientated, specialised courses for the general public (Peak Board, Education Authorities).

18.67 Links with other study centres will be maintained. Other agencies will be encouraged to ensure that their programmes reflect the Board's policies (Peak Board, Education Authorities).

18.68 An effective marketing strategy and public image will be promoted in order to project the National Park Study Centre into the 1990s, to review deficiencies on the premises, ensure prudent capital investment and to continue the sound administrative, financial, catering and domestic operation (Peak Board).

18.69 The training needs of the Board's staff and other countryside staff will be assessed and resources provided to plan, initiate and develop an effective training programme (Peak Board).

18.70 Specialist training for countryside staff nationwide will be developed (Peak Board, Countryside Commission).

18.71 The central booking service for the camping barns project will be maintained (see **17.73**) (Peak Board, camping barn owners).

18.72 The Board's own camping barn at Losehill Hall will be maintained (Peak Board).

Introduction

19.1 The Board's ranger service operates primarily in the field, in close contact with visitors and with those who live and work in the Park. Rangers are supported by a professional and administration staff at Aldern House with whom they have radio-telephone contact and regular meetings. The service works alongside ranger or warden services provided by other agencies, such as the National Trust, the Water Authorities and neighbouring County Councils, and the various emergency services including police, fire, mountain and cave rescue.

19.2 The ranger service is well-placed to identify and manage a wide variety of practical works needed to improve the Park particularly the footpath network. Included in the ranger service are the footpaths officer (who oversees much of the work outlined in Chapter 11) and the organiser of the Peak Park Conservation Volunteers.

19.3 This chapter is divided into two parts dealing firstly with the ranger services in the Park, and secondly with voluntary conservation work.

Ranger Services

19.4 The functions of the Park's ranger service are still substantially as set out in the 1978 Plan and are updated as follows:

(a) Providing information interpretation and friendly advice to visitors with a view to adding to their enjoyment, appreciation and understanding of the Park

(b) Maintaining a presence in areas of the Park popular with visitors, to resolve immediate problems created by visitor pressure, and to monitor levels of visitor use

(c) By agreement with owners and tenants, providing assistance with general protection to property and livestock, advising visitors of the Country Code, and, where necessary, liaising with police

(d) Carrying out practical countryside work such as waymaking and footpath maintenance, and wildlife and heritage conservation, monitoring and interpretation

(e) Carrying out agreed management work and byelaw enforcement in areas subject to access agreements or other management schemes

(f) Providing search, rescue and aid throughout the Park, in collaboration with the emergency services as required in any particular situation

(g) Maintaining a close working liaison with farmers, keepers, water bailiffs and other agencies operating within the Park

(h) Developing contacts with the other sectors of the local community, including schools and parish councils

(i) Assisting in the development and implementation of management proposals by other sections of the Board's staff.

19.5 To carry out these functions, the Board's ranger service divides the Park into four districts, each headed by a district ranger. The districts are in turn sub-divided into areas, each managed by an area ranger who co-ordinates the work of part-time and volunteer rangers — see Map 19.1. The chief ranger, district rangers, volunteers organiser and footpaths

officer, together with clerical support, co-ordinate the overall deployment of the service from Aldern House.

19.6 A number of other agencies also provide ranger or warden services in the Park. these include County Councils, Water Authorities, the Forestry Commission, the National Trust, the Nature Conservancy Council, County Nature Conservation Trusts and private estates. Co-operation is maintained with and between these various agencies.

19.7 The 1978 Plan marked a change in attitude which seeks to balance the patrolling, byelaw enforcement image of rangers with a more outgoing positive attitude, emphasising contact with visitors and local people throughout the Park, and based on the list of tasks set out above. This has been achieved by extra resources, without any reduction in the commitment to the contract to maintain access agreements. The Plan proposed negotiation with other services to ensure a consistent approach within the Park.

19.8 Since then, the ranger service has both expanded and diversified. The Park ranger service is now operated jointly in certain areas with the two water authorities, North West and Severn Trent, and with the Forestry Commission. Full-time and part-time rangers operate under a contract agreement. Community programme teams, managed by field rangers on behalf of other authorities, deal with footpath obstruction and the enormous backlog of repair work to footpaths (see Chapter 11 for a fuller account of work on the public path network).

19.9 Mountain rescue and cave rescue services are co-ordinated by the police through controllers nominated by the Peak District Mountain Rescue Organisation (PDMRO) and the Derbyshire Caving Organisation (cave rescue) as appropriate. The ranger service plays an active role in rescue work and provides controllers and members of mountain rescue teams.

19.10 For the future, during the period of this Review, there is a recognised need to further refine the work of the ranger service and its relationship to the other services operating in the Park. In particular it may be appropriate to consider the relative priorities of the various functions listed in paragraph **19.4**, according to the different problems and opportunities of each ranger district. The service could increase the level at which it works with other staff and other agencies to improve the amount and quality of interpretation for visitors. Discussions are in hand in other areas of the Park for more joint ranger services, which will further realise the overall

The helpful approach is as important as the Rangers' basic duties in bye-law enforcement.

Map 19.1
Ranger Service Organisation

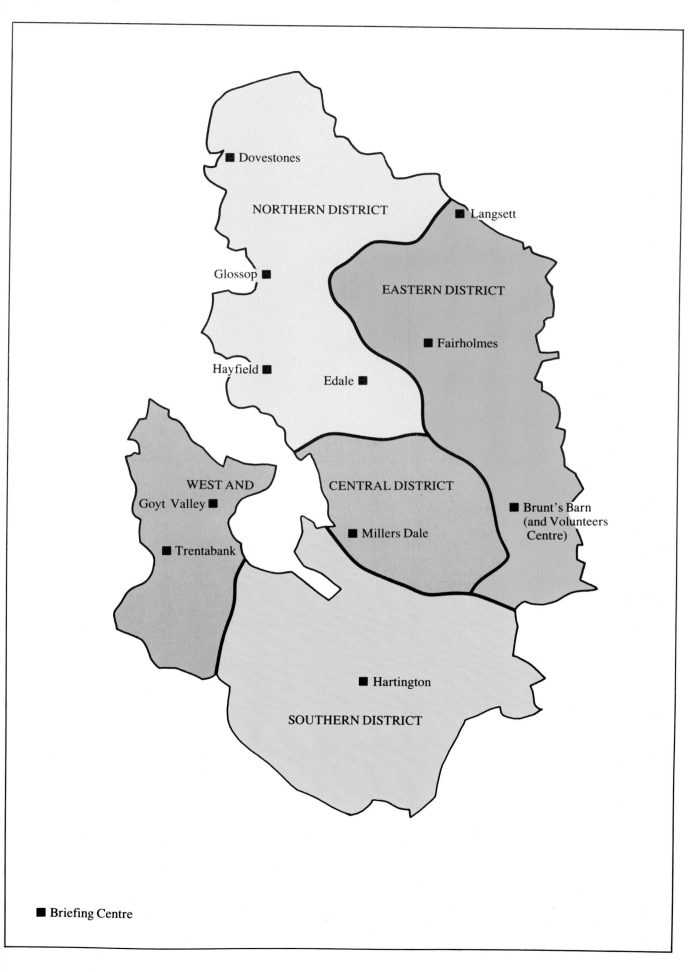

Dovestones

NORTHERN DISTRICT

Langsett

Glossop

EASTERN DISTRICT

Fairholmes

Hayfield

Edale

WEST AND
Goyt Valley

CENTRAL DISTRICT

Brunt's Barn
(and Volunteers
Centre)

Trentabank

Millers Dale

Hartington

SOUTHERN DISTRICT

■ Briefing Centre

The ranger service works closely with the emergency services, applying joint skills in wild country.

objective of a service for the Park (see Chapters 28, 29 and 30). As mentioned at **12.17**, the scope and nature of access byelaws may need to be reviewed, and further patrolling may be needed.

19.11 A review of the Board's own ranger service was completed in early 1988. The objective and policies set out below will form the basis for the ranger services in the Park.

Objective

19.12 To maintain an effective, well trained Park-wide ranger service, capable of handling emergencies, day-to-day contact with visitors and residents, and undertaking practical countryside work.

Policies

19.13 The Park ranger service will continue to be developed on the lines defined above, and priorities in their activities will be identified in relation to the character of the different Districts (Peak Board).

19.14 The Board will seek to maintain and where possible expand the liaison and contract arrangements between its own rangers and those of other agencies to provide a better-integrated and more comprehensive ranger service for the Park (Peak Board, Water Authorities, Forestry Commission, National Trust, County and District Councils, NCC).

Voluntary Conservation Work

19.15 The past decade has seen rapid growth of popular interest in voluntary work, helping to conserve the natural beauty of the countryside through direct practical conservation projects. Three main groups operate in the National Park — Peak Park Conservation Volunteers (PPCV); British Trust for Conservation Volunteers (BTCV); and the National Trust Volunteers on their own land holdings.

19.16 The 1978 Plan encouraged the promotion of voluntary conservation work throughout the Park (which has later come to include nature reserve management, erosion control and archaeological work) and the establishment of a volunteers' base with accommodation. The organisation of volunteers has concentrated on the provision of skills training, practical opportunities for voluntary work and companionship for conservationists, under the 'umbrella' of PPCV. PPCV draws from local conservation groups, sporting, educational or armed forces organisations, job creation schemes, handicapped or socially disadvantaged groups and considerable numbers of individuals.

19.17 Since 1977, PPCV has grown 3-fold from less than 1,000 workdays per year to well over 3,000 in recent years. During that time other conservation bodies operating in the Park, such as the National Trust, County Nature Conservation Trusts and the NCC have also increased their yearly use of conservation volunteers from several hundred to nearly 5,000, in several cases on the Board's initiative. With widely-published programmes of conservation work, there has been little need to actively recruit volunteers in recent years.

19.18 The PPCV expansion has been accomplished by the development of a centralised, trained team of part-time ranger supervisors working at weekends, supplemented by efforts from the Board's ranger service and other members of the Board's staff where appropriate.

19.19 The opening in 1981 of the Brunt's Barn Volunteers Centre, a self-catering hostel designed to accommodate 12 people, has been a great success with local conservation groups and has added significantly to the numbers of motivated and experienced volunteers tackling projects in the Park. This facility has helped to consolidate the joint PPCV/BTCV Summer Workcamps started in the early '80s, which helped to tackle projects such as the Dovedale Footpath restoration scheme. Recently groups from overseas have established joint programmes of work with PPCV, and international volunteers are increasingly active in the Park.

Over 8,000 workdays each year help with a backlog of conservation and other work in the countryside.

19.20 Controlled expansion of voluntary conservation work has been secured in the following ways:

(a) The volunteers organiser's supervision team was joined until August 1988 by an MSC-funded Conservation Action Team undertaking projects of local community and wildlife conservation value. It is hoped that this can continue under the Training Commission's (TC) Employment Training Scheme, or by other means.

(b) With grant-aid from the Board and others, BTCV have appointed a senior field officer based in Wirksworth, to develop conservation volunteer work in the southern half of the Park, mainly on privately owned land and working in close partnership with the volunteer organiser's team. (The field officer covers the whole of Derbyshire.)

(c) Organisations such as County Nature Conservation Trusts, NCC, and Water Authorities have developed their own voluntary programmes. A main thrust of expansion of volunteers work is at 'grass roots' level helping rangers, land managers and owners to make contact and work with groups local to their areas. This is already proving successful in the western and more remote northern parts of the Park.

19.21 However, further growth is being stemmed by the lack of resources on the part of these organisations to set-up or fund the increasing amount of work suitable for volunteers. Demand among volunteers has increased further recently, as people offer to help in growing numbers. This has spread the conservation work programmes throughout the year, 7 days a week.

19.22 The overall expansion of conservation action is proving a valuable asset in managing the Board's growing estates, especially with respect to wildlife conservation and protection, and in tackling conservation work elsewhere in the Park. The work experience and education gained by these volunteers makes practical conservation action one of the Board's major contributions to social well-being, as well as enhancing the natural beauty of the area itself. Volunteer work is to some degree catalytic encouraging landowners and farmers to undertake consrvation work themselves, with the benefit of grant-aid where applicable. Volunteers should not deprive local people or contractors of paid work.

19.23 The Board is conscious that a large amount of the work which volunteers undertake requires ongoing maintenance. To undertake remedial work with volunteers and then to see the work deteriorate through lack of maintenance is a waste of resources, and demoralising.

19.24 Future improvement of the conservation action process should concentrate on:

(a) Continued refinement of the opportunity for voluntary work as a 'countryside experience' developing rural skills and knowledge, and as a social and cultural exchange

(b) Encouraging the 'clients' — public and private landowners — to commit themselves to maintaining project work wherever reasonable

(c) Further refinement of the processes by which tasks are identified, allocated, equipped and supervised

(d) A continued search for sponsors for initial tasks, and adoption of sites to ensure continued maintenance

(e) Clarifying in all projects who carries the insurance and maintenance liabilities.

19.25 The range of tasks, the number of organisations involved, the number of sources of funds, the sheer number of projects and the need for effective maintenance follow-up may imply the need for a more clearly declared organisation or forum of interested parties to ensure best future use of resources.

Objectives

19.26 To maintain an efficient, adequately equipped and carefully supervised conservation volunteer force; and to pursue the work programmes of this major force in partnership with other countryside user and conservation groups.

Policies

19.27 A conservation volunteers forum should be considered which would encourage, nurture and co-ordinate local, national and international interest in practical conservation action within the Park (Peak Board, BTCV, National Trust, TC, County Nature Conservation Trusts).

19.28 Projects for voluntary conservation action will be identified, organised and equipped in long-term rolling work programmes throughout the Park (Peak Board, BTCV, National Trust, TC).

19.29 Voluntary conservation work initiatives will be supported, and technical advice and expertise will be provided to managers or organisations involved in conservation of the countryside throughout the Park (Peak Board).

19.30 In considering the use of volunteers for conservation projects, the possibility of the work being undertaken on a paid basis by local people or contractors will first be assessed. Volunteers should not be used if paid employment is a practical alternative within a reasonable term of years (Peak Board).

19.31 In considering volunteer projects, the longer term maintenance commitment will be critically examined. Projects should not be started without reasonable assurance that maintenance will be adequately carried out (Peak Board, CLA).

RURAL DEVELOPMENT

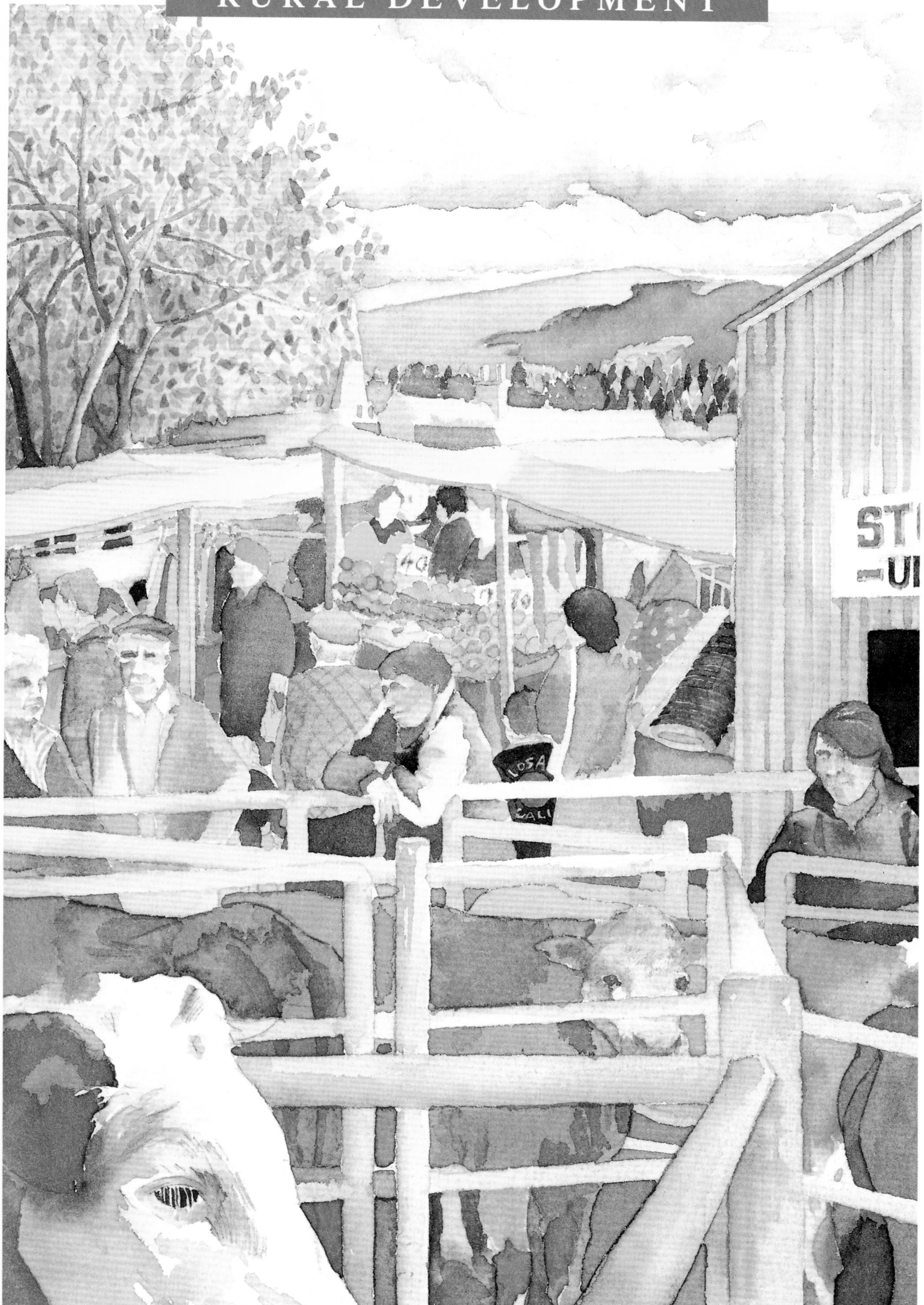

20 A STRATEGY FOR RURAL DEVELOPMENT

Introduction

20.1 The Peak Board is both a national park authority and a local planning authority. The Countryside Act of 1968 requires the Board to 'have regard to the needs of agriculture and forestry and to the economic and social interests of the local community'. The Town and Country Planning Acts confer the duties and provide the powers to plan for the proper development and use of land in the public interest.

20.2 The National Park is designated for its landscape, wildlife and recreational importance, but it also contains about 38,000 residents, 100 villages, 2,000 farms, 14,000 households and 12,000 jobs. The Board's strategic policies set out principally in the Structure Plan seek to support this population, to resist too much inward migration, and to make provision for the growth and change of the resident community.

20.3 The needs of the rural community, combined with demands for resources from the regional and national economy, generate a continuing need for rural development. The main local needs are for additional housing, employment and community facilities, and the improvement and maintenance of existing premises. There are also continuing demands for minerals, water storage, traffic across the Park and other demands from the country's industrial population in the surrounding lowlands.

20.4 The needs of the local community are often complementary to the needs of conservation and recreation. For example, farm businesses can be rewarded for meeting the national need for attractive scenery as well as for producing food. Staying visitors are attracted, amongst other things, by flower-rich fields and well-maintained stone walls, and can be accommodated in premises which might otherwise be neglected.

20.5 This Chapter describes the development planning system and sets out the overall Rural Development Strategy. Chapter 21 deals in more detail with housing, employment and services within the Park. Chapter 22 describes the basic pressures on the Park from outside — the regional and national needs.

The Development Planning System

20.6 The main planning document for the Peak Park is the Structure Plan. It was prepared during the mid 1970's, submitted for approval in 1976, and approved by the Secretary of State in 1979. It was designed for a life of about 15 years, and is thus due to be reviewed by 1991. The Structure Plan is part of the national development plan system, which also includes local plans. The only local plan which has been prepared is the Bakewell District Plan also due to be reviewed by 1991. However, in view of the recent pressures for development and for the resolution of traffic and other problems in Bakewell, a working party will be re-convened to discuss those issues of most urgent concern within the context of the District Plan. No further local plans are proposed. Government has recently suggested (1988) greater use of local plans (see **24.10-24.12**). The housing, employment and minerals content of the Structure Plan were not dealt with as main topics in the 1978 Plan.

20.7 The status of Development Plans and National Park Plans differ. Development Plans are prepared under the Town and Country Planning Act; go through a formal public participation process; and require the approval of the Secretary of State for the Environment before their policies become operative. The land use policies in the Development Plan are strengthened by this formal approval. By contrast National Park Plans are statutory documents produced and reviewed in accordance with the provisions of the Local Government Act 1972; contain policies which are formulated following wide consultations with many partners and the public, the Countryside Commission and District Councils; and are submitted to the Secretary of State for the Environment for information only, not needing to be formally approved.

20.8 The key to the inter-relationship of the National Park Plan and the Structure Plan rests in the Local Government Act of 1972, which states that NPP's should set out national park authority policies 'for the management of the park and for the exercise of the functions exercisable by them as respects the park'. Those functions include the local planning function.

20.9 A straight summary or reprint of Structure Plan policies is not, however, considered appropriate in this Plan. The imminent review of the Structure Plan itself would mean that such a summary would be out of date for most of the life of this Plan. A reprint of the policies is however available from the National Park Office.

20.10 The Structure Plan has provided the backbone and the strength for the Board's work — appropriate rural development has been encouraged particularly in areas of rural decline, and inappropriate development has been refused permission, or modified by the issue of conditional planning permissions.

A Rural Development Strategy

20.11 Development plans are implemented by two main means — the control of development, and the selective encouragement of development. Since 1975, on average

The needs of the local communities are met by many agencies. Strategy will be reviewed in the next Development Plan. Action is co-ordinated in various Rural Development Programmes.

some 800 planning applications have been determined each year, ranging from minor house extensions to major recreational and quarry proposals. Most of this work has been positive, consisting in each case of negotiation with the applicant and other public and private interested parties, and leading to an approval rate (with conditions) of over 80%. Some refusals have been the subject of an appeal, and most appeals have been dismissed. In virtually all of these cases, the statutorily approved Development Plan policies have been a material consideration. Thus consistency and fairness have been achieved, which is in the local, regional or national public interest.

20.12 The Board's responsibilities as Local Planning Authority include provision for the needs of the local community. The Board has only limited powers for implementation, and operates by enabling and encouraging appropriate development. The main national agency for assisting rural development is the Rural Development Commission (RDC). The RDC concentrates its resources in the most needy rural areas which have been designated as Rural Development Areas (RDA's). Much of the southern part of the National Park (see Fig. 21.1) is within either the Derbyshire RDA or North East Staffordshire RDA. A very small area around Wessenden Head and Meltham is within the Pennine RDA. The Board has worked closely with the Rural Development Commission, County and District Councils and others to prepare Rural Development Programmes which are focussed on social and economic development (see 23.24), but which also seek to further land conservation and land management.

20.13 The RDC provides grant-aid for administration and for special projects to the Rural Community Councils, and encourages economic development through its Business Service (formally the Council for Small Industries in Rural Areas (COSIRA). English Estates act as the RDC's agents in the provision of workshop space in the RDA's. Housing development to meet local needs is generally carried out by the District Councils, or by Housing Associations.

Objectives
20.14 To establish and maintain economically viable and socially balanced village and farming communities throughout the Park, by encouraging business investment and social development of a form and type which does not detract from, and should contribute to, the conservation and recreation objectives for the Park.

20.15 To maintain strategic planning policy for the development and use of land in order to plan and provide for the social and economic needs of the local community, to assess the balance of national interest in proposals generated by needs originating outside the Park, and to implement these policies through develpment control and by new development mainly by other agencies.

Policies
20.16 The policies in the Structure Plan remain relevant and are used as the basis of this Plan. The next review of the Structure Plan will carefully consider any indications for policy change suggested by this Plan (Peak Board).

20.17 The policies in the Structure Plan and Bakewell District Plan will be implemented through the Board's development control powers, and through liaison with the other agencies which have the powers to implement housing, employment and social programmes (Peak Board, County and District.Councils, RDC, RCC's).

20.18 The joint planning advisory group for Bakewell will be reconvened to consider outstanding proposals and policies in Bakewell in the context of the District Plan, and whether a formal review is needed after the review of the Structure Plan (Peak Board, County, District and Town Councils).

20.19 As required by the Countryside Act 1968, regard will be paid to the needs of the local community for housing, jobs and community facilities at a level appropriate to the current population of the Park. Efforts will be made to sustain balanced and economically viable communities and a viable multi-purpose farming industry, for their own sake and to the benefit of the conservation and recreation objectives for the Park (Peak Board, MAFF, Tourist Boards, County and District Councils, RDC).

20.20 Support for the local community will be pursued in the formation of strategic policies; the preparation and implementation of village management schemes; the conservation of historic buildings and ancient monuments; the determination of applications for planning permission, and the response to notification of farm grant applications (Peak Board, District Councils, RDC, MAFF, EH).

20.21 The Board will continue its active contribution to the Rural Development Programmes and encourage integrated rural development (RDC, County, District and Parish Council, RCC's, Peak Board, MAFF).

Introduction

21.1 Chapter 20 has set out the Board's overall strategy for rural development, within the Development Plan system. This chapter deals in more detail with housing, employment and services.

Population and Housing

21.2 The Board is required to have regard to the social and economic well being of the residents of the National Park, but it is not primarily responsible for functions such as housing. Policies for the local community are contained in the Structure Plan and the Bakewell District Plan.

21.3 The resident population in the National Park was 37,610 in 1971 and increased to 38,290 in 1981. The proportion of the population over 65 increased fro 16% in 1971, to 17.7% in 1981. This compares with figures for England and Wales as a whole of 13% and 15%. The widely held view that the Park as a whole has an abnormally high elderly population is thus not correct.

21.4 The Structure Plan divides the National Park into population sub-areas. Within these, the change in resident population between 1971 and 1981 is set out in Table 21.1. The table shows an increase in population of the 'commuter' areas of the Hope and Derwent Valleys and a decrease in the remoter areas of the plateau and the south west.

Table 21.1
Changes in the population living in the National Peak, 1971/81

Sub-Area	1971 Population	1981 Population	Change
Cheshire Moorlands	1,310	1,460	+150
High Peak East	3,330	3,490	+160
High Peak West	2,620	2,740	+120
W. Derbyshire: North	9.090	9,320	+230
W. Derbyshire: Limestone Plateau	8,820	8,790	−30
W. Derbyshire: Bakewell/Matlock	6,820	7,000	+180
Staffordshire Moorlands	4,120	3,990	−130
Residual	1,500	1,500	—
Total	**37,610**	**38,290**	**+680**

21.5 The Board's policy is generally to restrict planning permission for new development to the settlements of the Park. The Structure Plan proposed that a total of 820 new dwellings be built in the period 1977 to 1991, distributed as shown in Table 21.2 below: these new dwelling were to be built mainly in Bakewell and the larger villages, which provide services for the surrounding area. In other villages and hamlets, future development was to be restricted to the essential needs of the village itself.

21.6 The Structure Plan seeks to ensure that the restraint policies for housing development should not result in a shortage of houses for those whose natural home is in the Park and who work in the area. However the Secretary of State did not accept the Board's proposal that there should be a development control policy focussed upon 'local need'. He determined that local need was best met by housing development by the local housing authorities and housing associations. The Board and housing agencies make their best efforts within these constraints.

21.7 Between 1977 and 1988, permission was granted for 1,553 dwellings; and 1,021 dwellings were built, significantly more than the rate implied by the 1991 target of 820.

21.8 Table 21.2 shows the distribution of housing permissions in the different areas of the Park, these areas being shown on Map 21.1. Permission has been granted in all sub-areas for more houses than specified in the Structure Plan. Of the permissions granted, 59% have been for dwellings in the 20 larger villages and Bakewell, and 41% outside them. Only 2% of permissions have been for developments of 10 or more dwellings, and some 82% have been for a single dwelling. 36% of the permissions have been for the conversion of existing buildings.

Table 21.2
Planning permissions given for housing 1977/88

Sub-Area (see Map 21.1)	Structure Plan Provision to 1991	Houses Approved to 1988	Approvals above target	Built by 1988
Cheshire Moorlands	0	33	33	15
High Peak East	90	138	48	76
High Peak West	60	108	48	50
W. Derbyshire: North	240	350	110	252
W. Derbyshire: Limestone Plateau	130	442	312	306
W. Derbyshire: Bakewell/Matlock	180	274	94	197
Staffordshire Moorlands	120	192	72	102
Residual	0	36	36	23
Total	**820**	**1,553**	**753**	**1,021**

21.9 The Structure Plan runs to 1991. The housing target figures have been exceeded in all areas by the number of permissions granted and, in the case of the three West Derbyshire sub-areas by the number of houses built. Circular 4/76 makes it clear that control must be strict but that greater help should be given to meet local needs). Thus, in much of the Park, there is now an effective presumption against further approvals. The Board's view is that wherever local housing need is identified, development should be carried out by the agencies committed to meeting local needs.

21.10 In the Structure Plan, it was assumed that the local housing authorities would play a major part in the provision of housing for local needs. In 1980, Government gave tenants the right to buy their own homes. The consequence has been a reduction of the public rented housing stock, both overall and within each district. Sales of some council or housing association houses are subject to limitations on subsequent

Map 21.1
Population Sub-areas and Rural Development Areas

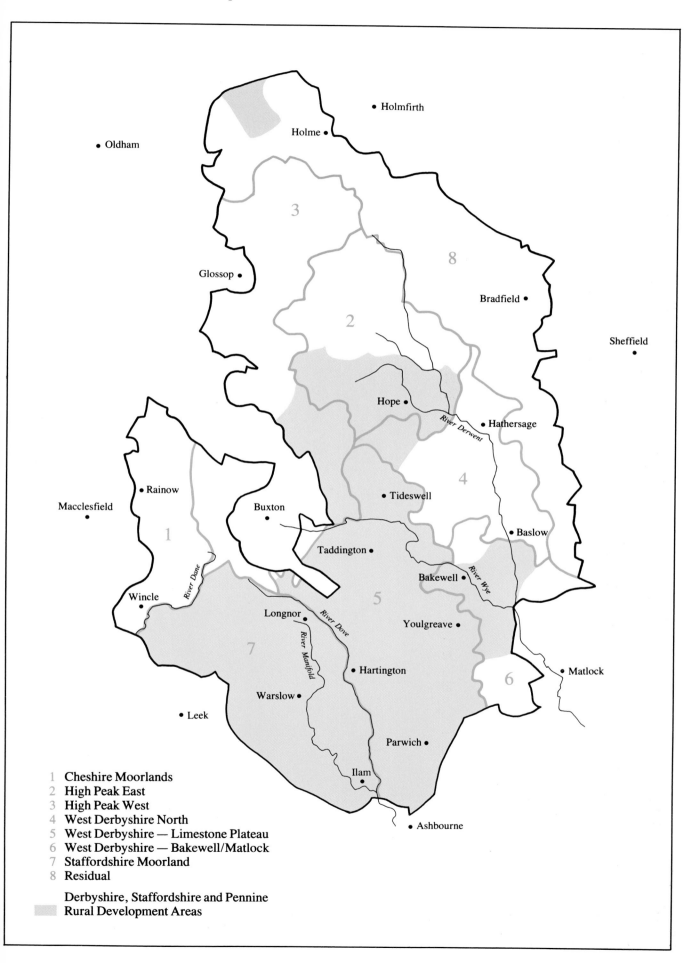

1 Cheshire Moorlands
2 High Peak East
3 High Peak West
4 West Derbyshire North
5 West Derbyshire — Limestone Plateau
6 West Derbyshire — Bakewell/Matlock
7 Staffordshire Moorland
8 Residual

Derbyshire, Staffordshire and Pennine
Rural Development Areas

Various sorts of affordable homes have been built in Tideswell, including shared equity schemes, houses for rent and conversions.

resales. Of the 5 Shire District Councils, Derbyshire Dales restricts resale to those living in the District Council area, and High Peak and Staffordshire Moorlands have retained the right to buy back the houses if sold within ten years of the original sale. To date there have been few cases of resale within the National Park, and none bought back by the District Councils. In rural areas there is a continuing decline in the role of local authorities as direct providers of housing, with an increasing role for housing associations. It is Government policy to revive the private rented sector.

21.11 The District Councils since 1980 have concentrated on the provision of housing to meet special needs, primarily for elderly people, and which is not subject to the right to buy. Partnership schemes with private builders have been developed, notably at Great Longstone and Stoney Middleton; these can provide low cost housing, but there is little or no control over subsequent sales to ensure that such housing remains available for local people. There are housing association schemes in Longnor, Tideswell, Hope and Bamford. There is a small and still declining amount of private rented accommodation, mainly associated with the largest estates, (Chatsworth, Haddon, Harpur Crewe) and with industrial concerns (Newburgh Engineering).

21.12 The provision of housing for local people whose incomes are too low to buy on the private market and for whom there is insuficient rented accommodation will continue to be a major concern of the Board. In the changing circumstances a number of ways of providing such housing may be developed and the Board will actively encourage such schemes, where a need has been shown. At present an

expansion of activity by Housing Associations seems the most promising means of securing housing in villages for local needs.

21.13 Second and holiday homes In 1974 it was estimated that there were 87 second and holiday homes in the Park. The 1981 census gave a total of 425, or 2.6% of households. This compares with an average for Great Britain of 1.0%, and of 16.2% in the Lake District. For most of the Park, second homes do not present a serious problem. But in some parishes the concentration is much higher than the 2.6% average: in 10 parishes, it is more than 10%. A survey carried out in 1983 showed that in the 15 parishes showing the highest concentration of second and holiday homes, there was a further increase of 3.4% in the preceding 2 years. These villages are generally those which are small, remote and attractive, mostly in the limestone plateau area of Derbyshire Dales, and in the Staffordshire Moorlands. The Board and the housing authorities have no means by which to control the use of existing property as a holiday or second home. Outside villages, the Board's policies favour the conversion of redundant buildings to recreation use rather than to permanent dwellings. This is a matter of growing concern which will be further examined as part of the review of the Structure Plan.

Objective
21.14 To safeguard or increase the housing supply for local people by use of the planning powers and housing investment available.

Policies

21.15 Further links will be developed with housing authorities and housing associations to provide housing for local needs. Where it is shown that there is a need for new housing, the Board will assist in identifying suitable buildings for conversion or sites for development, and will encourage action by housing authorities or by housing associations in line with Structure Plan policies (Peak Board, District Councils, Housing Associations, NAC Rural Trust).

21.16 The increase of houses occupied for holiday use will be monitored and, if necessary, Government will be urged to provide the means to discourage an imbalanced growth in the proportion of holiday and second homes in villages (Peak Board).

21.17 When necessary, the Board will continue to convene meetings of representatives of the councils and agencies involved in meeting the housing needs of the Park (Peak Board).

Employment

21.18 The Structure Plan states that the Board will consider favourably proposals for development which creates jobs, providing that these are mainly in settlements and will not be damaging to the character of the area. In areas where there has been a decline in agricultural or mining employment, specially sympathetic consideration is given to proposals for small-scale developments which provide new jobs. Craft industries are encouraged in settlements, and tourism is also important (see Chapter 17). Light industry is also to be encouraged in selected locations, concentrating on areas which are losing population.

21.19 Official statistics are inadequate for the study of employment in small areas. Only one employment office area (Bakewell) lies wholly within the National Park. The Employment Record which is available for this area covers only employees, and not those who are self-employed. The 1981 Census provides the widest coverage, but this is based on a 10% sample and is thus subject to error and is out of date. However, the census showed that the number of economically active residents had fallen from 16,453 in 1971 to 15,077 in 1981. The percentage working in different sectors of the economy is shown in Table 21.3.

Table 21.3
Employment by main classes

(Percentages from 1971 and 1981 censuses of employed people *living* in the National Park)

	1971	1981	Change
Agriculture	13.7	9.7	−4.0
Manufacturing	25.4	2.59	−0.5
Construction	5.3	5.9	+0.3
Quarrying and allied categories	10.3	5.5	−4.8
Other Services	39.8	45.4	+5.6

21.20 The employment structure of the Park is difficult to quantify. It is estimated that some 12,000 people work inside the Park. About 8,000 of these jobs are held by residents of the Park, and a similar number of residents travel out to work in the surrounding towns and cities: of the 12,000 jobs within the Park in 1981 about

10% were in agriculture.

18% in mining and quarrying (excluding haulage).

19% in manufacturing industry.

15% in tourism.

38% in other service industries, energy, construction, transport and miscellaneous occupations.

21.21 Employment in primary industries (agriculture, forestry, mining and quarrying) has been falling since the war, mainly because of mechanisation and the amalgamation of enterprises. Decline in these industries has been balanced by a growth in other types of work — mainly in the manufacturing and service industries. There is some evidence of a continuing shift away from the primary and secondary sectors toward service employment including those in the tourist industry.

21.22 Unemployment is generally lower in the National Park than in the constituent District Councils as a whole, or than in the counties; and significantly lower than the average for Great Britain and much lower than in some neighbouring metropolitan districts and the Derbyshire coalfield. In June 1988 for instance unemployment in Bakewell Ward was 3.2%, in Derbyshire Dales 4.6%, in Derbyshire 9.2%, and in Great Britain 8.8%. Unemployment figures, however, do not tell the full story. Access to jobs, limited variety of employment, low levels of pay or profitability need to be considered in any economic strategy.

21.23 The Board has worked closely with other agencies (English Estates, RDC, County and District Councils), through Action Plans and the Rural Development Programmes, to develop small industrial estates. Workshops have been provided in Bakewell, Tideswell, Longnor and Warslow. By June 1988, a total of 64,000 sq. ft. of workshops had been provided, creating 150 new jobs. The RDC Business Service is able to offer grants towards the costs of converting redundant buildings to employment uses in the

Microplants at Longnor — new industries can succeed even in more remote villages.

RDA's as well as business loans and an advice service. One of the most successful examples of conversion is the farm buildings at Pilsey on the Chatsworth Estate to provide workshop units and increased space for a farm shop. In 1987, the principle of providing special 'high technology' workspace in Bakewell was agreed, but a site which meets all parties' resources, policies and objectives is still being sought.

21.24 In some instances, however, workshops provided to encourage local employment have not been let for a sustained period after (for example some of those built at Warslow in 1981 were still not let in 1988). This leaves a decision to be made between waiting for the right tenant to arrive, providing further resources to attract tenants, or accepting that advance workshops are not the solution in some cases.

21.25 The Board can buy land in certain circumstances to enable development to take place but does not have the employment promotion powers available to County and District Councils. The Rural Development Programmes submitted jointly by a number of agencies provide one means for achieving the development of new small units, mainly in the larger settlements. The Government has stressed the importance of a positive approach by local planning authorities to the generation of employment. The White Paper 'Lifting the Burden', DoE Circular14/85 'Development and Employment' and the relevant planning policy guidance note (PPG 7: Rural Enterprise and Development) urge this approach. The DoE Circular 16/87 'Development involving Agricultural Land' encourages the re-use of redundant farm buildings for small businesses but with strict scrutiny of proposals in National Parks. The Board has not interpreted this to include modern wide-spanned farm buildings.

21.26 The pursuit of the main statutory responsibilities of landscape enhancement and recreational provision can help to some degree to meet local needs for jobs. For instance, woodland management may lead to jobs or income from timber production (see 5.29). Grants to repair historic buildings or convert redundant barns may create space for new enterprises (see 4.32). Landscape and building conservation work itself often uses local contractors or farm businesses employing local people.

21.27 The Government Report 'Pleasure, Leisure and Jobs — the Business of Tourism' emphasised the contribution which a vigorous tourism and leisure sector can make to employment. It is estimated that some 2,000 jobs are provided in tourism in the National Park. A continued modest growth in this sector, is envisaged particularly in the RDA's (see 17.17). Jobs in tourism are however often seasonal and low paid, and the need remains to provide higher-quality jobs in other sectors.

Objective
21.28 To provide a wider and more varied employment base to compensate for losses in the primary industries of agriculture and quarrying and to counteract current patterns of limited job opportunities, low wages and seasonal work.

Policies
21.29 The provision of new workspace, the development of tourism enterprises, the expansion of existing business; the use of redundant buildings; farm diversification and the development of a conservation economy will be encouraged to the extent that this is compatible with the

character of the area and the policies of the Structure Plan (RDC, Peak Board, County and District Councils, MAFF, Tourist Boards).

Community Services

21.30 The Board and its rural development partners view sympathetically proposals for the development of community services within villages; and advocate the retention of existing schools, village halls, shops and other services. In areas of the Park suffering from rural decline, particularly the South West, the Board is concerned that services should improve. Greater use of primary schools and village halls as community facilities and the joint use of facilities by local residents and visitors is also encouraged. These can provide economic support to the school, strengthen the links between school and community, and provide community facilities more cheaply by using existing buildings. This approach is encouraged. In Derbyshire for example, the development of Community Education will help to provide access to educational facilities for all groups in the community.

21.31 The responsibility for these services lies with other authorities. School closures have occurred, particularly in Staffordshire. A scheme for co-operation between the small moorland first and primary schools is now operating in the Staffordshire Rural Development Area, and the future of the remaining 5 primary schools would appear to be better than for some time. However, Warslow and Waterhouses Middle Schools closed in August 1988. Some of the schools closed in Staffordshire have become village halls, replacing poorer buildings, or providing a hall for the first time. In Derbyshire considerable commitment has been shown to rural schools and only Birchover School (with 5 pupils) has closed. Castleton, Chelmorton, Litton and Cressbrook schools have been proposed for closure, but have remained open following active campaigns.

21.32 However small schools with fewer than 50 pupils on roll remain vulnerable. The reasons for this are:

(a) The difficulty in smaller schools (particularly those with a single teacher) of providing a broad, balanced relevant curriculum appropriate to the needs of individual children.

(b) Social reasons — age groups are very small and this limits opportunities for shared learning among pupils of the same age.

(c) Financial — the unit costs of operating small schools are high.

The Board is not expert in educational matters, but as part of the wider social considerations the retention of a school (particularly infant and junior schools) is seen as being of great importance to the vitality of the village itself, and this should be balanced against other factors in any review.

21.33 There is a continuing programme of replacing and extending village halls, with grant aid from the District and County Councils and the RDC. In some of the smaller villages, it is difficult to maintain existing community buildings. Multi-purpose centres such as the one developed at Swythamley, can help meet local needs more economically.

21.34 The closure of village shops has continued, but most larger villages retain at least one. The Peak District Rural Shopkeepers association was established with assistance from the Derbyshire Rural Community Council and CoSIRA, and is active in the Park. It will continue to be supported, particularly in efforts to increase the links between local food production and sales (see Chapter 4) and in providing tourist and local information (see Chapter 18).

21.35 Post Offices fulfil a valuable purpose providing counter services, including banking and payment of benefits for people who do not have transport to the larger settlements. Post Office Counters have recently introduced a 'Community Office Contract' which reduces the income from post office work and so threatens the future of the network and can further weaken the social and economic integrity of the village.

21.36 Payphone kiosks are important to the less well-off and to the visitor. In popular walking areas, a farmer may be approached to allow a visitor to use the 'phone, which has on occasions led to theft or abuse if the caller is refused. Kiosks in remote areas can be vital in an emergency. Kiosks should be retained, and there may be a case for the provision of additional kiosks in some more remote areas.

Objective

21.37 To help maintain community services and facilities.

Policies

21.38 There will be a co-ordinated approach to the identification of needs, problems and opportunities. The provision or retention of community facilities such as shops, post office counters, payphone kiosks and village halls will be encouraged, particularly where these serve both the local community and visitors (RDC, Rural Community Councils, Peak Board, County & District Councils).

21.39 The communities of the National Park should be served by an educational network relevant to their needs. When closure of a school is first proposed, an appraisal based on likely housing and employment provision in the area will be provided, and the importance of the school as a community facility will be stressed (County Councils, Rural Community Councils, Peak Board).

Cressbrook village school was not closed by the Secretary of State, following a local campaign.

22 REGIONAL AND NATIONAL NEEDS

Introduction

22.1 The Peak District is subject to pressure for the use of its land for purposes which threaten to harm the character of the area, to generate traffic on the roads, to spoil the enjoyment of visitors and disrupt the life of local residents. The conservation of National Park qualities in the national interest is the prime consideration for the Board. These external demands are discussed below:

    (a) Mineral Extraction (**22.4-22.8**).

    (b) Waste Disposal (**22.9-22.10**).

    (c) Water supply reservoirs, gathering grounds and main rivers (**22.11-22.13**).

    (d) Pumped storage power scheme (**22.14**).

    (e) Power Transmission (**22.15**).

    (f) Heavy cross-Park traffic and through routes (**22.16-22.21**).

    (g) Military Training and Use (**22.22-22.29**).

22.2 The Board's main policies for most of these activities are in the Structure Plan, but they are briefly considered in the chapter. The Structure Plan is due to be reviewed by 1991. Until then, for the convenience of those who want a short reference document, the formal policies of the Plan have been reprinted as a separate publication.

22.3 In July 1988 a system of Environmental Assessment (EAs) was introduced by the Government. The purpose of EAs is to ensure that firstly the developer and then the planning authority give full consideration to all the effects of 'significant' development on the environment. A number of proposals generated by external pressures on the Park may be seen to represent a 'significant' threat to the Park. The Board will be seeking the submission of the EA in appropriate cases and will not approve significant departures from National Park policies without the most rigorous examination. In such cases, the Secretary of State can call an application in for his own decision, possibly following a public local inquiry.

Mineral extraction

22.4 The strongest conflict is with mineral extraction. The landscape of the White Peak is founded on carboniferous limestone, which has two qualities of use to industrial society — its chemical purity as calcium carbonate, an essential raw material in chemical and manufacturing industries; and its hardness as a bearing material in road construction and as an aggregate in concrete. The Park contains several other minerals in demand, including fluorspar, silica sand, fireclays and gritstone. The Board's policies for the control of mineral extraction are stated in the Structure Plan and have been reinforced by several ministerial decisions, statements and circulars.

22.5 These policies have provided the basis for a series of decisions upon proposals to extend quarries, or to open new quarries or mines. These decisions fall into two main groups — those concerning the extraction of limestone or gritstone as a roadstone, landfill or aggregate, and those concerning the use of purer limestone, gritstone, fluorspar and silica sand fo their unique or rare mineral qualities or as masonry stone. Extraction of the latter group has generally been accepted by the Board as being in the regional or national interest, and not available elsewhere. Such applications have been approved, where transport, landscape and restoration measures have seemed adequate at the time.

22.6 Proposals for mineral working to meet the aggregates market have usually been resisted as a matter of principle, on the grounds that adequate supplies of hard rock can be won elsewhere. This approach has recently been supported on appeal by the Secretary of State, after exhaustive examination at two public local inquiries related to Topley Pike Quarry (1985) and Eldon Hill Quarry (1986). Exceptions to this approach have been made only where other compelling circumstances have prevailed, such as opportunities to repair past damage, or where the local economy has been especially dependant on the quarry. The Board has been more favourably inclined to approve an extension where there has been a strong indication or guarantee that it represents a 'last bite' at a particular deposit.

22.7 There are more than 60 active quarries and mines in the National Park. It is anticipated that many of these will continue to operate for the period of this plan, managed in the light of Structure Plan policies, strong development control, and best quarry management practice. They provide employment for people, many of whom live within the National Park.

22.8 Substantial resources will continue to be committed by the Board to minerals planning control and to the review of mineral sites and conditions. Priorities will be selected for negotiating improvements. (See Chapter 7 and policies **22.30** and **22.32** below).

A new scheme for the better design and landscaping of Hope cement works quarries was agreed in 1988.

Waste Disposal

22.9 The Structure Plan contains no specific policies on waste disposal. In 1981, the Board's Planning Control Committee, faced with proposals to dispose of used car tyres in old quarries, adopted a policy. This established the principles that waste disposal is only acceptable in the Park when it will be of benefit in National Park terms (e.g. by creating new farmland or nature reserves or other acceptable land use); will not destroy existing national park characteristics; is not disruptive; and is adequately controlled.

22.10 The County Councils and Metropolitan District Councils are responsible for waste disposal plans — Derbyshire County Council for example are currently reviewing their waste disposal plans, which will consider

Agreements result in good management for recreation and conservation at existing reservoirs and catchments. We ask that private sales do not undo this good work.

sites within the Park. There have been no new proposals for some time, but pressures for waste disposal from the towns and cities around the Park are likely to increase. Transport cost is a factor which may result in more favourable consideration being given to any site proposed mainly to meet local needs, but proposals for the disposal of waste generated outside the Peak District should be resisted. Waste disposal policy will be considered in the review of the Structure Plan, and the Board will continue to participate in the preparation of neighbouring authorities' waste disposal plans.

Water supply reservoirs, gathering grounds and main rivers

22.11 The Peak District provides an accessible resource for clean water and economical storage of that water. The cities around have taken full advantage of this. There are 48 larger reservoirs. About 15% of the National Park belongs to Water Authorities as gathering grounds (see Chapters 1 and 23 on land sales and privatisation). Many main rivers are controlled by the three Water Authorities that operate within the Peak District.

22.12 The Structure Plan sets out the Board's presumption against the establishment of new reservoirs, to protect the remaining 'natural' valleys. There have been three occasions in the last 20 years when new reservoirs or extensions have been explored or proposed — at Manifold Valley, Hassop and Upper Derwent. These were successfully resisted by the Board. In other cases, reservoirs have been built or extended, for example at Winscar, which was accepted as a reasonable improvement of an untidy area.

22.13 There are no known or anticipated proposals to create additional storage or compensatory reservoirs. The North West Water Authority has looked at its long term needs and has no proposals within the Peak District. The Carsington Reservoir (outside the National Park) is expected to meet the needs of the Severn Trent Water Authority for the management of the River Derwent for the foreseeable future. Alternative sources of supply (such as underground sources in the Bunter sandstones east of the Peak District) will be advocated by the Board in the event of future increases in demand.

Pumped Storage Power Scheme

22.14 Allied to water storage, the Central Electricity Generating Board (CEGB) has carried out preliminary investigation into the possibility of substantially enlarging several reservoirs in the Longdendale Valley, together with a new reservoir on the moor above, to create a pumped storage power scheme. In the Peak Board's view, the environmental and recreational disadvantages make this scheme totally unacceptable. The investigations have been deferred — the CEGB has confirmed that it does not now envisage needing such a scheme until at least the end of the century. The Peak Board has urged national investigation of alternative power strategies or alternative methods or sites for power storage.

Power Transmission

22.15 There is one national electricity grid power line across the Park, in the Longdendale Valley. It is a major intrusion in the landscape, and should be removed or placed entirely underground at the first practicable opportunity (see Chapter 27). No further national grid lines are likely to be proposed, nor to be acceptable. Policies for the improvement of other public utility installations and local overhead lines are in Chapter 7 (**7.17-7.24**).

Heavy cross-Park traffic and through routes

22.16 The hilly nature of the Peak District is an obstacle on the direct line of communication between several conurbations and major towns around the Park. The Park is crossed by several primary routes (Class A roads). It is also the 'home base' for many lorries, on farms and at other countryside and village locations, providing significant employment. Many of the goods carried are local farm and quarry products. The following paragraphs briefly review current issues relating to cross-Park traffic and through routes. (Chapter 15 deals with traffic management, and Chapter 7 (**7.42-7.47**) deals with road verges and roadside 'furniture').

22.17 The relevant policies for the Park were developed in the Transport Study, a major joint research initiative carried out by consultants, of which the policy conclusions were accepted by the Highway Authorities and by British Rail. The key policies are:

(a) Cross-Park traffic is to be generally confined by weight restriction orders to trunk and primary roads.

(b) Major new provision for cross-Park traffic should be made only in the most compelling regional need, where no reasonable alternative exists, (in line with Circular 4/76). There is potentially a satisfactory motorway/trunk road 'box' outside the Park.

(c) There is no foreseen need for road improvements to a standard higher than 7.3 metres wide single carriageway (except crawler lanes on steep hills on the A628).

(d) Rail traffic is generally less environmentally damaging than road. The Board supports use of the rail network in preference to road, and in particular the payment of central government grants to any scheme which diverts heavy goods from road to rail.

The residents of Stoney Middleton and other villages are concerned at the continuing growth in heavy goods traffic.

(e) In any highway improvement design, environmental and safety factors take precedure over speed, convenience and economics (again, in line with Circular 4/76).

(f) There is, in the Study, an agreed list of improvements to the trunk and primary road networks, which will lead to environmental gains particularly through several by-passes to towns and villages.

22.18 Since the 1978 Plan, there have been several significant road improvements carried out with full regard to these policies. Major road developments outside the Park have been assessed by use of the data and programmes developed in the Transport Study, and kept up to date with main-road traffic counters.

22.19 Town or village by-passes or relief roads are still awaited for Bakewell, Baslow and Stoney Middleton. A new route is needed in the upper Hope Valley to replace the A625 at Mam Tor, which collapsed beyond repair and led to the diversion of traffic through Bradwell village. The recent Government proposal to reassess the tourist/environmental factor in such schemes is welcome, but has yet to produce any progress. The full list of road schemes which are desirable in the National Park interest is set out in the Transport Study.

22.20 Government priorities for improvement of routes for cross-Park traffic seem to be changing, with continued interest in the A628 Longdendale corridor and greater emphasis on the A6/A619/A623 corridor. Concern is growing both for impact on the Park's natural qualities and their enjoyment, and on the villages most affected. Survey, analysis and predictions of traffic flows (and the generation of new traffic by improvements outside the Park) is in hand or being sought.

22.21 The proposed application of the principles established in the Routes for People scheme (which itself included major traffic diversion and a village relief road) is described in Chapter 15.

Military Training and Use

22.22 Neither the Structure Plan nor the 1978 Park Plan have policies on military use other than low flying aircraft. However, in common with every other National Park, the Peak District has been subject to military use for many years. The three main forms of use are training and shooting on land held for those purposes; use of the wilder areas of the Park for 'adventure' training; and low flying aircraft.

22.23 Military Land Holdings There are only two areas, both long established, held by the armed forces. Totley Rifle Range comprises 45 ha leasehold, plus 38 ha where rights are held. The Board acquired the freehold in 1984 as part of the Eastern Moors Estate and this is leased to the Ministry of Defence (MoD) via private lessees. Upper Hulme Training Area and Firing Range extends to over 1,000 ha with firing rights over 200 ha, of which 28 ha are permanently closed to the public for safety reasons. The base is the recently refurbished Anzio Camp, Blackshaw Moor, just outside the National Park. About 60% of the area (620 ha) is now owned by the Peak Board, following transference of part of the Harpur Crewe Estate in 1986 (see **44.14**). The acquisition of the estate was conditional upon the continued training use by the Ministry of Defence (MoD), as part of these lands. A Management Plan for the military land is being prepared (see **44.14**), which includes an existing commitment that total use of all military land shall not exceed 1979 levels of use. A considerable part of the Upper Hulme training area lies within the Leek Moors SSSI (ornithological and botanical interest).

22.24 Adventure Training This includes navigation, rock climbing and camping expeditions and involves groups from all over the country. Each month there may be several groups somewhere in the National Park. A prior notification scheme for all service training exercises outside MoD land is operated. The Board advises the military on rights of way, camping and parking within the Park, and military use of access land is subject to the Board's approval. This category of military use is no different from that of many other civilian groups ranging from rambling parties to organised mass walks, and the Broad uses its powers and persuasion to minimise damage to the environment and nuisance to other users.

22.25 Low Flying Aircraft National Parks offer a challenging low flight training experience and thus are often heavily used. There is less of such flying in the Peak District than in some other National Parks and upland areas, reflecting perhaps the higher density of settlement and greater number of visitors, but disturbance is still caused to residents, livestock and visitors.

22.26 The overall impact and need for a policy The main objections to military activity include noise, restriction on public access, danger, visual intrusion, and harm to wildlife and sites of ecological, geological or archaeological importance. Military developments are not subject to formal planning control but the MoD is requested to consult the National Park Authority, under Circular 18(84 procedures, over any proposals it may have for new buildings or land use change. Generally, relations are good between the military and the National Park Authority. The armed forces also help with a variety of conservation and recreation projects.

22.27 The retention of land by the MoD for military training purposes produces some difficulties in securing National Park objectives, particularly access to wander at will in open country. The effect of military training on the conservation value of such land is less easy to determine, although

disturbance during critical periods may be detrimental to some bird species. The Report of the Defence Lands Committee 1971-3 (Nugent Report) was the last major review on this subject. It concluded that MoD use could continue in National Parks but no intensification of use, major expansion or new development should take place, without consultation with the National Park Authority and Countryside Commission. The Report recommended that both Upper Hulme and Totley be retained, but that the Upper Hulme ranges should not be used on any weekend each year between May and September inclusive.

22.28 The Board will continue to seek to minimise any adverse impact of military activity, through existing liaison procedures and through co-operation with MoD. It will oppose an increase in the amount of land used for military training activity unless, by mutual arrangement between MoD and the Board, alternatives are required to lessen demands upon areas of a particularly sensitive nature. Such arrangements should not produce a net increase in the amount of land in military use. The Board will press for visual and environmental improvements, and increased public access wherever possible including the resiting of activities where justified.

Objective
22.29 To minimise the impact of all external demands upon the Park.

Policies
22.30 All proposals for development in the Park generated by external regional or national needs will be most rigorously examined in the light of the national or regional need, the availability of alternative sites, routes or methods and the impact of the proposal upon the Park, consistent with Structure Plan policies and the Transport Study. These proposals include mineral extraction, waste disposal, water storage, power storage or generation, power transmission, movement of people and goods between surrounding urban areas and military use. Environmental Impact Assessments will be required in 'significant' cases (Peak Board, County and District Councils).

22.31 Relief from the impact of existing heavy and through traffic on the settlements and countryside of the Park will be sought by the early construction of the schemes referred to in para. **22.19** (Peak Board, Highways Authorities).

22.32 Reduction of the impact of other existing developments will be sought, including mineral sites and local overhead lines (see Chapter 7) and the national grid line in Longdendale (see Chapter 27) (Peak Board, CEGB, Electricity Boards BACMI).

22.33 Close co-operation with the Ministry of Defence will continue to minimise conflicts between military training and National Park objectives. There will be a presumption against any increase in the amount of land used for military training. Intensification of military training beyond agreed limits will be resisted (Peak Board, MoD).

WAYS AND MEANS

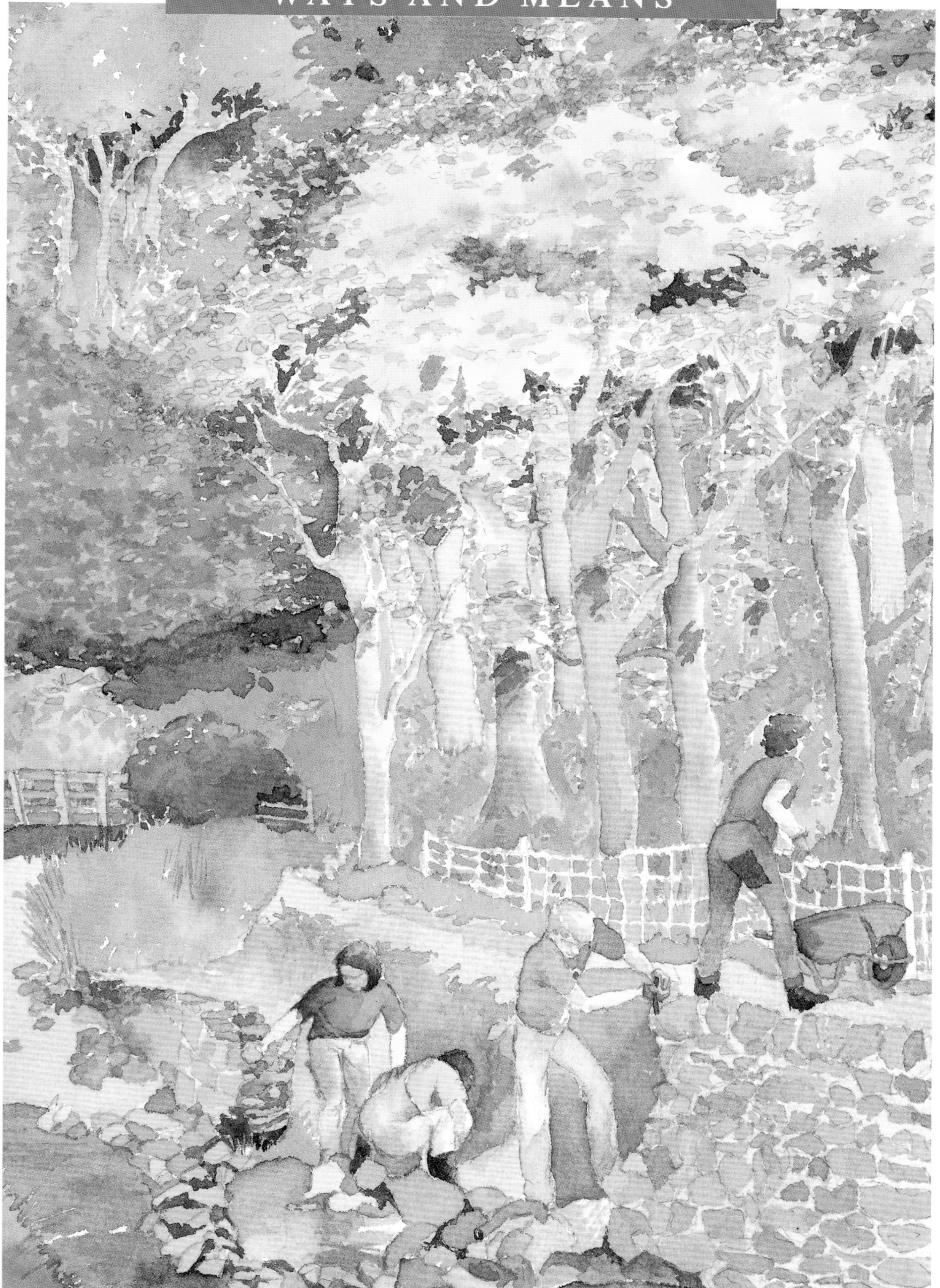

23 WAYS AND MEANS

Introduction

23.1 Chapters 1-22 outline objectives and policies for management of the Park over the next 5 and more years. We now consider how these policies may be implemented.

23.2 Throughout this Review, it has been emphasised that this is a Plan for the National Park, for all who are involved in it, not merely for the action of the Board. A great land area like this, with 38,000 residents and many thousands of different land owners, depends for its management upon the actions and resources of very many agencies. The Board, owning only 4% of the Park and spending (in 1987-88) a mere £4 million, is only one factor among many.

23.3 For that reason, each policy in this review is expressed in terms of which bodies may mainly implement it. Sometimes, the Board will lead: elsewhere, others may lead, and the Board's role may be quite limited. Throughout, the emphasis is on partnership. This emphasis is justified because others have the main stake — of landownership, or private interest, or statutory responsibility — in many fields; but also because of the high degree of convergence or overlap between the interests of different parties . Increasingly, the interests of the National Park coincide with those of farmers, or property owners, or public bodies concerned with (say) the rural economy or tourism. Partnership with other local authorities is especially important.

23.4 The Board's basic assumption, therefore, is that this is a plan to be implemented by all who work, live in, or have responsibilities within the National Park. Success in carrying out its purposes will depend on their willingness to pursue policies which will have been prepared in consultation with them; and to allocate their own, alongside the Board's resources.

23.5 The Board's role will be played in the same spirit — that is, as part of an overall effort, aiming to serve the interests of others at the same time as the purposes which the Board is specifically briefed to pursue.

23.6 Closely related to this principle of partnership is that of resources. The job of managing the Park is complex, highly varied, detailed and demanding. The Board and its many partners know that much has been achieved, but there is still much to be done. This is shown, for example, by the scope for improvement of many footpaths, historic buildings, farm woodlands, dry-stone walls, street surfaces or items of street furniture, ancient monuments and some villages and farms. Paragraph **1.10** records the Board's recognition of the need to ensure, through grant aid and practical assistance, that landowners are encouraged to contribute to conservation objectives.

23.7 In tackling these problems, we therefore need to draw on whatever resources we can get. The Board, in particular, will continue to press government for increase in its own Grant, and ask its constituent local authorities to match such increases. It will continue, where it can, to seek grants from other sources; to use the energy of volunteers and of Training Agency personnel (but see **1.23**), and to seek direct income from the public where that is appropriate. It will encourage others to do the same, and will use all legitimate means at its disposal to harness resources to the management of the Park. It is particularly encouraged by the new grant aid available from MAFF for conservation work in ESAs and for farm diversification.

23.8 The Board's contribution to the partnership which this Plan requires will be made in eight main ways:

(a) Direct action (**23.9-23.21**).

(b) Joint action with others (**23.20-23.37**).

(c) Grant-aid (**23.38-23.43**).

(d) Advice, information and research (**23.44-23.49**).

(e) Statutory influence (**23.50-23.51**).

(f) Consultation (**23.52-23.55**).

(g) Monitoring (**23.56-23.57**).

The rest of this chapter briefly expands on each of these types of activity, cross-referring where appropriate to more detailed statements in other chapters. Note especially the *Priorities for action* in Chapter 1 (**1.37, 1-17**).

Direct Action

23.9 The Board's direct action is of two main kinds — the management of land; and the provision of services.

23.10 Land management Following its recent aquisition of two major estates — Eastern Moors in 1984, Warslow Moors in 1986 — the Board now owns about 5,940 ha of land. This includes:

(a) 4 main estates — North Lees, 525 ha; The Roaches, 395 ha; Eastern Moors, 2,460 ha; Warslow Moors, 1899 ha.

(b) About 243 ha of woodlands, in 100 different lots widely scattered through the Park.

(c) Three disused railways, now converted into trails for walking and cycling — High Peak Trail; Tissington Trail; Monsal Trail.

(d) Many smaller properties, including 45 car parks (some with picnic sites), 17 toilet blocks, information centres, and specific features such as Windgather Rocks in Cheshire, the archaeological sites of Roystone Grange near Ballidon, Grindsbrook Meadows and the Sheepwash and field at Bakewell.

Practical action on a smaller scale — the rehabilitation of Heathcote Mere by the Parish Council, with a little help from others.

Map 23.1
Land Ownership

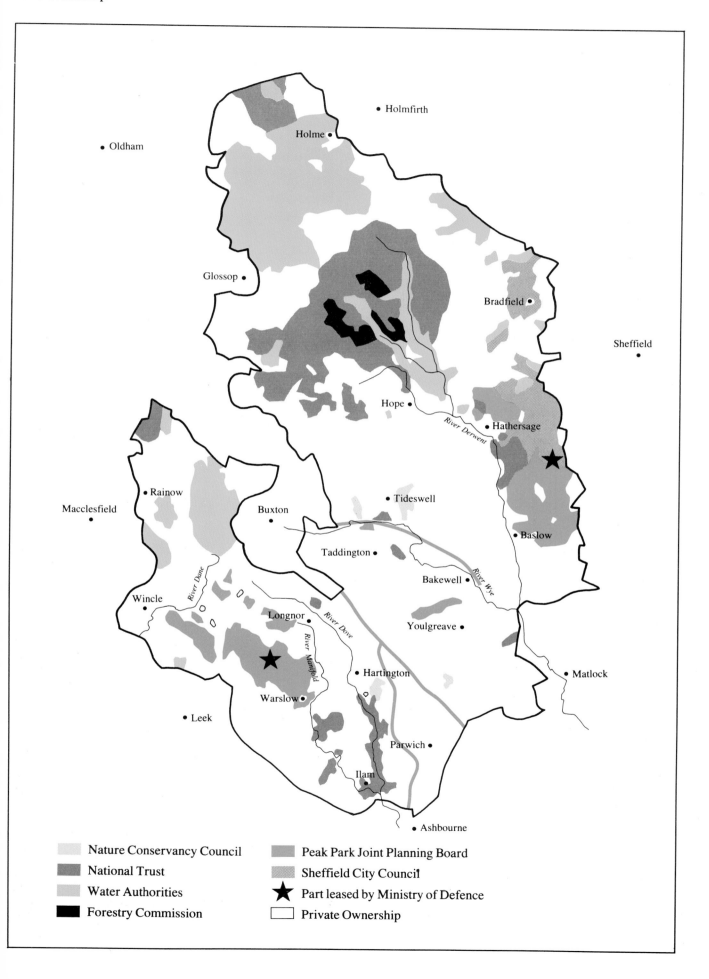

Nature Conservancy Council

National Trust

Water Authorities

Forestry Commission

Peak Park Joint Planning Board

Sheffield City Council

★ Part leased by Ministry of Defence

Private Ownership

(e) The buildings and grounds at Aldern House, the Board's headquarters in Bakewell; and Losehill Hall, the National Park Study Centre at Castleton.

(Map 23.1 shows the main public sector and National Trust land holdings).

23.11 The Board has acquired these properties over the years either for specific operational reasons or because acquisition was seen as the best or only means of achieving National Park purposes. These criteria will continue to guide the Board in relation to possible future additions to its estates. Conversely, where it feels that it can wisely dispose of property while safeguarding National Park purposes, it will consider doing so, imposing covenants where necessary.

23.12 The Board's broad objective in managing its main estates, woodlands and trails is to achieve high standards of land management which serve National Park purposes while meeting the proper needs of tenants, agister graziers and others with interest in the land. The Board is conscious that its own management will be looked to as a demonstration of what it expects of others within the National Park.

23.13 Provision of services The services to the public directly provided by the Board include:

(a) Information centres, free and saleable publications, and other information services (see Chapter 18)

(b) The National Park Study Centre at Losehill Hall, Castleton, which offers courses to the general public; training courses for countryside staff from all over the country and abroad; specialist conferences; advice to youth groups, schools and other educational parties visiting the Park; and a day visits service (see Chapter 18)

(c) 8 Caravan and Camping sites, some of which are run directly by the Board, some on lease or licence by the Camping Club or the Caravan Club (see Chapter 17)

(d) Two youth hostels, one (Hagg Farm) leased to Nottinghamshire County Council, and the other (Crowden) leased to the Youth Hostel Association (see Chapter 17)

(e) A camping barn at Losehill Hall, which is one of the series of such barns created otherwise on farms in the Park: Losehill Hall provides the central booking service for all of them (see Chapter 17)

(f) Cycle hire services at four locations (Parsley Hay, Ashbourne, Fairholmes and Waterhouses) (see Chapter 13).

23.14 The Board has developed these services over the years as a response to perceived need, and in the absence of (or as a stimulus to) others. In financial terms, the Board's approach is that income from such services should broadly cover their own operating costs (apart from the the basic costs of the information service and the educational staff costs at Losehill Hall). This purpose has been broadly achieved, and the combined income for all the services in 1977-78 was about £1.2 million. The Board has kept the services under review, and has expanded or contracted them according to perceived demand. It will continue to review them; and, in doing so, will keep in mind both opportunities for developing new services, and also the option of shifting existing services into others' hands in order to release resources for other work.

"Once there was a valley" . . . now the Board owns the Monsal Viaduct, a vital part of the Monsal Trail.

Policies

23.15 The policies in this Plan wil be implemented by a wide range of agencies, public and private, with an emphasis on partnership and resourcefulness in the pursuit of the well-being of the National Park (All agencies).

23.16 The Board's contribution to the implementation of policies will be made through direct action; joint action with others; grant-aid and other practical assistance; advice, information and research; statutory influence; and consultation (Peak Board).

23.17 To fund this contribution, the Board will continue to press Government to sustain and increase its Grant, and to ask the County Councils and Metropolitan District Councils to match such increases. It will use all means at its disposal to harness resources to the management of the Park (Peak Board).

23.18 Where acquisition of property by the Board appears necessary for specific operational reasons or as the best or only means of achieving National Park purposes, the Board will pursue that acquisition. Conversely, where it feels that it can wisely dispose of property while safeguarding National Park purposes, it will consider doing so (Peak Board).

23.19 The Board will continue to provide direct services for the visiting public; and will keep those services under review, developing new services or shifting existing ones into others' hands where appropriate (Peak Board).

Joint action with others

23.20 Over the years, the Board has developed or participated in a range of joint programmes of action, through which National Park purposes are served, often alongside the objectives of other organisations. The National Park has gained greatly from these joint programmes; and the Board is strongly committed to continuing collaboration of this kind. These joint programmes of action are described in the following paragraphs.

23.21 **Area Management Schemes** These cover various areas of the Park, and are aimed mainly at conservation, landscape enhancement and recreational provision. Partners in these schemes have included the Peak Board; North West , Severn Trent and Yorkshire Water Authorities; the National Trust; the Forestry Commission; County, District and Parish Councils; and other bodies. Much capital investment has been committed to these schemes, with contributions from all parties; and many of them also have joint programmes of annual expenditure, for example contract ranger services, (see Chapter 19). The intention is to continue these schemes and to extend the principle into other parts of the Park (see Chapters 24 to 47). Particular attention will be given to the anticipated consequences of the proposals to encourage water authorities to sell land and the intended privatisation of the water industry.

23.22 **Public Path** programmes through which the Highway Authorities, District and Parish Councils, the Board, the National Trust and other landowners and voluntary bodies collaborate to repair and maintain footpaths. The pattern of this collaboration varies between the different parts of the Park. Substantial use is made, in some areas, of volunteers or, formerly, of Manpower Services Commission teams and

Ideas through partnership into action: the leading partners receive the Times/RICS award for the Upper Derwent Management Scheme.

will, we hope, continue under the Training Commission or its successor. While encouraging progress is being made, the overall effort is far from adequate. Significant expansion of this joint activity is needed (see Chapter 11).

23.23 **Enhancement of Conservation areas** A successful pattern of collaboration has developed between the Board, Electricity Boards, British Telecom, Highway Authorities, Parish Councils and other local organisations in conceiving and carrying out enhancement schemes in and around Conservation Areas. The intention is to continue the programme of designating such areas within the settlements of the Park, and of joint action on enhancement schemes (see Chapter 9).

23.24 **Rural Development Programmes** A range of agencies, including the County and District Councils, the Rural Development Commission, English Estates, Rural Community Councils, MAFF and the Board are involved together in preparing each year, and implementing, Rural Development Programmes (RDPs) for each of the Derbyshire and Staffordshire Rural Development Areas. Between them, these Areas embrace much of the southern part of the Park. These Programmes, which have evolved from the earlier Action Plans, have their focus on social and economic development in these needy areas. The programmes are formulated and implementation is co-ordinated by officer working parties. The formal bids are approved by member steering committees on which all the contributing agencies and authorities are represented. There has been an encouraging extension in scope of the RDPs, for example to embrace tourism projects. A further extension, currently being considered for part of the Staffordshire RDA, would see the application of the principles successfully pioneered in the Integrated Rural Development project (see **23.26** below). The Board is keen to see the RDP process or principles continue, flourish and extend in subject scope and area of operation (see Chapter 20).

23.25 **Tourism Action Programme** An offshoot of the RDP process (and covering the same geographical area) is the Tourism Action Programme. The TAP was published in late 1987. This Programme was commissioned by the Board, the County and District Councils and the Development Commission, and has been prepared by the two regional Tourist Boards (Heart of England and East Midlands) in consultation with representatives of the tourism industry. It highlights needs and opportunities for tourism development and marketing, of kinds which will benefit the local economy and are compatible with the character of the National Park and adjoining areas (see also Chapter 17). The sponsoring authorities have accepted the report, and are considering how to implement it together with the private sector.

23.26 Integrated Rural Development Project In 1981, in response to an EEC initiative, a group of agencies (Development Commission, Department of the Environment, Ministry of Agriculture, Nature Conservancy Council, Peak Board, National Farmers' Union, Country Landowners' Association, and the Rural Community Councils of Derbyshire and Staffordshire, Forestry Commission and CoSIRA) jointly launched a 3-year experimental project in Integrated Rural Development (IRD). Funds came from the European Economic Community and from the first 4 of the agencies listed above. The Board provided professional , secretarial and financial services. The purpose was to test, initially in the two parishes of Monyash and Longnor, a new method of rural development, in which public agencies worked closely together and with the local communities, and in which efforts were made to encourage projects which produced benefits in social, economic and environmental terms simultaneously.

23.27 By 1984, the project had shown encouraging results, which are recorded in the report 'A Tale of Two Villages', published by the Board on behalf of the Project Steering Group. This first phase had established that local communities can be encouraged to achieve conservation objectives while improving their own quality of life and creating many new job opportunities at the same time. It had proved the validity of three principles, which can now be more widely followed, for example in Rural Development Programmes and Village Management Schemes (see paragraphs **9.18-9.29**). These principles are:

(a) **Individuality** Basing work on the character and needs of each place and not seeking to impose standard solutions

(b) **Involvement** Seeking the active participation of the local community in developing schemes and putting them into effect: encouraging community pride through self-help

(c) **Interdependence** Ensuring that work carried out does not damage social or economic or environmental interests and, more positively, devising schemes that benefit all threee interests simultaneously.

23.28 Funds were then put up by all the original sponsors (except the EEC), plus the English Tourist Board, the Countryside Commission and the Peak Board, for a second phase of the project starting in 1985. This second phase saw further evolution of the project, including its extension into a third area in the northern part of the Park; and widespread recognition of the project, including Awards from Europa Nostra and other bodies. Joint funding for the project ceased in March 1988.

23.29 This kind of collaborative, flexible action, which is easily understood by local communities, farmers and businessmen at local level, has high promise for the achievement of National Park purposes and the social and economic well-being of communities in the Park. However, translating experimental work into a broader-based programme of work is fraught with difficulties. The recent attempts to broaden the scope of the IRD work show that:

(a) The legal powers available to different agencies sometimes make it difficult for one agency to cover for the gaps in other agencies' work (for example the Peak Board can only act indirectly in most social and economic development work).

(b) The different priorities and budgets available for different sectors of public administration make it difficult to agree on integrated programmes of work.

(c) Professional attitudes can be sectoral and may have to be prompted to see the possibilities for generating a 'greater good' by amending their own objectives for an integrated programme of work.

However joint working has achieved significant successes in the former Action Plans, through the IRDP and in the continuing Rural Development Programmes. Efforts are now being concentrated in the North East Staffordshire Rural Development Area.

23.30 Community Action in the Rural Environment (CARE) This 3-year project was launched by the Countryside Commission, and is co-funded by the Commission, Barnsley Metropolitan District Council, the Board and a number of parish councils. It focusses on parishes in the western part of Barnsley Metropolitan District, including Langsett which lies partly within the Park. A project officer has been at work since late 1986, and is stimulating practical work by local people to improve their own circumstances and environment, such as the community minibus, tree planting and footpath improvements. The project has won a number of awards — the Carnegie 'Interpret Britain' award scheme in 1987, a Yorkshire Village Ventures award in 1987, came second in Yorkshire Television's Operation Eyesore in 1988 and was commended in the 1988 Times/RICS Conservation Awards.

23.31 Village Appraisals and Parish Maps The Board is particularly keen to work with parish councils on village appraisals and parish maps. These were given national encouragement in 1987 by the RDC, the Countryside Commission and Rural Community Councils. The preparation of such appraisals is best mainly carried out at the grass roots level of the parish, but the Board is pleased to assist (see also para. **9.33**).

23.32 Moorland Restoration and Management As a result of concern about the problems posed by large-scale moorland erosion in the Park, a group of organisations (Peak Board, MAFF, NFU, CLA, FC, NCC, Countryside Commission, National Trust, Peak Park Moorland Owners and Tenants Association, Severn Trent, and North West Water Authorities) came together in 1978 to fund and oversee the Peak District Moorland Erosion Study — a further example of co-operative action (see also Chapter 3, **3.2-3.30**).

23.33 Phase 1 of the study showed that about 8% (or 12.5 square miles) of the Park's moorland is bare or severely eroding. It also identified causes of erosion, including atmospheric pollution, large scale accidental fires, grazing pressure and, in places, heavy recreation pressure (see Phase1 Report, 1981). Phase 2 was concerned with practical experiments into methods of restoration. It demonstrated that restoration of heather moorland is achievable, at least on an experimental basis, if the correct techniques of establishment and aftercare are used (see Phase 2 Report, 1983). With this crucial discovery, the project was renamed the Moorland Restoration Project as its emphasis shifted to programmes of positive action. Since then, the Project has concentrated on developing ways of scaling up the experimental techniques, so they can be applied over larger areas. It has also commissioned and published (1987) a major study into the problems of accidental moorland fires in the Peak District. The National Trust have been particularly active in applying the findings of the project to tackle large scale erosion on their Kinder estate (see 'Kinder, the first 4 years', published by National Trust, 1986).

23.34 Work on the restoration of eroded ground is to continue, and the scope and role of the project is being broadened to cover the promotion of other aspects of good moorland management. In particular, it will provide expert advice on the best ways of balancing and, where appropriate, integrating, the multiple uses of moorland (farming, grouse shooting, water catchment, nature conservation and recreation), so as to ensure the long term survival of their semi-natural vegetation, wildlife and landscape character. This new emphasis to the project will be particularly significant in the context of the recently designated North Peak Environmentally Sensitive Area (ESA), and will continue to be developed in subject scope.

Policies

23.35 The programme of Area Management Schemes will be continued and extended into other parts of the Park, within the scope outlined in Chapters 24 to 47 (Peak Board, Water Authorities, National Trust, Forestry Commission, County Councils, District Councils, Parish Councils, other bodies).

23.36 The co-sponsors of the Integrated Rural Development Project will strive to secure the widespread application of the lessons which have been learned through the project as described in para. 23.26-29 (RDC, DoE, FC, MAFF, NCC, NFU, CLA, Rural Community Councils of Derbyshire and Staffordshire, Peak Board).

23.37 The co-sponsors of the Community Action in the Rural Environment project will seek to further its benefits, and to secure widespread application of successful techniques pioneered by it (Countryside Commission, Barnsley Metropolitan District Council, Peak Board, Parish Councils).

Grant Aid

23.38 **Capital Grants** The Board has for many years, and particularly since the 1978 Plan, used grants as a means to encourage and help capital works by other people which serve National Park purposes. Grants have been given, for example, for:

(a) Planting or management of woodlands (see Chapters 3, 4, & 5)

(b) Purchase of, or conservation works within, nature reserves (see Chapter 6)

(c) Landscape enhancement of unsightly areas, pond restoration, tree planting etc. (see Chapter 7)

(d) Repair or consolidation of historic features in the landscape, such as lime-kilns, pinfolds or relics of lead mining (see Chapter 8)

(e) Repair of historic buildings by their owners (see Chapter 9)

(f) Provision of car parks, toilets, picnic areas and other public facilities (see Chapter 14).

23.39 Such grants have covered widely varying proportions of the capital cost of projects (usually between 25% and 80%). Sometimes the Board's grant is reinforced by grant from other public bodies: indeed the Board is often instrumental in pointing an applicant towards sources of such grants, or acts as agent of other bodies in assessing applications (see Chapter 9). But even a modest grant may suffice to stimulate the project, thus securing a gain with little cost to the public purse. Conditions attached to grants serve to ensure that the gain is sustained by sound management thereafter.

23.40 **Annual grants and other payments** The Board has made extensive use of annual grants or other 'revenue' payments to stimulate continuing actions by others which serve National Park purposes. Such payments have been made, for example, in the context of:

(a) Access agreements, to secure public access to open land (see Chapter 12)

(b) Management agreements (capital grants or annual payments under the Farm Conservation Scheme) to secure protection or active maintenance by farmers of heritage features such as dry-stone walls, flower-rich meadows or woodlands (see Chapter 4)

(c) Support to voluntary organizations for safeguarding the nests of rare birds of prey, excavating key archaeological sites, providing advice to farmers (Farming and Wildlife Advisory Groups), organizing conservation work by volunteers (British Trust for Conservation Volunteers), or general community work (Rural Community Councils).

(d) Support for recreational public transport (see Chapter 16).

23.41 Annual payments of this kind have not until recent years represented a major call on the Board's resources. The recent growth in the number of management agreements, and the periodic reviews of levels of compensation for access agreements, have significantly increased the total sums flowing out in this way. The Board will continue to use this method of stimulus to action by others.

23.42 Where the Board feels that the stimulus would be better given by other agencies, it will press for this. An example of such pressure was the Board's success in persuading the Ministry of Agriculture to increase the capital grants for dry-stone walls; to accept top-wiring of walls as eligible for higher rates of grant; and (later) to place the North Peak area on the short-list for designation of Environmentally Sensitive Areas. Payments to farmers by the Ministry of Agriculture could reduce the necessity for the Board to make further management agreements, at least within the designated ESA (see Chapter 4).

Policy

23.43 Grant aid will be used by the Board and other agencies where it can bring clear gains to National Park purposes and is consistent with other calls upon resources (Peak Board, MAFF, EH, NCC, and other agencies).

Advice, Information and Research

23.44 **Advice** The offer of expert advice has increasingly been used by the Board as a means to influence and assist actions by landowners, property owners and others. Often, this advice is proffered in the context of statutory provisions

— such as development control, or farm grant notifications —
which oblige people to approach the Board. But the Board's
experience has been that informal and positive-minded
advice, if offered before decisions are made, can produce
environmental and other gains which statutory action alone
might never achieve. Moreover, landowners and others
welcome expert advice which may save them difficulties later
and may permit them to achieve a variety of purposes.

23.45 For these reasons, the Board will continue to make
advice readily available, subject to constraints on staff
resources and to encouraging where appropriate the use of
other agencies or professional consultants. Key examples are:

(a) Advice to farmers on all aspects of farm conservation
and diversification, within the context of the Linked Advice
Network (described in Chapter 4)

(b) Advice, including limited architectural guidance , to
the owners of those listed historic buildings in the Park
which are 'at risk' by reason of being unused or becoming
derelict, in order to help them find new uses, or if necessary
new owners or tenants (see Chapter 9)

(c) Technical support to the Peak Park Trust, which was
set up in 1987 to bring new life to disused historic buildings
in the Park and to pursue related initiatives

(d) Architectural or Landscape Design Services (on a
recharge basis) to other authorities

(e) Managaement (on an agency basis) of woodlands
belonging to other public bodies in the Park

(f) Advice to owners of property, on developments which
they may have in mind: simple advice proffered to them
prior to formal planning applications can often save cost
and give much higher standards of development.

23.46 Information and research Very often, advice is only
as good as the information on which it is based. This point has
been underlined since the Board's contact with farmers was
sharply increased following the introduction of the farm grant
notification process in 1980. In order to assess the potential
impact of proposed farm improvements upon wildlife habitats
and field monuments, the Board needed detailed information
(often on a field by field basis) on the pattern and quality of
these features.In 1980 this information was not available on a
systematic basis, and the advice to farmers had often to be
tentative or based on rushed survey information. To remedy
this, the Board has over the last five years been building up a
data base on wildlife habitats, field monuments and other
features, with survey work by trained teams funded by the
Manpower Services Commission. It is hoped this can
continue under the Employment Training Schemes of the
Training Commission.

23.47 In other fields as well, the Board is constantly up-dating
and extending its base of information and its methods of
storing and retrieving this. It commissioned or co-sponsored
research in specific fields — for example the major survey of
visitors to the National Park which has illuminated this Plan;
the study of the impact of public access upon moorland
wildlife; and the experimental work on moorland restoration.
The Board will continue to update and improve its base of
information, and to make information available to assist the
pursuit of National Park purposes.

Policies
23.48 The Board and other agencies will continue to make
advice readily available to farmers, owners of historic

buildings and others, where this will serve National Park
purposes, subject to constraints on staff resources
(RLMEG agencies and others).

23.49 The Board will continue to update and improve its
base of information, and to make it available to assist the
pursuit of National Park purposes (Peak Board).

Statutory Influence

23.50 The Board influences some key aspects of development
and land management in the Park by use of its statutory
powers or formal rights of consultation. Of these, the most
significant are:

(a) **Planning Control** The Board is able to give or
withhold permission for changes in land use, or
construction or alteration of buildings, or mineral working;
and to impose conditions to ensure acceptable
development. The policies which guide our decisions are
set out in the Development Plan First Review and Structure
Plan and (for Bakewell) in the Bakewell District Plan. The
underlying aim is to ensure that local needs for
development and change are met, in so far as they are
compatible with the beauty of the Park and with sound
standards. 80% of applications are approved (See Chapter
20).

(b) **Forestry operations** The Board is asked to advise the
Forestry Commission on Plans of Operation submitted by
owners of dedicated woodlands and on applications for
forestry or woodland grants (see Chapter 5).

(c) **Farm grant notifications** The Board is able to
comment upon and influence proposals by farmers for
improvement works on which they are seeking Ministry of
Agriculture grant. A high proportion of these proposals
gain our agreement, often after the farmer has agreed to
modifications which benefit the National Park (see **4.43**).

(d) **Agricultural and forestry buildings and roads** The
Board is able to influence the siting, design, and materials
of all such proposals. These are processed in conjunction
with farm grant notifications(see **4.44**).

We see these statutory processes not as isolated regulatory
activities, but rather as part of the overall pattern of our
partnership with the Park community and other agencies,
driving always towards positive goals. The Board will
continue to exercise these powers in this spirit.

Policy
23.51 Statutory powers or formal rights of intervention in
the context and spirit of partnership with the Park
community will continue to be exercised by relevant
agencies (RLMEG agencies and others).

Consultation

23.52 The final element in the Board's contribution to the
partnership which this Review requires is consultation. It is
not sufficient to agree the goals of a plan with one's partners
and then to move off into isolated action and correspondence.
There must be regular consultation.

23.53 The Board and its partners have developed a broadly
effective pattern of consultative mechanisms and liaison
meetings. The most significant of these are:

(a) The Peak Park Liaison Committee, comprising the Board and the five Shire District Councils with territory in the Park

(b) Meetings between the Board and the seven County or Metropolitan District Councils from which the Board levies a precept

(c) The Steering Group and Working Groups of the Rural Development Programmes for Staffordshire and Derbyshire (see 23.24)

(d) Annual (or more frequent) meetings between the Board and:

— National Farmers' Union

— Parish Councils

— Amenity organisations

— Ramblers' organisations

— Horse riding organisations

— Wildlife conservation organisations

— Peak Park Moorland Owners and Tenants Association

— Derbyshire Archaeological Advisory Committee

— Housing agencies

(e) Meetings for joint working on tourism, which bring together representatives of the Board, County and District Councils and Regional Tourist Boards and others. These may take on board the work of the Camping and Caravanning Study, which brings together organisations concerned with the supply of sites for these purposes in or near the Park

(f) The Rural Land Management Executive Group (see paragraph 1.32)

(g) Regular liaison meetings with partners in Area Management Schemes (see Chapters 24 to 47).

23.54 The Board sees these and other consultations as essential to oil the wheels of partnership, to defuse issues which could become contentious, and to focus energies on positive achievements. We will continue to play an active part in such consultations.

Policy

23.55 Consultation processes will continue to oil the wheels of partnership in pusuit of National Park purposes (All partners).

Monitoring

23.56 A system for monitoring the implementation of the National Park Plan is needed, in order:

(a) to give an indication of changes that may significantly affect the plan

(b) to determine whether the policies contained in the plan are being implemented

(c) to assess whether the policies and the projects set up to implement policies are effective in achieving the objectives and strategy of the plan.

A regular programme for the collection and analysis of information and statistics is being established. This programme will identify areas where review may be needed and where fresh impetus is required to implement policy related to the Functional Strategies system (see 1.20).

Policy

23.57 A system for monitoring the implementation of this Plan will be established. Reports will be brought forward to the Board's executive committees and to its partners on steps needed to ensure the effective pursuit of the Plan's objectives (Peak Board).

Introduction

24.1 In the 1978 Plan, Chapter 13 indicated how general policies would be implemented in various parts of the Park. The remaining chapters of this Plan indicate what progress has been made, describe current circumstances and issues, and contain suggestions for future policy and action. They deal with 23 areas which are identified on Map 24.1. Some include land outside the National Park where joint action is being taken (e.g. Macclesfield Forest, Chapter 43). Buxton (Chapter 47) is completely outside the National Park, but is included because it is in the heart of the Peak District, and provides major services to visitors to the National Park. Consultation replies on the Draft National Park Plan have helped the Peak Board to clarify and improve these Area Summaries, with the benefit of local information and comments. In many cases, more detailed policies still need to be worked up in further local studies and consultations.

Work to Date and Current Situation

24.2 Much has been achieved in 10 years since the 1978 Plan by joint studies and action with other authorities and agencies (e.g. Longdendale, Chapter 27; and Upper Derwent, Chapter 31). Continued joint working is important to build on successes in those areas, and review the need for any changes. There is also scope for progress in other areas (e.g. the Upper Don in Yorkshire, Chapter 30; and the Board's Warslow Moors Estate, Chapter 44). Some areas in this review have been adjusted since the 1978 Plan, largely to reflect new joint study arrangements. This is made clear in the sections concerned.

24.3 Since the 1978 Plan, the abolition of the Metropolitan County Councils in 1986 has brought the Peak Board into closer partnership with the Metropolitan Districts or City Councils of Barnsley, Kirklees, Oldham and Sheffield. This is reflected in relevant chapters.

24.4 The 3 Regional Water Authorities (North West, Severn Trent and Yorkshire), with major holdings in the National Park, have achieved much through Area Management schemes in partnership with the Peak Board and others. Government pressure on the Water Authorities concerning land

disposal and privatisation is referred to in Chapter 1. The Peak Board is seeking appropriate consultation arrangements from Water Authorities and the government to safeguard what has been achieved, and to ensure that future potential for conservation and recreation can be realised.

24.5 Surveys of motorists and traffic counts in 1986/87 have indicated that there are about 18½ million visits each year to the National Park (see **10.14** and Appendix 5). Visitor distribution figures for the area in Chapter 25-46 are given as estimates in these Chapters (see also Map 24.2). There is confidence in the estimates for central areas within the Park since there was a comprehensive cordon around them. However, there is less certainty about those quoted for peripheral areas where it was difficult to pick up flows to an area. There were no comparative figures for the areas in the 1978 Plan. Other information however indicates a significant change since 1978 in two areas — a fall in volume of traffic in Dovedale, and a rise in Chatsworth. The fall in traffic flows in Dovedale is particularly encouraging as the first evidence of the success of measures to limit visitor impact on an over-used area.

Policies and Proposals

24.6 The policies and proposals in this chapter are related primarily to the detailed application of conservation policies (Chapters 2 to 9), recreation policies (Chapters 10 to 19) and socio-economic policies (Chapters 20 to 21) of this Plan. Whilst the Area Summaries reflect key issues and policies relevant to particular areas, they do not cover everthing in the topic chapters which come earlier in this Plan. Readers are encouraged to look at these earlier chapters which apply Park-wide. If particular points from those chapters have not been repeated in these Area Summaries, it does not reduce their importance in the topic chapters.

24.7 The recreation zoning policies in the 1978 Plan remain valid and are re-stated in this Plan (see Chapter 10, policy **10.28**). The zoning for individual areas (with few amendments since the 1978 Plan), is included as guidance to policies and proposals. They are illustrated on Diagram 10.1, and are briefly summarised below:

Zone I — low intensity active recreation. No facilities normally provided.

Zone II — low intensity active recreation; with simple related facilities.

Zone III — low intensity informal recreation; active recreation opportunities developed. Small-scale related facilities.

Zone IV — modest intensity informal recreation; and modest scale facilities.

Zone V — larger scale facilities and major focus for informal recreation.

Most of the Zone IV and V areas have existing recreation facilities. The statements in Chapters 25 to 47 indicate where additional facilities are proposed or should be investigated.

24.8 Each area contains a number of Sites of Special Scientific Interest and Scheduled Ancient Monuments, as well as other heritage features which have no statutory protection at present (see Chapter 8). Priority will be given to the conservation and appropriate management of all land within each area in line with policies already stated in this Plan (Chapters 2-9 inclusive).

24.9 In all areas, there will be a concern to promote the economic and social well being of the Park communities (see Chapters 20 to 22). However, only substantial initiatives taken or planned are highlighted in the Area Summaries which follow. Broad policies particularly relevant to circumstances in local areas are also identified.

24.10 Government recently suggested that local plans are a useful bridge between strategic policies (the Structure Plan and the National Park Plan in the Park) and development control. It is keen that there should be greater coverage of the country by Local Plans and that 'bottom drawer' plans should be brought into public light and a proper democratic process.

24.11 In the Park, there is a good coverage of 'local plans' in the sense that there are either landscape and recreation management plans or village conservation studies (now to be broadened into 'village management schemes') for most parts of the Park in which there is sufficient activity or development to merit them. Most of them have been the subject of wide discussion and agreement between users, owners and public agencies and are published. Thus the government's objectives are being met. Consideration will be given throughout the Park to up dating, broadening and adding to these plans and schemes where necessary.

24.12 Each area summary indicates a statement as to the current status of schemes or studies and proposals to improve or sustain them to meet the objectives of Government's advice.

24.13 Chapters 25 to 47 deal, in turn, with the areas indicated on Map 24.1. Each has the following format:

(a) **Introduction** − including description of the area, and the main points from the 1978 Plan

(b) **Work to Date** − summarising the main activities and action since the 1978 Plan

(c) **Current Circumstances** − identifying key issues and facts forming a basis for policies and proposals

(d) **Policies and Proposals** − these include recreation zoning as a guidance, along with specific policies and proposals. Policy statements and proposals have been indented and underlined. The organisations listed in brackets after them are only those primarily involved in implementation, and the Board hopes for their co-operation and agreement. They do not indicate the range of bodies to be consulted.

24.14 The only exception to this is the statement for the Buxton Area outside the National Park where Local Planning Authority responsibilities are shared by Derbyshire County Council and the Borough of High Peak. For this area, the Plan suggests 'Topics for Investigation' which have been agreed with the two adjoining authorities.

24.15 Other area summaries refer to joint working arrangements across the Park boundary. The wider principle of the interdependence of the Park and its surrounding countryside and towns rests in Policy **10.17** and is developed further in Chapter 17, particularly **17.19**, **17.28**, **17.36**, **17.82**.

24.16 Buxton is only one town of many fulfilling this role interdependently with the National Park. Others which already have a substantial tourist function or potential include Meltham, Holmfirth, Penistone, Sheffield (linked to 'business tourism'), Chesterfield, Matlock, Wirksworth, Ashbourne, Leek, Macclesfield, Whaley Bridge, Chapel-en-le-Frith, New Mills, Hayfield, Glossop and Uppermill.

24.17 The following table lists the chapter number and title of each of the area summaries which follow this chapter. The table also names the more significant existing area and estate management plans which exist or are being prepared. (It does not list the conservation area or village management schemes. These are dealt with in Chapter 9, and introduced individually in the area summaries).

Chapter number	Area Title	Area or estate management plans at 14.10.88
25	Northern Moors	
26	Dove Stone	Dove Stone Management Study
27	Longdendale	Upper Longdendale Study
28	Wessenden and Marsden Area	
29	Meltham and Holmfirth Fringes	
30	Upper Don Tributaries	Upper Don Study
31	Upper Derwent and Woodlands Valleys	Upper Derwent Management Plan
32	Edale Valley	
33	High Peak Fringe	
34	Hope Valley	
35	Eastern Moors	Eastern Moors and North Lees Estate Management Plans
36	Northern Limestone Plateau	
37	Lower Derwent Valley	Chatsworth Inheritance Tax Management Plan
38	Wye Valley	Bakewell District Plan
39	Southern Limestone Plateau	
40	Stanton and Birchover	
41	Lyme Hall and Park	Lyme Hall and Park Management Plan in course of preparation
42	Goyt/Todd Brook/Lamaload	
43	Macclesfield Forest, Wildboarclough Wincle	Macclesfield Forest and Wildboarclough Joint Management Plan
44	South West Moors	Warslow Moors and Roaches Estate Management Plans
45	Upper Dove and Manifold Valleys	
46	Lower Dove and Manifold Valleys	
47	Buxton Area (outside the National Park)	

Map 24.1
Area Sub-divisions

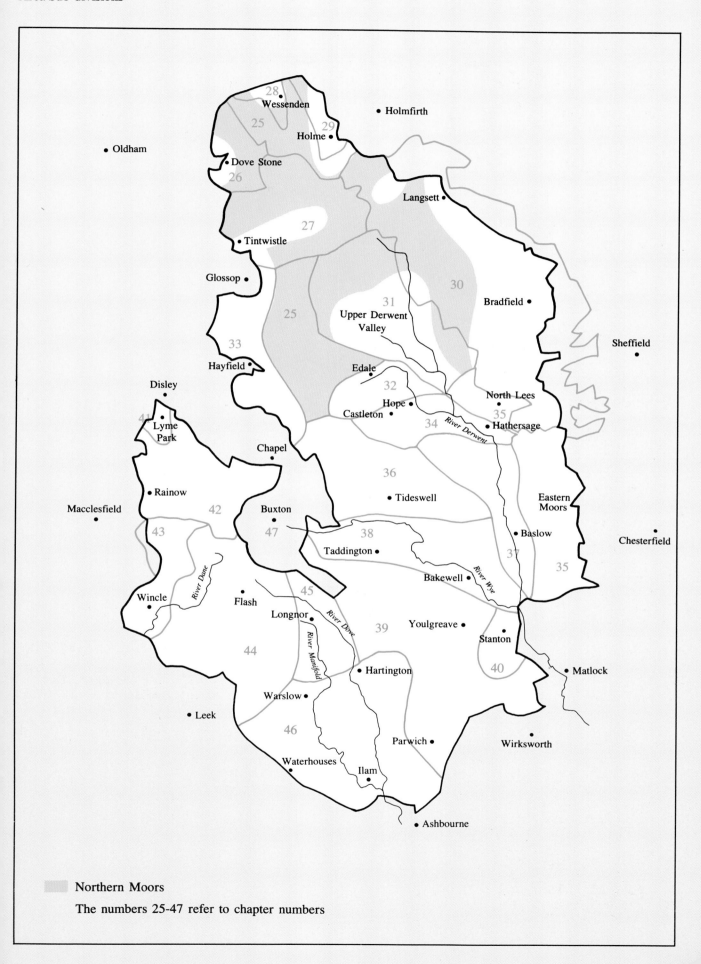

Northern Moors

The numbers 25-47 refer to chapter numbers

Map 24.2
Visitor Distribution

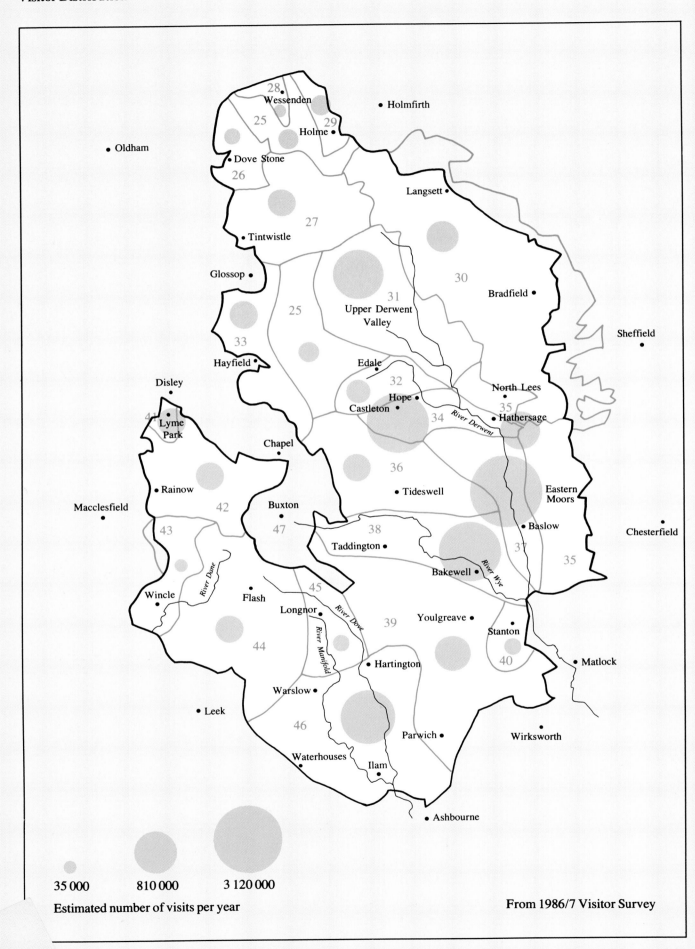

Oldham

Wessenden
Holme
28
25
29
Dove Stone
26
27
Tintwistle

Holmfirth

Langsett

Bradfield

Sheffield

Glossop
25
31
Upper Derwent
Valley
30

33
Hayfield
Edale
32
Hope
Castleton
34
River Derwent
North Lees
35
Hathersage

Disley
41
Lyme
Park
Chapel
36
Tideswell
Eastern
Moors
Baslow

Macclesfield
Rainow
42
Buxton
47
38
Taddington
37
35
Chesterfield

43
River Dane
45
River Dove
River Wye
Bakewell

Wincle
Flash
Longnor
River Manifold
39
Youlgreave
Stanton
Matlock
40

Leek
44
Hartington
46
Warslow

Waterhouses
Ilam
Parwich
Wirksworth

Ashbourne

35 000   810 000   3 120 000

Estimated number of visits per year

From 1986/7 Visitor Survey

25 Northern Moors

Introduction

25.1 The Northern Moors are the main area of gritstone moorland in the Peak District. This area consists almost entirely of uninhabited moorland and excludes the main valleys. In some cases it overlaps with Area Management Studies (e.g. in Dove Stone and Longdendale, Chapters 26 and 27 respectively). A summary here saves repetition in other chapters which follow. Much information and policy also cross relates to Chapters 3, 4, 6, 12 and 22 of this Review. General policies for moorland management are set out in Chapter 3.

25.2 Apart from some boundaries, a few roads, and the Holme Moss tv transmitter, the Northern Moors area is as near to wilderness as occurs in England. It is prized for recreation on this account, and for the challenge of navigating over featureless open country. Much of the land is owned by the National Trust, or by Water Authorities which acquired land to protect reservoir catchments. Sheep grazing and grouse management are the main economic uses.

25.3 Much of the area is a Site of Special Scientific Interest, and land not within the SSSI is known to have similar nature conservation interest. The area also has archaeological interest, particularly for signs of activity in Mesolithic times.

25.4 Most of the land within the Northern Moors is subject to Access Agreements, or otherwise open to free public access on foot. The 1986/87 surveys suggest there are over 190,000 visitors each year to the Northern Moors, approaching from neighbouring areas like Longdendale, Dove Stone, Holmfirth, Upper Derwent, Edale and Hayfield. The Pennine Way starting from Edale runs across Kinder, Bleaklow and Black Hill and is a major focus for walkers.

25.5 In the 1978 Plan, the whole area was shown as Zone 1 to cater only for low intensities of active recreation, with no facilities normally provided. The 1978 Plan provided for:

> (a) Safeguarding the wild qualities by avoiding or reducing the impact of man-made features
> (b) Providing opportunities for walking and nature study, while pointing out that an alternative to Access Agreements might be appropriate in certain circumstances
> (c) Tackling the problem of moorland erosion.

Work to Date

25.6 The Section 3 Map (see **2.22**) defines nearly all the area as "particularly important to conserve".

25.7 The Moorland Erosion Study considered the reasons for erosion of the blanket bog. Conservation of the vegetation is in the best long-term interests of all users and it has been demonstrated that erosion can be halted and reversed. The Study therefore went into a more positive phase and became the Moorland Restoration Project (see **3.25** and **23.32** to **34**).

25.8 The National Trust acquired the Hayfield Estate (Kinder Scout) in 1982 and, as a condition of Countryside Commission grant, prepared a Management Plan in consultation with the Peak Board. Among other improvements, the Trust has carefully managed moorland vegetation to permit heather to recover. This was recognised by a Ford European Conservation Award in 1987.

25.9 Additional access areas have been the subject of detailed discussions with the owners of land not open to the public, and agreement has been reached on land south and east of Kinder Reservoir.

25.10 A few sections of the Pennine Way have been surfaced to prevent the development of wide swathes of exposed peat.

25.11 In a few cases, proposals for agricultural improvement and fencing have been resisted under the Farm Grant Notification Scheme, though some roadside fencing and some re-improvement of reverting land has been accepted. Agreement was reached with some owners and farmers to substitute cattle grids for a proposal to ring-fence a land holding or to erect roadside fences (e.g. North Lees and Ringinglow). This helps to maintain the open character of moors crossed by minor roads.

25.12 Planning permission was given for a replacement TV transmitter at Holme Moss, and an unplanned car parking area nearby was improved and defined to prevent it spreading (see Chapter 29).

Current Circumstances

25.13 The Section 3 Map has replaced the Moor and Heath Map and will show virtually all land in this area as "particularly important to conserve" (see paragraphs **2.16-2.18**).

25.14 The participants in the Moorland Management Project (see Chapter 3) have decided that the best way to ensure the long-term conservation of the vegetation is to widen the scope of the Project to advise on moorland management generally.

25.15 Naturalists have expressed concern that public access to moorlands affects wildlife, particularly the characteristic ground-nesting birds such as golden plover and wintering birds of prey. A study has been started to try to understand the relationship and to suggest action. As with most biological interactions, the situation is complicated and will take time to evaluate. In the meantime, the Board will continue to seek a balance between the interests of wildlife, landscape and recreation. It is adopting the principle of sanctuary areas to conserve areas of importance for wildlife (see **12.27**).

25.16 The Countryside Commission has appointed a Project Officer for the Pennine Way to prepare a strategy for coping with the popularity of this long-distance path. She is employed under the direction of the Board's Chief Ranger and is based at Edale. Parking of cars related to the Pennine Way, in use at places like Snake Summit and Wessenden Head, needs careful consideration to avoid spoiling the moorland environment.

25.17 The Ministry of Agriculture has included this area as part of an Environmentally Sensitive Area (ESA). The response to MAFF so far has been encouraging, and this will allow for payments to landowners, farmers and shooting tenants to conserve their land (see **4.19**).

Policies and Proposals

25.18 Zone I policies are still relevant to the Northern Moors (see 10.28).

25.19 Section 3 Map policies (see Chapter 2) will be applied particularly to this area by means of ESA status, the Moorland Management Project, continued action in Area Management Studies and in responding to farm grant notifications (Peak Board, MAFF and other participants in Moorland Management Project).

25.20 New fences in the natural zone moorland areas will continue to be resisted unless:

(a) there are good conservation reasons for them (e.g. temporary fencing to aid recovery of fire damaged, eroded or overgrazed moorland).

(b) the fence is part of an agreed land improvement; or

(c) the fence is an essential safety measure along major roads.

(Peak Board, Ministry of Agriculture, Peak Park Moorland Owners and Tenants Association).

25.21 As the whole area forms part of the Natural Zone (see Chapter 2), great care will be taken to avoid new developments which would affect the wild qualities of the area. Where works are essential, or changes to existing man-made features are desirable, they will be carefully designed so as to have minimum effect on the landscape. This applies particularly to surfacing of the Pennine Way and other footpaths, and parking related to moorland routes (Peak Board).

25.22 Increased public access will be sought in accordance with the objective stated in 12.25 (Peak Board).

25.23 Further bird surveys will be encouraged (see 6.67) (Peak Board, NCC).

Most of the land in the Northern Moors is subject to Access Agreement, or otherwise open to free public access on foot.

26 Dove Stone

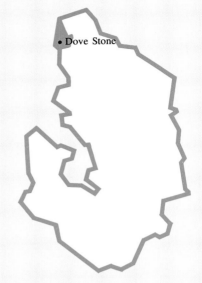

• Dove Stone

Introduction

26.1 This north-west corner of the National Park has high gritstone moorland surrounding a network of reservoirs. It contrasts strongly with the adjacent urban areas outside the National Park. Much of the area is in the ownership of North West Water, with the land farmed predominantly for sheep.

26.2 The moorland has a peat blanket, carrying a fragile vegetation of heather, mosses, lichens and cotton grasses. Parts of the moorland have suffered from erosion. The slopes above the reservoirs are mainly agricultural grassland, but include an extensive patchwork of tree-planting. There are 4 reservoirs — 3 in the valley between Saddleworth Moor and Greenfield, and a fourth (Chew) Reservoir at a high level on the edge of the moor. Only the lowest reservoir — Dove Stone — is used for recreation, with a sailing club established on its southern shore. Below this reservoir is a large public car park — for about 70 cars — and a separate car park for the sailing club. Further car parking spaces are provided along the roadside. There is also a toilet block and a ranger briefing centre. The car park is a starting point for walks around the lower reservoirs, and onto an access track to Chew Reservoir. The moorland to the east is included in an Access Agreement.

26.3 Additional car parking and toilets for the area are provided on high ground to the west of the reservoirs, at Binn Green. The access is from the A635 road which links Greenfield with Yorkshire.

26.4 The 1978 Plan referred to a Joint Study which was examining the future development and management of this area, and anticipated the publication of a Management Plan. This Management Plan was published in early 1978, following approval by the authorities whose officers had worked together to produce it — the Peak Board, North West Water, Oldham MBC, Greater Manchester Council, and North West Regional Council for Sport and Recreation. Other organisations had helped in producing the plan, including the Ministry of Agriculture and representatives of local interest groups.

26.5 The 1978 Plan referred to the need to find a new future for Ashway Gap House. Despite various efforts by a number of organisations, the building proved to be beyond repair. It was therefore demolished and the site landscaped.

Work to Date

26.6 The Management Plan has formed the basis for implementation in Dove Stone. Action has progressed slowly, mainly due to the limited resources available to the participating authorities. Even so, significant achievements can be recorded:

(a) Extension of the Peak Board's ranger service to improve visitor advice and liaison in the Dove Stone area. A full-time ranger is now based in the area, with part funding by North West Water. He is supported by part-time staff, within the contract Ranger Service provided by the Peak Board.

(b) Improvements to public car parking below Dove Stone Reservoir. This was a problem site for many years, until the Peak Board and, more recently, Oldham MBC carried out major landscaping works to the car parks to improve traffic circulation and to improve their appearance.

(c) Improved footpath facilities, for the able and the disabled visitor. These include a new concession path around Yeoman Hey and Greenfield reservoirs and a recently completed wheelchair route on the northern side of Dove Stone Reservoir. Major improvement works have been carried out on the existing footpath network, including surface and bridge works, stiles, gates and drainage.

(d) Landscaping and tree-planting to enhance the overall appearance of the area.

The Trinacle Stones on access moorland, high above Dove Stone Reservoir.

(e) The publication of a free 'visitors guide', available from rangers and from information points in surrounding areas.

(f) Liaison with neighbouring areas to cope with the demand for lightweight camping, with provision in the Tame Valley area to the west rather than in the National Park.

Current Circumstances
26.7 The 1986/87 surveys suggest there are about 80,000 visitors to this area each year. However, it has a limited capacity to absorb recreation pressure due to shortage of suitable car parking areas. Improved parking is only likely to come about by reorganisation of the activity areas around the Dove Stone reservoir. Any further attraction of, or provision for, visitors would threaten the fragile network of main recreation routes. These are already heavily used at busy times, and there is little sense of isolation or wilderness, save for those visitors who wander onto the moors.

26.8 Most visitors are casual walkers, staying close to the Dove Stone reservoir to watch the sailing. In hot weather the reservoir becomes a bathing area, despite Water Authority efforts in the past to prevent this because of the risk of drowning or accidents. The Authority erect warning notices, and rescue lines are carried by staff and rangers.

26.9 A further wheelchair route on the eastern side of Dove Stone reservoir will follow when negotiations are complete. A later stage may see the completion of a full circuit around the reservoir.

26.10 Following the abolition of Greater Manchester Council in March 1986, Oldham MBC gained a member's place on the Peak Board. The Council quickly sought new action in its part of the National Park. Member level meetings have been held, and an Advisory Steering Committee has been established to give increased impetus to the activities of the Officer Group and to extend its remit to cover the whole of the Oldham part of the National Park. The Members Advisory Steering Committee includes Oldham MBC, North West Water and Peak Board representatives.

26.11 In 1988, new treatment works planned for the reservoirs in the valley will mean less restriction on recreation activity. However, this is likely to have little effect as Dove Stone reservoir is already well used and more activity would not be appropriate on the other reservoirs.

Policies and Proposals
26.12 The broad zoning policies previously defined in the National Park Plan and Dove Stone Plan still apply:

(a) The moorland and the higher slopes of the valleys are most appropriate for low intensity agriculture, with recreational use linked to moorland access — Zone I.

(b) The middle and lower valley slopes are appropriate for a mixture of grassland agriculture and plantation woodland, with recreation limited to a clearly defined network of walking routes — Zone II.

(c) The surrounds of Dove Stone Reservoir are already well used, and this area requires positive management to integrate this activity with the maintenance of an attractive part of the National Park landscape — Zone IV.

26.13 For the future, most attention will centre on the area around Dove Stone Reservoir:

(a) Car parking will need to be rationalized — there is the opportunity to improve public provision by reorganising the sailing club's boat and car parking.

(b) The toilets should be improved to include facilities for the disabled.

(c) The recreation route network will continue to be improved, to provide for walkers and the disabled. It is not, however, felt that horse-riding can be accommodated off the metalled routes. Nor does the area readily lend itself to cycling. Links for walkers, cyclists and horse riders into the area from the adjacent urban areas are being considered.

(d) Information and interpretation for visitors must be improved.

(e) There is also the possibility of extended public access to moorlands in the area, subject to full consideration of any wildlife and primary land use interests.

(f) Motor cycling activity will be considered in the light of some complaints.

26.14 The extension of the Dove Stone Officer Group's remit will give the opportunity to consider land use and management requirements over a wider area. However, most of this additional area is regarded as Zone I insofar as broad zoning policies are concerned.

26.15 The Dove Stone Management Plan will continue to provide a basis for decision making and investment of funds for recreation, conservation, land and water management in the area. A new appraisal will be made to cover all the Oldham MBC area within the National Park (Peak Board, Oldham MBC, North West Water).

26.16 The Plan will be monitored and reviewed by the Officer Group, reporting annually to a Member Advisory Steering Committee (Peak Board, Oldham MBC, North West Water).

27 Longdendale

• Tintwistle

Introduction

27.1 'Long', 'den', and 'dale' all imply a 'valley', and this elongated name well characterizes this area. A deep valley cuts into the heart of the Peak District gritstone moorlands from the west, reaching some seven miles into the National Park. The valley contains a string of five major reservoirs, and parallel to these are the major communication and service links — the A628 trunk road, the Woodhead railway (closed in recent years), and a 400 kV overhead electricity line — all running west-east. Other important roads leave the area — to the north the A6024 to Holme Moss, and to the south the B6105 to Glossop.

27.2 The slopes of the lower valley rise almost immediately from the reservoir margins, and are mainly enclosed grassland which has been managed at a low intensity. The land continues to rise up onto the surrounding moorland plateau, with Bleaklow to the south and Black Hill to the north. The valley is largely shared among half-a-dozen main farms, primarily sheep, but with two cattle enterprises. Most of these farms are tenanted from North West Water.

27.3 Other than the farms, the few residents in the area are at Woodhead in the east, Crowden in the centre, and Tintwistle in the west. Crowden is also the base for many of the recreation activities in the valley, and Woodhead has long been a major attraction to car-borne visitors at weekends. The Pennine Way crosses Longdendale north-south, passing through Crowden. It was for this reason that a Youth Hostel was established there by the Peak Board, and a lightweight camp site was added in 1977.

27.4 The valley has a limited network of public footpaths plus a number of routes to public access land — most of the moorlands around are open to access. One of the most popular areas — the Black Cloughs at Woodhead — is also within a major Site of Special Scientific Interest.

27.5 In the 1970s, a sailing club site was developed on Bottoms Reservoir, with a plan to move eventually to the larger Torside Reservoir. North West Water also agreed to fishing on Valehouse Reservoir.

27.6 The 1978 Plan recognised the need for a comprehensive and co-ordinated approach to action and management of this area, and proposed a Joint Working Party.

Work to Date

27.7 Many public and local bodies were involved in a study, which was led by North West Water and the Peak Board, and guided by an Advisory Steering Committee of members drawn from ten bodies. A study report was published in 1981, and provided the basis for a major implementation programme. The Peak Board chairs this Steering Committee which also includes representatives of North West Water, High Peak BC, Derbyshire CC, Charlesworth PC, Tintwistle PC, Sports Council, Countryside Commission, Barnsley MBC, Tameside MC and Kirklees MDC.

27.8 The most significant achievements are:

(a) Improvement of the coverage provided by the Peak Board's ranger service, with a full-time ranger and part-time staff, part funded by North West Water.

(b) Opening up of some reservoir margins to the visitor.

(c) Improvements and additions to the network of walking and horse-riding routes, with concessionary links supplementing the public rights of way.

(d) The establishment of a major sailing facility on Torside Reservoir, run as a club but with arrangements for public use. Adjacent to the site is a public car park for over 100 cars, a toilet block and information room. An informal picnic area has been provided, and there is a wheelchair access to the reservoir edge.

(e) Approval has been given — subject to constraints on levels of use and noise — for water sports on Bottoms Reservoir. This will be based on the former sailing club site, and can provide sailing, water-skiing, canoeing and fishing. It is intended that public and educational groups would be able to make use of the facility. Permission for water skiing was granted by the Peak Board as an exception to normal policy in view of the location of the site. A proposal for more intensive recreation and leisure use of Bottoms Reservoir and its environs was refused planning permission in June 1988.

(f) A small public car park and toilets have been provided at Crowden, catering for the active recreation seeker — walkers and climbers.

(g) A number of small woodlands have been established as landscape features.

(h) Some existing small woodlands have been enclosed to exclude stock and encourage natural regeneration. One large 40 ha. block of relict oak and birch has also been enclosed.

(i) A management agreement has been concluded within the Site of Special Scientific Interest at Black Clough.

(j) Restoration works have been carried out at St. James Church, Woodhead.

(k) An eighteenth century turnpike bridge at Saltersbrook has been restored, and in 1987 this project received a CPRE commendation.

(l) The framework provided by the Study helped to guide the Water Authority and its consultants in their satisfactory resolution of the problems posed by the need to carry out flood prevention measures in the Valley. These will commence in 1988.

(m) A Guide to the area was produced in 1988 for visitors to the Valley.

Current Circumstances

27.9 Implementation of projects is now slowing down, partly due to competing demands for resources within the participating authorities, and partly due to attention being redirected to other land use issues. The Advisory Steering Committee of members continues to meet once a year to guide implementation.

27.10 The 1986/87 surveys suggest there are about 370,000 visitors to this area each year.

27.11 There is still a need to complete the tree planting, car parking, toilet, information, walking, horse-riding and cycling projects identified in the 1981 study. Changing local circumstances have affected these programmes, the most significant of which is the closure of the Woodhead railway line through the valley. This should give opportunities for new recreation routes, avoiding some of the conflicts of interest encountered in creating routes elsewhere in the valley. The recreation potential of the line will not be prevented by the major reservoir safety works programmed for the valley, though some minor modifications to routes may be needed. The railway closure could enable links to be improved with the Upper Don Valley, where there is recreation potential for the disused line to the east of Dunford Bridge. There is also a proposal in a report produced by consultants for Barnsley MBC to include the Woodhead line in a long distance recreation route between York and Liverpool.

27.12 The future of the disused Woodhead tunnel between Dunford Bridge and Longdendale is uncertain. However, the Board supported a call by the Derbyshire CC and Barnsley MBC for studies of possible alternative uses — in particular a shared transport/powerline route.

27.13 The Department of Transport has recently dropped an earlier plan for a Mottram, Hollingworth, Tintwistle bypass and stated that there are no proposals for new roads through the Park and there is a Government presumption against new roads in National Parks. It has declined a feasibility study related to the tunnel, but is looking again at the A628(T) with a view to minor improvements. The future of the tunnel therefore remains uncertain.

27.14 The valley has been threatened by other major changes in recent years. In 1977 a proposed new road through the valley was abandoned by the Department of Transport. In 1983 the Central Electricity Generating Board (CEGB), postponed plans for a pumped storage power generation project. The Steering Committee believe that the existence of the Longdendale Study was a major factor in causing the CEGB to reconsider its proposals. This illustrates pressures that always lurk in and around the Peak District, and the outcome justifies the attention the Peak Board and other bodies have given to enhancing the

valley. The Peak Board will need to remain vigilant against either of the above major threats being proposed again (see **27.22**).

27.15 Discussions on the possible privatisation of water authorities and the disposal of their holdings was a major subject of concern in the valley in 1986. This is dealt with as a wider issue earlier in the Plan (see **1.19** and **23.21**). Specific proposals may arise within the valley — at the present time consideration is being given to future uses of Holybank Quarry, a disused site just outside Tintwistle. A recent planning application for a rifle range in the quarry was refused.

27.16 The Longdendale Officer Study Group and Members Advisory Steering Committee are excellent samples of co-operation between the various authorities involved, and the achievements would not have been possible without these joint bodies.

Policies and Proposals

27.17 The 1978 Plan provisionally defined broad recreation zoning policies for Longdendale. Following the more detailed Local Study, these were adjusted. They can now be defined as follows:

(a) The moorland and the higher slopes of the valleys are most appropriate for low intensive agriculture on well-managed heather and grassland. Recreational use linked to moorland acess is appropriate — Zone I.

(b) The middle and lower valley slopes are appropriate for a mixture of grassland agriculture and woodland with recreation limited to a clearly defined network of routes — Zone II.

(c) Small areas at Woodhead and Crowden are quite heavily used for informal recreation — Zone III.

(d) The lower valley floor from Torside westwards is most able to accommodate intensive recreation facilities — water recreation, major car parks, well-used recreation routes — Zone IV.

27.18 Proposals for Zones I and II will be closely linked to policies fo the natural zone. Non-traditional methods of farming will be resisted, and traditional methods encouraged (Peak Board, MAFF, Longdendale Advisory Steering Committee, North West Water).

27.19 At Woodhead, a scheme will be prepared to improve visitor management, accommodating the existing activity by improvements to the car parking, and by providing toilets and information (North West Water, Peak Board).

27.20 Elsewhere in the valley, work will continue to implement the proposals in the 1981 Study related to car parking, recreation route, environmental conservation and information. This will be monitored and reviewed by the Officer Working Group, which will continue to report annually to the Members Advisory Steering Committee (Peak Board, Longdendale Advisory Steering Committee).

27.21 A scheme will be devised to make use of the recreation potential of the disused Woodhead Railway line. This will be linked to a similar scheme being investigated from Dunford Bridge eastwards. The future use of the Woodhead tunnel will also be clarified (Peak Board, North West Water, Derbyshire CC, High Peak BC, British Rail). (See also **30.23**).

27.22 Any proposals for new communication links or services (including a Pumped Storage Power Station) in Longdendale will be resisted in line with established policies **22.30-22.32** (Peak Board).

27.23 The 1981 study has a long term aim that the 400 kV power lines running through the valley should be put underground, and this will be pursued (Peak Board).

A major sailing base has been established on Torside Reservoir, run as a club, but with arrangements for public use.

28 Wessenden and Marsden Area

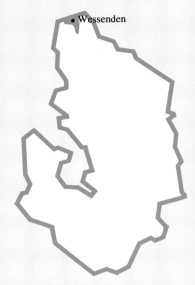

• Wessenden

Introduction

28.1 This northern area lies between the A635 road and Marsden, a town just outside the National Park. It includes a deeply cut valley containing three reservoirs between the A635 and Marsden, and some moorland adjoining reservoirs and roads which link into the Northern Moors (Chapter 25). The alternative route for the Pennine Way is a track running the complete length of the valley. Much of this area is owned by the National Trust and Yorkshire Water Authority. The A62 trunk road leads westwards from Marsden over the Pennine Ridge at Standedge, while the railway and canal tunnel pass underneath. Redbrook Reservoir is used as a sailing club, and Pule Hill just outside the National Park is a popular area with visitors.

28.2 The 1978 Plan proposed the character of the area should be maintained with limited provision for active recreation and associated small-scale facilities. It suggested investigation of additional accommodation in the Marsden area and treatment of a derelict site. It called for consultation by adjoining authorities about recreation proposals which might affect the National Park, particularly by increasing pressure on the Moors.

Work to Date

28.3 Marsden Youth Hostel has closed since 1978, but Pennine Way accommodation is presently provided at Globe Farm, Standedge. The Board acted to restore fly tipping sites on moorland adjoining the Wessenden Moor road to Meltham. At Wessenden Head, a derelict but screened quarry area used

for parking has been improved by the Board, with a contribution from the National Trust as owners. A car park adjoining Standedge cutting has recently been landscaped by Oldham MBC. A Standedge Trail is being promoted and interpreted by Kirklees MBC and Oldham MBC as a joint project using robust routes. At Naze Top Wood in the Wessenden Valley, the Peak Board and Yorkshire Water jointly funded fencing and tree planting by Huddersfield Conservation Volunteers. Work has been done by National Park Rangers to prevent trespass by motor bikes and horses on the Pennine Way alternative route.

28.4 Prior to its abolition in April 1986, West Yorkshire MCC sought views on a proposed 90 miles circular walk in Kirklees District, to be known as the Kirklees Way. It included the Wessenden Valley and the adjoining moorland near Holme (see also **29.4**). Kirklees MBC took over responsibility for this project from West Yorkshire MCC. The Kirklees Way opened in May 1988. Its usage and condition will be carefully monitored and reviewed.

Current Circumstances

28.5 The 1986/87 surveys suggest there are about 35,000 visitors to this area each year.

28.6 Yorkshire Water are to review their Divisional Recreation Strategy, which could include consideration of improved access to water areas. The appointment of a Pennine Way Project Officer (see **11.3**) provides an opportunity to review, with the Kirklees MBC's countryside rangers, the action needed on this section of the Pennine Way. The possibility of new legislation on Common Land is relevant to Wessenden Moor, where access and management will be discussed with the National Trust.

28.7 The Peak Board approved an application for oil exploration at a site near Wessenden Head. This was without prejudice to any subsequent application to exploit any oil that might be found in the area. Drilling was carried out in early 1988. No further work is proposed and the site has been restored.

28.8 Meltham Moor is popular locally and improved public access arrangements would be desirable. However, there are higher priorities for Access Agreements in other parts of the National Park (see Chapter 12).

28.9 In 1987, the National Trust appointed a Warden whose area includes Wessenden Moor. The possibility of more comprehensive National Peak Ranger Service coverage, as achieved elsewhere in the Peak District, should be examined with Yorkshire Water.

Policies and Proposals

28.10 The 1978 Plan remains valid for an area which is only capable of accommodating limited recreational facilities and activity. The wild qualities of the moors must continue to be safeguarded and policies for them applied to that end (see Chapter 2, 3 and 25). On valley sides, as at Naze Top Wood, regeneration of existing woods needs to be encouraged by fencing against sheep and by some additional planting (see Chapter 3).

28.11 The recreation zoning of the 1978 Plan is still appropriate to the character of this area:

(a) The moorlands on the higher valley sides and in the upper valley — Zone I.

(b) The area around Butterley Reservoir may be suitable for small scale recreation facilities — Zone II.

28.12 The existing character of the area should be maintained. Close liaison will be maintained to consider action on recreation facilities and routes (e.g. reservoir access), modest accommodation (e.g. back-pack campsites), landscape improvements, management of Common Land, and ranger services within and close to the National Park (Peak Board, Kirklees MBC, Yorkshire Water, National Trust).

28.13 Consideration will be given to seeking improved public access to Meltham Moor subject to careful consideration of conservation interests (Peak Board).

28.14 Consideration will be given to establishing contract ranger arrangements in the area based upon existing joint funding schemes for the National Park Ranger Service which operate in other parts of the Peak District (Peak Board, Yorkshire Water).

29 Meltham and Holmfirth Fringes

Holme •

Introduction
29.1 This area in the north of the National Park contains several reservoirs supplying parts of West Yorkshire, the village of Holme and sloping land adjoining the Northern Moors. There is enclosed and improved farmland on the fringe of Meltham, with degenerating farmland and barns around Bradshaw to the south of the A635 and in the vicinity of Digley Reservoir. Improved farmland around Holme leads up to poorer land around the Yateholme Reservoirs where there are substantial conifer woods. A number of minor roads and tracks link Meltham, Holmfirth and Holme and the various farmsteads. Much of the land in this area is owned by the Yorkshire Water Authority.

29.2 The 1978 Plan suggested small-scale accommodation and parking facilities, route improvements, improved management of farmland, additional tree planting and improvement of existing plantations.

Work to Date
29.3 Since 1978 the Yorkshire Water Authority has improved car parking at Holme Moss, Ramsden Reservoir (with help from Kirklees MBC), and Digley Reservoir (with design advice and grant-aid from the Peak Board). Information for visitors in this area, a much filmed location for the 'Last of the Summer Wine' tv series, has been improved. Kirklees MBC propose information boards at Digley and Ramsden Reservoir car parks, for which leaflets in their Countryside Link series are now available. The Peak Board has provided an information board in Holme Village,

and also constructed a viewfinder at Holme Moss with help from the Automobile Association and Yorkshire Water.

29.4 The footpath network has been improved, especially around Ramsden and Digley Reservoir car parks. Walks are well signed and waymarked. They are described in a booklet called 'Enjoying Yorkshire's Waters' produced by Yorkshire Water. The former West Yorkshire MCC proposed a 90 mile circuit path called the Kirklees Way largely using existing routes (see also **28.4**). This would have included some sensitive parts of moorland between the A635 and Holme. Kirklees MBC took over responsibility for this project from West Yorkshire MCC and agreed to route changes suggested by the Board to avoid moorland near Holme. The Kirklees Way opened in May 1988.

29.5 A waste tip at Royd Edge, Meltham was reclaimed by West Yorkshire MCC and the Peak Board to provide grazing land and trees.

29.6 A Conservation Area was designated in Holme village, and the Peak Board has co-ordinated an improvement package with local agreement. This has included removal of overhead wires, and renewing the stone setts at The Green following construction of an alternative area for buses to turn round at the southern end of the village. The retention of the village school in Holme is important to the community, who have also expressed concern about possible loss of the village shop and post office. A possible site has been identified for a car park requested by the Parish Council as an alternative to parking on The Green.

29.7 It is understood that the Forestry Commission is disposing of its Yateholme Forest to Yorkshire Water to manage with their adjoining woods. Yorkshire Water currently have no specialist landscape or forestry staff, but have agreed to consider guidelines put forward by the Peak Board.

29.8 Kirklees MBC are looking at the possibility of landscaping and forming a streamside path called the Meltham Linear Park running westwards from Meltham into the National Park.

Current Circumstances
29.9 Yorkshire Water has completed may improvements in line with its Recreation Strategy, which is to be reviewed. There is also the possibility of land disposal or privatisation which makes it vital for the Board to maintain close liaison and co-operation with Yorkshire Water (see **1.15**). There is a particular need to safeguard facilities jointly provided (e.g. Digley car park), sites of conservation value, and areas with further potential for action (e.g. the Yateholme area — see **29.12**).

29.10 The possibility of more comprehensive National Park Ranger service coverage, as achieved elsewhere in the Peak District, should be examined with Yorkshire Water.

29.11 The 1986/87 surveys suggest there are about 200,000 visitors to this area each year.

Policies and Proposals
29.12 The zoning set out in the 1978 Plan is unchanged. It is as follows:
  (a) The upper valley sides and moorland — Zone I.

Holme village. Overhead wires have been removed, and The Green has been re-surfaced with stone setts.

(b) Much of the area is suitable for small scale recreation facilities related to moorland recreation (if suitable sites are available) — Zone II.

(c) Areas around Digley, Ramsden and Yateholme Reservoirs and Holme Village, have already proved suitable for small scale car parks and picnic sites — Zone III.

29.13 The main issues for possible action in this area include:

(a) Modest additional recreation facilities and routes (especially related to reservoirs, access to Ramsden Clough, Yateholme woodlands and a circuit from Meltham).

(b) Scope for development of small-scale accommodation facilities (e.g. farmhouse accommodation, back-pack camp sites and camping barns).

(c) Improvement of existing plantations by introduction of more broadleaved trees, providing new woodlands.

(d) Continuing environmental improvement work in Holme, including better parking arrangements.

29.14 The character of the area, and existing recreation facilities and routes, should be maintained and enhanced. Further improvements should be considered along the lines set out in 29.12. Any proposals should be lined, where appropriate, to the area of Kirklees outside the National Park (Peak Board, Kirklees MBC, Yorkshire Water Authority).

29.15 Consideration will be given to establishing contract ranger arrangements in the area, based upon existing joint schemes for the National Park Ranger Service which operate in other parts of the Peak District (Peak Board, Yorkshire Water).

30 Upper Don Tributaries

Introduction

30.1 This area is dissected by numerous tributary watercourses which feed the River Don. These watercourses are now used for water supply purposes and 14 reservoirs have been created in this part of the National Park. Water catchment areas have been extensively planted, and the characteristic landscape is one of wooded valleys and improved farmland with moorland and rough pasture above. The area contains a number of small settlements (chiefly Langsett, Low Bradfield and High Bradfield), linked by a maze of minor roads. The Sheffield/South Yorkshire conurbation lies immediately to the east and three major trans-Pennine routes cross the area — A625, A57 and A628(T). The road linking the A57 to Langsett on the A616(T) is a popular scenic drive.

30.2 Proximity to urban areas such as Sheffield and Barnsley ensures that the area is popular with local visitors. Recreational use is generally limited to a few water areas (e.g. Damflask), reservoir margins and woodlands. Elsewhere, prevention of access, narrow roads and lack of facilities may act as a deterrent to some visitors. Sheffield City Council and Yorkshire Water have significant land holdings in the area. This Chapter covers the following areas from the 1978 Plan — areas 4 (Dunford Bridge/Winscar), 5 (Bradfield/Broom-head/Langsett), 6 (Redmires/Rivelin), and the part of area 13 dealing with Sheffield City Council's Moors.

30.3 The 1978 Plan suggested that there was scope for additional recreation facilities and activities, and proposed local studies of much of this area and its

immediate periphery. These were to be carried out jointly by the major agencies involved. A sailing base was proposed at Winscar Reservoir.

Work to Date
30.4 Yorkshire Water produced a Recreation Strategy in 1981 for its reservoirs and land within and outside the National Park. The Local Planning Authorities and Yorkshire Water agreed that a more comprehensive area study was desirable to build upon this. Thus the Upper Don Tributaries Joint Study covering 94 square miles within and outside the National Park was started in 1982. Work on the study was delayed by other commitments and the abolition of South Yorkshire MCC.

30.5 In the meantime, work on a number of small schemes has been implemented. These are mainly environmental improvements. At Winscar a car park and picnic area have been provided together with extensive tree planting. Near Langsett Reservoir a woodland has been fenced to allow natural regeneration, and a lay-by improvement backed by tree planting has been carried out opposite Midhope reservoir.

30.6 Langsett Parish now benefits from inclusion in the Community Action in the Rural Environment (CARE) Project. This is an experimental project established by the Countryside Commission (with support from Barnsley MBC, the Peak Board and local parishes), for a 3 year period from July 1986. The Project is described in Chapter 23, and is proving very successful.

30.7 Parts of both Low and High Bradfield, Langsett and Upper Midhope have been designated as Conservation Areas (see **9.12**). Enhancement schemes implemented in recent years include surface improvements to the car park and tree planting in Low Bradfield, and a stone sett paving project in High Bradfiel. Langsett is split by the National Park boundary, and has therefore required close liaison between the Board and Barnsley MBC. A village brief for future development opportunities and for enhancement ideas has been jointly agreed and houses are being built.

30.8 The Board persuaded Sheffield City Council and its tenant to install a cattle grid rather than fence across Hallam Moors next to the Board's North Lees Estate (see **25.11**). Access Agreement negotiations are continuing with Sheffield City Council for Hathersage and Burbage Moors, and discussions are also continuing with private moorland owners in this area (see Chapter 12). The City Council has re-affirmed that Blacka Moor is available for recreation including peripheral car parks and walking and riding opportunities.

Current Circumstances

30.9 The Manchester — Sheffield (Woodhead) railway line has closed, and British Rail are seeking to dispose of about 19 miles of the route. Within the National Park almost all the line lies in Longdendale, although there is a very short length within the Park on the east side of the Woodhead Tunnel at Dunford Bridge. Beyond this point, there is a 3½ mile length of the line immediately adjacent to the National Park boundary which Barnsley MBC hope to aquire as the basis of a major recreational use extending westwards from Penistone. The possibility of the disused Woodhead line forming part of a formally designated long distance walking, horse riding and cycling route between York and Liverpool is being looked at. Barnsley MBC engaged SUSTRANS Ltd. (the Railway Paths Project) as their consultants on this with the help of the Countryside Commission. A meeting of local authorities and other interests has been held at Barnsley to discuss the SUSTRANS report. Ongoing action is likely to be co-ordinated by Officer and Member Steering Committees which Barnsley MBC will service. (See also Chapter 27 — Longdendale).

30.10 Yorkshire Water has completed construction of a new treatment works at Langsett Reservoir. Whilst the need to safeguard the quality of the water in this reservoir is now less paramount than before, there are overriding conservation interests to be considered in comtemplating any increased recreational use of the water. Provision for sailing, canoeing and fishing is available at the nearby Underbank Reservoir.

30.11 At Langsett, a woodland car park beside the village has been completed and a path round the reservoir. The conversion of the adjoining historic Langsett Barn to an information, ranger briefing and community centre is progressing. This is a jointly funded scheme supported by the Peak Board, Yorkshire Water, Barnsley MBC and the Countryside Commission, and involving the Peak Park Trust.

30.12 Water based recreation is concentrated on More Hall and Damflask Reservoirs, although angling is more widely spread. There has been no de-

mand for a sailing base at Winscar Reservoir. This must place doubt on the need for such a facility in this location, since there are now such facilities at Torside to the west and Rother Valley to the east.

30.13 A number of reservoirs and their surrounding woodlands have potential for increased recreational use, provided wildlife interests are safeguarded. Yorkshire Water has completed the constructed of a new treatment works at Redmires Reservoirs. It is currently considering designating a nature reserve in the area because of its great ornithological value. With Sheffield City Council, they proposed viewing hides (including facilities for the disabled) to overlook the reservoir. One hide has been erected, and parking opportunities are being investigated elsewhere around the reservoirs.

30.14 A general problem throughout the area is uncontrolled roadside parking which gives rise to damage to roadside land and can be a hazard to both pedestrians and other vehicles. The proximity of the area to Sheffield and Barnsley suggests that its popularity will be maintained and that use could well increase. Visitor surveys carried out by the Board in the area in summer 1987 suggest that about 270,000 visitors use the National Park part of this area each year. The completion of the Stocksbridge by-pass-M1 link has improved communications, and visitors may well be attracted from further afield as a result.

30.15 The Working Group for the Upper Don Joint Tributaries Study reconvened in 1987, and work has gained momentum because of:

(a) The success of the CARE Project and the opportunity to build upon it.

(b) A successful series of joint projects carried out with Yorkshire Water.

(c) The closer working links with Sheffield City Council and Barnsley MBC since they became constituent authorities in 1986.

(d) The extensive land holdings of two public agencies — Sheffield City Council and Yorkshire Water — in the Study area, and the opportunity for them to contribute further to National Park purposes.

(e) The possibility of land disposal and privatisation of Yorkshire Water, and the need to identify

conservation and recreation interests to be safeguarded.

(f) The appointment by Yorkshire Water in November 1987 of an Access Officer as a 3 year project with support from the Countryside Commission.

30.16 A Members Advisory Steering Committee has been formed, and has agreed that a draft report be considered by its parent bodies as a basis for formal consultation and public comment later in 1988. Local parish councils are being invited to be represented at future Steering Committee meetings.

Policies and Proposals

30.17 The following broad zoning policies should provisionally apply to the area, pending completion of the Upper Don Study. This zoning is broadly as defined in the 1978 Plan, although the conservation value of Langsett Reservoir suggests it should be reclassified as Zone IV:

(a) Moorland Areas — Zone I.

(b) Less accessible moorland fringe farmland and woodland — Zone II.

(c) Accessible fringe areas with limited tree cover, viewpoints and possible access points to moorland — Zone III.

(d) Areas supporting existing recreational activities but with limited potential for additional use, e.g. Redmires/Rivelin, Bradfield, Dunford Bridge/Winscar Reservoir, Langsett — Zone IV.

(e) Areas with extensive tree cover adjacent to water areas with good access and scope to accommodate large scale formal and informal recreational activities, e.g. Damflask Reservoir — Zone V.

30.18 It is hoped that this recreation zoning might be extended to cover the remainder of the Upper Don Study area outside the Park if Sheffield and Barnsley Councils agree in the light of specific zoning suggestions which are being made in this Study.

30.19 In particular, consideration should be given to the following:

(a) The use of water areas and the desirability of reducing current restrictions on access to reservoir margins and catchment areas, where compatible with conservation interests.

(b) Additional moorland access areas and paths where this is compatible with conservation interests, given the substantial areas of open country close to Sheffield which are not covered by such arrangements at present.

(c) In popular areas, the scope for better parking, picnic and toilet facilities (perhaps linked to traffic management), segregated and improved walking, riding or cycling routes, and opportunities for cycle hire.

(d) The management of woodlands, to achieve a balance between commercial, landscape, conservation and recreation objectives.

(e) The value of forest areas for birds, and need for care with access (perhaps having some sanctuary areas excluded from recreation activity), especially on moorlands and related to Langsett and Broomhead reservoirs.

(f) The recreational use of Winscar Reservoir and surrounding land.

(g) Schemes for the environmental improvement and new use of surplus railway land at Dunford Bridge, and along the former Woodhead line to Penistone.

(h) Continuation of village Conservation Area work, and action to conserve barns of architectural and historic merit.

(i) The possibilities of a more comprehensive National Park Ranger service cover as achieved with Water Authorities and the Forestry Com-

mission in similar areas elsewhere in the Park (see **19.10**).

30.20 The Upper Don Tributaries Joint Study should be completed as soon as possible, by means of an Officer Working Group and Advisory Steering Committee of members (Peak Board, Barnsley MBC, Sheffield City Council, Yorkshire Water).

30.21 Consideration will be given to establishing contract ranger arrangements in the area, based upon existing joint funding schemes for the National Park Ranger service which operate in other parts of the National Park (Peak Board, Yorkshire Water, Sheffield City Council).

30.22 The Community Action in the Rural Environment (CARE) Project in western Barnsley will continue to be supported. Lessons learned from CARE should be considered for wider application in the Upper Don specifically, and the National Park in general (Peak Board).

30.23 The future use and recreation potential of the disused Woodhead railway line to the east of Dunford Bridge will be pursued, in close liaison with the authorities involved in assessments of the Woodhead tunnel and Longdendale sections (Barnsley MBC, Peak Board) (see also **27.21**).

30.24 Conservation Area enhancement programmes will be extended and implemented in association with Parish Councils in Langsett (jointly with Barnsley MBC), High Bradfield, Low Bradfield and Upper Midhope (Peak Board, Barnsley MBC, Sheffield City Council).

31 Upper Derwent and Woodlands Valleys

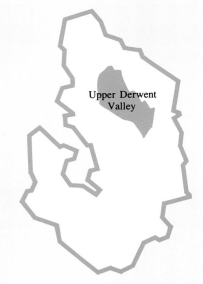

Introduction
31.1 This area covers the Derwent Valley north of Bamford, and the Woodlands Valley leading up to the Snake Summit. It includes 3 large reservoirs — Derwent, Howden and Ladybower — covering some 340 hectares. They provide water for Derby, Nottingham, Leicester and Sheffield. The reservoirs are surrounded by farmland and plantation woodlands, stretching up to wild gritstone moorlands (see Chapter 25). Farming is a major activity, with concentration on hill sheep. Extensive woodlands are managed by Severn Trent Water, the Forestry Commission and the National Trust. Some areas are within a Site of Special Scientific Interest (see **6.24**).

31.2 The A57 is the main road between Sheffield and Glossop, with the A6013 from Bamford to Ladybower, and a cul-de-sac north from Ashopton Viaduct to Kings Tree. Based on visitor surveys done by the Peak Board in 1986, it is estimated that there are now about 1.25 million visits to the whole Derwent and Woodlands Valley area each year. A number of access points lead to the moors and there are many popular paths.

31.3 Most land is owned by Severn Trent Water, the Forestry Commission or the National Trust. The 1978 Plan referred to problems of traffic congestion and parking, and the general lack of adequate facilities and routes. It called for a local study.

Work to Date
31.4 The Peak Board published a Draft Management Plan in 1979. It included

Walling work being carried out as part of the Western Barnsley Community Action project (CARE).

proposals to re-organise parking at sites related to Ladybower Reservoir, reduce motor vehicle access for visitors north and east of Fairholmes, enhance the distinctive environment, and safeguard local community interests.

31.5 Most of the proposals were widely supported. An Officer Working Group was formed early in 1980 to sort out details and co-ordinate implementation. It includes representatives of the Peak Board, Derbyshire CC, Sheffield City Council, High Peak BC, Derwent and Hope Woodlands PC, Bamford with Thornhill PC, Nature Conservancy Council, Sports Council, Countryside Commission, Severn Trent Water, National Trust and Forestry Commission. Three more interested parties joined in 1988. The Group has proceeded with agreed action, based on subsequent Committee decisions by member authorities. Much has been achieved to improve the environment for local people and visitors, and to create better recreational opportunities. Joint action and funding has been a key point in successful implementation. The regional significance and achievements of this scheme were highly commended in a Sir Mark Henig Award for Tourism Enterprise in 1982, given by the English Tourist Board. In 1988, the Management Plan achievements won a first prize in the Times/RICS Conservation Awards. The judges welcomed the quality of work and value for money achieved by a wide partnership.

31.6 The chief measures and work carried out so far include:

(a) Traffic restrictions on 6½ miles of road in the northern part of the Valley. Motor access for local interests, emergency services and the disabled is still allowed. Coaches can park at Fairholmes but cannot go on narrow roads beyond there. The 'closed' roads are ideal for walking, cycling and horse riding.

(b) Bus services from surrounding towns and cities have been improved. They link with a regular minibus service available between Fairholmes and Kings Tree when that road is closed on Sundays and Bank Holiday Mondays in the summer (about 35 days each year).

(c) Cycle hire was established by the Peak Board at Fairholmes in 1981, with 50 bicycles available. Following average hirings of 10,000 each year, a permanent building with 75 bicycles available was completed in 1987,

with Sports Council and English Tourist Board grants.

(d) Parking and picnic facilities have been greatly improved, with major sits provided by Severn Trent at Fairholmes (200 cars and 3 coaches) and Heatherdene (100 cars) overlooking Ladybower Reservoir. Other improvements to parking areas at Bridge End Pasture, King Tree (both Severn Trent), Derwent Overlook, Birchen Clough and Hurst Clough (Peak Board) provide a further 170 car spaces. Separate parking areas exist for anglers around Ladybower.

(e) Information, refreshment and toilet facilities are included in a new building at Fairholmes. The information centre was enlarged in 1986 to help cope with the needs of a site having 250,000 visitors a year, with costs being shared by Severn Trent, Peak Board and Countryside Commission. In addition to these interests, others represented on the Working Group contributed to the displays (Nature Conservancy, the National Trust, the Sports Council, the Forestry Commission, and the Derwent and Hope Woodlands Parish Council). The Centre had 51,500 visitors in 1987. It has recently been awarded a commendation for interpretation under the Carnegie 'Interpret Britain' Award Scheme 1987. The refreshment room is currently let to a local person. Elsewhere roadside vending has been restricted by High Peak BC designating, for the first time in this National Park, routes where trading is not allowed; trading from three parking areas is permitted under licences.

(f) In 1981, Severn Trent Water agreed to meet half the costs of the Peak Board's National Park Ranger Service in the Valley, with a full-time ranger and part-time staff for a 5 year period, in return for Ranger cover of Water Authority interests. This joint funding arrangement was the first in this National Park. It proved successful, and has been renewed with additional financial support from the Forestry Commission. There is close liaison and a good relationship with National Trust Wardens.

(g) Several miles of new concession routes have been provided chiefly for walking, but also for wheelchairs and for horse riding. Adequate safeguards for these routes are being considered. Other path improvements are plann-

ed. In addition some reservoir margins have been opened up to visitors.

(h) Many sponsored walks and events have been held and there have been some problems of disturbance, damage and litter. The Working Group has produced guidelines for such events and provides a corporate response to try to steer organisers away from the busiest times and sensitive places (see **13.46-13.53**).

(i) Landscape improvement schemes have been carried out at several sites in the Valley. In particular, 3 miles of concrete post and wire fencing was removed between the A57 and Fairholmes, where cattle grids were installed to allow a 'Parkland Grazing' regime.

(j) Woodland management and tree planting programmes are being implemented by Severn Trent and the National Trust to protect broadleaved woods against stock, to improve the shape and appearance of plantations, and to enhance their landscape and wildlife value. The Forestry Commission is devising similar plans for its woods. The Snake Plantations are the first priority. Felling and replanting plans have been agreed and have started.

(k) The old restrictive signs are gradually being replaced by attractive information boards, interpreting popular features and sites. Also produced have been a free illustrated visitors guide and several publications on local history and walks (all available from the Fairholmes Information Centre).

(l) Boat fishing has been introduced by Severn Trent, who also allow the use of Ladybower for sub aqua diving. A platform for disabled anglers has been provided at Ladybower Reservoir.

31.7 Surveys have shown that the work carried out has generally been appreciated. Many people who had been critical about the original proposals, admitted to being happy with the results.

31.8 Sailing and canoeing on Ladybower Reservoir were elements in the 1979 proposals. Two proposed Sailing Club sites have been turned down on appeal by the Secretary of State for the Environment. (Neither proposal was for the site identified at Ashopton in the 1979 draft plan which is no longer available) (see **13.79**). The Working

Cyclists enjoy the traffic-free roads in the Upper Derwent.

Group feels there is no site available which is acceptable to all interests. Canoeing is catered for at Ramsley Reservoir, and Severn Trent has invited the British Canoe Union to consider using the outfall from Ladybower Reservoir.

31.9 Plans by the Forestry Commission for extending their plantations a further mile up the West End Valley were resisted by the Peak Board on grounds of landscape, conservation and recreation. The Commission accepted this advice, but are looking at the Woodlands Valley where there is some potential for new planting.

31.10 Severn Trent Water has established Nature Conservation Liaison meetings intended to bring together local naturalists and nature conservation organisations (e.g. NCC, RSPB, Sheffield Bird Study Group, County Nature Conservation Trusts and Peak Board), as well as major local landowning and managing interests. The aim is to ensure that management activities are sympathetic to the considerable wildlife value of the valley. On behalf of this Group, the Peak Board has overseen a small MSC funded survey team to bring existing biological information together, and to fill major gaps in knowledge. Since then, the MSC project has ceased, but some of the team have been employed to finish the work.

31.11 The Integrated Rural Development Project (see paragraph **23.26**) was extended in 1986 to the parishes of Derwent and Hope Woodlands, where a trial alternative grant scheme was introduced to reflect local needs. A number of community projects were

assisted including refurbishment of the village hall, and improved television reception. Five of the nine eligible farmers joined the scheme. Several new jobs were created.

31.12 A hostel and camp site at Hagg Farm, operated by the Peak Board since the early 1970s has recently been transferred to Nottinghamshire Education Authority which is using it as an outdoor centre for secondary children, with some public use. In the 1980s a camping barn was opened at Alport Castles Farm (see **17.73, 74**).

Current Circumstances

31.13 A great deal of work has been carried out in this area since 1978. There remain several issues which need to be acted upon, including:

(a) The future of redundant properties — e.g. barns and water authority installations. Yorkshire Bridge Filter House building and the sludge lagoons opposite will become redundant in September 1988. Severn Trent are commissioning a study of future possibilities in conjunction with the Peak Board.

(b) Woodland Management, enhancement and further planting plans, which still demand much work and careful negotiation over details.

(c) Parking, traffic management and storage sites for highway chippings related to the A57 road. This will include tackling problems at Ashopton, and also at Birchin Clough where parking improvements have been carried out. Sites have been agreed in the forest to store road chippings. Parking problems at Ashopton need solving.

(d) Motor cycling activity on sensitive routes in the area.

(e) Completion of further walking, cycling and horse riding routes.

(f) The current reviews of, and likely proposals to extend, Sites of Special Scientific Interest by the Nature Conservancy Council.

31.14 Water Authorities and the Forestry Commission have been under pressure from government to dispose of their land holdings. Both have said there are no plans for disposal in the Upper Derwent at present, but it is important to safeguard conservation and recreation interests (e.g. new recreation routes and parking areas) and to ensure that future plans can be achieved.

31.15 The Officer Working Group (see **31.5**) meets twice yearly to co-ordinate management work and consider what new initiatives are needed. This group will continue to be the main means for promoting and developing the aims of this Plan in this area.

31.16 The IRD Project ran until the end of March 1988 and ideas for future action building on that work are being considered. The Ministry of Agriculture's North Peak Environmentally Sensitive Area (see **4.19**) started in 1988 includes Derwent and Hope Woodlands; this will help to provide positive incentives for farm and moorland conservation management. The business development and community elements of the IRD scheme will need to be taken up by relevant agencies. Being outside the Rural Development Area, there was no obvious mechanism for continuing an 'integrated initiative', unless the Upper Derwent Group expanded its brief. This was done in 1988, and the Ministry of Agriculture, Derbyshire Rural Community Council and the Rural Development Commission were added to the membership of the Officer Group referred to in **31.5**.

Policies and Proposals

31.17 The following broad recreation zoning policies in the 1978 Plan should continue to apply to this area:

(a) Moorland Areas and Higher Valley Sides – limited informal recreation linked to moorland access is appropriate – Zone I.

(b) Remoter farmland of the Woodlands Valley and the eastern shore of the reservoirs north of the A57 – Zone II.

(c) Areas around the Snake Inn and the road beyond Fairholmes cater for limited informal recreation as a base for active recreation – Zone III.

(d) More intensive recreation activity related to Ladybower Reservoir, with major visitor facilities in the Fairholmes area – Zone V.

Recreation activities around certain stretches of reservoir margin need to be carefully controlled during the bird breeding season because of the presence of several particularly sensitive species.

31.18 The Management Plan for the area should be updated (perhaps by annual review statements) by the interests represented on the Officer Working Group, so that there is a clear record of policies and achievements, an ongoing basis for reacting to new plans, and guidance for investment by those involved (Peak Board, Upper Derwent Officer Group see 31.5).

31.19 The Officer Working Group should continue to consider progress, the need for any changes and new initiatives, and future priorities having broadened its involvement and membership to reflect land management, community and socio-economic issues (Peak Board, Upper Derwent Officer Group).

31.20 The Nature Conservation Liaison Group's link to the main Officer Group should be strengthened. It should continue to receive and consider information on nature conservation issues, and report its findings to the main Officer Working Group (Severn Trent, Peak Board).

32 Edale Valley

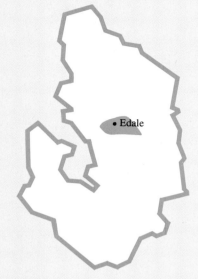

Introduction
32.1 Edale is a dramatic shale valley about 3 miles long, enclosed by the southern edge of the Northern Moors and the ridge which runs from Rushup Edge to Lose Hill. It contains traditional farms and farmland, much of which is owned by the National Trust. There are 6 'booths' or hamlets, including the area around the Mill and the cottages. Grindsbrook Booth is the main settlement, popularly known as Edale village. The valley contains a complete community with parish council, school, shops, public houses and church. It is under major pressure from visitors and 'comers' – those who choose to come to live here, but were born and work elsewhere. Several of the cloughs (e.g. Jaggers Clough), which run into the main valley, are of outstanding nature conservation value.

32.2 Visitor pressures are severe because of the popularity of the walks in and starting from Edale, especially the Pennine Way. Large numbers of visitors arrive at Edale station on the Manchester-Sheffield railway. There are many signs of visitor activity including camping and bed and breakfast businesses, two hostels, an information centre and two information points, a major car park at Grindsbrook road end (with allied parking restrictions), and two thriving pubs.

32.3 The basic policy in the 1978 Plan was to maintain the distinctive character of the Valley, and restrain the further development of recreation facilities.

Work to Date
32.4 The Peak Board and the National Trust have worked in co-operation.

Both bodies provide some visitor facilities; have agreed landscape management measures; and provide separate Ranger or Warden services, working in co-operation to different but compatible objectives. The National Trust has acquired additional land to safeguard the beauty of the area, and works with its tenant farmers. The Trust and the Board carry out landscape work, often using conservation volunteers. The Trust ran an agency for a Manpower Services Commission Community Programme, which was based in the Edale Valley and provided 200 work places throughout the Peak District. The Board carried out remedial works including stone paving where there was severe erosion of the southern end of the Pennine Way, at Grindsbrook Meadows: the Trust has carried out a more ambitious scheme at Jacob's Ladder.

32.5 The Joint Working Party on camping and caravanning (see paras. **17.31-43**), prompted in part by the difficulties in Edale, identified the valley as an area of constraint and, amongst other measures, set up a voluntary system to control caravan rallies. High Peak BC and the Peak Board have enforced controls over camping use. A proposal to gain special control over camping in and around Grindsbrook Booth by the use of an Article 4 Direction was not successful, but a new limited planning permission was negotiated with the main site operator.

32.6 The Peak Board carried out a study of the booths in Edale with a view to their designation as a Conservation Area. Such designation is normally followed by an enhancement scheme including environmental and practical improvements (see **9.30**). However, the Parish Council were opposed to the proposal, which is therefore being held in abeyance.

32.7 Derbyshire CC imposed a clearway order between the Barber Booth road junction and Mam Nick because of severe congestion related to hang gliding and visitor parking. There is also a Prohibition of Driving Order between the Barber Booth car park and Hayfield (via Jacob's Ladder).

Current Circumstances
32.8 The balance of the valley community is still changing. The close-knit farming, railway and mill families have seen the arrival of more holiday businesses and commuters. The school, with about 30 children, is probably not

at immediate risk — the journey time to Hope should help its protection.

32.9 British Rail have promoted the Hope Valley line as a 'scenic railway', with walks between the stations also identified. The improvement of Edale Station to make it more suitable for a recreation role should be considered in the context of traffic and visitor management in Edale (see also **34.16** & **34.27**).

32.10 Based upon surveys of car parking, traffic counts, visitor questionnaire surveys and observations (including those of the resident Ranger), the valley is used to its recreational capacity, overall and year round. The 1986/87 survey suggests that there are about 250,000 visitors for this area each year. Further specific measures, such as footpath development can be taken to manage recreational use better, but not in order to increase overall levels of use. At peak periods the valley's public use is in excess of capacity which may justify additional measures to ease particular problems (see policy **32.13**, a restatement of the policy in the 1978 Plan).

Policies and Proposals
32.11 The recreation zones in the 1978 Plan still apply in the Edale Valley as follows:

(a) The slopes of Kinder associated with the Northern Moors — Zone I.

(b) The Mam Tor/Losehill ridge is intensively used by walkers and also for riding — Zone II.

(c) The majority of the Valley floor is used to some degree for both informal and active recreation, and some small-scale parking areas might be provided — Zone III.

(d) The area around Grindsbrook Booth contains the majority of parking facilities and overnight accommodation — Zone IV.

32.12 The key issues to consider are:

(a) Footpath and bridleway improvements, concentrating (initially at least) on the existing network). The scope for a path link along the valley between Edale and Hope away from the road will be considered.

(b) The need for traffic management measures to solve particular problems.

(c) The possible improvement of Edale Station in relation to the recreational use of the Hope Valley line, and related footpath network.

(d) Continued health and planning control over caravans and tented camping. Promotion of camping barns as an alternative to tented camping.

32.13 The distinctive character of the valley should be maintained and its enhancement encouraged, further development of visitor facilities and attractions should generally be resisted and further steps should be taken to improve visitor management (Peak Board, National Trust, High Peak BC, Edale PC).

The Edale Valley enclosed by the southern edge of the Northern Moors and the ridge from Rushup Edge to Lose Hill.

33 High Peak Fringe

Hayfield•

Introduction
33.1 To the west of the main block of the Northern Moors, the land slopes to form river basins in which are located Chapel-en-le-Frith, New Mills, Whaley Bridge, Hayfield, and Glossop. These settlements, all outside the National Park, are connected by the A6 and A624 roads. They are employment centres surrounded by numerous small farmsteads and small settlements associated with mills (e.g. Little Hayfield and Rowarth).

33.2 Each settlement provides a gateway into the National Park. In particular, Hayfield is an important centre for both active and informal recreation, and for approach to the Kinder plateau. There is a good network of tracks and rights of way throughout the area.

33.3 The 1978 Plan drew attention to the likelihood of local studies by Derbyshire CC and High Peak BC outside the Park in these areas. It also highlighted the scope for significant improvements to the recreation route network, and for more overnight accommodation.

Work to Date
33.4 Just outside Hayfield, the Peak Board provided a lightweight campsite and a small car park in the late 1970s, adjoining Kinder Road. This includes a Ranger Briefing Centre and information board. Visitors entering the National Park this way climb past Kinder Reservoir, using recently improved and landscaped footpaths.

33.5 Since 1978 the Hayfield relief road has been constructed. The village is linked to the urban areas to the west by the Sett Valley Trail, developed by Derbyshire CC along a disused railway in the 1970s. They have added toilets, an information centre and cycles for hire based on the former Hayfield Station site, where there is also a coach and car park. In New Mills a visitor centre opened in 1988, providing a year round information point.

33.6 The Board has established a Ranger Briefing Centre at Glossop, by shared use of a Scout Hut.

Current Circumstances

33.7 The 1986/87 surveys suggest there are about 390,000 visitors to this area each year.

33.8 The attraction of Kinder continues to place a strain on the limited visitor facilities close to Hayfield. The Peak Board has resisted extending the car parking provision on Kinder Road, recognizing that there could never be enough space to absorb all the likely visitor pressure in that area. Detailed examination of this problem, and of possible toilet provision, is proposed with survey and traffic counts being made in summer, 1988. The main parking areas should continue to be at the old station site within Hayfield. Consideration will be given to the provision of a minibus service.

33.9 Agreement has recently been reached by the Board for an additional access area to the east and south of Kinder Reservoir. This adjoins National Trust access land, and will be closely related to a footpath route being developed with North West Water around Kinder Reservoir.

33.10 It is hoped to carry out improvements to an informal viewpoint, parking area and adjoining land at Monks Road, Charlesworth.

33.11 Otherwise, the circumstances of this area are mainly dictated by its farming activity, its proximity to urban areas and the demands for extended recreation facilities.

33.12 The A6 by-pass of Chapel-en-le-Frith and Whaley Bridge opened in August 1987. High Peak BC's policy to develop these towns as tourist centres is supported. Local Councils are co-operating in a project designed to provide a network of paths in the Goyt basin outside the National Park, extending north and west to Stockport. Links into the National Park will also need to be considered as part of Derbyshire County Council's Recreational Paths Project.

33.13 The recreation zoning in the 1978 Plan remains relevant. It has been somewhat refined as follows:

(a) The moorland areas and higher valley slopes are most appropriate for low-intensity use — Zone I.

(b) The remoter farmland areas away from the main settlements have a generally attractive nature which should be safeguarded. Any recreation provision should be linked to existing rights of way — Zone II.

(c) The fringes of the smaller settlements have scope for small scale recreation facilities — Zone III.

(d) The immediate vicinities of New Mills, Chapel-en-le-Frith, Hayfield, Glossop and Whaley Bridge provide (or could provide) the bases for recreation and general visitor activity — Zone IV.

(e) The main settlements of New Mills, Glossop, Chapel-en-le-Frith, Whaley Bridge and Hayfield are areas in which High Peak BC intends to encourage development of tourism and related facilities — Zone V.

33.14 Liaison will continue between the relevant local authorities and action will be taken in accordance with the above recreation zoning (High Peak BC, Derbyshire CC, Peak Board).

33.15 The demands for extra car parking and for toilet facilities in the Hayfield area will be examined (Peak Board, Derbyshire CC, High Peak BC, Hayfield PC).

33.16 Improvements will be sought to the informal car parking area alongside Monks Road, Charlesworth. (Peak Board).

33.17 Improvements will be sought to the path network in the area, including links to adjoining areas in the Goyt basin and Stockport outside the National Park (Derbyshire CC, High Peak BC, Peak Board, New Mills Town Council).

34 Hope Valley

Introduction

34.1 This area is one of the most densely populated parts of the National Park. It includes the villages of Bamford, Bradwell, Castleton, Hope and Hathersage and a number of industrial enterprises. Castleton is perhaps the most popular tourist centre in the Park. The 1986/87 surveys suggest that the Hope Valley area gets about 2.25 million visits each year. Informal recreation use is intensive, and the area forms a starting point for active recreation pursuits. The A625 runs the length of the valley, but has been closed since 1977 to the west of Castleton by the landslip at Mam Tor. The Winnats Pass is therefore the main link to Castleton from the west. The A6013 links to Bamford and the A57 to the north. The B6049 runs south to Bradwell and Tideswell. The main bus links are to Sheffield. Hope, Bamford and Hathersage are linked to Sheffield and Manchester by the Park's only passenger railway service.

34.2 Easy access to places like Sheffield and Buxton places considerable pressure on the local housing market. Major sources of local employment include Hope Cement Works — a prominent feature in the landscape. Other firms at Castleton, Bamford and Bradwell also provide considerable numbers of jobs. The local economy benefits considerably from visitor spending, notably the hotels, guest houses, gift shops, and camp and caravan sites. The valley is also one of the most prosperous farming areas in the Park.

34.3 There are problems of congestion in Castleton, especially on Sunday afternoons, Bank Holidays, and at special events such as the traditional Garland Ceremony. Notable attractions are the caverns, the Winnats Pass, Mam Tor and Peveril Castle. Castleton is also a good starting point for walks, and particularly popular for coach excursions – especially by school parties. Losehill Hall, the National Park Study Centre located on the edge of the village, is an important source of local employment as well as providing the education service described in Chapter 18. Other features of interest in the valley include the Roman Fort and its adjacent settlement near Brough, and the alleged Little John's grave at Hathersage.

34.4 The 1978 Plan proposed a series of local studies for the Hope Valley related to the Winnats Pass, the local road problem and need for improvements, parking arrangements at Mam Tor and in Castleton, and better public transport.

Work to Date
34.5 Strict control over development has been maintained to prevent dramatic change in the character of the valley. Development to meet local housing needs has been promoted, with notable examples at Bamford and Hathersage. Consent has been granted for new factories at Hathersage and on the site of Hope Station. A major revision to the shape of Hope Cement Works quarry to improve its final appearance has been agreed in 1988.

34.6 The Peak Board has designated Conservation Areas in Castleton, Bradwell and Hathersage. Designation has been followed by enhancement works, including paving, tree planting, the removal of overhead wires and the renovation of the Square in Castleton. Traffic and parking problems need careful consideration in these villages.

34.7 The closure of A625 over Mam Tor frustrated the Peak Board's attempts to seek further closure of the Winnats Pass to traffic at peak periods (such a scheme operated successfully in 1975 and 1976). It has also created problems for access to the three caverns outside the village. Diverted traffic from the A625 has added to traffic volumes in the Winnats and to problems in Bradwell and Bamford (see paragraphs **22.16-22.21**). There are no obvious solutions. Derbyshire County Council has indicated that the Mam Tor road will not be reconstructed; and that no priority can be given to the most practicable alternative solution, namely the construction of a new road through Pindale linking Hope to the Rushup area. This is regretted, particularly by

the National Trust. Bamford and Bradwell cannot easily be by-passed – indeed an earlier by-pass line in Bradwell has now been built upon. The Peak Board, Derbyshire CC and the National Trust are keen to see the old road over Mam Tor managed as a bridle route, and for parking and landscape improvements to be made on the two cul-de-sac roads. Some sections of the landslip-affected road could be retained for interpretation as a reminder of the power of geological processes.

34.8 The Board's car park at Mam Nick has proved popular as an access point for walkers to Mam Tor. Following the implementation of a clearway on the Mam Nick road, this car park was extended in 1988. Footpath improvements have been undertaken on routes previously suffering major problems of erosion, including the surfacing in local stone of the path to Mam Tor by the National Trust.

34.9 Improvement projects at Bamford have included a major new footbridge over the River Derwent by Bamford Mill, which won a CPRE design award; tree planting in a verge alongside the A6013; and erection of old toll gate posts and an information plaque by the roadside. The schemes all involved joint efforts and funding by the Peak Board with Derbyshire CC, and Parish Council support.

34.10 Losehill Hall has developed its role as a Study Centre and important source of local employment (see Chapter 18). Work on youth and schools liaison, close contacts with the Hope Valley Community College and the local community, including farmers, have developed considerably since 1978.

34.11 Attempts to improve information facilities for visitors to Castleton have not proved successful. A possible heritage centre promoted by the Peak Board and the National Trust was investigated, but a suitable site has not been found.

Current Circumstances
34.12 Housing pressures are likely to continue and the interests of the local community must be carefully considered. There are further Housing Association schemes proposed in Bamford and Bradwell. Local employment needs careful consideration particularly with the decrease in employment at Hope Cement Works. An enterprise agency was assessing needs and offering advice during 1988. However, the

special character of this area must be protected. Pressures to develop industry in the open countryside are increasing nationally. The effect is already noticeable in the Hope Valley. A balanced approach to this is essential. Site selection is crucial, and use of derelict or despoiled sites has clear advantages. Traffic considerations are also vital, and the scale of development must not prompt major additional housing demands to spoil the character of the area.

34.13 While there may be some opportunities to develop the local tourist industry, the ability of the area to absorb increased numbers of visitors is in doubt. Castleton in particular experiences considerable congestion at peak periods, but the need for improved information services remains for the very large numbers of visitors who currently use the area. The importance of tourism in the local economy needs to be balanced against the danger of over commercialisation and congestion.

34.14 Losehill Hall is now clearly established as a major study centre. A number of other field study centres and similar establishments are run by other organisations. Careful control over these is essential since they can generate considerable pressures on the area. School parties further increase these pressures and can lead, for example, to physical damage to the unique character of the area by collection of rock samples.

34.15 Many of the problems and opportunities outlined above relate closely to the issues of traffic circulation and parking provision. Decisions need to be made on the status of various roads in the area to set the context for future development. Parking congestion at peak times in Castleton spoils the character of the village and affects enjoyment by locals and visitors. However, it is an effective regulator of visitor numbers: increased parking provision may only serve to increase visitor numbers and to create new problems. Careful study of this problem is clearly essential.

34.16 British Rail have in recent years promoted the Hope Valley line as a 'scenic railway', with walks between the stations also identified (see also **32.9** and **32.12**(c)). Improvements to the various station sites would be desirable to fit them for a new role related to recreational use. Scope also seems to exist for improved visitor parking related to the railway and local walks.

34.17 Additional through traffic in Bamford and Bradwell has increased problems of parking congestion. Hathersage also has traffic and parking problems and the lack of a direct pedestrian link from the car park to the Main Street makes it worse. A new path connection to improve this situation was likely to go ahead in 1988.

Policies and Proposals

34.18 The basic recreation zones in the 1978 Plan remain valid as follows:

(a) Areas around Mam Tor and The Winnats — Zone I

(b) The Losehill Ridge — Zone II

(c) Most of the valley farmland is unsuited to major visitor facilities, but there is scope for limited facilities and improvement of walking, riding and cycling routes — Zone III

(d) Some additional modest scale recreation facilities might be appropriate in the Bamford area — Zone IV

(e) The major centres for recreation activity are the Castleton/Hope/Bradwell area and Hathersage — Zone V.

34.19 The main emphasis in this area will be on socio-economic issues and traffic circulation. These are essentially land use planning matters, more properly covered in the Structure Plan Review, which will need to take account of:

(a) The need to maintain strict control over development to protect the character of the area. Large scale and intrusive development must be firmly resisted. Within this context, the needs of the local population for houses and jobs must be carefully considered.

(b) The status of the main roads in the area will have to be carefully decided in the context of the abandonment of Mam Tor and the increased pressures on the Winnats, the A6013 and the B6049. Derbyshire CC has agreed that this study must begin in advance of the Structure Plan Review. Close liaison will need to be maintained between the Board and local Parish Councils.

34.20 Enhancement proposals in the Castleton, Bradwell and Hathersage Conservation Areas should continue to be implemented (Peak Board, Parish Councils).

34.21 Village management schemes will be considered at Bamford and Hope (Peak Board, Parish Councils).

34.22 Efforts to remove eyesores and restore derelict land should continue. This applies particularly to parking improvements and treatment of the Mam Tor roadway and its future management as a bridle route (Peak Board, Derbyshire CC, National Trust).

34.23 The information and interpretation services at present in Castleton need to be reviewed and possibly extended (Peak Board, National Trust, HMBC).

34.24 Within established planning policies, the development of field study centres in the Hope Valley will be strictly controlled to contain their impact (Peak Board).

34.25 Visitor parking in Castleton and related to the Caverns needs to be re-examined. Parking for the caverns also needs considering in relation to future arrangements at Mam Tor and the future road pattern in the area (see 34.19b and 34.21). (Peak Board, Derbyshire CC, High Peak BC).

34.26 Problems of parking for visitors and residents in Bamford, Bradwell, Hathersage and Hope should be resolved as and when opportunities arise (Peak Board, Derbyshire CC, High Peak BC, Derbyshire Dales DC).

34.27 Consideration will be given to improving parking and the footpath network related to the station sites along the Hope Valley line and linked to any promotional work carried out in relation to the railway service (Peak Board, British Rail).

35 Eastern Moors

Introduction

35.1 The majority of this area is a gritstone plateau dominated by relatively small individual blocks of moorland, between Curbar and Stanage. These are largely of heather and rough grasses, grazed by sheep. However, there are also extensive areas of recently established semi-natural woodland (e.g. on Ramsley Moor); smaller areas of enclosed pasture (e.g. near Curbar Gap); and two small reservoirs on the moorland, Ramsley and Barbrook. Several public roads provide good access and divide the moors into distinct blocks, and there is therefore not the same degree of remoteness as there is on the northern moors (Chapter 25). The area includes the Longshaw Estate Country Park and North Lees Hall and Estate, and is extremely popular for informal recreation.

35.2 The dramatic Eastern Edges dominate the western boundary, with the wooded Derwent Valley below. These cliffs provide the most extensive and varied gritstone climbs in the country, and are the most heavily used climbing areas of the Park. There are also many popular walking routes (particularly along the Edges) and moorland access areas. There are car parks at Curbar Gap, Froggatt Edge, Birchen Edge and Hollin Bank and (provided by the National Trust) at Longshaw. Towards the east are areas of improved, enclosed farmland and woodland as the land drops down to the lowlands of North East Derbyshire.

35.3 Much of the moorland has particularly high archaeological and wildlife value. White Path Moss is a site of Special Scientific Interest (SSSI). Big

Moor, Totley Moss, Leash Fen and Ramsley Moor were also designated as an SSSI in 1986. The moors are an especially important habitat for migratory birds and for several rare species of birds.

35.4 Ownership of the area is to a large extent in the hands of the Peak Board and National Trust, with Chatsworth Estate owning the remainder at the southern end.

35.5 The 1978 Plan called for a local study to develop land use management policies and appropriate recreational opportunities. It also suggested greater public access; a Management Plan for North Lees Estate with facilities related primarily to active recreation pursuits; and continued action on the Management Plan for the National Trust's Longshaw Estate.

Work to Date

35.6 In 1984 the Peak Board acquired from the Severn Trent Water Authority a 2,590 ha moorland estate comprising Big Moor, Eaglestone Flat, East Moor, Leash Fen, Ramsley Moor and Totley Moss. A Management Plan for the Eastern Moors was adopted by the Peak Board after widespread consultation and is being implemented. A main principle is the conservation of the high wildlife value. The moors continue to be grazed, but the traditional agisted sheep grazing system is being modified to secure conservation benefits. Additional areas have been opened for public access and concession footpaths and horse riding routes have been provided, taking care to protect core 'wildlife sanctuary' areas from visitor disturbance. The car park at Curbar Gap has been extended, with a picnic area nearby and a wheelchair route onto Baslow

Edge. The need for parking restrictions at Curbar Gap is being reviewed now that the extended car park is in use.

35.7 North Lees provides a fine opportunity for the development of educational and interpretive programmes, carefully planned to develop these areas for the current level of use and to avoid creating further visitor pressure. It also gives a splendid chance to conserve, use and manage the fine North Lees Hall, listed Grade II*. The Elizabethan tower house is the best historic building owned by the Peak Board.

35.8 A Management Plan for the Board's 524 ha North Lees Estate was produced in 1988 following consultation with other authorities and interests. It introduces new proposals for educational use and for agricultural management at a level appropriate to

Eastern Moors Estate. An attractive mixture of rock, gritstone edges, woodland, farmland and moorland.

the conservation value of the farm. The Board has concluded leases with the Derbyshire College of Agriculture for an agricultural tenancy of 470 ha of the Estate, and to the Vivat Trust to convert and manage the Hall for holiday lettings in two self-catering units. The estate continues to be extremely popular for active recreation, and a 45 pitch tented campsite with ablution block has been developed by the Board. The present level of recreational provision and use of the Estate is appropriate and should not be greatly expanded.

35.9 Development of the National Trust's Longshaw Country Park has been carried out along the lines of the Management Plan. A new Information Centre/Cafe/Shop has been provided. Car parks have been provided at 3 locations on the Estate and further walks and horse routes have been developed. The Site of Special Scientific Interest within Padley Gorge has been enclosed to exclude sheep grazing for the benefit of natural oak regeneration (see 3.31-42).

35.10 There have thus been 3 local studies for Longshaw, Eastern Moors and North Lees. Additional and separate Management Plans have been prepared for the Chatsworth Estate (see Chapter 37), and are being drafted for the Sheffield Moors in the Upper Don (Chapter 30).

Current Situation
35.11 Due to its location close to Sheffield and Chesterfield, the area receives a high level of visitor pressure. The 1986/87 Visitor Survey suggests that there are about 810,000 visits to the area. Areas such as Curbar, Froggatt and Stanage Edges are subject to particularly high use, (with resulting problems of congestion, verge parking and footpath erosion. Unofficial use of areas of high ground for hang-gliding is an increasing concern, particularly on Stanage Edge. Pressure for further public access to moorland must continue to be balanced with the need to conserve landscape and wildlife values.

35.12 Visitor pressure will continue in this area and consideration needs to be given to providing additional car parking in the congested areas. Parking facilities at Shillito Wood on the Eastern Moors Estate were being improved during 1988. To protect unspoilt areas of open moor, recreation will be directed to areas such as Longshaw Country Park where there is some spare capacity. Activities such as hang-gliding will be carefully regulated.

35.13 Areas of surface erosion will be identified with positive steps taken to divert visitor pressure off them and carry out improvement works.

35.14 The large area of heather moorland now owned by the Board presents an opportunity for detailed monitoring of heather management and for applying techniques developed by the Moorland Management Project (see 3.25).

Policies
35.15 The recreation zoning from the 1978 Plan remains valid and is being reflected in local Management Plans:

(a) The moorland areas and semi-natural woodlands — Zone I.

(b) Remoter farmland (e.g. near North Lees) is suitable for riding, walking and small-scale recreation facilities — Zone II.

(c) The more accessible areas of farmland and plantation woodland such as the Cordwell Valley may be suited for informal recreation facilities — Zone III.

(d) The already popular Longshaw Country Park — Zone V.

35.16 Public access should be directed to areas with capacity to meet the pressures of use. In particularly popular areas, further car parking should be considered and traffic management investigated to relieve congestion (Peak Board, National Trust, Chatsworth Estate, Derbyshire CC).

35.17 The North Lees Estate Management Plan proposals will be implemented, and will be carefully monitored (Peak Board).

35.18 The Eastern Moors Management Plan proposals will continue to be implemented, and will be carefully monitored (Peak Board).

35.19 Longshaw Country Park will continue to provide informal recreation to relieve other areas of pressure, but use there will be carefully regulated according to existing activity and conservation interests, in line with the Management Plan for the estate (National Trust, Peak Board).

35.20 The Board will actively apply new heather management techniques in the conservation of its moorland where these offer benefits. Core areas of wildlife interest will continue to be protected from public access (Peak Board).

36 Northern Limestone Plateau

Introduction
36.1 This area consists of the limestone plateau lying north of the Wye Valley. It includes Tideswell and the smaller villages of Litton, Foolow, Great Hucklow, Peak Forest, Wormhill and Wardlow. The gentle rolling plateau is dissected by small dales, such as Combs Dale and Bradwell Dale (several of which contain grasslands of high wildlife value), and by the start of the Dale system running into the River Wye. On the higher land there are some areas of semi-natural vegetation, including areas of limestone heath such as Longstone Moor and Bradwell Moor — but the main feature is enclosed farmland with a few clumps of broadleaved trees. The Northern Limestone plateau is particularly important for flower-rich fields (see 3.89). Much of the land has been or is still being worked for vein minerals: while many former workings have been restored, there are others still in need of remedial treatment. At Tideswell Dale, the Peak Board has a popular car park and picnic area, with footpath routes and a wheelchair route.

36.2 The Structure Plan contains policies aimed at halting the population decline (SP 10.91) and at encouraging new employment opportunities, particularly in the Tideswell area. It also contains policies to promote the controlled use of minor roads and tracks for walking, riding and cycling. The 1978 Plan emphasised these policies, and also encouraged the development of small-scale farm tourism enterprises. It proposed continued effort to reclaim derelict land, and renew and increase small woodlands, using primarily native hardwood species. Management agreements were suggested for the limestone heaths.

Work to Date

36.3 Since the mid 1970s a number of small advance factories have been built on an industrial estate in Tideswell, creating about 80 new jobs. Frontage land detracts from the overall appearance of this Estate, and improvements are needed. The population decline has reversed. Tideswell was designated as a Conservation Area in 1980 and has benefited from an enhancement programme, including a major repaving scheme in Cherry Tree Square. Litton has recently been designated a Conservation Area, and an enhancement programme agreed.

36.4 The area forms part of the Derbyshire Rural Development Area (RDA), where a series of co-ordinated social and economic initiatives are being followed with the help of the Development Commission for Rural England.

36.5 Since the 1978 Plan, the Peak Board has reclaimed a number of minor eyesores. By the use of Management Agreements and also by direct management, the Board has also continued to encourage the regeneration of older woodlands and the planting of new ones.

36.6 A study of limestone heaths which was completed for the Peak Board in 1984, shows the location and importance of all remaining examples. Negotiations are in progress for management agreements on a number of these heaths, and Longstone Moor is now a Site of Special Scientific Interest. The Section 3 Conservation Map (see **2.16-2.22**) includes the limestone heaths and other limestone hills such as Wardlow Hay Cop.

Current Circumstances

36.7 The 1986/87 surveys suggest there are about 340,000 visits to this area each year.

36.8 In recreation terms the area has an extensive network of paths and tracks, but many are overgrown and obstructed or poorly signposted and waymarked. Improvements are badly needed. A number of farms and hotels in the area offer self-catering or bed and breakfast accommodation. More farms offer bed and breakfast than at the time of the 1978 Plan. There is scope for additional ventures, particularly at the quality end of the market which is in demand according to the English Tourist Board.

36.9 A major extension of Tunstead Quarry into the Old Moor area near Wormhill was refused by the Peak Board but after a Public Inquiry, was approved by the Secretary of State for the Environment in 1978. A large new underground fluorspar mine at Great Hucklow gained planning consent in 1986 thus protecting existing jobs. It has resulted in restoration of an unsightly derelict area which the Board had earlier proposed for compulsory purchase. It received an award from 'Planning Newspaper' in 1988. However the Board refused consent for further extensions to Eldon Hill Quarry in 1985 and was supported by the Secretary of State at appeal, so that a limit is now confirmed on the life of this quarry.

36.10 There are still a number of old unrestored vein mineral workings. Tideslow Rake, one of the largest veins, is now a scheduled Ancient Monument because it shows a variety of old mining techniques. The worst in environmental terms is Dirtlow Rake, where a restoration scheme prepared by Derbyshire CC with the Board is underway and should be completed in 1989. The County is carrying out basic remedial works here, using DoE derelict land grant. The Board will contribute to additional enhancement measures and the interpretation of features of historic interest; and will also take on future management of the site.

36.11 In Tideswell, there is pressure for additional workspace and housing development. General social and economic development issues are dealt with as part of the RDA process (see paras. **23.24-23.29**). The Officer Working Party and the Committee of Members of the relevant local authorities try to co-ordinate work in the area. An extension to the industrial estate has been agreed in principle by the Board and two sites for housing are under discussion. One of these belongs to the District Council and a detailed proposal is imminent.

Policies and Proposals

36.12 The recreation zoning in the 1978 Plan remains valid as follows:-

(a) The Natural Zone areas of limestone dales, limestone upland and heaths — Zone I.

(b) The majority of the area has potential for recreation related to tracks and minor roads and limited scale recreation facilities — Zone III.

(c) Tideswell could continue to develop as a centre for recreation activity with modest scale activities — Zone IV.

36.13 The Rural Development Area (RDA) Programme will continue to be used to promote the economic and social well being of the area. Further housing development and additional workshops will be provided under the programme for the RDA, particularly at Tideswell, and additional tourism development will be encouraged, particularly farm tourism (see Chapter 17). (Peak Board and RDA Working Party)

36.14 Conservation Area enhancement work will continue in Tideswell and Litton in association with the Parish Councils, and improvement packages will be devised and implemented in local consultation with other villages such as Taddington (Peak Board, Parish Councils).

36.15 Attention should be given to improving the local public rights of way network in accordance with the policies and priorities set out in Chapter 11 (Peak Board, Derbyshire CC).

Cherry Tree Square, Tideswell. A major repaving scheme carried out with Parish Council support.

37 Lower Derwent Valley

Baslow •

Introduction

37.1 The area includes the Derwent Valley from south of Hathersage to Beeley (including Chatsworth Estate), together with Abney/Offerton Moor, and the Eyam and Stoney Middleton area. Much of the valley is enclosed improved farmland, with woodlands on some of the steeper land. Many of the villages in this area, such as Baslow and Grindleford, have expanded considerably in recent years, with many residents taking advantage of the easy commuting distance to work in Sheffield and Chesterfield. This has placed considerable pressures on the local housing market.

37.2 Chatsworth House is the home of the Duke and Duchess of Devonshire. It dominates the southern end of the Derwent Valley, with 405 ha of open parkland surrounding the house and a garden covering 40 ha. Woodland areas cover the high land both to the east and west, with the Eastern Moors forming a skyline in some places. Chatsworth House is a major tourist attraction. There are large car parks near the House, and at Calton Lees at the southern end of the park. The parkland is open to the public, there are attractive walks in park and woodlands, and a touring caravan site has recently been opened. The farming and forestry exhibition is a further attraction, and Chatsworth is a popular venue for Horse Trials, Game Fairs etc. It also provided a fitting spot for the climax of the National Park Awareness Campaign in September 1987.

37.3 Eyam is a popular tourist village for both individual visitors and organised parties. The main reason is its association with the Plague of 1665-66. The Church alone receives over 100,000 visitors a year. Baslow is also much visited because of its proximity to Chatsworth. All the villages are used as bases for walks particularly along the river and on surrounding moorland. Eyam and Offerton Moors and the Abney/Bretton Clough are quiet places for hill walkers. Tourism generates employment notably linked to the various Chatsworth enterprises (see **37.7**). Other employment sources are at Calver Mill, in Eyam village, and the minerals industry around Eyam and Stoney Middleton.

37.4 Main traffic routes include the A619/A623 running east to west and the B6001 north to south. The A619 between the two roundabouts in Baslow is the most heavily used section of road in the Park. The A623/A619 is a major cross-Park route and its use has increased since the Chapel By-Pass opened. Representatives of Stoney Middleton, Baslow and Calver have expressed greater concern recently. The area is relatively well served by public transport with good bus links to Sheffield, Chesterfield, Bakewell and Buxton and direct services to Liverpool and Lincoln. Grindleford station lies on the Sheffield to Manchester railway line (see Chapter 34).

37.5 The 1978 Plan suggested improved public car parking and public transport related to Chatsworth Park, improved information for the Eyam area, possible landscape treatment and recreational use of quarries (as they become disused) in Stoney Middleton Dale, and improved visitor facilities in the Calver/Grindleford area.

Work to Date

37.6 Strict control over developoment is essential if the character of the area is to be protected. Pressures for large scale development have been resisted in recent years, although previous commitments have led to substantial housing developments in Baslow and Calver. Development related directly to local needs has been promoted, notably in a recent housing development at Stoney Middleton. There has been little recent pressure for industrial development, although negotiations with the minerals industry have produced environmental improvements while maintaining employment.

37.7 Tourism-related development has been chiefly at Chatsworth with improved signing (now from the M1), a touring caravan site developed and managed by the Caravan Club, camping barns, a garden centre, and craft workshops and shops at the farm near Pilsey. Future plans include a major visitor centre and cafe in woodland overlooking the House and Park. Recreation development at Chatsworth may be having an effect on Baslow for example through approaching traffic. The access to the caravan site from the A619 within the village was opened in 1987. Overall traffic levels may be increasing as roads into the National Park are improved. Monitoring will continue.

37.8 Attempts to negotiate canoe access have failed so far to open up one of the most suitable rivers in the Park for canoeing — i.e. the Derwent. A further attempt at appropriate arrangements is planned, in the knowledge that landowning and fishing interests have expressed their concern (see **13.90-13.100**).

37.9 Eyam has a designated Conservation Area, within which enhancement proposals are being implemented in cooperation with local interests. The centre of the village is also eligible for special grants from HMBC. The local community have erected a series of plaques in the village identifying features of local historic interest, especially related to the plague story. There are Conservation Areas in Stoney Middleton and Beeley. These are more recent designations where programmes of village improvement work have been devised and agreed for Stoney Middleton, and are likely to be agreed soon at Beeley.

Current Circumstances

37.10 The 1986/87 surveys indicate there are over 3 million visits to the Lower Derwent Valley area each year.

37.11 Discussions are well advanced between the Countryside Commission, other Government agencies and the Chatsworth Estate on the production of a Management Plan for the core of the Estate. This will include commitments to conserve the distinctive character of the area, and to maintain and develop recreation opportunities. The Estate will receive exemption from certain aspects of Inheritance Tax regulations to enable the special landscape for which exemption has been claimed to be kept in its traditional ownership and with consistent management set out in this Inheritance Tax Management Plan. It has been agreed that the Board should act as agent for the relevant government agencies in ensuring that the provisions of the plan are carried out.

37.12 Improved information services in Eyam are being considered. Apart from further improvements at Chatsworth, and possible scope to use old quarries in Stoney Middleton Dale for recreation, no major changes in visitor provision seem necessary.

37.13 Traffic will continue to be a major issue particularly as the use of the A623/A619 corridor increases. Further road improvements are proposed outside the National Park. This will emphasise existing traffic problems in Baslow and Stoney Middleton in particular. Residents have formed an action committee and surveys are in hand. At busy times Baslow is heavily congested and this problem seems likely to worsen (see Chapter 15 and **22.16-22.21**).

37.14 Pressures for new housing develoment are likely to continue. The changing needs of existing industrial and commercial firms may need to be accommodated in ways that safeguard the character of the area. Unless strict control over development is maintained, the character of the area could change dramatically.

37.15 Further enhancement work in Eyam is progressing, and may be needed in other villages in the area (see **9.26-9.28**).

Policies and Proposals
37.16 The recreation zoning pattern in the 1978 Plan for this area remains relevant as follows:

(a) Remote areas of Eyam and Offerton Moors — Zone I.

(b) Remoter farmland and woodland areas — e.g. around Abney and beyond Calton Lees — Zone II.

(c) Most remaining farmland and woodland has potential for limited scale recreation facilities — Zone III.

(d) Modest scale facilites might be appropriate in the Grindleford-Calver area — Zone IV.

(e) The existing heavy use of Chatsworth (including Calton Lees), and Baslow, together with the potential of Stoney Middleton area, suggests a Zone V definition.

37.17 Apart from further improvements to visitor facilities and increased attention to conservation issues, the main emphasis in the area will be on socio-economic and traffic issues. These are land use planning matters more properly covered in the Structure Plan Review, which will need to take account of:

(a) The need to maintain strict control over development to protect the character of the area. Within this context the needs of the local people for houses and jobs must continue to be carefully considered. The needs of the minerals industry must be balanced against the long term interests of landscape conservation.

(b) The status of the A623/A619 and traffic problems in Baslow and Stoney Middleton.

37.18 As quarries in Stoney Middleton Dale reach the end of their life, their finished appearance in the landscape will need to be carefully planned. The emphasis will be on landscape and nature conservation, but should leave options open for recreation use, including climbing (Peak Board in conjunction with mineral operators).

37.19 The status of the A623/A619 and traffic problems in Baslow and Stoney Middleton will be investigated linked to other work in these villages (Peak Board, Derbyshire CC).

37.20 Enhancement work in Conservation Areas will continue in Eyam, and will be pursued in Stoney Middleton, Beeley and other villages, in close co-operation with local interests (Peak Board).

37.21 The inheritance Tax Mangement Plan for the core area of the Chatsworth Estate will be monitored on behalf of Government agencies (Countryside Commission, Peak Board).

37.22 Information provision in Eyam will be improved (Peak Board, Parish Council, Eyam Sports Association and Eyam Village Society).

37.23 Arrangements for canoe access to the River Derwent will be pursued subject to consideration of conservation and fishing interests (British Canoe Union, Sports Council, riparian interests, Peak Board).

38 Wye Valley

Taddington •   • Bakewell

Introduction
38.1 The River Wye rises near Buxton and flows east to join the Derwent at Rowsley. East of Buxton the Wye follows a series of deep and attractive dales cut into the limestone plateau. The character of these varies markedly. Deep Dale and Cressbrook Dale are wild areas with few signs of human activity. By contrast Millers Dale and Monsal Dale contain minor roads, farmsteads and small settlements. Some areas such as Monsal Dale are extremely popular with visitors, others are less accessible. The dales are outstanding for their wildlife interest, and also offer some of the best limestone climbing faces in the country.

38.2 Bakewell, a small market town of about 4,000 people, is the largest settlement in the National Park. It lies at the junction of the limestone outcrop with the shale/grit area to the east. Here the Wye emerges from the confines of the limestone dales into the broader shale valley, where it flows in numerous meanders to Rowsley. The gentler gritstone slopes leading up to Stanton Moor are mainly pasture, while the slopes on the northern side of the valley are extensively wooded. Haddon Hall, the Derbyshire seat of the Duke of Rutland, dates back to the 14th century and earlier, and is set in beautiful countryside, south of Bakewell, overlooking the River Wye. Visitor facilities there have been improved, (including parking and a restaurant), and business facilities (including small conferences) are now available. Guided tours are popular and special information is available for school project work.

38.3 Parts of the Wye Valley, particularly the Limestone Dales, have outstanding nature conservation value. Cressbrook Dale and Monks Dale form part of the Derbyshire Dales National Nature Reserve. Many of the remaining limestone dales are Sites of Special Scientific Interest.

38.4 The valley is followed in part by the A6 trunk road, and the area is extensively used for informal recreation motoring. Bakewell in particular suffers problems of traffic congestion, due to through traffic, recreation traffic and local traffic (particularly on market days, weekends and Bank Holidays). The former Midland Railway line follows the valley, and is an outstanding example of railway engineering including the Monsal Dale viaduct.

38.5 In the 1978 Plan, the future management of the valley was seen to be linked closely to the future of the railway. Traffic management was also a major consideration related to Ashford,

Millers Dale, and also Monsal Dale where a Management Agreement was proposed. Means of reconciling the needs of rock climbing, rambling, nature conservation and field studies were to be sought. Preparation of a Local Plan for Bakewell was proposed.

Work to Date

38.6 In 1980, the Board acquired some 8 ½ miles of the former Midland Railway, from Blackwell Mill to Coombs Road with £154,000 from British Rail to assist with essential maintenance of major strucures. The old railway, re-christened the 'Monsal Trail', was opened to the public in 1982, but the cost of making safe the four major tunnels meant that they were sealed off, and alternative routes were provided for walkers. Bakewell Station has been developed as a small industrial estate, and a car park provided for the Trail. At Millers Dale, a car park, ranger centre and toilets have been provided, and limekilns stabilised as interesting historic features connected to

the railway. The old concrete platforms and ballast have been removed with Derelict Land Grant from the DoE. Other sections of the line have been acquired by Haddon Estate (Coombs Road viaduct to Rowsley), and Derbyshire Dales DC (Rowsley to Matlock).

38.7 Work has been completed recently on widening the A6 between White Lodge and the dual carriageway at Taddington. A short stretch of new road on the east side of Ashford was built to enable traffic to be diverted away form the village, which now has a Conservation Area. The Board has provided a car park at Upper Dale where Derbyshire Dales DC in consultation with Chatsworth Estate and the Peak Board is considering providing new public toilets. The Board has agreed to assist Derbyshire Dales DC with planned improvements to two parking and picnic areas at Monsal Head in 1988.

Cressbrook Mill. A major cause for concern in which an historic building is in a very poor state of repair.

38.8 The central part of Bakewell was made a Conservation Area in 1980. The related enhancement proposals agreed are being implemented. A major paving scheme for the area by the Market Hall was completed in 1987. A District Plan for Bakewell was approved by the Board in 1982 to deal with land use issues and allocations. In 1985 a combined National Park and Tourist Information Centre was reopened, by joint initiative of the Peak Board and the (then) West Derbyshire District Council. This Centre, located in the historic Market Hall, now has some 120,000 visits per year. Many other historic buildings in the town have been repaired or restored with grant-aid from the Peak Board and (in some cases) from English Heritage.

38.9 Conservation Area status, and enhancement packages, also exist in Rowsley, Cressbrook and Ravensdale.

38.10 The Board refused consent for further extension of the Topley Pike Quarry near King Sterndale in 1985, and was supported by the Secretary of State at appeal. The quarry will probably close in the late 1990's and ways in which the site can be treated will need to be discussed. It needs to be integrated back into the landscape in a new use, possibly linked to the Monsal Trail. Climbing use should be considered.

Current Circumstances
38.11 The 1986/87 surveys indicated that there are over 2.5 million visits each year to this area of the Park.

38.12 Bakewell is a focus for activity and visitors. Problems of traffic management and car parking are particularly acute on Market days, Bank Holidays and weekends. The District Council have bought a field to the east of the Wye to provide extra car parking in the short term and to assist comprehensive planning in the long term. There is a need for greater investment in community facilities, including a permant library, as well as some new housing (particularly for young people and families). Sites for further industrial development are being sought. The District Plan provides the framework for these proposals, but there is need for co-ordinated working both to implement the Plan and to consider the need for review in the light of changing circumstances, and Rural Development Area initiatives.

38.13 The opening of the Monsal Trail has greatly increased the recreational use of the area, particularly by walkers.

The heaviest use of the trail occurs at Monsal Viaduct and Millers Dale. Use of the section around Bakewell and west of Millers Dale is much less heavy. The lack of continuity of the Trail because of the tunnels and the steep narrow paths that link the Trail either side of them has restricted its use by cyclists and horseriders. Some of the viaducts are used for authorised abseiling.

38.14 Future use of the Trail is related to proposals by Peak Rail for re-opening the line from Matlock to Buxton as a working railway. A planning application was approved in principle in 1988 despite some objections, notably from Haddon Estate. Should the line be re-opened, this would have a major impact at Bakewell and Millers Dale in particular. The track bed is sufficiently wide to allow the rail use and the existing trail use to co-exist, with suitable segregation. Care would be taken to protect areas and features of conservation value along and adjoining the route.

38.15 Discussions between nature conservation bodies (which now own dales with major rock faces) and the British Mountaineering Council over conflicts between climbing and nature conservation proved inconclusive. However, climbers are now more willing to consider closed seasons for specific reasons, and some progress has been made.

38.16 The area has considerable industrial history, particularly linked to the use of water power. Two mills, Caudwell's Mill at Rowsley (Corn Mill) and Cressbrook Mill (formerly textiles), are of particular significance. The Board and other agencies have recently assisted the Caudwell's Mill Trust in developing better information and parking facilities, and extra employment opportunities linked to a restored working corn mill and craft workshops. At Cressbrook Mill the situation is becoming critical as this major historic building is in a very poor state of repair. After negotiations with the owners, and an enforcement appeal, some essential repairs are underway, but the long term future use and maintenance of the Mill is not yet assured. The Mill Pond at Lumford Mill (established by Arkwright) is of national historic importance. This feature is threatened by flood protection requirements. Local authorities and other agencies are trying to find a suitable solution with the owners.

38.17 At all these Mills, there is a great deal of scope for interpreting the history

of the area. The Monsal Trail also provides opportunities for interpretation, at present limited to a few plaques. The small museum in Bakewell has expanded. There is scope for self-guided trails, in Bakewell and in the other main villages of the valley (Rowsley, Ashford and Cressbrook) which all contain Conservation Areas. Care will be taken to consider parking and traffic issues in such villages, and this is already being assessed in relation to the Ashford area.

38.18 The area is within the Derbyshire Rural Development area (RDA) (see **20.11**-**20.13**). There are currently proposals for further industrial development in Bakewell using former tipped land off Ashford Road (for which a derelict land reclamation grant has been sought), and possible sites for a prestigious 'High Tech' industrial development are also under urgent investigation. Land at the Bakewell riverside is currently under review to meet car parking and other needs. The joint planning advisory group, set up to draft the District Plan, will be reconvened to explore its implementation and consider any future review.

Policies and Proposals
38.19 The recreation zoning should remain essentially as set out in the 1978 Plan, namely:

(a) The limestone dales — Zone I.

(b) The higher valley sides of the shale grit area to the east of Bakewell — Zone II.

(c) The limestone plateau and enclosed farmland are suitable for limited recreation facilities — Zone III.

(d) Topley Pike area and the station areas of Millers Dale, Hassop and Rowsley — Zone IV.

(e) The Bakewell-Ashford area — Zone V.

38.20 Important wildlife sites in the limestone dales will continue to be safeguarded, and the levels of recreational use limited (Nature Conservancy Council, Peak Board).

38.21 The Bakewell Plan provides the statutory framework for future development in the town, but expires in 1991. A joint planning advisory group will be reconvened. Investigations of traffic management and the provision of additional car parking will be carried out. The Rural Development Programme will continue to be a means of implementing the proposals in Bakewell District Plan, and providing for community needs in the area (Peak Board, Derbyshire RDP Working Party).

38.22 Conservation Area enhancement works will continue in association with the Parish or Town Councils in Bakewell, Ashford, Rowsley, Cressbrook and Ravensdale. (Peak Board, Parish Councils).

38.23 Village management schemes will be considered at Great Longstone and Taddington (Peak Board, Parish Councils).

38.24 The Monsal Trail will be maintained as a footpath and bridleway, and ways will be investigated of improving facilities related to the Trail as well as improving its continuity and providing links to other areas. The principle of re-opening the railway from Matlock to Buxton is supported. Areas and features of conservation value along and adjoining this route will continue to be safeguarded. Action will be taken to prevent unauthorised uses such as swinging from viaducts (Peak Board).

38.25 Interpretation of the area will be developed and based upon:

(a) Monsal Trail and the stations , particularly Millers Dale and Bakewell

(b) Industrial history, particularly related to the use of water power in the valley

(c) The wildlife and geological interest of the limestone dales.

(Peak Board, English Heritage, Nature Conservancy Council).

38.26 Efforts will continue to ensure the long term future conservation and best use of Cressbrook Mill (Peak Board).

39 Southern Limestone Plateau

Youlgreave •

Parwich •

Introduction

39.1 This large area of limestone plateau stretches from the Wye Valley in the north to the National Park Boundary in the south east. It includes the settlements of Chelmorton, Flagg, Monyash, Over Haddon, Youlgreave, Elton, Winster and Parwich. There are problems of population imbalance, and employment opportunities are still limited in variety. Limestone dales such as Lathkill Dale, Bradford Dale and Gratton Dale are of national ecological importance. Parishes with striking historic landscape features include Chelmorton, Winster and Ballidon (see **8.17-8.18**).

39.2 This area was the core of the 'Routes for people' experiment and contains a number of car parks and picnic sites, waymarked routes, information facilities, and a 'White Peak' scenic motor route linking places of interest (see **15.4**). The area is well used for leisure motoring, picnicking, walking, cycling and horse-riding, using the extensive network of minor roads and green lanes supplemented by the High Peak and Tissington Trails. These Trails were created on old railway lines by the Peak Board in the late 1960s and early 1970s. The Board operates a cycle hire scheme at Parsley Hay, at the junction of these Trails.

39.3 The 1978 Plan contained policies aimed at consolidating the recreation opportunities provided under the 'Routes for People' scheme. These included the encouragement of limited visitor facilities such as overnight accommodation and craft shops, the pro-

vision of additional parking, and development of Magpie Mine as an interpretive centre. There was also emphasis on renewing and increasing small woodlands, and continued restoration and enhancement of derelict land.

Work to Date

39.4 The area is within the Derbyshire Rural Development Area, where joint action by many public agencies has been tackling the problems of unemployment, population loss, declining services and isolation through a co-ordinated programme of work. The current programme includes workshop provision in Youlgreave, support for small businesses, encouragement for rural tourism, help with housing and transport and support for community facilities and services.

39.5 The Integrated Rural Development (IRD) Experiment (see **23.26-23.29**), included Monyash and started in 1982. A Trial Alternative Grant Scheme was worked out to suit local needs for business development, community action, farming and land management. Schemes carried out include conversion of barns to craft and holiday use, maintenance of characteristic landscape features such as stone walls, woodlands and flower-rich meadows, the building of a village hall and provision of a play area.

39.6 Monyash, Youlgreave, Alport and Winster are established Conservation Areas and have benefited from enhancement programmes. Parwich was designated in 1986, and an enhancement package has been agreed. Village Guidelines were produced for Youlgreave in consultation with the District and Parish Councils.

39.7 Cycle hire at Parsley Hay started as an experiment in 1975 linked to the Trails. It proved so popular that the Peak Board retained it as a permanent facility and there are now 100 cycles with about 15,000 hirings a year. A Pathfinder 'bike and ride' bus service, linking cycle hire centres at Parsley Hay and Ashbourne, was discontinued after 1978 because of lack of demand.

39.8 An extension of Ballidon Quarry, within the National Park but close to the boundary, was approved in 1986, with stringent conditions including extensive tree planting. This is almost certain to be the last extension which will be acceptable as the quarry is prominent and is close to an 'Historic Landscape' (see **39.1**).

39.9 The Peak Board has restored a number of derelict sites, notably Green Lane Pits near Friden in 1986/7. With DoE grant, it removed dumped tyres and other rubbish to conserve this Site of Special Scientific Interest which has both geological and botanical value, and carried out extensive walling and tree planting. The Board acquired an important site nearby at Blake Moor, and carried out positive works to enhance its conservation value. These were safeguarded by covenants when it was resold in 1988. A number of woodlands have been planted and several regenerated.

39.10 The area contains many archaeological and historical remains. At Roystone Grange near Parwich the Board has helped to develop a self-guided archaeological trail which shows five different ages of farming settlement as well as other features. In 1987 it acquired the farm; resold part of it, subject to covenants to conserve features of importance; and retained the section which has the prime archaeological sites. This was achieved by the use of delegated powers from Derbyshire CC, and with help from the Countryside Commission, English Heritage and the National Heritage Memorial Fund.

39.11 Proposals for action in the Winster historic lead mining landscape are proceeding, with restoration of the Ore House and a nearby mere. Conservation of Pitts Mine, some old barns and provision of a self-guided footpath interpreting the various features, remain to be carried out. At Chelmorton, agreements have been made with farmers to ensure the upkeep of the drystone walls which mark the boundaries of the medieval strip field system.

39.12 The Board has also recorded surviving features of local interest such as limekilns and pinfolds and helped restore some of the best examples. However, Magpie Mine's potential for interpreting the lead mining history of the area is only partly developed. An ambitious scheme was not implemented because of lack of finance and limited security of tenure.

39.13 Derbyshire County Council has carried out a substantial mineshaft capping programme. Many dangerous old lead mineshafts in this area have been capped in the Winster and Bonsall Moor area, with care to protect wildlife and historic interests.

Current Circumstances
39.14 Surveys in 1986/87 suggest over 600,000 visits to this area each year.

39.15 This area has many examples of the conversion of redundant farm buildings to tourist accommodation, with an increasing tendency for farm buildings to be sold separately from their land and converted to multi-unit tourist developments.

39.16 Ways to safeguard and build upon the success of the IRD Scheme were considered, given that joint funding of the project on its present basis ended in March 1988 (see 23.26-23.29). Wall and meadow management payments have been made under the Board's Farm Conservation Scheme, and additional farms have been included in the parish.

39.17 There is a serious problem of scrub invasion of the limestone dales; and some of the dales, for example Lathkill Dale, are under strong and increasing visitor pressure. Agricultural changes mean that only a relatively small number of flower-rich pastures and hay meadows still survive on the plateau: they should be conserved to illustrate the traditional farming practice, and in view of their landscape and nature conservation value. Appropriate arrangements and incentives to ensure that this happens are made where possible under the Farm Conservation Scheme, or by Management Agreements.

Policies and Proposals
39.18 The recreation zoning policies for the area in the 1978 Plan remain valid and are:

(a) The Natural Zone areas of Bonsall Moor, Gratton Dale, Lathkill Dale, and Bradford Dale — Zone I.

(b) The majority of the remainder of the area is suitable for riding, walking and cycling, and limited scale informal recreation facilities — Zone III.

(c) The settlements of Youlgreave, Monyash, Winster and Parwich already serve as local centres with visitor facilities and limited additional provision could be appropriate, provided the car parking capacity is not exceeded. Great care must be taken not to spoil the traditional character and local communities of these villages — Zone IV.

39.19 The Peak Board will continue to work closely with its RDA partners to promote the economic and social well-being of the area consistent with Structure Plan policies. The re-use of good quality redundant traditional buildings will be encouraged (Peak Board, Derbyshire RDP Working Party).

39.20 The Farm Conservation Scheme, the Rural Development Programme and other ways of maintaining and extending the improvements to the economy, environment and quality of community life which have been helped by the IRD Project will continue to be considered (Peak Board).

39.21 Conservation Area enhancement works will continue in association with Parish Councils and landowners in Monyash, Youlgreave, Alport, Winster and Parwich (Peak Board and Parish Councils).

39.22 Limited visitor facilities such as overnight accommodation and craft shops may be appropriate in suitable locations, such as Youlgreave, Over Haddon, Monyash, Winster and Parwich and by the diversification of farm businesses (Peak Board).

39.23 The wildlife of the limestone dales and other unimproved grasslands (including flower-rich fields) will be conserved and, where appropriate, interpreted (Nature Conservancy Council, Peak Board, Ministry of Agriculture).

39.24 Continued efforts will be made to safeguard and interpret the archaeological and historical features of the area. Initial priorities will include the historic landscapes of Chelmorton, Winster and Ballidon; and better visitor interpretation at Magpie Mine. Similar action could then be taken in other mining heritage areas such as Bonsall Leys and Elton (Peak Board, English Heritage and Sheffield Museums Service, Peak District Mines Historical Society).

39.25 The scope for implementing traffic management measures in Youlgreave will be pursued in the light of the published 'Guidelines' for the village (Derbyshire CC, Peak Board).

The new Village Hall at Monyash, built as part of the IRD Project. It is used by many groups, including the local school.

40 Stanton and Birchover

Introduction

40.1 This area consists of the gritstone hills which rise up to Stanton and Harthill Moors. The villages of Stanton and Birchover lie on the western slopes of Stanton Moor, and provide small-scale services for both local people and tourists. The hamlet of Stanton Lees overlooks the Derwent Valley in the east. Much of this area is served by narrow hilly lanes. Most of the higher land forms open heather and bilberry moorland with some semi-natural woodland. There are many sites of archaeological and wildlife interest, especially on the moors.

40.2 The gritstone outcrops in several places form distinctive landscape features, especially at Robin Hood's Stride and Rowter Rocks near Birchover. The moors and the network of rights of way are popular with walkers and car-borne visitors. The rock has been quarried for building stone in several sites and there are still stone cutting workshops in Birchover. Many of the quarries have been disused for some years and have revegetated, but several have recently reopened due to a revival in the market for dressed gritstone.

40.3 The 1978 Plan suggested possible improvements in visitor facilities related to Robin Hood's Stride and Stanton Moor together with modest additional recreational facilities in the area generally.

Work to Date

40.4 A camping barn has been opened at Birchover near an existing camp site which has been improved. Both are popular. There have been no specific projects to provide extra car parks or other visitor facilities, and existing informal car parking has continued.

40.5 A small number of houses have been built in the area over the last 10 years, particularly in Birchover on infill plots. In 1986 the Peak Board proposed that Stanton village should be designated a Conservation Area in order to further protect and enhance its character. This did not meet with favour locally and this proposal has been held in abeyance. The school in Birchover was closed by Derbyshire County Council in summer 1987, and has permission in outline for conversion to a house.

40.6 Stanton Moor has been fenced and sheep graze the moor. Public access is available on public rights of way and informal access has continued. Earl Grey's tower on the northern edge of the moor is a prominent landmark in need of repair. The Nine Ladies Stone Circle is an important historic feature, and there are also other Ancient Monuments on the Moor.

Current Circumstances

40.7 The wealth of archaeological and historical interest in this area deserves protection and provides scope for interpretation.

40.8 Many of the gritstone quarries on Stanton Moor are still covered by valid planning permissions dating from the early 1950s. Some of these have continued working, in some cases sporadically, to the present day. Some have recently reopened, especially on the north east side of the moor. The narrow roads are generally unsuitable for the associated heavy lorry traffic and routing agreements are being sought with the various operators to try to minimise the problem.

40.9 Recent use of an intensive clay pigeon shoot in a former quarry further illustrates the uncertain future of the quarries in the area, and prompted a review of the policies on shooting in Chapter 13 of this Plan (see paragraphs **13.101-13.106**).

40.10 The 1986/87 surveys suggest this area has about 70,000 visits each year.

40.11 There seems to be scope for some additional small-scale farm tourism or tourist accommodation subject to appropriate siting and design (see **4.25/6** and **17.53-17.60**).

40.12 Positive action to improve facilities, particularly parking related to

Harthill Standing Stone is one of many features of archaeological interest in the Stanton and Birchover area

Robin Hood's Stride and Stanton Moor, should be considered.

Policies and Proposals

40.13 The recreation zoning for this small area in the 1978 Plan remains valid as follows:

(a) Stanton Moor, Harthill Moor and semi-natural woodlands – Zone I.

(b) Much of the area has scope for both informal and active recreation at carefully selected locations – Zone III.

(c) The Stanton/Birchover locality is already the focus for most of the recreation activity in the area, and should be the location for any significant recreation facilities – Zone IV.

40.14 Around Stanton and Birchover, limited additional parking and visitor facilities such as small campsites, farm tourism and accommodation may be appropriate but great care will be needed in selection of sites (Peak Board, MAFF).

40.15 Limited improvements in car parking related to Stanton Moor and Robin Hood's Stride should be considered in consultation with local interests (Peak Board).

40.16 The archaeological, ecological and historical heritage of the area (especially of Stanton Moor) needs to be safeguarded and interpreted more fully (HMBC, Peak Board, Museums Services).

40.17 Efforts will continue to get better routes for heavy lorry traffic serving the quarries. (Peak Board, Derbyshire CC).

41 Lyme Hall and Park

• Lyme Park

Introduction
41.1 Lyme Hall and Park is just within the National Park to the south of the A6 trunk road. Lord Newton gave it to the National Trust in 1946 for the 'health, education and delight of the people', and the Trust leased it to Stockport Council in 1947. Lyme Hall dates back to Elizabethan times and is a Grade 1 listed building. There are other buildings (many listed) and about 526 ha of parkland, woodland and moorland. The extensive areas of semi-natural unimproved rough grassland (over 400 ha) are of particular nature conservation value. One of the main interests of Lyme lies in its historical continuity of management as a deer park. It was emparked some time after 1388 from the Forest of Macclesfield, enclosing red deer and wild white cattle. The red deer herd is still a feature of Lyme, and a stag's head forms the logo for this area which the Countryside Commission designated a Country Park.

41.2 Lyme has some 350,000 visitors a year providing an attraction in its own right, particularly for visitors from Stockport and the Manchester conurbation. The 1978 Plan noted the Hall and other buildings were in much need of repair, and a Management Plan was proposed. This was to be produced by a Joint Management Committee of Greater Manchester (GMC) and Stockport MBC, with assistance from the National Trust and Peak Board.

Work to Date
41.3 Much has been achieved in restoring the Hall, its rooms and contents, and the adjacent garden and orangery. Parking, information and other visitor facilities have also been improved. The Joint Management Committee continued its work, with capital and revenue expenditure being split between GMC and Stockport MBC; and with some assistance form the Historic Buildings and Monuments Commission, Countryside Commission and National Trust. However, GMC was abolished in April 1986. Since then, Stockport MBC has been largely responsible for meeting running costs which currently amount to some £500,000 net per annum. It has maintained joint working arrangements, with an Officer Group (including the Peak Board, National Trust and Greater Manchester Countryside Unit), providing advice to the relevant Committee of the Council.

Current Circumstances
41.4 Facilities available include the Hall and gardens, parking areas, toilets and information points, refreshment facilities, an adventure playground, pitch and putt course, and orienteering course. There is a good network of paths, and visitors can wander at will over much of the parkland. Lyme caters for events such as sheep dog trials, horse trials, an annual festival and traction engine rallies. The Hall itself is used for concerts, functions, seminars and promotion days for businesses. Additional information about visitors came from a survey in 1987 which the Board carried out for Stockport MBC. It showed that 34% of visitors were from the Stockport area, and 42% from the rest of Greater Manchester. The uncommercialised wildness of Lyme is the aspect which most visitors feel is of greatest importance and enjoyment. This provided useful background to the preparation of a Management Plan.

41.5 The Hall and Orangery are now in good condition, but a quinquennial review in 1987 highlighted the need for action on other buildings, including the Cage which is a prominent landmark. A rolling programme of repairs to buildings is under way, with some changes of use being considered. A keeper has been appointed to the Hall, and displays and features are being improved. The shop has been put in a more suitable place inside the Hall. Cycle hire which was opened in the 1970s has now closed because of lack of use. The Nursery area became redundant in 1987, and greenhouses have been demolished. This presented an opportunity to consider alternative uses including a caravan and camp site (which Stockport MBC has discounted as not being viable at this stage), and a parking and events area.

41.6 A number of actions are being pursued to improve promotion and administration and to establish a 'Friends of Lyme'. The production of a Management Plan has been delayed, but is being produced in 1988. This should guide future development and investment by Stockport MBC, and be helpful to the Peak Board in considering future planning applications, and proposals for woodland management and tree planting.

Policies and Proposals
41.7 The following objectives for the Management Plan have evolved through the Officer Group, bearing in mind the outstanding importance of Lyme Hall and Park in historic and landscape terms, visitor survey findings, and the need to pay close attention to presenting the Hall and Park as amenities for the people of Stockport:

(a) To ensure the conservation of the historical, landscape, ecological and architectural features of the estate and Hall and their best presentation, resulting in maximum public enjoyment at minimum cost.

(b) To pay particular attention to presenting the Park and Hall as amenities for the people of Stockport, identifying the area more closely with the Borough and encouraging greater use of it by its residents.

(c) To introduce measures to reduce the net revenue deficit to Stockport MBC by 25%, principally by increasing income through:

— attracting paying half day visitors.

— encouraging repeat visits.

— encourage visitor spending.

— having a cost effective charging system.

— utilising effective marketing practices.

— maximising funding from national bodies and external agencies.

(d) To manage the land, the historic landscape and the wildlife consistent with good husbandry and conservation practice.

(e) To manage the estate within the terms of the lease from the National Trust.

41.8 Given the character of the area and management decisions already taken, the following recreation zones are relevant:

(a) On Park Moor, natural qualities should be maintained and only low intensities of use related to active recreation pursuits are appropriate — Zone I.

(b) Most Parkland, Meadow and Woodland is able to accommodate low intensities of receational use and facilities, subject to careful site selection and management — Zone III.

(c) The Central Area of the Hall and Park is capable of taking extra visitors — Zone V. This would be welcome to sustain the Hall, associated buildings and the Park as a major attraction on the edge of the National Park. Major developments should however be in carefully selected areas closely related to the building complex, Lyme Hall and the nearby parking area. They should make use of existing buildings wherever possible.

41.9 The main topics being investigated in the Management Plan include:

(a) Uses to be made of the Hall, and appropriate means of preserving and interpreting its special interest.

(b) Renovation and uses of other buildings, including the Stable Block, Cage, Shepherds Cottage, Lantern and Kennels. A feasibility Study to consider the future use of the Stable Block in the context of use of other buildings for interpretation, refreshments etc. is being commissioned related especially to the Central Area of the Park. This will be considered as part of the Management Plan process.

(c) Improvement of recreation facilities including the location of parking, refeshment and information facilities for visitors, and a clear hierarchy of routes for vehicles and users on foot, cycle or horseback within and around the Park.

(d) Provision of a caravan and campsite; or other special facilities (e.g. to cater for events), and a new use for the Nursery area.

(e) Conservation and enhancement of the Parkland, Woodland and Moor.

(f) Improved promotion of Lyme and public transport links.

(g) Further developemnt of facilities for the educational use of the area, which is rich in historic, landscape and ecological interest and offers opportunities for practical research and projects.

(h) Exploring ways of increasing the efficiency and effectiveness of services provided at Lyme, consistent with the environmental standards appropriate to an Historic House and Country Park.

(i) Scope for funding from outside bodies, including sponsorship and the approach to charging for facilities at Lyme.

(j) Vehicular access to Lyme Park from the A6, including consideration of current plans for a Disley by-pass which include an option for a route at the northern end of Lyme. The Lyme route is supported by Stockport MBC, but opposed by the National Trust and Peak Board.

41.10 A Management Plan will be produced as a priority to provide detailed policies and proposals for Lyme taking into account the issues, objectives and zoning referred to above. It should be the subject of liaison with appropriate interests including the Countryside Commission, English Heritage, Macclesfield B.C. and local Parish Councils, and must be monitored and reviewed in the light of experience (Stockport MBC, National Trust, Peak Board, Greater Manchester Countryside Unit).

The red deer herd is a feature of Lyme Country Park. Managed by Stockport MBC, it attracts 350,000 visitors a year.

42 Goyt/Todd Brook/Lamaload

• Rainow

Introduction

42.1 This area straddles the Derbyshire/Cheshire border within the National Park. High moorland ridges separate the Todd Brook, Lamaload, and Goyt Valleys. There are reservoirs in each of the valleys. There is therefore little high-quality in-bye farmland, and sheep farming predominates. The enclosed land is often ranch-grazed, and many of the dry-stone walls which have long characterized the area are in poor repair. In the Goyt Valley, large areas of Forestry Commission plantations dominate much of the western side. The Lamaload and Todd Brook valleys contain only limited woodland. The middle and upper Goyt Valley is designated a Site of Special Scientific Interest, reflecting diversity of habitats found in the valley. The moorland at Coombs Moss is of considerable landscape and wildlife value.

42.2 Three major 'A' roads — the A5002 (Long Hill), A54 and A537 — provide easy access into the area. Many public footpaths link through the area. Most of the recreation pressure centres on the Goyt Valley, which has been a major attraction to visitors for generations. Much of the activity is nowadays concentrated around Errwood Reservoir, which offers sailing and fishing.

42.3 Visitor pressure on this area led to the introduction of a Traffic Management Scheme in 1970, involving the closure of the central section of valley road at peak times. This scheme still operates, but has been modified many times. A minibus link from Buxton Station and Macclesfield is available on summer Sundays and Bank Holiday Mondays.

42.4 The 1978 Plan suggested that a Joint Management Plan might be needed for the Goyt. Continuation of the Traffic Scheme and a moorland Access Agreement were proposed. Other proposals were to seek improved public access to moorlands such as Coombs Moss and Castle Naze, more riding and cycling routes, and better public transport. Lamaload Reservoir was identified as a potential location for sailing, together with improved footpath access and tree planting.

Work to Date

42.5 The last major review of the traffic scheme was carried out in 1976, and heralded the gradual removal of the park-and-ride minibus service during the late 1970's and early 1980's. A system of park-and-walk replaced it, and has been well accepted. The removal of the minibuses, and the extension of the peak time traffic-free area to include the section of road from Errwood to The Street, allowed the designation of a wheelchair route alongside the reservoir for the disabled during the hours of road closure. The starting point is a small car park for the disabled at The Street.

42.6 In response to an approach by Buxton Round Table, a second wheelchair route was constructed winding into the heart of the high moorland, along the track of the former High Peak Railway. Again a small car park for the disabled was provided. The whole project gained a CPRE commendation.

42.7 One attraction in the Goyt Valley is the site of Errwood Hall, a 19th century mansion which is now a ruin. Situated amongst its rhododendron gardens, the site is still evocative of the valley's past. A nature trail was developed in the vicinity by the Forestry Commission in the 1970's and relaunched in 1987 as a woodland walk.

42.8 The Peak Bord's information point in the valley at Derbyshire Bridge was closed at the end of 1986 because of low usage. New information boards have been placed at key sites in the valley, and a new free 'Visitors Guide' has been published.

42.9 These new information services were the results of the efforts of an Officer Liaison Group for the Goyt which was set up in 1984. The Peak Board, the Forestry commission (major land leaseholder) and North West Water (major landowner) were represented at that time. They were joined in 1986 by the Nature Conservancy Council, who are also currently reviewing the Goyt Valley SSSI. The Liaison Group's remit is only the Goyt Valley and its catchment, and excludes villages and other areas covered in this chapter.

42.10 The Ranger Service provided by the Peak Board in this area was extended in 1986. This was made possible by part funding from North West Water and — for the first time in the National Park — a contribution to the ranger service by the Forestry Commission.

42.11 An established sailing club had been keen to expand onto Lamaload,

Brian Redhead (President of the Council for National Parks) leads children on an improved woodland walk at Errwood Hall.

and there was interest in schools' sailing. The Water Authority, however, revised its draw-down arrangements to leave a relatively small area of water suited to sailing. The sailing proposal was not therefore acted upon. The Board has a car park, picnic area and toilets, and plans for further paths and planting are being prepared.

42.12 The village of Pott Shrigley has a designated Conservation Area, which includes the parkland of the Hall and woodland around the village. It is split for planning and improvement purposes between the Peak Board and Macclesfield BC, as it straddles the National Park boundary. Improvements have included a paving scheme near the church, and repairs to the school building. Rainow also straddles the Park boundary. Over the past 3 years extensive tree planting has been carried out in Rainow parish by agreement with owners and joint funding from Peak Board, Cheshire CC, Macclesfield BC and Rainow PC. A National Park millstone boundary sign was erected at the Park boundary at the Parish Council's request.

Current Circumstances
42.13 The 1986/87 surveys suggest about 390,000 visits each year to the Goyt, Lamaload, Todd Brook area.

42.14 The Goyt is one of the most sensitive areas in the National Park, being an area of outstanding landscape and wildlife value, and a magnet to visitors. Lamaload and Todd Brook are quieter areas, and the limited facilities for visitors have contained any pressure on those areas.

42.15 The recreation facilities in the Goyt Valley work at maximum capacity, and any increases in facilities could cause great harm to what is at present a finely balanced mix of land uses. Until now, most of the casual visitor pressure has been absorbed around Errwood Reservoir, with the more active visitor attracted to Derbyshire Bridge. In recent years pressure has increased on the area around Fernilee Reservoir. This is viewed with concern, since the western side in particular has been deliberately set-aside as a quiet wildlife refuge in the heart of the valley.

42.16 General agreement has been reached on the need to maintain the careful balance of land use, with agriculture, forestry, water supply, nature conservation and recreation existing in harmony. Demands for changes to the network of recreation routes, including specific suggesions for horse riding, are being resisted until the SSSI review is complete is complete.

42.17 The ruins of Errwood Hall will be consolidated and an information board provided about its history.

42.18 Negotiations since the 1970's have yet to result in an access agreement in the Goyt. Obstacles to agreement were first the danger of uncapped mineshafts, and now unresolved concerns about public liability. The existence of the SSSI also calls for a balanced approach to the recreation and nature conservation interests.

42.19 Responses to the Draft National Park Plan Review suggest that the conservation interest at Combs Moss is considerable. This will clearly need further survey and consideration in relation to any improved access for walkers.

42.20 Consideration has been given over the years to extending the High Peak Trail northwards from Dowlow, south of Buxton (where it currently terminates) via the Goyt to Whaley Bridge. The initiative currently rests with Derbyshire CC. There is a proposition for a 'Shires Way' long distance route from Greater Manchester to and through the East Midlands. Progress will be difficult because of the present uses of the old rail track bed.

Policies and Proposals
42.21 As in the 1978 Plan, the broad zoning policies for this area are:

(a) The moorland areas are most appropriate for low-intensive agriculture on well-managed heather and grassland. Recreation activities linked to moorland walking are appropriate. A possible Access Agreement over part of the moorland is still being investigated — Zone I.

(b) The moorland fringes, Fernilee Reservoir vicinity (other than the east bank), and Lamaload Reservoir vicinity (other than the east bank) are relatively remote. Any recreation provision should be carefully contained — Zone II.

(c) In the enclosed land throughout the area and the afforested land — recreation facilities generally should not be extended beyond those already present — Zone III.

(d) The immediate vicinity of Errwood Reservoir accommodates intensive recreation pressure at busy times. Facilities should not be significantly extended beyond those already present — Zone IV.

42.22 Every effort will be made to maintain the existing balance of land uses and their management in the Goyt Valley, through the work of the Officer Liaison Group in consultation with the County, District and Parish Councils. Works will be carried out to enhance existing woodlands, farmland, moorland or recreation facilities and routes. (Peak Board, North West Water, Forestry Commission, Nature Conservancy Council).

42.23 The conclusion of the Access Agreement negotiations for the Goyt Moors will be sought, subject to safeguarding conservation interests (Peak Board, North West Water, Nature Conservancy Council).

42.24 The ruins of Errwood Hall will be consolidated and an information plaque provided (Forestry Commission, Peak Board, North West Water).

42.25 Further liaison and appropriate action will be pursued to enhance recreation and conservation interests in the Lamaload area in consultation with the Cheshire CC, Macclesfield BC and Parish Councils (Peak Board, North West Water).

42.26 Consideration will be given to seeking improved public access to moorlands such as Combs Moss and Castle Naze, as proposed in the 1978 Plan, subject to careful consideration of conservation interests (Peak Board).

42.27 Consideration will be given to improving the walking, cycling and horse-riding links between the High Peak Trail and Whaley Bridge (Derbyshire CC, Peak Board).

42.28 Conservation Area enhancement will continue in Pott Shrigley in association with the Parish Council. Other opportunities to involve Parish Councils in environmental work, following the success of work in Rainow, will be considered (Peak Board, Macclesfield BC, Cheshire CC).

43 Macclesfield Forest, Wildboarclough and Wincle

Wincle

Introduction

43.1 This area is close to Macclesfield and includes land within and outside the National Park. It includes Tegg's Nose Country Park, Macclesfield Forest and Reservoirs, Shutlingsloe, Wildboarclough and Wincle. The mixture (within a relatively small area) of moorland, enclosed farmland, plantation woodland, four reservoirs and The Clough makes it extremely attractive. The area is crossed by narrow minor roads, public and concession recreation routes. The Gritstone Trail linking Lyme Park via Tegg's Nose to the Staffordshire Way runs to the west of the Forest. Most land is owned by North West Water (Macclesfield Forest), Cheshire CC (Tegg's Nose), and the Earl of Derby's Estates (much of Wildboarclough and Shutlingsloe).

43.2 The 1978 Plan referred to work then in hand on a Joint Study by Macclesfield BC, Cheshire CC, North West Water and the Peak Board. It identified topics for investigation in a proposed Management Plan. Because this Management Plan includes Wildboarclough, the area described in this Chapter also includes Wildboarclough. (In the 1978 Plan this had been covered in the 'South West Moors' area). The Wincle/Danebridge area has also been added as a result of Macclesfield BC's response to the Draft National Park Plan Review. They felt consideration of it here would be more appropriate than in the South West which is chiefly Staffordshire Moorlands. Some rationalisation and

development of recreation facilities around Wincle and Danebridge seemed possible in the 1978 Plan.

Work to Date

43.3 A Draft Management Plan for Macclesfield Forest and Wildboarclough was the subject of widespread consultation and public participation in 1978. It was revised and approved by the four authorities participating in the Study, and published in 1982.

43.4 Conservation and landscape management are the Management Plan's primary aims, with small-scale recreational facilities and management improvements to ease traffic flow, parking and trespass problems. Teggs Nose Country Park is specifically designed and advertised to attract increasing levels of activity, but the scale of recreation use is to be broadly maintained at existing levels in the Forest and Clough.

43.5 Much has been achieved — chiefly by investment on the part of North West Water Authority, the Peak Board and Cheshire CC in improved recreational facilities, with support and guidance from Macclesfield BC and in consultation with local parishes. Action includes:

(a) The Peak Board has improved existing informal parking and picnic areas at Vicarage Quarry, Clough House Farm, Nab Quarry and a layby near Brookside Cafe. In the Forest, North West Water has constructed lay-bys at Topclose and Ridgegate Reservoir; and both a car park and lay-by at Trentabank Reservoir. These sites provide a total of about 150 car spaces.

(b) Information and toilet facilities have been greatly improved at Tegg's Nose by Cheshire CC. New facilities were provided by North West Water at Trentabank, where there is a ranger briefing centre and information point. The Trentabank picnic area, along with toilets, may be managed under a lease to the Peak Board.

(c) Recreation routes have been improved, and extra waymarked concession routes provided for walkers, horse riders and disabled people in the Forest. The design of the disabled route and information display overlooking Trentabank was helped by suggestions from the local disabled group.

(d) An area surrounding the Trentabank Reservoir has been licensed to the Cheshire Conservation Trust by the Water Authority as a nature reserve. It includes a heronry.

(e) The Forest is used for orienteering events and training by local groups.

(f) The National Park Ranger Service in this area is jointly funded by the Peak Board and Water Authority, and is based on the Briefing Centre at Trentabank. Good working relationships exist between National Park Rangers and Cheshire Countryside Rangers who operate at Tegg's Nose, on the Gritstone Trail and public rights of way.

(g) A leaflet about the Forest has been produced and paid for by the Peak Board, North West Water and Macclesfield Borough Council.

43.6 Concern to avoid adding pressure to narrow roads in the Wincle area means that no significant recreation facilities have been developed there.

Current Circumstances

43.7 A recent report to Cheshire CC indicates that Teggs Nose received 150,000 visitors in 1986/87, mostly from a 40 mile radius. The main attractions were walking, picnicking, the views and guided walks.

43.8 Further visitor survey information was collected by the Peak Board in the Forest in 1987, and it indicated in the region of 51,000 visits each year. However, the weather and number of interviewees were not conducive to reliable predictions. Further surveys took place during summer 1988, together with parking and traffic counts, for comparison with those done before the production of the Management Plan.

43.9 The Officer Group meets twice yearly to review problems and progress, consider future priorities, and coordinate action.

43.10 Macclesfield BC has requested more detailed studies of the Wincle area.

Policies and Proposals

43.11 The 1978 Plan's zoning system and policies were extended to the whole Management Plan area, including land outside the National Park. They remain valid as follows:

(a) The wilder moorland areas of Shutlingsloe and Piggford Moor — Zone I.

(b) Areas of remote enclosed farmland and plantation woodland below the high moors — Zone II.

(c) Much of the rest of the area has opportunities and scope for walking, riding and limited associated facilities — Zone III.

(d) Tegg's Nose, the reservoir margins and Wincle/Danebridge area are a focus for informal recreation use, but selection of areas to be used needs great care — Zone IV.

43.12 The Officer Working Group is considering implementation of other items in the Plan:

(a) Car parks at Standing Stone, Ridgegate, and scope for public use of the Hanging Gate Inn parking areas.

(b) The provision of toilets at Trentabank may mean that toilets are not needed at the proposed Standing Stone and Ridgegate car parks. However, toilets need to be considered for Wildboarclough.

(c) Further improvements to recreation routes, together with guided and self-guided trails.

(d) Traffic Management measures, if improved off-road parking arrangements do not satisfactorily relieve earlier problems.

(e) North West Water has recently produced revised management plans for the Forest, which they have submitted to the Forestry Commission for approval in consultation with the Peak Board, Cheshire CC, Macclesfield BC, and local parish councils. Amendments have been requested to ensure they are consistent with the Management Plan proposals, which suggested ways in which landscape and wildlife improvements could be achieved, to create a more attractive forest. Other owners of woodland and tree groups in the rest of the area will be encouraged to pursue positive planting and management plans.

43.13 The Macclesfield Forest and Wildboarclough Joint Management Plan will continue to be used to guide decision-making and investment of funds for recreation, conservation, land and water management in the area. It will be monitored and progress reviewed by the Officer Group, who will report back to parent authorities when necessary (Macclesfield BC, Peak Board, North West Water, Cheshire CC).

43.14 As staff resources permit, existing features of interest and recreation activities and traffic issues in the Wincle/Danebridge area will be considered and any action needed discussed with local councils and other interests (Peak Board, Macclesfield BC, Cheshire CC).

44 South West Moors

Introduction

44.1 This area contains the high moorlands stretching along the route of the main A53 Buxton to Leek road, from Axe Edge in the North to Upper Hulme in the South. The peat-covered moorlands have relatively limited plateau areas, and are deeply dissected by the headwaters of rivers flowing in all directions. Much of the land is over 1,000 ft. above sea level. The area therefore contains elements characteristic of the northern part of the Park but on a smaller and more intimate scale. The River Dane, which flows through the heart of the area, is the only major river in the shale/grit area of the Park that remains essentially unexploited for water resources. There are popular recreation areas at Tittesworth Reservoir, at the Roaches with its fine climbing outcrops, and at Morridge where there is gliding.

44.2 The population of the area has been declining. The farms are mainly small and some are rapidly degenerating as rush, bracken and scrub invade formerly enclosed farmland. There is considerable wildlife interest on both the moorland, in-bye land and woodlands.

44.3 The Structure Plan proposed a variety of initiatives to prevent the continued decline of the rural population, to generate fresh employment opportunities, and to encourage the development of recreational facilities.

44.4 The 1978 Plan proposed continued work on a Local Study (the South West Study) for the area, under the co-ordination of the Rural Land Management Executive Group. The potential for developing farm tourism and staying

Wildboarclough Valley and Shutlingsloe. This part of the National Park is much used by Macclesfield folk.

Part of the Warslow Moors Estate for which the
Peak Board is preparing a Management Plan.

visitor accommodation was to be integrated into this. Problems related to the recreational use of the Roaches were to be examined, along with further recreation opportunities in the Tittesworth Reservoir/Blackshaw Moor area. Some rationalisation and development of recreation facilities seemed possible in the Wincle and Danebridge/ Swythamley area. The 1978 Plan included Wildboarclough in this area, but this is now dealt with in Chapter 43.

Work to date
44.5 The South West Study was begun, but not completed because of other initiatives. For example, the area forms part of the North East Staffordshire RDA, and a joint working party (the North East Staffordshire Working Party – NESTWOP) was formed to help the

social and economic revival of the whole of the Staffordshire part of the Park. NESTWOP's activities also include areas within Chapters 45 and 46, relating to the Dove and Manifold Valleys.

44.6 Many of the issues due to be covered in the South West Study will now be picked up in the Warslow Moors Estate Management Plan (see **44.14**).

44.7 The area contains many small marginal family farms which are affected by economic pressures such as the imposition of milk quotas in 1984. Farm incomes have been falling in the area, and some farmers may go out of business. A handful of farms now run scrap and lorry businesses, which are difficult to fit into the landscape of the area.

44.8 Four Management Agreements have been concluded in the area, the most notable being agreement not to improve Gun Moor, the southernmost area of predominantly heather moorland on the Pennine Chain. The NCC have included a substantial area of land rich in wildlife and rare species in their proposed Leeks Moors SSSI.

44.9 The Peak Board has provided a small car park at Gradbach, and a lay-by beneath the Roaches. Concern to avoid adding pressure on the narrow roads in the Swythamley area means that no significant recreation facilities have been developed there.

44.10 Tittesworth Reservoir is well served by road, and the reservoir is now managed for angling and informal recreation. Picnic sites, information and refreshment facilities have been provided by Severn Trent Water. This work was commended in the 1988 Times/RICS conservation awards.

44.11 The Peak Board developed a touring caravan site with 60 pitches at Blackshaw Moor, just south of the National Peak boundary adjoining the A53 Leek-Buxton road. This was done in co-operation with The Caravan Club, who manage the site, and are now buying it from the Board. It is hoped to increase the size of this site to 90 pitches. The Youth Hostels Association has converted Gradbach Mill to a hostel, with grant from the Peak Board. There is also a Scout Camp adjoining The Roaches.

44.12 The Peak and Moorlands Farm Holiday Group, which was fostered by NESTWOP, has helped improve staying visitor accommodation, adopting a co-operative approach to promotion and marketing. This initiative is helping to sustain farm incomes as well as contributing to environmental objectives by finding new uses for existing buildings.

44.13 Recreation problems in the Roaches area were examined following the acquisition of the 395 ha estate by the Peak Board in 1980. A Management Plan was adopted in 1981, which provided for the Estate's future development and gave special emphasis to nature conservation. It imposed controls to resolve the apparent conflict between conservation and recreation, particularly climbing and hang gliding. A programme of walling works, heather and burning and bracken control was drawn up. Following a review of the Management Plan in 1982, a system was developed to permit specific areas to be grazed during the appropriate season. The Peak Board is to further review this Management Plan, and future parking arrangements.

44.14 In 1986, the Warslow Moors Estate was transferred to the Peak Board by the Government in lieu of capital taxation from the Harpur-Crewe family — 1,899 ha of land being classified as of 'heritage quality'. Some of the Estate lies in the Dove and Manifold Valley areas which are dealt with in Chapters 45 and 46 of this Plan. An Estate Management Plan is being prepared for the property as a whole, to provide for public access and recreation where this is compatible with the outstanding conservation values of the area. The needs of the Estate tenants and the wider local community are also

a major consideration. About 620 ha of the Estate is either let or licensed to the Ministry of Defence for use as a Military Training Area based on its camp at Blackshaw Moor. Within the context of the overall Estate Management Plan, a separate plan is being agreed with the Ministry of Defence which seeks to minimise the conflicts between military training and National Park objectives for the long-term benefit of the area and the public.

44.15 In 1986, the Peak Board also acquired, with the Nature Conservancy Council, an adjoining farm running to 74 ha. A Management Plan has been agreed, principally to ensure conservation of the area's outstanding wildlife value.

44.16 A joint Staffordshire CC and Peak Board scheme using MSC workers was set up in 1984 to improve the footpath and bridleway sytem in the area. It has done a considerable amount to remove path obstructions, to improve stiles and path surfaces, and generally to reverse decades of neglect. This work is continuing, under the new Employment Training Scheme under Staffordshire County Council's management. Staffordshire Moorlands District Council has also been active in footpath, verge and wall improvements in conjunction with the MSC.

Current Circumstances
44.17 Many initiatives are going ahead in this area. This is a special challenge, given the substantial areas of land at Warslow Moors and the Roaches owned by the Board and the RDA work. Links need to be forged between these Estate Management Plans and wider initiatives arising from the RDA. Meanwhile, the Board has approved a major extension to a cement-mixer factory to secure existing jobs.

44.18 The 1986/87 surveys suggest about 335,000 visits to this south west area of the Park each year.

Policies and Proposals
44.12 The recreation zoning for the area is unchanged from the 1978 Plan and set out below. It will form part of the framework for the Estate Management Plans for Warslow Moors and the Roaches, and will need to be refined as these studies progress:

(a) The areas of Axe Edge, the Roaches and Gun Hill — Zone I.

(b) The remoter farmland areas such as around Brandside and Morridge — Zone II.

(c) The majority of the farmland has some scope for recreation facilities in appropriate locations — Zone III.

(d) The area around Danebridge is already subject to moderate intensities of use — Zone IV.

(e) The Tittesworth/Blackshaw Moor area — Zone IV. (Further recreation development could result in the area being reclassified as Zone V).

44.20 The Peak Board, in partnership with other public agencies and the local communities and through the Rural Development Programme, will endeavour to promote a revival in the economy, environment and quality of community life in the area (Peak Board, NESTWOP).

44.21 The potential for developing farm tourism and staying visitor accommodation will continue to be examined and integrated into this area, in the context of a Tourism Action Programme (Peak Board, NESTWOP, Heart of England Tourist Board).

44.22 Encouragement will be given to development of recreational facilities (especially where this helps to sustain existing businesses), where this is consistent with the special character and qualities of this area and complies with Structure Plan policies (Peak Board)

44.23 Forms of farm diversification will be examined and promoted to ensure the continued future of the family farm in the area, subject to the policies in the Structure Plan (see also 4.32-4.35) (Peak Board, MAFF).

44.24 The Management Plan for the Warslow Moors Estate will be completed in the wider context of this South West area, subject to widespread consultation and public comment. This will include a separate Management Plan for land held by the Ministry of Defence under lease and licence (Peak Board, MoD).

44.25 The Management Plan for the Roaches Estate will be reviewed in consultation with appropriate interests (Peak Board)

44.26 The footpath and bridleway system will continue to be improved, and its use will be carefully promoted as an important asset to the local tourist industry (see Chapter 11) (Peak Board, Staffordshire CC, Staffordshire Moorlands DC).

45 Upper Dove and Manifold Valleys

Introduction

45.1 The area is characterised by enclosed improved farmland but there are large outcrops of limestone rough grazing on the high ground including Chrome Hill and Parkhouse Hill. In the 16th and 17th Centuries, Longnor was a market town and the focus of settlement in the area, which consisted of small farms with linked cottage industries. In more recent times, the area has lost population and employment opportunities and Longnor has lost its market function and the service industries that went with it.

45.2 The Structure Plan and the 1978 Plan proposed a variety of initiatives to stabilise the population, generate new employment opportunities and develop recreation opportunities. In particular it was proposed to develop staying visitor accommodation as a new use for the large number of disused buildings in the area. Better information facilities were suggested for Longnor. It was also proposed to extend the 'Routes for People' approach to this area of the Park (see **15.4** and Chapter 39).

Work to date

45.3 The Board introduced a grant scheme for tourist accommodation (see **17.4**) which assisted in the development of a number of tourist businesses particularly in the Staffordshire Moorlands part of the National Park. It was later phased out as Tourist Board schemes provided an alternative source of help. Longnor was the focus of much of this activity. The village was designated a Conservation Area and a major programme of environmental improvement

The Old Market Hall, Longnor before conversion into a ceramics workshop as part of the IRD project.

was carried out in consultation with the local community and in partnership with other public agencies. Notable was the Chapel Street scheme which converted a street of derelict houses into tourist accommodation, houses and a cafe.

45.4 The role of the inter-authority working party (the North East Staffordshire Working Party — NESTWOP) is referred to earlier (see **44.5**). A Housing Association was encouraged to provide 14 new houses for rent at Windy Ridge, Longnor primarily for young couples. The Council for Small Industries in Rural Areas (COSIRA) agreed to develop Advance Factories for rent on Buxton Road, Longnor, financed by the Development Commission. These factories had remained empty for two years when the Board and other agencies, and with help from the EEC, were able to launch funds for an experimental programme of Integrated Rural Development (IRD) in 1982 (see also Chapter 23).

45.5 The IRD scheme helped still further in the rejuvenation of Longnor.

The advance factories were occupied by a new firm, which is a high technology plant propagation business. The Old Market Hall, empty for 30 years, was converted into a workshop by English Estates with financial assistance from the Development Commission and the Peak Board: it now houses a ceramics workshop. Other businesses were helped to establish or expand. The community restarted its well-dressing tradition which lapsed nearly 30 years earlier, and carried out a large number of other community schemes. A variety of community-run tourist schemes was also implemented e.g. craft demonstrations and an information point in the village shop. Overall some 40 new full-time or part-time jobs have been created, and Longnor has re-established its role as a thriving centre for the surrounding area.

45.6 At Parkhouse Hill, an important Management Agreement was concluded to install a cattle grid and leave the narrow road unfenced and open. Efforts are being made to overcome problems of fossil collecting at Chrome Hill and

Parkhouse Hill by reference to the Geologists Association's 'Code for Geological Field Work', and by the vigilance of Rangers.

Current Circumstances

45.7 The 1978 Plan's policies and proposals have been successfully applied and have been translated into a comprehensive programme of action. The revival of the area has created recreation facilities and improved the environment, notably the considerable number of building restoration schemes completed or in progress. It has also generated many new employment opportunities in a short period of time. The community has a new spirit of confidence.

45.8 Visitor pressure in Longnor now means that the Market Square, which is also the main car park for the village, is often full and congested. The Parish Council requested a new car park and identified a possible site in woodland owned by the Peak Board. However, this proposal aroused strong local opposition and the Board therefore withdrew its planning application. Further ideas from the village to solve parking problems may be forthcoming. The Board would not normally proceed with a scheme that does not have general support in the locality.

45.9 A joint Staffordshire County Council and Peak Board scheme using MSC workers was set up in 1984 to improve the footpath and bridleway system in the area (and in adjacent areas in the Staffordshire part of the Park). Based in Longnor it has removed path obstructions, improved stiles and path surfaces and generally reversed decades of neglect (see also **44.16**). Staffordshire Moorlands District Council has also been actively involved in footpath works in this area.

45.10 The existing policy to maintain reasonable population levels and improve the economy, environment and quality of life in the area has achieved a great deal in a short period of time. This policy will be maintained, with careful management of the area. The lessons of the IRD approach to environmental improvement, economic development and community enterprise in the Longnor area are to be applied in other parts of the Staffordshire Peak District (see **23.26-23.29**). The Staffordshire RDA officer working party has approached one village, and intended to approach other villages as part of a rolling programme in the RDA.

45.11 The 1986/87 surveys suggest that about 110,000 visits are made each year to this area.

Policies and Proposals

45.12 The recreation zoning in the 1978 Plan remains appropriate as follows:

(a) The Chrome Hill/Parkhouse Hill area — Zone I.

(b) The remoter farmland of the Dove Valley — Zone II.

(c) Continued scope exists for active recreation and related accommodation in selected locations over much of the area — Zone III.

(d) Longnor is the best centre for recreation services — Zone IV.

45.13 The Peak Board, in partnership with other public agencies and the local communities and through the Rural Development Programme, will endeavour to promote a revival in the economy, environment and quality of community life in the area (Peak Board, NESTWOP).

45.14 The potential for developing farm tourism and staying visitor accommodation will continue to be examined and integrated into this area in the context of a Tourism Action Programme (Peak Board, NESTWOP, Heart of England Tourist Board).

45.15 Encouragement will be given to the development of recreational facilities (especially where this helps to sustain existing businesses), where this is consistent with the special character and qualities of this area and complies with Structure Plan policies. (Peak Board).

45.16 Forms of farm diversification will be examined and promoted to ensure the continued future of the family farm in the area, subject to the policies in the Structure Plan (see also **4.32**). (Peak Board, MAFF).

45.17 A small car park and picnic site may be developed at Longnor to relieve congestion problems in the centre of the village, if there is general agreement on a site (Peak Board, Staffordshire Moorlands DC, Longnor P.C.).

45.18 The footpath and bridleway system will continue to be improved, and its use will be carefully promoted as an important asset to the local tourist industry (see Chapter 11) (Peak Board, Staffordshire CC, Staffordshire Moorlands DC).

46 Lower Dove and Manifold Valleys

Introduction

46.1 This area contains spectacular limestone scenery, including the deep limestone dales of the Rivers Dove and Manifold and a number of very attractive villages. It is virtually defined by a triangle of roads — A515, A52(T) and B5054 — and includes the villages of Hartington, Fenny Bentley, Warslow, Waterhouses, Thorpe, Ilam, Alstonefield, Grindon and Butterton. Tissington (to the east of the A515) is also included.

46.2 The area is popular with visitors. The 1986/87 surveys indicate there are just over 2 million visits to this area each year. In the dales, traffic generation and parking problems can become acute at peak periods. Dovedale, and the National Trust's Ilam Country Park, are major focal points for visitors. Walking and riding are major activities: the Tissington Trail and Manifold Track provide largely traffic-free routes for walkers and cyclists.

46.3 There is much of geological and wildlife interest particularly in the dales, including some of the finest semi-natural woodlands in the National Park. In this context the high level of recreational activities may be viewed as a potential threat. The area is popular with staying visitors, there being a number of camping and touring caravan sites, together with considerable resources of farmhouse and self-catering accommodation. A lot of land is owned by the National Trust, whose holding in the Dove/Manifold area has increased since 1978.

46.4 The 1978 Plan proposed continuing work on management plans for the areas around Dovedale, Milldale, Alstonefield and the Manifold Valley, with a strong emphasis on the need for traffic management and car parking schemes. It also proposed an information centre at Dovedale, better information about the Manifold Valley, recognition for the use of the Manifold Track for cycling, permanent extension of the Tissington Trail into Ashbourne, and measures to improve traffic conditions in Tissington. It also highlighted scope for caravan and camp sites in the Hartington/Newhaven areas.

Work to date
46.5 Considerable progress has been made towards achieving these aims. Landscape, parking and traffic management improvements have been completed at Milldale and at the southern end of Dovedale. Parking space has been reduced near the Dale entrance, including removal of cars and landscape restoration of the slope below Bunster Hill. These measures appear to have brought about a general reduction in traffic. New car parks have been provided by the Peak Board at Hulme End and Waterhouses in the Manifold Valley. A small car park has been provided by the Parish Council in Grindon, with grant from the Peak Board for this and other landscape improvements. The Parish Council would now like to see public toilets provided in the village.

46.6 Cycling is now officially recognised on the Manifold Track. An additional cycle hire centre has been opened by the Board at Waterhouses. Cycles are also on hire locally by private operators. Major improvements are being carried out to re-construct the main valley footpath between Dovedale and Hartington: it has been completed between Dovedale and Milldale, and works are now underway in Wolfscote Dale and Beresford Dale. A suggested footpath route between Milldale and Lode Mill on the Derbyshire bank of the River Dove, as an alternative to the road on the Staffordshire side, has been the subject of much discussion. It has been resisted by the National Trust, as owners, and by fishing, farming and conservation interests. The Board will discuss with the Trust and other interests possible ways of improving links with Milldale and Lode Mill for walkers.

46.7 The Joint Study on Camping and Caravanning published in 1980 suggested measures for tackling problems of overuse of areas like Wetton and Alstonefield, and provision of new sites to relieve pressure on more sensitive places in the dales. Planning consents have been given for large new sites at former quarries near Hartington and Alsop, but these have yet to be taken up. Co-ordination and consultation on rally sites has improved.

46.8 A permanent extension of the Tissington Trail to Ashbourne has not proved possible through the tunnel. The Peak Board has therefore relocated its cycle hire base out from the centre of the town to the outskirts at its Mapleton Lane car park.

46.9 The role of the inter authority working party (the North East Staffordshire Working Party — NESTWOP) is referred to earlier (see **44.5**). In Hartington, within the Derbyshire Rural Development Area, CoSIRA provided a workshop by a conversion of a large traditional building. This is now used by a pottery firm.

Current Circumstances
46.10 The area seems certain to maintain its popularity and traffic congestion will continue to be a problem. The 'Routes for People' principle has not been extended to this area and there may still be scope for adopting this or a similar approach to traffic management (see **15.4**). Local improvements to car parks in heavily used areas such as the Manifold Valley will help traffic management and visual amenity. Wear and tear on major recreational routes is also likely to be heavy and will need management.

46.11 The need to achieve the right balance between local needs and those of visitors is of fundamental importance. There has been a population decline, but the area now derives considerable economic benefit from visitors. Staying visitors generally contribute more to the local economy than day trippers. However, the heavy and often unauthorised use of some camping and caravan sites, particularly around Wetton and Alstonefield, causes considerable problems for the local community. This is a matter for the Staffordshire Moorlands DC and the Peak Board to tackle.

46.12 Local discussions have been held about ways of easing conflicts between vehicles and walkers, cyclists and disabled people in the Manifold Valley. Local people are reluctant to see changes, but a package of improvements has been worked out with the County Surveyor and local interests. Mining areas at Ecton are significant, and in some cases would benefit from schemes to reclaim dereliction, enable interpretation and safeguard historic interest and valuable habitats which may have evolved.

46.13 The area falls within parts of two Rural Development Areas — Staffordshire and Derbyshire. Rural Development Commission Advance Factories have been built at Warslow and at Waterhouses, just outside the National Park boundary, but they have proved difficult to let and are not fully occupied. The Hartington Pottery has been helped to establish in the area through RDA work (see **46.9**). One of the issues under consideration is housing, and there are proposals for small-scale housing developments in Hartington, Alstonefield and Butterton. Staffordshire Moorlands District Council has bought land for housing in Warslow to provide accommodation for elderly people and young families.

46.14 The funds available to the District Councils for meeting local housing needs by public sector housebuilding or acquisition are becoming more limited. The role and funds of the Housing Corporation and housing associations or trusts is expanding. The Board's role is as facilitator, particularly by the careful encouragement and approval of planning applications designed to meet local needs.

46.15 Although Warslow Middle School avoided closure in 1984, both Warslow and Waterhouses middle schools were subsequently proposed for closure in a reorganisation of schools in the Leek area by Staffordshire CC. The Secretary of State agreed, despite local objections. The schools closed in September 1988, and the future use of the properties will be carefully considered with a presumption in favour of local community use or benefit.

46.16 Conservation Area designations have been made for parts of Alstonefield, Ilam, Butterton and Hartington. Enhancement programmes have been agreed for Alstonefield and Ilam, where most of the improvements have been done. An improvement programme for Butterton has recently been agreed locally. Improvement of parking on the outskirts of Hartington is planned as a priority, linked to reduction of parking and environmental improvements in the centre of the village. It is hoped these discussions may progress to devise an enhancement programme for the Conservation Area. Tissington was proposed as a Conservation Area, but no action has been taken on this following strong local objections. Local traffic and parking problems there would seem more likely to be solved if it had Conservation Area status.

46.17 A key proposal in the plans for Dovedale was an information centre at the parking areas near the Dale entrance. Lack of funds and disagreement on details meant it did not proceed. This proposal needs further study as part of an overall review of visitor information in this area.

46.18 Staffordshire CC is planning to organise a scheme to stabilise the remaining structure of Throwley Old Hall ancient monument and to provide a small parking area, interpretation and improved footpath circuits in the area, with help from the Peak Board and other interests.

Policies and Proposals
46.19 The recreation zoning outlined in the 1978 Plan is still relevant as follows:

(a) The Natural Zone areas of Dovedale and the Manifold Valley — Zone I.

(b) The remote farmland to the south of the area — Zone II.

(c) The majority of the remainder of the area has scope for active recreation and limited scale recreation facilities in suitable locations — Zone III.

(d) Areas already providing moderate-scale recreation facilities — e.g. Milldale, Alstonefield, Wetton Mill and Weags Bridge — together with those areas which have potential for such facilities, e.g. areas around Warslow/Ecton/Hulme End and Onecote — Zone IV.

(e) Those areas where essential larger scale activities may be accommodated in carefully defined locations, e.g. Ashbourne/Thorpe/Ilam area, Waterhouses and the Hartington/Newhaven area — Zone V.

46.20 This area relies very much on income from two main sources — farming and visitors. The need to maximise income from these sources to maintain a healthy local economy must be viewed against the possible effects such a policy may have on the landscape and environmental quality of the area generally. A number of principles are suggested to guide future action and management:

Volunteers carrying out river revetment work as part of a 10 year programme to reconstruct the heavily used Dovedale-Hartington footpath.

(a) The development and use of recreational facilities and roads in the area should relate to the conservation of the distinctive environment of the area. There is little scope for major new facilities close to the Dales. Monitoring will be important to consider the need for traffic management and conservation schemes, particularly in the most sensitive limestone dales such as the Manifold Valley and Dovedale.

(b) The level of provision and use of visitor accommodation in the area should be monitored to provide information to guide decisions on additional provision, relocation/extension of existing facilities and action against unauthorised use.

(c) In view of the extent of informal recreational activity throughout the area, particular attention should be paid to maintaining a high level and quality of on-site information at all recreational sites.

46.21 Maintenance of work carried out, or in the course of implementation in the Dovedale and Milldale areas (see 46.5 and 46.6) should con-

tinue using present working arrangements. (Peak Board, Staffordshire CC, Derbyshire CC and the National Trust).

46.22 A programme of traffic management, environmental improvement work and information provision will be pursued in the Manifold Valley (Peak Board, Staffordshire CC).

46.23 The Peak Board, in partnership with other public agencies and the local communities and through the Rural Development Programme, will endeavour to promote further revival in the economy, environment and quality of community life in the area (Peak Board, NESTWOP).

46.24 Proposals will include small-scale housing developments in the villages of Hartington, Butterton, Alstonefield and Warslow, if appropriate sites can be identified (Peak Board, NESTWOP, Derbyshire RDA Working Party).

46.25 The potential for developing farm tourism and staying visitor accommodation will continue to be examined and integrated into this area, in the context of a Tourism Action

Programme (Peak Board, NESTWOP, Heart of England Tourist Board).

46.26 Encouragement will be given to development of recreational facilities (especially where this helps to sustain existing businesses), where this is consistent with the special character and qualities of this area and complies with Structure Plan policies (Peak Board, Parish Councils).

46.27 Conservation Area enhancement works will continue to be implemented in association with local Parish Councils in Hartington, Alstonefield, Ilam and Butterton (Peak Board, Parish Councils).

46.28 Village management schemes will be considered at Warslow and Wetton (Peak Board, Parish Councils).

46.29 At Hartington, action to improve parking facilities, linked to traffic management and environmental improvements will be pursued as a priority (Peak Board, Derbyshire Dales DC, Derbyshire CC, Hartington PC).

46.30 Camping and caravanning activity in the Wetton and Alstonefield areas will be restricted to existing levels of provision in line with the Joint Study on Camping and Caravanning (Peak Board, Staffordshire Moorlands DC).

46.31 At Dovedale, further discussions will be held about information for visitors (Peak Board, National Trust, Nature Conservancy Council, Countryside Commission).

46.32 Action will be taken to stabilise the remains of Throwley Old Hall, and to provide a related small parking area, footpath improvements, and appropriate interpretation (Staffordshire CC, Peak Board).

46.33 At Grindon, consideration will be given to developing toilets if a clear demand exists, a suitable site can be found and funds are available (Staffordshire Moorlands DC, Peak Board).

46.34 The footpath and bridleway system will continue to be improved, and the use will be carefully promoted as an important asset to the local tourist industry (see Chapter 11) (Peak Board, Staffordshire CC, Staffordshire Moorlands DC).

46.35 Early consideration will be given to future use of the Warslow school and also to that of Waterhouses school, which will have an impact on Park residents (Staffordshire CC, Staffordshire Moorlands DC, Peak Board).

47 Buxton Area

Introduction

47.1 The whole of this area lies outside the National Park, which bounds it on three sides. However, geographically, Buxton is close to the heart of the Peak District and there are many links between the Park and the Town.

47.2 Buxton provides a large proportion of the guest house and hotel accommodation in the Peak District, has main shopping facilities, swimming baths and an information centre. It is also the centre for much of the surrounding road and transport network. Within Buxton there are many facilities for recreation use, such as the town parks and the Country Park at Poole's Cavern. The centre of Buxton is an outstanding Conservation Area with much of historic interest, particularly related to its development as a Spa Town. Thus Buxton is closely related to the Park in recreation and tourist terms.

47.3 The 1978 Plan suggested investigation by the appropriate authorities of continuing development of recreation facilities and services, coordination of information provision, improving traffic conditions, and better recreation routes in and around Buxton.

Work to Date

47.4 Much has been done by others to improve the attractiveness and competitiveness of Buxton as a Spa Town. In particular:

(a) The new Spring Gardens Shopping Centre and Car park (1986)

(b) The Spring Gardens Relief Road (1987)

(c) The Cavendish Shopping Centre (1987)

(d) The upgrading of much of the hotel accommodation (about 800 bedspaces in serviced accommodation in Buxton).

(e) The establishment of the Buxton and District Tourist Association

(f) The development of Buxton Steam Centre by Peak Rail

(g) The renovation of the Opera House and the launch of the annual Buxton International Festival

(h) The improvements at the Buxton Museum and Art Gallery and, in particular, the development of an exhibition on the Peak District.

47.5 There are increasing links between the National Park and the Buxton International Festival, with emphasis in the Festival marketing of the role which Buxton can play as a base for touring in the Peak District during the day, and attending the Buxton Festival in the evenings.

47.6 Some of the Board's sponsored recreation bus services go through Buxton, thus assisting travel for visitors and locals alike. Apart from this, the Board has done little within Buxton since the 1978 Plan. Various meetings have been held, and in particular Buxton was the base for the 1982 Conference of National Park Authorities.

47.7 Attempts were made to establish a major new Tourist Information Centre in a shop unit in Buxton, and the Board voted money for a joint venture with the Borough Council. However, in 1988 High Peak BC opened a new and larger Tourist Information Centre at the Natural Baths site in Buxton. Arrangements between the Board and the District Council are currently under discussion.

Current Circumstances

47.8 Buxton is an historic Spa Town which is now putting considerable efforts to modernise and improve its facilities, whilst keeping the very beautiful 'Spa Town in the hills' quality. Tourism is increasingly a major element of the local economy and employment.

47.9 There is still much to be done in improving the facilities and accommodation in the Town. Buxton is likely to grow in importance as a day visitor centre for shopping and leisure, and as a base for longer visits. In particular, a number of the larger hotels are striving to attract conferences to the area.

The Pavilion Gardens have been renovated, increasing the attractiveness and competitiveness of Buxton as a Spa Town.

47.10 This marketing of Buxton is likely to be assisted by a much increased marketing and availability of Buxton Spa water, following a change in ownership of the bottling rights in 1987.

47.11 The traffic problems of the central area were greatly improved by the Spring Gardens relief road in 1987. However, there are still severe traffic problems especially on the A6 (Fairfield Road) which is the subject of a study being undertaken by DCC. The impact of the new Chapel by-pass is being carefully monitored.

47.12 The Manchester to Buxton railway line continues to have great importance to the town and to the wider Peak District; and is receiving increased marketing by British Rail as a 'scenic railway'. The activities of Peak Rail at Buxton are already increasing the attraction of the town to railway enthusiasts: and this would be greatly enhanced should Peak Rail succeed in its plans to reopen the old Midland Railway between Matlock and Buxton.

47.13 The footpath links from Buxton to the footpath and bridleway system of

the National Park still need improvement. Walkers use the busy A6 road in large numbers but there is no footway. The possibility of establishing improved links between Buxton and the Monsal Trail should be considered when Topley Pike quarry closes, as there is a good potential link.

Possible Topics for Investigation
47.14 The Buxton area is outside the National Park and the responsible Local Authorities are Derbyshire CC and High Peak BC. In view of the close relationship of Buxton to the National Park, it is suggested that the following topics might be investigated by the appropriate authorities. The Peak Board will be pleased to co-operate in the investigation and development of any of these suggestions:

(a) Development of an improved Tourist Information Centre in Buxton and the co-ordination of information services in Buxton with those provided in the Park.

(b) Close involvement with the marketing of Buxton as a Tourist location, including working with Buxton and District Tourist Associa-

tion. Joint working through the meeting of groups of authorities and agencies with common interests (see paragraph **17.12**).

(c) Increased working with the Buxton International Festival, and emphasis upon Buxton as a base for exploring the National Park during the Festival.

(d) Improved footpath links (**47.13** above).

(e) Monitoring of the traffic leaving the Peak Park area, so as to contribute towards the case for improved roads within Buxton, and related to proposed road improvements elsewhere on the A6, A619 and A623 and in Manchester.

(f) The introduction of new and improved trains on the Buxton to Manchester Railway line, and the opportunity this presents for visitors to Buxton and the National Park.

(g) The proposed reopening of the Buxton to Matlock railway line by Peak Rail, approved in principle by the relevant planning authorities.

Appendix 1
Report of Public Consultation and Participation

1. The public consultation and participation process had three distinct parts: formal written consultations; the distribution of a summary booklet and questionnaire; and 16 public exhibitions and meetings. The substance of the comments made in all three parts was taken into account in preparing the final Plan.

Formal Written consultations

2. The draft Plan was sent to a total of 290 formal consultees (see Appendix 2). These were constituent local authorities, parish councils, government departments and a wide range of bodies representing many interests including land and conservation, sport and recreation, accommodation and transport. In all a total of 113 replies were received from the 290 bodies who were asked to comment.

Summary Booklet and Questionnaire

3. A summary booklet was published, entitled Your Chance to be Heard containing statements that summarised the Plan's aims and intentions in each of 23 topic areas, together with a reply-paid, pull-out questionnaire. A copy of this booklet was delivered to the vast majority of households in the National Park. It was also made freely available at the public exhibitions and meetings that took place in and around the Park, and to interested members of the public. Over 20,000 booklets were distributed or picked up. A total of 1,071 replies were received by the cut-off date. Of these 893 were from National Park residents, a response of just under 5%. The questionnaire returns lack authority because of the uneven profile of the respondents and the low response rate. However, the general support for most of the topic statements was welcome and encouraging, and many additional comments were taken into account.

Public Exhibitions and Meetings

4. Sixteen public exhibitions and meetings were held at a variety of venues, including Sunday Schools, Council Chambers, theatres and museums in villages, towns and cities in and around the Park (see Appendix 3). In each case evening meetings were supported by a small exhibition on the afternoon of the same day, and on the preceding day as well at the five city venues. This 'roadshow' was publicised by a variety of methods including press releases, press advertisement and a substantial poster campaign, using the logo from the summary booklet.

5. Attendances at meetings varied from fewer than 20 at some of the city venues to over 70 at three of the venues inside the Park. On every occasion there were lively debates with a good range of topics covered.

6. The Exhibition comprised a set of purpose-designed panels summarising the Plan, backed up by a video recording of the slide-tape presentation and a selection of National Park publications.

7. Knowledge of the plan-making process reached many more people as a result of the meetings and associated newspaper articles, radio interviews and posters. The Board was welcomed at all venues and, on some occasions, it was suggested that it should visit more frequently. This point is to be considered in deciding the future pattern of the Board's public meetings.

8. The public meetings and exhibitions were held at the following places:

Location	Venue
Huddersfield	Venn Street Arts Centre
Bradfield	Village Hall
Macclesfield	Town Hall (Assembly Rooms)
Holme	Sunday School
Stockport	Town Hall (Council Chamber)
Hope	Hope Valley College
Oldham	Civic Hall, Upper Mill
Stoke-on-Trent	City Museum, Hanley
Ashbourne	Compton Offices (Council Chamber)
Derby	Assembly Rooms
Tideswell	Wesley Church Hall
Sheffield	Town Hall (Reception Room)
Bakewell	Town Hall (Court Room)
Buxton	Paxton Suite, Pavilion Gardens
Leek	Moorlands House (Meeting Hall)
Glossop	Town Hall (Glossop Room)

PEAK PARK JOINT PLANNING BOARD 1988

Your chance to be heard

NATIONAL PARK PLAN DRAFT 1ST REVIEW

SUMMARY

Cover of summary booklet with questionnaire, sent to over 18,000 addresses in and around the National Park.

Appendix 2
Consultees

The following organisations were consulted during preparation of this Plan.

County Councils
Derbyshire County Council
Staffordshire County Council
Cheshire County Council

District Councils
Derbyshire Dales District Council
High Peak Borough Council
North East Derbyshire District Council
Macclesfield Borough Council
Staffordshire Moorlands District Council
Sheffield Metropolitan District Council
Kirklees Metropolitan District Council
Oldham Metropolitan Borough Council
Barnsley Metropolitan District Council

Parish and Community Councils
All Parish Councils and meetings wholly or partly in the National Park
Derbyshire Rural Community Council
Yorkshire Rural Community Council
Community Council for Staffordshire
Cheshire Community Council

Land and Conservation Interests
National Farmers Union
Ministry of Agriculture, Fisheries and Food
Country Landowner's Association
Forestry Commission
Timber Growers (UK)
Nature Conservancy Council
Severn Trent Water Authority
Yorkshire Water Authority
North West Water Authority
English Heritage
National Trust
Council for the Protection of Rural England
Council for National Parks
County Wildlife Trusts
Royal Society for the Protection of Birds
The Moorland Association
Peak Park Moorland Owners and Tenants Association
Derbyshire Archaeological Advisory Committee
Derbyshire Historic Buildings Trust
Hallamshire Historic Buildings Trust
Staffordshire Historic Buildings Trust
Derbyshire Archaeological Society
Hunter Archaeological Society
Derbyshire Ornithological Society
Peak District Mines Historical Society
Chatsworth Estates
Civic Societies: Bakewell and District Holme Valley
Meltham Saddleworth
Hayfield Youlgreave
Centre for Conservation of Historic Parks and Gardens
Archaeological Officers
Peak Park Wildlife Advisory Group

Sport and Recreation Interests
East Midlands Regional Council for Sport and Recreation (Co-ordinator for other Regional Councils' Views)
Derbyshire Caving Association
British Mountaineering Council
Cyclists Touring Club

British Hang Gliding Association
Peak Hang Gliding Association
Sheffield Hang Gliding Association
British Horse Society
Autocycle Union
Land Access and Rights Association (LARA)
Trail Riders Fellowship
British Orienteering Federation (East Midlands Association)
Orienteering Clubs: Manchester and District
Derwent Valley
South Yorkshire
National
Ramblers' Association: South Yorks and NE Derbyshire
Manchester
Staffordshire
West Derbyshire (Derbyshire Dales)
National Director
Peak and Northern Footpaths Society:
Derbyshire Footpaths Preservation Society
Open Spaces Society
Byways and Bridleways Trust
Sheffield Campaign for Access to Moorland
British Field Sports Society
National Federation of Anglers
British Canoe Union
Royal Yachting Association
Peak District Mountain Rescue Organisation

Accommodation Interests
Caravan Club
Camping and Caravanning Club
YHA
Boys Scouts Association
Girl Guides Association

Transport Interests
Department of Transport
British Rail
South Yorks PTE
West Yorks PTE
Great Manchester PTE
Transport 2000
Trent Motor Traction
Peak Rail
Automobile Association
Royal Automobile Club
County Public Transport Officers

Police
Derbyshire
Staffordshire
Cheshire
South Yorkshire
West Yorkshire
Greater Manchester

Public Bodies and Government Departments
Department of Environment (Regional Office)
Directorate of Rural Affairs
Countryside Commission
Rural Development Commission
English Tourist Board
Regional Tourist Boards: East Midlands
Heart of England
Yorkshire and Humberside
North West

Rural Development Commission Business Service:
                          Derbyshire
                          Staffordshire and Cheshire
English Estates
Ministry of Defence
East Midlands Electricity Board
Yorkshire Electricity Board
Midlands Electricity Board
North West Electricity Board
British Telecom
Manpower Services Commission
Central Electricity Generating Board

Other Interests
Royal National Institute for the Blind
Derbyshire Association for the Blind
Derbyshire Centre for Integrated Living
Royal Association for Disabled and Rehabilitation (RADAR)
Derbyshire Association for the Disabled
Derby and Derbyshire Chamber of Commerce and Industry
Bakewell Chamber of Trade
British Trust for Conservation Volunteers
Greater Manchester Countryside Unit
Macclesfield Groundwork Trust

Appendix 3
Extract from the Report of the National Parks Committee 1947

1. The following extract from the report of the National Parks Committee of 1947 (the Hobhouse Report) is included to give an historical dimension to this plan for the 1990's. The following brief review of this report's description of the Peak District will perhaps help to strengthen a longer-term view of the tasks facing those people and organisations committed to the maintenance of a National Park landscape for future generations.

2. The report's content is remarkably familiar in its description of the qualities, problems and opportunities of the area. It is a timely reminder that a ten-year plan is only a small step along a long road.

3. Paragraphs 1 and 2 describe the contrasts between the 'weird loneliness' of the Dark Peak and the 'solace by the quiet rivers of the dales' in the White Peak, which lie within a day's travel of each other. Paragraphs 3 to 5 record man's enrichment of the landscape through the creation of fields, farmsteads, villages, cultural traditions and the discovery of geological interests. This plan's first section deals at length and in detail with the conservation of all these unique qualities.

4. Paragraphs 6 and 7 remark upon the proximity of half of England's population to the Peak National Park, and the vigorous steps taken to preserve it. By 1947, 12 amenity societies had joined to form the voluntary Joint Committee for the Peak District National Park. Its successor met the representatives of the National Park Authority during the preparation of this Plan.

5. Paragraphs 8 and 9 consider the demands for minerals and conclude that the area near Buxton, excluded from the National Park, should contain enough accessible limestone of high quality to last for several generations. With only one major exception, at Old Moor, the Park has fulfilled that arrangement to date. One company has been invited on appeal to concentrate its investment on its approved quarry in the Buxton area and to run down its quarry in the Park.

6. Paragraph 10 reviews the impact of water catchment and storage on landscape and access. Since then, no further valleys have been flooded. Measures for conservation and access have improved greatly, but are again at risk from proposed land disposals or by transfer to private sector management.

7. Paragraph 11 expressed fears that further suburban development, particularly in the Hope Valley, would damage landscape and spoil the character of traditional architecture and village. The flood was stemmed by the 1960's, and design control improved by the 1970's. Work now continues through the adoption of integrated village management schemes, and through attempts to limit housing development to local needs.

8. Paragraph 12 and 13 summarised the linked problems of closed moorlands — 'an altercation with a game keeper may mar a day's serenity' — and of ill-educated visitors causing unwarranted damage and disturbance to wildlife. Since 1974, four major processes have substantially improved that situation — access agreements, the ranger service, the information service and the youth and schools service at Losehill Hall national park study centre. In the next few years, the right balance between farming, gamekeeping, visitors and wildlife will be sought, particularly on those moors where an agreement has not yet been concluded.

9. Paragraphs 14 to 16 conclude with a 'call for balanced judgement and firm decisions made without fear or favour. No potential National Park is in more pressing need of protective planning and of expert and careful management'. The report recommends a single body to carry forward the pioneering work of the CPRE, National Trust and the Joint Planning Committee. The Peak Board has taken up the challenge over 37 years. This plan takes one more step, towards the end of the 20th century.

"3. The Peak District (including Dovedale)
1. The attraction of this popular region of hill country, which is formed by the southernmost block of the Pennines, is enhanced by the contrast between the two chief component elements of its scenery. On the north and west rise the gritstone moors with their austere, solitary plateaux, falling away abruptly in scarped edges, their grotesque groups of stones, folded valleys and broken cloughs; on the south and east are the upland limestone pastures and exquisite dales. Thus within the space of a day or so the traveller may battle with the invigorating winds on Wessenden Head, Kinder Scout or Shutlingslow and laze under the cliffs of Dovedale or Chee Tor, refreshed by the completeness of the two-fold scene — 'the White Peak and the Dark Peak' as it has been aptly named.

2. The gritstone landscape is most impressive on Kinder, whose remarkable peaty plain, trenched by 'groughs', scored by sluggish streams and edged by black crags, presents some of the most difficult country in England at night or in mist. The weird loneliness of this tableland, which lies between Manchester and Sheffield, has a compelling attraction for the more vigorous inhabitants of these smoky cities. Others find solace by the quiet rivers of the dales or the fantastically shaped limestone rocks, such as the Peter Stone in Cressbrook Dale, the Apostles, or Thor's Cave.

3. The essential background of the Peak District, providing its vitality and much of its beauty, is the farm — the moorland sheep-runs, and the cattle pastures of the vales, the chequered pattern made by the stone walls, the small copses hanging to the hillsides and the sycamore-sheltered farmhouses and barns. No less is the district enriched by the homely beauty of its villages, both those of the gritstone such as Hathersage and Stanton-in-Peak, and those of the limestone, such as Winster, Monyash, and Tissington. Haddon Hall and Chatsworth are its architectural triumphs, but the country owes even more to the modest manor houses, known as 'Halls', with their low-pitched gables and stone roofs.

4. On the flat hill tops are frequently to be found the remains of early man, varying in range from the massive temple at Arbor Low to small stone circles and innumerable burial mounds called 'lows', a word which figures in many

local place names. The Norman keep of Peveril Castle hangs on the precipitous edge of the Peak Cavern. There are pleasing mediaeval churches, and the moors have still their ancient crosses, 'hollow gates' and paved packhorse ways. On 29th May, called 'Garland Day' at Castleton, a Morris dance is performed, led by a 'King and Queen' mounted on horseback. The village of Eyam holds memories of the Plague of 1666, and the once pagan custom of dressing the wells is celebrated at Tissington, Barlow and other villages. Old millstones still lie below the rocks from which they were hewn, and on the Sheffield side the ruined grinding wheels of the 'little mesters' tell of the early cutlers' trade.

5. Much geological interest centres in the caverns, which are a great attraction to tourists, at Matlock, Buxton and especially Castleton, where they contain the rare variety of fluorspar known as 'Blue John'. While the many caves and potholes provide ample scope for exploration, climbers who prefer the upper air may spend long days on the gritstone crags.

6. But beyond its intrinsic qualities, the Park has a unique value as a National Park, surrounded as it is on all sides by industrial towns and cities. Sheffield, Manchester, Huddersfield, Derby and the Potteries lie on its borders; indeed it is estimated that half the population of England lives within 60 miles of Buxton. Communications are good and it is feasible for neighbouring city dwellers to be in the Park within an hour by road or rail. The very large membership of the Ramblers' and Youth Hostels Associations within its range testifies to the use that is now being made of this district.

7. There is no other area which has evoked more strenuous public effort to safeguard its beauty. Twelve rural amenity societies have formed a Joint Committee for the Peak District National Park, and it is mainly due to their efforts in recent years that the region has more or less retained its rural character. Its very proximity to the industrial towns renders it as vulnerable as it is valuable.

Problems and Requirements
8. The most serious menace to the landscape of the Peak District comes undoubtedly from the exploitation of its minerals. From ancient times it has been worked for lime and for lead, but these old workings were on a small scale and seldom led to major disfigurement. But today the increased power of modern machinery is visibly reducing the hills and scooping out the fertile soil of the dales at a progressively accelerated rate. The heights round Buxton emit black smoke, Dove Holes is raw and heaped with tips, the famous Hope Valley contains a vast scar, a recent quarry gashes the side of Eldon Hill. This is an area where limestone is of the highest grade and the demand for it is at present unlimited.

9. We have taken evidence both from representatives of the industry and from independent experts, on the basis of which we have excluded the district containing most of the major workings with room for expansion. Our conclusions are that within this area there is enough accessible limestone of high quality to last for several generations and that it should therefore be possible to exclude fresh quarrying on any large scale from the National Park. There are, however, notable instances of damage to scenery by the industry within the proposed Park, and wherever

possible, measures should be taken to check the defacement which is now in progress and to remedy what has already been inflicted. In one or two cases we recommend that workings should be discontinued and compensation paid.

10. Another increasing threat is that of the catchment and impounding of water. The nearby cities already draw vast supplies from this area and others are now looking to its few untapped watersheds. A dozen large reservoirs now cover much land that was once fertile and lovely, resulting in the loss of numbers of farms and the eviction of their inhabitants — the loss too of villages where visitors would have found much needed accommodation under true country conditions. Moreover the fear of pollution has led to curtailment of popular access to the catchment areas. Many schemes have been executed with little appreciation of the finer landscape values, particularly in the treatment of fencing, roads and viaducts, and in the formal planting of conifers, where native hardwoods might have gradually made a more natural setting to these artificial lakes. The time has come to consider whether this region should suffer further intrusion of this kind. It will certainly be essential that the National Parks Commission should be consulted, and their advice given full weight, on any new proposals for water catchment within the National Park.

11. Perhaps the most distressing injury to Peak landscape, because it could most easily have been avoided, is that inflicted by residential building unsuitable in materials and design. The area is peculiarly susceptible because of its small scale and quiet tone. The traditional villages and farms, with their stone walls and stone-slate roofs, are often of high architectural quality and the introduction of incongruous building can do deplorable damage. The worst danger lies in the acquisition of land near villages for development of the suburban type. The Hope Valley which lies across the National Park is chiefly endangered. Other disfigurement is also sprinkled about the region in the form of advertisements, garish filling stations and shacks. Strict planning control must be directed to the mitigation of disfigurement and its prevention in the future. Stone is acknowledged to be the fitting local material and the utmost efforts should be made to ensure the right use of stone for new houses, which may affect the appearance of the whole area for generations.

12. The controversy over access to uncultivated lands reaches its height in the Peak, where landowners may draw their most remunerative rents from the lease of grouse moors, and where at the same time large areas are sterilised for water catchment. Many of the finest moorlands, where thousands wish to wander, are closed against 'trespassers' and an altercation with a gamekeeper may often mar a day's serenity. A National Park in the Peak District will not justify its name unless this problem is satisfactorily solved. The Footpath and Access Special Committee is devoting careful study to this subject, which is based on broader issues than the peculiar conflict in the Peak. Increased privileges for the public must, however, be accompanied by a greater sense of responsibility. Certain ignorant young folk in this area cause unwarrantable damage to walls, hedges, haystacks, trees and stock, and disturb the peace of the villages with their rowdiness. An adequate staff of wardens, reinforced by a first class Public Information service, will be needed to protect the farmer and those who know how to enjoy the country from those who, as yet, do not.

13. The intensive preservation of grouse and the influx of visitors have had a damaging effect on the wild life of this district. A hundred years ago a dozen different species of raptorial birds, including the golden eagle, the hen-harrier and the hobby, were recorded in the Peak, and wild lilies-of-the-valley were abundant in some of the limestone dales. To-day but few hawks survive the gamekeeper's hostility, and the famous lilies are hardly to be found.

14. The formidable list of problems which have forced themselves upon our attention indicate that the management of the Peak District National Park will call for balanced judgment and firm decisions made without fear or favour; for here, more than in any other area, powerful claims for the economic exploitation of the land will come into conflict with the primary purpose of the National Park — to provide open-air enjoyment in a setting of unspoilt beauty for surrounding urban populations of exceptional density.

15. The protection and restoration of natural beauty, and of access to it, rather than the development of recreational facilities must be regarded as the immediate and paramount consideration in the Peak District. No potential National Park is in more pressing need of protective planning and of expert and careful management.

16. Four County Councils and one County Borough will constitute, with the representatives of the National Parks Commission, the new Park Committee. This will be the body to carry on the pioneer activity of the Council for the Preservation of Rural England, the National Trust and the Peak Joint Planning Committee, in preventing and mitigating defacement, in educating and enlisting a public opinion which can help in the restoration of natural beauty, and in the maintenance of the architectural standards, the wild life and the sound farming which once enriched this land.''

Appendix 4
Summary of the 1986/87 Visitor Survey (Publication March 1988)

1. The survey forms an integral part of the review of recreational policy for the Peak Park.

2. The survey was carried out in two stages. The first stage involved a series of roadside interviews during the period from June to September 1986. The second stage involved roadside interviews during November 1986 and March and April 1987.

3. 14,856 drivers or riders of vehicles were interviewed.

4. There are about 18½ million visits to the Park each year.

5. There are strong seasonal and daily variations in the number of visits made to the National Park.

6. Over 95% of visitors have been to the Peak District before.

7. Regular visitors account for 5 million visits to the Park each year.

8. 65% of day visitors are from the surrounding conurbations.

9. Some sectors of the car-owning community are under-represented amongst visitors.

10. Members of countryside related organisations account for 21% of Park visits.

11. Over 10% of visits to the Peak District are made by staying visitors.

12. The holiday season is concentrated within the summer months.

13. 80% of holidays made are short breaks of less than 7 days.

14. Nearly half of all staying visitors to the National Park stay in the surrounding towns and villages.

15. In summer over half of all visitor nights spent in the Park were on camping or caravanning holidays.

16. The average size of recreational groups has decreased from 3.3 persons in 1971/2 to 2.8 persons in 1986/87.

17. Visitors are attracted to the Peak District's unspoilt open countryside and to its villages and towns, for example 60% rate 'uncommercialised areas' as very important.

18. The most popular areas for visitors are the Lower Derwent, Wye and Hope Valleys.

19. The major recreational activities in the National Park are sightseeing and hiking.

20. Each year visitor spending generates over £75 million for the local economy.

21. Over 80% of visitors who use facilities are satisfied with their provision.

22. Over 40% of visitors set out to visit a particular area.

23. Visitors return to areas they have been to on a previous occasion.

24. Visitor spending has risen in real terms by 38% during the period 1971/2 to 1986/87.

INDEX

References to policies are shown in bold type

number of 36, 37, 138
part-time 36, 37
profitability of 37
size of 36, 37
visitor accommodation on 82, 122-3
visits 130
Farm and Countryside Initiative (1986) 40
Building Design Guide 42
Community Link (FCL) 130
Conservation Scheme 15, 26, 28, 30, 35, 38, 39, **43-44**,
45, 48, 52, 54, 60, 67, 157, 158
Diversification Grant Scheme 37, 38, 40, 118
Grant Notification Scheme 10, 14, 26, 34, 35, 38, 39,
40-43, 49, 50, 52, 66, 67, 158
Woodlands Scheme 47
farmers 24, 36, 38, 32
advice for 39, 43, **44**, 67, 158
and conservation 36, 38, 39, 40, 43, 54
and public paths 83, 85
farmhouse accommodation **122-3**
farmhouse teas 107, 108
farming 11, 14, 18, 24, 26, 35, **36-44**, 58, 59, 64, 127, 128,
138, 157
and education 130
changes in 37, 55
dairy 31, 35, 36, 37
environmentally sensitive 23, 32, **39**
livestock 36
woodlands as part of 45
Farming and Wildlife Advisory Groups (FWAG) 43, 157
farmland 20, 34
enclosed 24, 26, 30, 32, 33, **34-5**, 36, 48
farmsteads 18, 20, 36, 122
Felling Licences 47
fences 32, 33, **35**, 38, 88
Fenny Bentley 60, 201
ferns 23, 35, 56
field study centres 118, **123**, 130
fields 35, 66
fires 25, 54, 90, 156, 157
fish 100, 103
fishing 79, 92, 100, 102, **103**, 109
Flagg 189
fluorspar 22, 146
flower-rich fields 20, 55, 157
grasslands 29, 34, 52, 54
folklore 65, 68
Foolow 183
footpaths 25, 68, 73, 82, 83, 84, **85**, **86**, 105, 107, 110, 132,
152
forestry 18, 42, **45-8**, 58, 127, 128, 138, 158
Forestry Commission 10, 14, 28, 29, 32, 33, 34, 43, 45, 47,
48, 54, 83, 105, 106, 128, 132, 134, 155, 156, 157, 171,
174, 175, 176, 194, 195, 197
Forestry Grant Scheme (FGS) 45, 47
forests 22, 24, **32-34**, 45
Froggatt Edge 181, 183
Functional Strategies 11, 15, 159

game 33, 45
gamekeepers 24, 132
gardens 70, 75, 124
geology 18, 31, 50, **57**, 92
geomorphology 50, **57**
gliding 79, 92, **95**
Glossop 114, 162, 178

golf courses 79
Goyt Valley 84, 109, 128, 194, **195**
Gradbach 123, 198, 199
grants 8, 43, 50, 52, 54, 66, 144, 152, 155, **157**
agricultural 36, 37, 42, **43**
building repair 71, 74, **75**
Derelict Land 58, 59
for archaeological research 67
for bus shelters **116**
for landscape enhancement **60**
for nature reserves 52
for parking **105**, 157
for picnic facilities 106
for ponds 55, 157
for public path maintenance 84
for public transport **116**
for rural enterprises **40**
for toilets 106
for tourism projects 118
for voluntary conservation work 135
for woodlands 37, 45, 47
Forestry Commission 32
in Conservation Areas 71
MAFF 35, 36, 39, 60, 117
new procedure for 38, 40, 42, 43
Peak Board scheme 43, **44**
planting 45, 47
grassland 24, 29, 34, 36, 49, 51
Gratton Dale 189, 190
grazing 25, 28, **29**, **31**, 90
Great Hucklow 183, 184
Great Longstone 73, 142, **189**
green lanes 55, 84, 99
Grindleford 185, 186
Grindon 60, 63, 73, 106, 201, 202, **204**
Grindsbrook Booth 110, 177, 178
gritstone 20, 33, 146
moorland **24-8**
grouse 24, 25, 26, 36, 54, 55, 56, 79, 90, 157
guesthouses 118, **120**

habitats 10, 15, 35, 42, 49, 88, 90
conservation of 28, 49, 50, **52-4**
management of 50, **54-5**, 57
semi-natural 30, 31, 49, 97
surveys of **50-2**
Haddon Hall 75, 142, 186, 187, 188
Hagg Farm Hostel 62, 123, 154, 176
hang-gliding 10, 79, 92, **95**
Harpur Crewe 142, 149
Hartington 71, 73, 105, 110, 112, 126, 127, 201, 202, **203**, **204**
Hathersage 69, 71, 73, 179, 180, **181**
Hayfield 106, 162, 165, 178, 179
Heathcote Mere 55, 60
heather 24, 25, 30, 156
heathland 20, 29, **30**
hedges **33**, 35, 62
herb-rich meadows 55
herbicides 34, 49
heritage, cultural 11, 14, 15, **64-9**, 67, 82, 90, 92, 124
High Peak
Borough Council 14, 106, 108, 142, 162, 168, 175, 177,
178, 179, 181
Trail 58, 84, 98, 107, 152, 195
highway(s) 112
furniture 62

Acknowledgements

Thanks are due to many people for their help with the production of this Plan, including:

Steering and advice by the National Park Plan Sub-Committee; Michael Dower and the managament team; John Anfield and the editorial team; and the Rural Land Management Executive Group.

Over 30 Authors at Aldern House and Losehill Hall, who wrote topic papers.

Editing by Helen Dimond, Martin Smith, John Thompson and others.

Word processing by Elaine Fisher and team.

The Roadshow, organised by Bob Braddock.

Production Editing by John Youatt.

Design by Karen Sayer.

Illustrations by Hannah Chesterman.

All photographs except those listed below by Ray Manley.

Anon
p.38 Castleton, p.75 Thornbridge Hall, p.78 Walking, p.114 Railway, p.116 Bus.

Care Project
p.174 Walling

David Hosking
p.57 Badger

Lyme Park
p.193 Stags

Judy Merryfield
p.30 Mine Capping

Peter Phillipson
p.54 Heath Burning

Richard Taylor
p.71 Eyam Square, p.73 Litton Chapel, p.73 Roof

Mike Williams
p.24 Noe Stool, p.29 Mam Tor road, p.32 Trees, p.34 Farmland, p.36 Ploughing, p.178 Edale Valley, p.191 Harthill Stone, p.197 Wildboarclough Valley.

Satellite photo © NRSC and Robertson McCarta publications.

Maps are based on the Ordnance Survey Map with the permission of the Controller of Her Majesty's Stationery Office. Crown Copyright reserved.

Typeset and printed by Witley Press Ltd., Hunstanton, Norfolk.

Whilst every effort has been made to ensure that the information contained within this Plan is accurate at the time of going to press, the Board does not accept responsibility for any errors or omissions.

Published by the Peak Park Joint Planning Board, Aldern House, Baslow Road, Bakewell, Derbyshire DE4 1AE.
April 1989.

ISBN: 0-907543-24-3